P9-CEA-339

FOR CRYING OUT LOUD

FOR CRYING OUT LOUD

Edited by
Rochelle Lefkowitz
and Ann Withorn

Women and Poverty in the United States

The Pilgrim Press
New York

Library of Congress Cataloging-in-Publication Data

For crying out loud.

Bibliography: p.
1. Women—United States—Economic conditions.
2. Women, Poor—United States—Attitudes. 3. Sex discrimination against women—United States. 4. Public welfare—United States. I. Lefkowitz, Rochelle, 1951– . II. Withorn, Ann, 1947– .
HQ1426.F757 1986 305.4'2'0973 86-9302
ISBN 0-8298-0581-8

The Pilgrim Press, 132 West 31st Street, New York, NY 10001

Dedicated
to Gwyne Withorn White
and to the memory of
Mamie Wilson

CONTENTS

FOR CRYING OUT LOUD

INTRODUCTION

Rochelle Lefkowitz and Ann Withorn

> *You know what really makes me mad? It's all these people saying I'm not poor because I get welfare and all these other so-called benefits.*
>
> *What do they mean, I'm not poor? What is poor if it's not having people in grocery lines comment on what you buy with your food stamps? What is poor if it's not staying home all weekend before the check comes, because you don't have the car fare to go anywhere? Or that you have to switch your child's dentist because the one you had doesn't want to take Medicaid any more?*
>
> *I'm poor because every time I see my welfare worker he tells me I'm poor. I'm poor because now they say I can't even go to school anymore, that I have to take any job I can find even if it has no future, no hope.*
>
> *It doesn't matter that maybe in some ways I get a little more now than I might have gotten years ago. I'm still poor and they won't let me forget it!*
>
> ———Boston welfare recipient

Today, two out of three poor adults in the United States of America are women. The "feminization of poverty" has become a catch phrase to be interjected in presidential and other political campaigns, and to be generally decried, if not defined, by everyone across a wide political spectrum.

This book was initially inspired by our complex reactions to the new attention being given to women's poverty. On the one hand, as feminists long concerned with social welfare and women's issues, we were pleased that both the women's movement and the broader society were beginning to pay attention to poor women. For too long women on welfare, older women, women of color, and other economically and socially vulnerable women had remained invisible. Between "dress for success" and Reaganomics we had seen poor women swept aside, ignored, and punished. Given this context, we found it encouraging to see the feminization of poverty attract so much attention.

On the other hand, as we heard the term used as a catchall for a wide variety of problems and needs, we began to worry that, once again, poor women would lose their voice, that others were going to simplify and define their reality. We could not help but feel concerned that even the popular term itself, coined by sociologist Diana Pearce in 1978, would mislead and misinform. Did the long-needed naming of the problem as the *feminization* of poverty—and not the impoverishment of women—tend to put a pink dress on issues that were somehow more serious when they affected men? Isn't the explanation for poverty more complex than that all women are but "one man away from welfare?" And, aren't the solutions somehow more complicated than either simply "putting women to work" or reforming the welfare system?

Our goal for this collection, then, is to unsnarl the tangled skeins of women's poverty and to provide a more complex picture than has emerged in the media or in the recent literature. Unifying all the essays and individual accounts that follow is the recognition that we live in a society where women's work is never done—and never paid in full, with either economic *or* social and psychological recognition. Here, therefore, we set out to examine all the varied strands: the historical, sociological, economic, psychological, and experiential.

This collection is, however, neither a laundry list of woes nor a distanced academic survey. Personal accounts give a slice of reality and a broad view—one that hopes to capture the single mother of young children, the aging widow, the black, Latina, lesbian, and rural woman with its wide-angle lens. The essays and accounts expose suffering, but they are also filled with courage, ingenuity, and hope. And we do more than catalogue the strength and the difficulty; the collection examines the traditional "solutions" to poverty—education, job training, electoral politics—with an urge to see beyond them to more fundamental change. In fact, the book expresses a single vision: beyond equity toward liberation. Together, the contributors provide the ingredients, if not the recipe, for change.

Major Themes

The essays and personal accounts in this collection were selected for their diversity and for the breadth and depth that they bring to an analysis of women's poverty. Yet their rich variety is bounded by several themes.

First, all embody the basic tension facing everyone concerned about women's issues: the need to discuss the common needs of *all* women while still recognizing and respecting the critical differences *among* women. The powerful sexism of society forces us to speak in generalities. As a group, women have been lumped together in countless ways: our psychology examined; our "natural" mothering instincts assumed; our intellectual, physical, and emotional capacities corseted by educational institutions and by family patterns. So our authors respond in kind, by making demands in the name of all women, by stressing the aggregate statistics that quantify the end results of discriminatory attitudes and policies. Many essays in this book, then, examine the fundamental economic and social vulnerability that unites all women—to explain how societal expectations have been embodied in formal and informal patterns that produce consistent wage inequality, persistently unequal family roles, and a widespread inability of society to value women's and men's lives equally.

At the same time, however, it is the differences among women that keep us from fighting our common battles. To deny the special history and needs of women of color, and among them of black, Latina, Asian, and Native American women, is to impose a false harmony that only serves to make women of color feel more isolated from white women. Likewise, women of all races from working-class backgrounds may experience real and potential poverty very differently, often seeking different solutions and approaches, from middle-class women who find themselves newly poor or newly aware of their risk of poverty. Lesbians, older women, and rural women all have discrete concerns, which, if denied, will lead to inadequate demands for change or, even worse, to demands that help some women at the expense of others. Other contributors, therefore, try to analyze the variance within women's poverty in order better to explain the whole.

A second, related theme is that women's poverty is a complex state of being, only partially defined economically. Therefore this book does not present page after page of statistical charts and graphs. There is some economic analysis, to be sure, but more often the contributors offer a mixture of sociological and psychological insight into the ways in which women experience their poverty and their heightened potential for poverty. There is wide-ranging analysis of the policies that contribute to the absolute and subjective problem at the same time that they attempt to "solve" it. And there is always an attempt to explain the political choices that have contributed to women's poverty as well as the political options for women seeking to change their situation.

Here another theme emerges in our discomfort with the "feminization of poverty" concept. Most of the current literature emphasizes how badly the welfare system hurts women and how better job programs—or more enforcement of child-support arrangements—are the way to get women off welfare and end the so-called cycle of dependence. Yet, given the lack of viable job options for women and the continuing psychological and physical requirements of caring for a family, such demands seem simplistic. Even worse, they seem, finally, to be less concerned with women's economic and social well-being than with expense to the taxpayers.

In the pages that follow, many authors examine the welfare state but from a different perspective. They make clear how fully the welfare system is enmeshed with "women's issues." Most recipients of all government social programs are women and their children. Most workers in the system are women. And most of the pertinent "social problems" are blamed on the failure of women's nurturing role. Unlike those who see "being on welfare," or dependence on the state, as the basic problem of women's poverty, our contributors take a more complex view. All see the welfare system as simultaneously offering relief from some aspects of women's traditional roles AND maintaining women's perpetually inferior status, through inadequate and punitive programs.

A major argument contained within this book, then, is that "public dependence" is a right for all citizens and should be treated as such, not as a punitive "last resort" for those poor souls who have failed at "independence." Many women at all stages of life do, and should, make rational choices to enter the welfare system. We support them in this decision and offer suggestions to make it less of a nightmare.

Finally, this book maintains throughout that poor women can speak for themselves. The obvious expertise of the poor women who speak in these pages demands acknowledgment that giving voice to one's life is as legitimate as writing from "objective" research data. Feminist professionals write here seeking to develop mutual relationships with poor women and their organizations in order to provide the "supportive service" of information flow, not to usurp others' experience. And poor women offer hard analysis as well as first-hand evidence about the nature of poverty.

Our anthology counters the "sympathetic" image of poor women contained in the "neediest cases" at Christmas time. Too often, such accounts are like the old TV show "Queen for a Day," where an applause meter registered audience response to each contestant's tragedies, and the woman in the most acute crisis won a crown, a bouquet of roses, and a washer/dryer for her pain. Instead, we propose a different basis for suggesting new kinds of solutions, which incorporate poor women's perspectives in their design and implementation. We therefore prefer alternatives that grow from the bottom up. In putting together this anthology, we became inspired anew by poor women's strength and imagination. We uncovered examples of middle- and working-class, black, Latina, Asian, white, old, and young feminists acting together to expand and redefine the goals for all women. The fruit of such efforts is a strategy that addresses poor women's needs by truly valuing women's work in all settings, by asserting the rights of all to have basic needs met, and by demanding, even in today's climate of reaction, that public resources be committed to making that happen. In turn, we hope our readers will take the evidence, analysis, and suggestions presented here and use them to continue to "cry out loud" so that together we can build a better future.

Rochelle Lefkowitz and Ann Withorn

Summary of the Collection

The book is organized into four parts, with approximately six selections in each. The authors discuss their topics without assuming the reader's prior background in economics, sociology, or social policy. As editors, we introduce each section, to point out the links between the selections and to suggest questions that they provoke.

In the first section, we present different perspectives on the notion of the "feminization of poverty." Diane Dujon crystalizes the problem by describing what it's like to be poor with either a welfare check or a paycheck. Next the authors who coined and popularized the term make the basic arguments about why women are increasingly poor. Then women from differing perspectives show the reasons why economists, feminists, and black activists may diverge in their view of women's poverty.

The second section presents some of the differing ways in which women actually experience poverty. These accounts go beyond the aggregate statistics to explain women's persisting poverty. Here authors insist on the need to understand the special circumstances of women of color, in regard to both economic and social aspects of their poverty. Older women and teenage mothers are the two fastest-growing groups of poor women, and both, for different reasons, are often caricatured by discussions of women's poverty. Here their concerns are examined, along with those of employed women living in poverty. The diversity is immense, but this section suggests that acknowledging rather than glossing over it is one fundamental step toward change.

The third section further humanizes the problem. Poor women live everyday lives, full of struggles, hopes, and accomplishments, just like other women. As willing and unwilling clients of the welfare system, however, their reality is complicated by the countless ways in which options are limited and actions thwarted by bureaucratic processes, policy decisions, and social stigma. Often the services feel like punishment, and the label "welfare recipient" seems to be one's only identity. The authors here challenge the stereotypes and provide readers with a deeper base for respecting the hard work poor women do in providing for themselves and their families.

Finally, we close with a consideration of strategies for change. Most often poor women are told to solve their problems by getting a job. Yet most know the cruel irony of such advice. Some suffer from age or racial discrimination, so that finding any job is difficult. All know that the jobs they find, as women, are unlikely to meet their own economic needs, much less those of their families. Education is also often offered as a solution, but again without recognition that most women need baccalaureate-level degrees even to begin earning breadwinners' wages. And welfare "reform" usually means new bureaucratized pressures on women to leave the system, not increases in basic benefits to end poverty.

So the suggestions offered here are not the usual ones. Instead, changes are suggested that *expand* the role of the state in providing basic supports for women. Pay equity and community education are advocated instead of narrow job training and low-level jobs. Instead of cheerful lectures on how to set "achievable goals" and to develop "marketable job skills," what women have the right to expect is radically recast.

Such solutions may sound "unreasonable" to policy makers, the general public, even to some self-identified "advocates for women." They may, however, be the only reasonable hopes poor women have for short- and long-term change. We hope that the essays and accounts in this volume establish some of the groundwork for such an "unrealistic" but essential agenda.

Acknowledgments

Most of all we would like to acknowledge each other. This book began in conversations during the early 1980s between a Boston professor and a New York journalist. We talked about Ronald Reagan, about our work in teaching and working with women on welfare, and about the problems we faced in our own lives. As we went through a frustrating process of conceptualizing and selling the proposed volume to publishers who wanted it to be either more "upbeat" or more "professional," we provided consistent support to each other. As one of us struggled with motherhood and a newly challenging work life, the other changed careers and dealt with deaths of close relatives as well as physical assault in the stairways of New York. Yet somehow we also were able to help each other stay focused—through gentle prodding—toward our mutual goal.

And as we helped each other, in turn, we received support from the women who have contributed to this volume. They never forgot us, and their questions about the book and their interest in the common task sustained us. In addition, there were many women who played a role in conceptualizing the book without finally being included in it, including Mary Jo Hetzel, Barbara Monty, Joanne Lukomnik, Barbara Joseph, Theresa Funiciello, Marian Darlington Hope, Winnie Breines, Grace Remy, Mary Quinn, Sylvia Smith, Kip Tiernan, Nancy Hoffman, and Ginnie Bullock. We would also like to recognize the efforts of three organizations whose work inspires poor women as well as ourselves. They are the Coalition for Basic Human Needs (CBHN) and Advocacy for Resources for Modern Suvival (ARMS)—both Boston welfare rights groups—and the New York Downtown Welfare Advocacy Center (DWAC).

More personally, we would like to thank Frances Goldin for her valuable advice, even if we did not always take it, and Ellen Prateger and Karen Vale for their technical assistance with word processing. And we cannot overestimate the contribution of Larry Kramer and George Abbott White, who gave unfailingly of their precious time and emotional support, especially when it seemed as if the book would never be finished.

PART ONE

Poverty's Pink Collar: Why Are Women Poor?

Long before displaced homemakers, teenage mothers, or even Aid to Families with Dependent Children (AFDC), there was poverty. In fairy tales like Hansel and Gretel, a poor couple abandon their young son and daughter in the woods because they cannot feed them. Neither beauty nor goodness saved Cinderella from having to clean chimneys after Mother died and Father remarried a Wicked Stepmother with two daughters of her own. The biblical story of Ruth describes how, in order to eat, poor, unmarried women had to glean in the wheat fields, trailing male harvesters to pick up what they dropped. Indeed, poverty among women and their children is as old as recorded history.

For fairy tale Cinderella and biblical Ruth, things ended happily ever after: poverty ended with marriage. But today, when nearly one out of two marriages ends in divorce, it is often the other way around—marriage ends in poverty, for women and their children.

In the past fifteen years, one of the most staggering trends in the United States has been the growth of households headed by women. From 1972 to 1982 alone, they increased by 57 percent. In other words, one out of every six American families is now maintained by a woman. By 1981, 47 percent of all low-income families in the United States were headed by women. For black and Latina families, these figures were as high as 70 percent and 50 percent.

In American society, families headed by one breadwinner are often likely to be poor. When that breadwinner is a woman, the odds increase. In 1978, sociologist Diana Pearce coined the now classic phrase to describe this alarming trend: the feminization of poverty.

For a while, this new name put poor women in the headlines once again and on the evening news. Yet while feminizing poverty did draw many women's groups from the National Organization of Women to the League of Women Voters to pay attention to a problem they had never before embraced so readily, some things didn't change for poor women when their name did.

Still, American society, like many others before it, expresses sorrow and responsibility for some poor women—and blames and punishes others. Now, as then, poor women are divided into two categories: good and bad. The worthy widows and their orphaned children, once the deserving poor, are now the truly needy. And the America of the 1980s chucked the wicked stepmother in favor of the "blended family," and turned the once-risqué divorcee into the valiant single mom. Yet one evil, poor woman remains: the welfare mother, "welfare" being the only adjective since "unwed" that has been able to tarnish motherhood.

So the debate began. Did the feminization of poverty help to highlight women's poverty, or does all the attention to women's poverty as something new somehow take away from the plight of women who have been poor for generations? And why can't everyone agree about how to talk about women's poverty?

In this section, we present the arguments that arise from looking at poverty through the lens of gender. We then turn to some of the debate that followed the "discovery" of the feminization of poverty, which challenges its proponents not to ignore race, class, or the dangers of creating a new way to divide poor women into the "good, new poor" and the "bad, long-term poor." We present this debate not to force a choice of which cause of women's poverty is more important—race, class, or gender—but in the hope that together, all these perspectives allow us better to understand and address women's poverty.

Welfare mother-turned-low-wage working mother Diane Dujon sets the terms for exploring the feminization of poverty by describing it. Then, feminist scholar Barbara Ehrenreich, in her essay on the new poor, describes the forces that push women into poverty.

Next we have reprinted sociologist Diana Pearce's ground-breaking essay here as a historic document to make the original case for the feminization of poverty. Then, economists Elaine Donovan and Mary Huff Stevenson explain how what people see as the causes and solutions to women's poverty depends a lot on the political outlook of the beholders. Finally, feminist economist Pamela Sparr and black scholar Linda Burnham end by critiquing the concept of the feminization of poverty, particularly as it applies to black women and others who have been poor for some time.

OUT OF THE FRYING PAN

Reflections of a Former Welfare Recipient

Diane Dujon

Many people consider me a welfare success story. But if I am, it is in spite of welfare, not because of it. I had to constantly fight the Welfare Department to earn my college degree while continuing to receive benefits. I was determined to be in a position where I could have a chance to become self-sufficient when I re-joined the work force.

The reality is that while I was fortunate enough to find employment as an administrative assistant immediately upon graduation, I still must rely heavily upon the networks and resources I established while surviving on welfare. I still shop for bargains, prepare many foods from scratch, and have little money for pleasure. My child-care expenses alone equal one week's take-home pay each month. My rent swallows up another week and half's pay; and I'm relatively lucky that I have lived in my apartment for more than ten years so that my rent is lower than most and my heat is included. The remaining one and a half weeks' pay goes toward clothing, health and dental care, utilities, school loans, and transportation. I am still in arrears with many of my utility bills, even after applying all of my tax refund to catch them up.

Another reality is that I have much less time for myself and my daughter. I always feel that the time I spend with my daughter now is spent coaxing her to rush to get ready for school or bed. Even on weekends and holidays I am busy trying to catch up on housework, the laundry, or clothes and food shopping. Too much time is spent being the breadwinner, and the nurturing falls by the wayside. I am always tired because I never get enough rest.

While there are definite differences between being on welfare and being on a payroll, I still don't have enough money to sustain myself and my family at a very basic level, and I have less time to compensate for my lack of finances. I still continue to be limited in my day-to-day decisions and choices. Although I am no longer dependent on the Welfare Department and the whims of politicians, I am now dependent on the work place and the whims of bosses! I have commited forty-plus hours a week of my precious time to a job to make my landlord rich. I still cannot afford to buy a car or go on "vacation" or pay a sitter while I go out.

I feel fortunate to have been on welfare because I learned how to survive using my wits. This type of creative thinking is invaluable to all poor people, especially single, female heads of households. I became an expert shopper, cook, and stitcher. I learned how to prioritize and set my own agenda. I also got to know my daughter in a way that would have been impossible if I had worked full time while she was younger. I concentrated on obtaining my degree and succeeded against a myriad of odds. I believe that these skills helped me to maintain my self-esteem and buoyed my sense of dignity through all the frustrations. I also grew spiritually while on welfare. I learned to rely on God when humankind was neither human nor kind. I call on these resources as much today as I did then.

As for whether there ought to be some supports for working mothers, I have lived four lives since becoming an adult: as a single working women, as a woman married to a poor man, as a welfare mother, and as a working single mother. I can truly say that in all these lives I have needed supports at one time or another. Returning to work after being on welfare was one of the most devastating adjustments I've ever had to make. Although the state does provide some child-care support for me, I feel that it's not enough. When I started working, my income rose by four times—but my child-care expenses rose by eight. This puts a tremendous financial burden on me. I also feel that the state should provide some rental or fuel assistance to people whose rent is in excess of 40 percent of their income. I believe too that medical and dental supports are essential for single heads of households because the premiums for family plans are astronomical, and the family's health and well-being are jeopardized as a result. Moreover, since I am now ineligible to recieve food stamps, my grocery expenses have quadrupled at least. When I was on welfare, I always felt that the Welfare Department was continuously probing to find out if I received a crust of bread to which I was not entitled; now, however, I feel that no one even cares if I get a crust of bread! The idea that because I work I need no supports is ludicrous, especially as a single mother. According to the National Commission on Working Women, 80 percent of women in the work force are employed at low-skilled, low-wage jobs. Hence, we represent a growing trend popularly referred to as "the feminization of poverty."

What's the solution? Well, I personally feel that forced-work programs—the Employment and Training Program (ET) in Massachusetts is a "liberal" example—are an example of how politicians waste the taxpayers' money. Why do we need a program to force women on welfare to find jobs when most women on welfare have an employment history, and the average stay on welfare is less than three years? ET now stresses choices—the same choices that every other American already has without such a program. The money would be put to better use by funding the supports needed by women who return to work. Since ET does not create jobs or address the barriers to employment faced by women—such as discrimination, sexism, racism, and classism—the most it can do is cause shifts in the unemployment population, leaving women feeling inadequate if they don't keep a job or harassed if they do.

What's more, as a black woman, I find minority women are especially oppressed in the labor force. I know numerous minority women in ET who are constantly being trained for months in the hopes of becoming employed. When the training period is over, the companies often decide not to hire them, and the women are placed in another training site to begin the cycle over again. Minority women find it difficult to find a job, and even when they do become employed, their road to upward mobility is rocky at best and nonexistent at worse. Now that the government is pulling away from its commitment to affirmative action, this situation is worsening daily.

I would suggest that women commit themselves to helping other women. The feminist movement has opened doors to women that have been closed to all women in the past. We women must train one another, educate one another, and communicate with one another. We must ensure that supports are in place to help overcome the barriers to self-sufficiency. Unfortunately, many of the women who have made breakthroughs in politics and the corporate ladder forget those behind them. While it is important for us to battle male chauvinism at every turn, we must also fight the tendency that some of us have toward female chauvinism. We must recognize welfare as a women's issue and child rearing as society's issue. Studies are now confirming what we have always known: women are the chief nurturers even in couples who consider the partners equal. Above all, we must allow women the choice of staying home and caring for our children whether we are financially independent or not. Our children are our greatest resource, and we must do whatever it takes to make sure that they develop into responsible citizens so that they can face the problems of adulthood and develop worthwhile solutions.

WHAT MAKES WOMEN POOR?

Barbara Ehrenreich

One morning, Brenda C. woke up crying. "I couldn't take it anymore," she explained. "My welfare check and food stamps were cut and I had to choose between paying the rent or buying food and school clothes for my growing kids—my oldest son's shoe size went from an eight to an eleven over one summer! Things had to be bought. What could I do?"

What Brenda did came as a shock to herself and her two sons, Kenny, thirteen, and Tony, eight. "I went down and enlisted in the army," she said. "It's my last chance to try and support my family. I don't know any other way." Soon afterwards, Brenda left for basic training, leaving Kenny and Tony in the care of a friend until she returned.

Brenda is black, a single parent in her thirties, and like many welfare recipients, she worked whenever she could. Her last job as

---

This essay is based on two previously published works. The editors thank Holly Sklar, Karin Stallard, South End Press, and Barbara Ehrenreich for permission to reprint sections of *Poverty in the American Dream: Women and Children First*, by Karin Stallard, Barbara Ehrenreich, and Holly Sklar (South End Press, 1983), pp. 5–7, 9; and "The Male Revolt: After the Breadwinner Vanishes," by Barbara Ehrenreich, *The Nation*, 26 February 1983, pp. 225, 240–42.

a Volunteers in Service to America (VISTA) worker, organizing community food and nutrition programs, was eliminated when the Reagan administration revamped VISTA. The string of low-paid jobs that Brenda held never paid enough to support her family without public assistance. And when she wasn't working, welfare payments alone barely covered rent, household items, and school supplies. Often the food stamps didn't last through the end of the month. Brenda and her children managed by doing without almost everything but the essentials. Once their income shrank, however, even the essentials were not affordable.

Avis Parke joined the ranks of the American poor after her divorce from a middle-class husband, a minister. Avis, in her early fifties, is white and college educated. Like many other "displaced homemakers," she found a cold greeting in the job market.

Parke v. *Parke* was a classic case of a middle-aged man leaving for a younger woman; and when the marriage dissolved, so did Avis' middle-class life-style. Now, Avis and her three youngest children (the oldest three live on their own) have made an unheated New England summer cottage their year-round home. Avis survives on a tenuous combination of welfare, food stamps, child support, and a lot of thriftiness.

Avis and Brenda are among the more than 32 million Americans who live below the official poverty level: $9,287 for a nonfarm family of four in 1981. Today, one out of seven Americans is poor according to official measures. Many people know that poverty is on the rise. What many do not know is that more and more of the poor are women and their dependent children.

The Increasing Impoverishment of Women

Two out of three poor adults in this country are women, and one out of five children is poor. Women head half of all poor families, and more than half the children in female-headed households are poor: 50 percent of white children, 68 percent of black and Latino children.[1] A woman over sixty is almost twice as likely as her male counterpart to be impoverished. One fifth of all elderly women are poor. For elderly black women, the poverty rate in 1981 was 43.5 percent; for elderly Latina women, 27.4 percent. Among black women over sixty-five living alone the 1982 poverty rate was about 82 percent.[2]

While the "feminization of poverty" isn't yet a household phrase, for growing numbers of women and their dependent children, it is an everyday reality. According to sociologist Diana Pearce, who tagged the trend in a 1978 study, 100,000 additional women with children fell below the poverty line each year from 1969 to 1978. In 1979, the number surged to 150,000, which was matched in 1980.[3] Households headed by women—now 15 percent of all American households—are the fastest growing type of family in the country.[4]

So clear is the spiraling pattern of women's impoverishment that the President's National Advisory Council on Economic Opportunity observed in September 1981: "All other things being equal, if the proportion of the poor in female-householder families were to continue to increase at the same rate as it did from 1967 to 1978, the poverty population would be composed solely of women and their children before the year 2000."

"All other things," of course, are not equal. Poverty is disproportionately borne by people of color, and with continued racial discrimination and high unemployment there will be many poor men in the year 2000. Yet, however many impoverished men there will be, there will still be many more poor women. Women are increasingly likely to carry primary responsibility for supporting themselves and their children as a result of rising divorce rates and nonmarital childbirths. At the same time, most women remain locked into dead-end jobs with wages too low to support themselves, let alone sustain a family. In 1980, the median income of a female household head, with no husband present, was $10,408; for black women it was $7,425 and for Latina women $7,031.

A 1977 government study found that if working women were paid what similarly qualified men earned, the number of poor families would decrease by half.[5] In 1980, the median income of a full-time, year-round working woman was $11,590—versus $19,172 for her male counterpart. In short, there is a fundamental difference between male and female poverty: for men, poverty is often the consequence of unemployment, and a job is generally an effective remedy, while female poverty often exists even when a woman works full-time.

Virtually all women are vulnerable—a divorce or widowhood is all it takes to throw many middle-class women into poverty. Yet as

Sally Michaels (not her real name), a divorced mother of three, points out, "There is a lot of denial among women. It's like how people are about seat belts. They don't want to wear them because they don't want to face the fact that they're in danger."

Decline of the Breadwinner Ethic

According to popular wisdom, it was women, and especially feminists, who brought about the "breakdown of the family."[6] What has gone almost unnoticed is that men, too, have changed and in a way that directly threatens the traditional family centered on the male breadwinner. In fact, in the last three decades, men have come to see themselves less and less as breadwinners and have ceased to measure their masculinity through their success as husbands and providers.

Yet, this drastic change in men, and in our cultural expectations of them, has been ignored, down-played, or else buried under the rubric of "changing sex roles." True, our expectations of adult womanhood have also altered dramatically in the last thirty years. The old feminine ideal—the full-time housewife with station wagon and suburban ranch house—has been largely replaced by the career woman with skirted suit and attaché case. Partly because the changes in the woman's role were given conscious articulation by the feminist movement, changes in men (and in the behavior expected of them) are usually believed to be derivative of, or merely reactive to, the changes in women. Yet what we could call "the male revolt" began well before the revival of feminism and stemmed from dissatisfactions every bit as deep, if not as idealistically expressed, as those that motivated the "second-wave" feminists.

Signs of male discontent began to emerge in the 1950s, a time when the media celebrated American "togetherness" and all men were expected to grow up only in order to settle down. To do anything else was less than grown-up, and the man who willfully deviated was judged, in both expert and popular opinion, to be "less than a man," someone about whom "you had to wonder." Yet, at the same time, middle-class men anguished over "conformity," which was covertly understood as acquiescence to the burdens of job and family. *Playboy* appeared, in 1953, as the first manifesto of open rebellion, describing wives as "parasites" and "gold diggers" that the free-spirited male eluded for life. By the end of the decade, the medical profession offered would-be male rebels a more respectable rationale than *Playboy*'s hedonism: the responsibility of breadwinning (combined with cholesterol) was what drove men to early deaths from heart disease. Soon after, psychology, the erstwhile champion of male heterosexual conformity, did an about-face, reclassifying responsibility as "guilt" and guilt as a psychic "toxin." By the end of the 1970s, the old ideological props for the male breadwinner ethic had crumbled. Today the man who postpones marriage and avoids women who are likely to become financial dependents is considered not deviant but healthy.

The greater prosperity men gained from the decline of the breadwinner ethic has not, however, been shared by women. A consequence of the changed economic relationship between the sexes has been the feminization of poverty. Indeed, for an increasing number of single mothers, there is only one thing left of the family-wage system, the fact that women, on the average, are paid less than a family (at current urban rents, less than a very small family) requires for a moderate standard of living.

The Goals of Feminism

If public policy cannot restore the breadwinner ethic and the male-centered family-wage system, then public policy can at least acknowledge their demise. To do so would require, for a start, a commitment to implementing some of the most elementary goals of feminism.

First, women should have the opportunity and the right to earn living wages, in fact, family wages, for many of them must support a family as well as themselves. This means the occupational segregation that locks 80 percent of women workers into low-paid "women's jobs" must be ended. It also means there must be greater financial recognition for those occupations that have come to be considered "women's work"—clerical, sales, light assembly, and service jobs. There must be an end to all forms of discrimination, subtle and otherwise, that have kept women out of men's higher-paid crafts and professions; and those who choose a "woman's job" such as nursing or clerical work, should receive pay equal to what men receive for jobs requiring comparable levels of skill and effort.

Nevertheless, the goal of financial independence for women, however elementary in the sense of having broad feminist support, is more radical than it may once have appeared. It is clear in the 1980s, if it was not in the more prosperous 1960s, that anti-discriminatory measures such as the Equal Rights Amendment are not enough to guarantee women's economic well-being. It will not help women to break out of their occupational ghetto if there are fewer and fewer well-paying jobs outside of it and it is hard to insist on higher pay from employers who are busily disinvesting, fleeing overseas, or replacing human labor with robots and microcomputers. For women (as well as for a growing number of men) the achievement of a family wage will require both a major redistribution of wealth and an economy planned to generate well-paying, useful employment—in short, an economic approach that is considerably to the left of anything in the current realm of American political discourse.

Second on the list of elementary goals, women need a variety of social supports before they will be able to enter the labor market on an equal footing with men. The most obvious and desperately needed service, both for women who are married and joint breadwinners and for those who are sole breadwinners, is reliable, high-quality child care. Job-training programs are another necessity, if only because so many of us, in all social classes, were educated for dependency and were never offered the skills that might sustain us through long stretches of financial independence, if not for a lifetime. Finally we must recognize that at least for the foreseeable future, many women will find themselves unable to enter the labor market at all, either because they have small children to care for or because they cannot find jobs that pay enough for material subsistence. This means there must be a government program of adequate income support, something far more generous and dignified than our present system of welfare. It is worth recalling that even before the recent wave of budget cutbacks, there was no state where the combined benefits of Aid to Families with Dependent Children (AFDC), the major form of public assistance, and food stamps were enough to bring a family up to the official poverty level. For women supporting families, unemployment means destitution, and a minimum-wage job is not much of an improvement.

Barbara Ehrenreich

The Need for Social Welfare

Feminists have demanded and fought for expanded social welfare programs from the beginning of our movement in the 1960s, a time when such a policy seemed reasonable and even inevitable, to a time when any expansion of government spending, other than military, is viewed as subversive to economic stability. Yet I believe that we need to push this set of demands even further. The collapse of the family-wage system requires nothing less than the creation of a welfare state, that is, a state committed to the welfare of its citizens and prepared to meet their needs—for financial assistance, medical care, education, child care, etc.—when they are unable to meet those needs themselves.

Those who believe that the country can no longer collectively afford such services should consider two obvious sources of revenue for social purposes: (1) increased corporate income taxes (corporate taxes have been declining steadily as a share of federal revenue since the 1950s while the burden of financing government activities has been shifted to individuals) and (2) drastically reduced military expenditures. As more and more people are coming to realize, our present stock of missiles and countermissiles does not constitute a "defense" but a standing invitation to annihilation. The kind of defense program we most urgently need is a program of defense against the mounting domestic dangers of poverty, unemployment, disease, and ignorance—that is, we need a welfare state.

If that phrase, "welfare state," has been made to sound morally distasteful by our current policy makers, we should recall that the family-wage system was itself a kind of private-sector welfare system, in which a woman's only "entitlement" was her share of her husband's wage. Those who believe that it is somehow more honorable to rely on an individual man than on agencies created by public wealth are simply clinging to an idealized memory of male paternalism. The breadwinner ethic never had the strength of law or even the transient support of public policy. If men cannot be held responsible as individuals—and there is no way consistent with democracy to do so—then we must all become more responsible collectively.

There are those who will argue that a welfare state only substitutes one sort of paternalism for another. The conservative analysis of the social welfare programs of the 1960s is that they failed, and that they failed because they engendered dependency and helplessness in their beneficiaries. (This, at least, is George Gilder's argument; others on the right argue that there is no need for further social welfare spending because the programs of the 1960s succeeded.) I am more impressed by the analysis of scholars such as Frances Fox Piven and Richard Cloward that the social welfare programs introduced in the 1960s, limited as they were, succeeded not only in lifting many of their direct beneficiaries out of poverty but in enabling working people in the "near poor" category, which includes so many women, to struggle for wage and benefit gains from their employers.

Not, as Piven and Cloward would agree, that those programs are in any way adequate models for the future. In fact, one of the most important feminist criticisms of the programs that constituted President Lyndon Johnson's Great Society is that they tended to assume a society of male breadwinners and female dependents. Thus, for example, Aid to Families with Dependent Children, whose beneficiaries are primarily single mothers and their children, continues to be based on the premise that the mere presence of a male in the household is a cure for poverty and a sufficient reason to suspend or reduce benefits. Job training programs such as the Comprehensive Employment and Training Act (CETA) have been faulted for tracking women toward low-wage service employment and away from potentially well-paying technical jobs. As Diana Pearce argues, social services must be based on the "acknowledgement that more and more women are financially on their own; that the female headed household is here to stay." Otherwise, government programs perpetuate the myth of male paternalism and the reality of female financial dependence.

Nor is there any reason why social welfare programs have to be intrinsically paternalisitic. Frank Riessman, Alan Gartner, and many others have made a convincing case over the past ten years that publicly sponsored services do not have to be bureaucratically or professionally dominated but can actually generate participatory citizenship and self-help initiatives. For example, instead of funding programs like Medicaid, which has served as a bountiful subsidy to the medical profession and associated industries, government health-care initiatives could focus on the direct provision of care, on preventive measures, and on environmental improvement. And surely financial assistance does not have to carry the stigma associated with welfare. Consider the contrast between unemployment insurance, which is collected by both men and women, and welfare, which is primarily collected by women. There is no reason why the institutions of an American welfare state could not be democratic, accountable, decentralized, and respectful of individual dignity—and there is no reason why liberals and feminists should abandon this as a goal.

I do not propose an expanded welfare state as an ultimate social goal but as a pragmatic step that circumstances have forced upon us. My utopian visions are far more socialistic, more democratic at every level of dialogue and decision making, more "disorderly," as Paul Goodman would have said, than anything that would ordinarily be described as a welfare state. Yet women like Brenda C. and Avis Parke have very few immediate alternatives. If they had won equality and economic independence before the collapse of the family-wage system, they might have been able to step right into the liberal feminist vision of an androgynous and fully capitalist society. But the collapse of the family-wage system came first, before either the economy or the culture was ready to admit the female breadwinner on equal terms. The result is that for an increasing number of women and children, the services that an adequate welfare state should provide have become essential to survival.

Relations With Men

But what about the men? For there is, of course, more at stake here than their wages. The collapse of the breadwinner ethic, and with it the notion of long-term emotional responsibility toward women, affects not only the homemaker who could be cut loose into poverty but the financially self-sufficient working woman, not to mention the children of either. For better or worse, most of us grew up expecting that our lives would be shared with those of the men in our generation; that we would marry or, in the modern vernacular, that we would have "long-term committed relationships." Only within those relationships could we imagine having children (and not only because of the financial consequences of motherhood) or finding the emotional support to do what we increasingly identified as our own things. Yet we—and the "we" here includes not only the educated urban women, feminists and others, whom conservatives might dismiss as members of marginal groups—face the prospect of briefer "relationships," punctuated by emotional dislocations and seldom offering the kind of loyalty that might extend into middle age. If we accept the male revolt as a fait accompli and begin to act on its economic consequences for women, are we not in some way giving up on men? Are we acquiescing to a future in which men will always be transients in the lives of women and never fully members of the human family?

To an extent, that is what women are beginning to do: look for emotional support and loyalty from other women, while remaining, in most instances, sexually inclined toward men. A neighbor, abandoned by her husband two years ago, still hopes to meet "a nice, reliable guy," but her daily needs for intimacy and companionship are met by a local women's group. An acquaintance, single and successful in her career, plans to have a baby with the help of women friends who are committed to serving as "co-parents." Two divorced women in their fifties decide that it will be both cheaper and less lonely to share the suburban house that one of them inherited from her marriage. According to Howard University professor Harriette McAdoo, there has always been a strong tradition of mutual support among urban black women, and a similar pattern is now emerging among the growing number of single women in the suburbs. That aid may involve practical help, like the exchange of babysitting or the loan of a credit card, and it usually involves affectionate support—friends to call in a moment of depression or to share a holiday meal. These are small steps, improvisations, but they grow out of a clear-headed recognition that there is no male breadwinner to lean on and probably not much use in waiting for one to appear.

Yet I would like to think that a reconciliation between the sexes is still possible. In fact, so long as we have sons as well as daughters, it will have to happen. "Grown-up", for men, should have some meaning for a boy other than "gone away"; and adulthood should mean more than moral vagrancy. If we cannot have—and do not want—a binding pact between the sexes, we still must have one between the generations, and that means there must be a renewal of loyalty and trust between adult men and women. But what would be the terms of such a reconciliation? We have seen the instability, and the indignity, of a bond based on a man's earnings and a woman's dependence. We cannot go back to a world where maturity meant "settling," often in stifled desperation, for a life perceived as a "role." Nor can we accept the nightmare anomie of the pop psychologists' vision: a world where other people are objects of consumption, a world of chance encounters of a "self" propelled by impulse alone.

I can see no other ethical basis for a reconciliation than the feminist principle often repeated—that women are also persons, with the same need for respect, for satisfying work, for love, and for pleasure as men. As it is, male culture seems to have abandoned the breadwinner role without overcoming the sexist attitudes that role has perpetuated: on the one hand, the expectation of female nurturance and submissive service as a matter of right; on the other hand, a misogynist contempt for women as "parasites" and entrappers of men. In a "world without a father," that is, without the private system of paternalism built into the family-wage system, we will have to learn to be brothers and sisters.

Finally, I would hope that we might meet as rebels together—not against one another but against a social order that condemns so many of us to meaningless or degrading work in return for a glimpse of commodified pleasures and condemns all of us to the prospect of mass annihilation. If we can do this, if we can make a common commitment to ourselves and future generations, then it may also be possible to rebuild the notion of personal commitment and to give new strength and meaning to the words we have lost—responsibility, maturity, and even, perhaps, manliness.

THE FEMINIZATION OF POVERTY
Women, Work, and Welfare

Diana Pearce

Poverty is rapidly becoming a female problem. Though many women have achieved economic independence from their spouses by their participation in the labor force (and in some cases, by divorce), for many the price of that independence has been their pauperization and dependence on welfare. In 1976, nearly two out of three of the 15 million poor persons over sixteen years old were women.[1] In certain groups, the imbalance was even greater: over 70 percent of the aged poor are women. Black women, who were only 6.1 percent of the population in 1975, accounted for 17 percent of the poor that year.[2]

The economic status of women has declined over the past several decades. At the same time, a number of important and relevant demographic changes (the increase in longevity, the increase in divorce, the increase in illegitimate births) have occurred. Perhaps

This essay is reprinted with permission from *Urban and Social Change Review* 11, no. 1 (February 1978): 28–36. The author is indebted to Frank Munger, who sparked interest in this problem, and to Bail Miller and George Wright, who reviewed early drafts.

the most striking of these trends is the increasing number of female-headed* families; the percentage of all families that were female headed rose from 10.1 in 1950 to 14 in 1976, an increase of almost 40 percent in a single generation.[3] At the same time, the economic well-being of this growing group has eroded. The ratio of median income of female-headed families has declined steadily from 56 percent in 1950 to 47 percent in 1974. Moreover, between 1950 and 1976 the number of families with incomes less than the poverty level that were female headed doubled. Today almost half of all poor families are female headed.[4]

Paradoxically, this decline occurs in a period when other trends suggest potential for improving women's status—trends such as the increase in women's labor-force participation, the mandating of affirmative action, and the increasing employment of better-educated women. Yet, women's earnings, relative to those of men, have decreased; the female/male ratio of full-time, year-round, civilian earnings has fallen from .61 to .59. Whereas in 1950, the unemployment rate of women was only slightly larger than that of men (5.7 vs. 5.1), by 1976 it was 8.6 compared to the male rate of 7.0.[5] Moreover, if one does not include workers under twenty, for whom unemployment rates are high for both sexes, the disparity becomes much greater; in 1974 the unemployment rate of women twenty years old and older was almost one-and-one-half times that of men.[6]

In sum, it is women who account for an increasingly large proportion of the economically disadvantaged. What these statistics do not reveal is that while many women are poor because they live in poor, male-headed households, an increasing number are becoming poor in their own right. I will concentrate here on the latter group, that is, those women who are poor because they are women. While many women are poor for reasons other than, or in addition to, their gender, in this paper I will focus on the question: What are the economic and social consequences of being female that result in higher rates of poverty? This does not mean that the problems of the millions of women in poor, male-headed households are insignificant or unimportant; on the contrary, much of

* This term will be used to refer to those families in which there is only an adult woman and no adult male; "male-headed" will be used to refer to families in which there is an adult male and perhaps an adult female. These are official Census Bureau terms, not descriptions of intrafamily dynamics.

what is said here can be applied to their problems as well. In particular, I will explore two aspects of the feminization of poverty: (1) the role of different sources of income—earned income, public transfer and private transfer income—in allowing women's poverty and (2) the role of the welfare system in perpetuating women's poverty.

Income and Poverty

Unlike earlier immigrant groups, who entered the urban labor market at the bottom and gradually improved their position, women have remained at the bottom.[7] As Oppenheimer has cogently argued, women's entry into the labor force in steadily increasing numbers, from less than one fifth of the work force in 1920 to nearly 40 percent today, has been bought at the price of economic advancement for women workers.[8] That is, within occupationally segregated "ghettos," the demand for cheap labor and the demand for female labor became synonymous. The rapid growth of jobs, particularly since World War II, has been in industries and occupations that are low wage and dead end—and open to women. Once in the labor force, women are confined to these jobs and are restricted from moving into better-paid (but traditionally male) jobs or moving up career ladders. As a result, women are much more concentrated in fewer occupations than are men; 60 percent of all women are in ten occupations. Moreover, this concentration has remained stable over time. Fourteen of seventeen occupations that were predominantly female in 1900 are still predominantly female, and a segregation index developed by Gross indicates that women are as occupationally segregated today as they were at the end of the Victorian era.[9]

Not only do women suffer limited occupational opportunity, but economic well-being is a price paid by women in the pink-collar[10] and other female ghettos (textile and electronics factories, banks and offices, household service and day care). Sometime ago, D. S. Knudsen showed that the higher the percentage of workers that are female in an occupation, the lower the average income in that occupation.[11] Fuchs maintains that most of the earnings gap between men and women can be accounted for by the different jobs held by men and women.[13] In short, women are concentrated in relatively few, generally low-paying occupations. Some specific examples are given in Table 1.

Table 1
Weekly Wages and Percent Female for Selected Industries, January 1973

	Average weekly earnings	Percent female
Apparel manufacture	$ 93	81
Transportation equipment	210	10
Malt liquor	229	7
Motor vehicle sales	152	11
Construction	223	6
Transportation and utilities	196	21

E. Waldman and B. J. McEaddy, "Where Women Work. An Analysis by Industry and Occupation," Monthly Labor Review, *May 1974, p. 10.*

The cost to women of occupational segregation is difficult to grasp. In 1970, when the poverty-level income for a family of four was about $3,700, there were 6 million women who worked full-time, year-round, and earned less than $4,000 per year. Such women were concentrated in a few of the lowest-paying jobs: sales workers.[13]

In terms of increased poverty of women, Sawhill presents two sets of findings that put a price tag on occupational segregation.[14] First, a study done by the Urban Institute calculated the earnings functions of female heads of families as if they were males but otherwise with the same age, race, education, and residence characteristics. It was found that women who head families would receive 36 percent more income if they were men, other things being equal. If male labor-force participation characteristics, such as hours worked, are also added into the equations, the women's incomes would also increase, but by much less (13 percent). Sawhill also calculated what could be considered to be the long-term institutional constraints on women's income imposed by occupational segregation. Classifying occupations from the detailed (three-digit) census code as predominantly male (80 percent or more of all workers are male), predominantly female (30 percent or less of all workers are male), or mixed, she calculated the number of occupations in which a female high school graduate, age twenty-five to thirty-four, would make less than $3,000 per year working full-time. She found that while only 20 percent of the predominantly male occupations were ones with such poverty-level wages, over half (54 percent) of the female-dominated occupations were ones with poverty-level wages.[15]

Although similar in their role in the labor force to previous ethnic, immigrant, and racial groups who were exploited for their cheap labor, particularly in the first generation of their participation in the urban industrial labor force, in at least one respect women are different from such past groups of new entrants to the labor force. Women are permanent temporary workers. That is, employers can and do flim-flam women to their (the employers') advantage, by simultaneously enticing them to enter the labor force (the help-wanted ads read "varied, interesting work, young company on the move"), but at the same time minimizing their commitment to the idea of an individual career ("earn that Acapulco vacation, send your kids to college"). As long as women, as well as their employers, view their work as temporary and secondary while their home and family is their permanent and primary commitment, they are less likely to engage in expensive-to-the-employer-type activities such as participating in labor unions and affirmative-action suits, making demands for advancement or skill development, and even simply working long enough to be eligible for a pension.

This interest on the part of employers in obtaining loyal but not long-term employees also accounts for their lack of interest, much less enthusiasm, for developing quality day care, even for welfare mothers. Such a service might permit a nearly uninterrupted work life, and/or commitment to the individual employer over a period of time long enough to acquire seniority, to demand a promotion, or otherwise to become expensive. Providing day care implies support for the permanent participation of women in the labor force, as well as acceptance of women, including mothers, as workers whose primary economic contribution is not in terms of child care. Without the provision of quality day care, on the other hand, women who drop out of the labor force or quit a job because of child-care problems can be seen as "less committed" workers. In turn, their lesser attachment to the labor force is identified as the cause of their disadvantaged status. Their interrupted work lives also make upward mobility difficult; they never achieve seniority, and career development suffers. Particularly, as fringe benefits become an increasingly large proportion of the employer's labor cost (estimates run as high as 40 percent), workers who are denied such benefits because of their temporary and/or part-time and/or short-term status are increasingly attractive economically. Temporary workers are cheap workers.

Related to the "temporary" status of women is their tendency to be employed in part-time work. Although clearly part-time work is the preference of many women, particularly middle-class women, there are many women who would prefer to work full-time but are unable to do so. In part, this is because the structure of the economy has changed. Many of the service industries that account for much of the recent increased labor demand, and especially for female labor,[16] are ones that have hours that require one or two part-time shifts of workers rather than a single eight-hour shift (for example, restaurants, transportation service, and retail stores). Such places frequently differentiate between part-time and full-time workers, not only in wages and benefits but in terms of opportunities for advancement and for upgrading of skills.

In addition to lower wages, women suffer from higher rates of unemployment and must wait longer periods of time between jobs. These patterns of instability, or what Wilensky called "disorderly work history,"[17] lead many women to become disillusioned and leave the labor force. Almost twice as many women as men are classified as discouraged workers: neither working nor actively looking for work.[18]

Finally, it should be noted that the effects of occupational segregation and wage discrimination are so strong that they tend to overwhelm other kinds of disadvantage. Thus, there is some evidence that black women earn somewhat more than white women of comparable education and occupation, apparently because black women tend to have more economic return-to-work experience than do white women (perhaps because it is less interrupted than the average white female's).[19] Apparently, for a woman, race is a relatively unimportant consideration in determining economic status.

Private Transfer Income

The second source of income to be considered here is that of private transfers. At one time, most of the private transfer was indeed private, that is, within the nuclear family. Working husbands gave their nonworking wives some portion of the paycheck to pay for the expenses of the home and child(ren). The rising divorce rate is such that it is estimated that about one in three marriages will fail; moreover, they will fail sooner, resulting more often in the early married and early divorced young mother with very young children. The internal transfer of resources for housekeeping and the needs of the children becomes institutionalized in the form of child-support payments (and, sometimes, alimony). For many women, the price of freedom from the marriage bond is therefore very steep, for the likelihood of the same rate of transfer of economic support continuing is very low. In one study done on behalf of the public welfare department office charged with enforcement of child support for welfare mothers, it was found that a minority of only 22 percent of spouses were fulfilling all of their obligations fully; half were contributing nothing. Moreover, in two out of three AFDC [Aid to Familes with Dependent Children] cases, there was no child-support agreement, formal or informal to be enforced.[20] In part because of this problem, in part because the fathers are either not accessible or do not have the resources themselves, concentrated efforts at increasing child-support payments on behalf of women on AFDC cases have very little effect. The total money collected in December 1976, after nearly a year of increased nationwide efforts, averaged about $6 per recipient, and about 1 percent of the AFDC cases closed that month were closed because of receipt of child support.[21]

It is clear that particularly in the case of AFDC mothers the lack of child support is in part due to the fathers' own poverty, for one study estimated that over a third were unemployed, almost a fifth had criminal records, and the majority had unskilled or semiskilled occupations.[22] Potential for support exists; a third of the AFDC parents providing no support had some college education, and a third had their high school diplomas.[23] This potential for support will not be realized because the social norms permit men to cease their support of their children when they leave their children. The poor father by no means has a monopoly on nonsupport, for the failure to provide (or cease to provide after a few years) is a practice widespread throughout American society. Forty percent of absent fathers contribute nothing, while the average payment provided by the other 60 percent is less than $2,000 per year (Urban Institute, 1976); this is at a time when the median income for all families is about $13,800. Thus, the poverty among female-headed families that is due to the lack of child support will not decrease unless there is real change in the societal context that condones and even encourages the absent father's neglect of his financial responsibilities to his children.[24]

Finally, women who head households are less likely to be the recipients of intergenerational transfers of resources. While many parents help out adult children in times of financial need or crisis, the single or divorced daughter is less likely to be the recipient of these transfers. Even if a woman received such help during marriage, the dissolution of the marriage often includes selling the house and other property. It is also true that while women have the same overall median level of education as men, the distribution is much more clustered around the median. Thus, not only do fewer women have very low levels of education, but also fewer women than men continue their education beyond the high school level. The lesser investment in daughters' than in sons' higher education robs women of a source for intergenerational transfer of resources.

Women and Public Transfers

Public transfers include all unearned income received from the government and can be divided into two basic types: that which is received as a consequence of participation in the labor force and that which is received as minimal income support, regardless of previous employment status.

In work-related benefits, women are generally underrepresented among the beneficiaries and are even more underrepresented in dollars received. Thus, while women are 52 percent of the beneficiaries of Social Security (which is underrepresentation because of the highly skewed sex distribution of the aged), they receive only 46 percent of the benefits.[25]

Unemployment insurance, however, is somewhat more of an enigma. Figures cited by officials state that women make up 38 percent of the total recipients[26], which compares favorably with their participation (40 percent) in the labor market. Yet, a number of factors point to the fact that a much larger number of women are not covered at all or are covered in a very limited way. First, there are certain occupations that are entirely excluded, such as household-service workers (that is, almost all women, or 1.7 million workers), and farm workers (who number 0.7 million). Second, unemployment insurance is predicated upon "willingness to work," which is usually defined as "willingness to work full-time." Since many women work in industries that structurally require part-time workers, many of them are excluded. Third, under similarly rigid logic, many states disenfranchise pregnant women entirely without considering individual differences in physical ability or willingness to work and regardless of month of pregnancy. Fourth, many women work in the "irregular economy," doing work that is not covered because it is semilegal or illegal, marginal, or bartered (prostitutes, babysitters, women who type at home). Finally, many women workers seem to use AFDC instead as unemployment insurance (see below).

Other forms of "work"-related, income-transfer programs support so few women that it becomes difficult to compare the relative inequality created thereby. How much, for example, is the free medical care and educational benefits available to veterans directly or indirectly a reason for their lesser rates of male poverty? A corollary question of policy interest is whether the incidence of poverty is reduced for those women who serve in the armed forces, as apparently it may be for men who enter the labor force via the armed forces.[27] As Black Lung coverage does for mine workers, would "Brown Lung" legislation and benefit programs for the largely female work force of textile mills have a measurable impact on women's poverty (due in this case to work-related ill health and consequent uncompensated unemployment)?

In discussing public assistance, that is, public transfers not conditioned on previous labor-force experience, it is necessary first to establish the extent and the adequacy of such public assistance. Although the number of AFDC recipients has risen dramatically in the last decade, as a percentage of the population it has remained stable at about 5 percent.[28] Benefit levels however, have been declining; using 1967 as the base (=100), benefits declined from $139 to $135, from 1974 to 1976, or about 1.4 percent per year. The actual average payment per family in 1977 was $235, or about $75 per recipient. By even the very conservative standards of state governments, benefit levels are inadequate. Each state determines its own standard of need based on cost-of-living estimates, but this standard is not necessarily tied to the Bureau of Labor Statistics poverty-level income cutoffs. Even so, the state is not required to provide families on relief with the full amount that the state has determined as their minimum need. Further, many states set an arbitrary top figure regardless of family size. The result is that, nationally, 23 percent of the AFDC case load receive cash benefits that total less than 40 percent of the poverty line (adjusting for family composition, etc.), and 24 percent were given benefits that put them between 40 and 70 percent of the poverty line.[29] Even including the cash equivalent of food stamps in the calculations left ten states in 1974 with maximum benefit levels less than 75 percent of the poverty line.[30] Finally, if one compares the poverty level of recipients before and after receiving welfare, there is relatively little escape from poverty via AFDC: whereas 92 percent of the families receiving AFDC were poor before, 76 percent of AFDC families remain poor after receiving aid.[31]

It seems clear, then, that whatever the source of income considered, women are frequently likely to receive less than they need, often much less than a poverty-level income. Child-support payments are, with rare exceptions, paid irregularly, frequently well below need (as well as below the absent parent's ability to pay), and are subject to premature demise. Welfare payments are below even that state's own determination of need in almost half the states, leaving almost all welfare families below poverty-level cash incomes. Even earned income, largely because of occupational segregation as well as discrimination, fails to provide above-poverty-level incomes for many women. In 1976, almost 20 percent of employed, female family heads were poor, and one third of black employed females who headed families were in poverty.[32]

As we have seen, each of the sources of income—and, therefore, of potential economic well-being—is likely to be inadequate and thus to contribute to women's poverty. The process of feminization of poverty is also a process of institutionalization of sexual inequality, focused in particular on the institution of public welfare. In order to understand, however, the role of public welfare in both the deterioration and the maintenance of women's poverty, it is necessary to put welfare's role in historical perspective.

The History of the American Welfare System

Over time, the American welfare system has moved through three stages of development, each of which can be characterized by its role in the larger society, in particular its role vis-à-vis the labor market. In the first stage of this federally constructed and subsidized system, welfare was conceived as a means to protect an already glutted Depression-era labor market from being further flooded by would-be workers, widows and deserted wives, the disabled, and the aged. Even the titles of the original state assistance programs revealed that welfare was predicated on motherhood: "Mother's Pensions," "Mothers' Aid." By the 1950s, however, the problem became not one of too many workers but of too much dependency.

At this second stage, welfare was seen as a temporary expedient, necessary to ease the transition from rural to urban (for example, for Southern black and white migrants) and from home to work (for the woman who heads the family). Welfare recipients at this juncture were not so clearly "deserving" as those in the first stage. Nevertheless, much of the policy debate centered on the adjustment problems of these families. Indeed, much of the rhetoric that frames today's policy questions comes out of this "tiding over" model of welfare; the "problem" of second-generation welfare families, the "vicious circle" of poverty, all imply that welfare had failed in its function as temporary expedient to tide one over a rough spot. This stage culminated in the 1962 amendments, which established social services for the welfare recipient. The object of these new services was to enhance the positive aspect of welfare, its role increasing the adjustment of the individual in crisis (for example, to urban life, to single parenthood, or both), while preventing the development of permanent dependency.

The third stage is somewhat more difficult to discern, for it continues to be clouded by the leftover rhetoric of the "tiding over" stage, the dominant policy question is, "Why don't welfare recipients work and get off of welfare as quickly as possible?" If instead we turn it around and ask, "Why are so many welfare recipients working?" we will be better able to comprehend the way in which welfare is not simply a temporary aid during a crisis or adjustment phase but a system that is creating a permanent underclass of welfare recipient/low-wage workers. For in spite of the enormous disincentives and severe labor-market handicaps of most recipients, an increasing proportion are working. Although, at any one point in time, only about 15 percent are working as well as receiving welfare, surveys indicate that the true figure is at least 25 percent, to which one must add those in training, awaiting training, or looking for work.[33]

Moreover, if one looks at even a relatively short span of time, it is clear that most welfare recipients in fact alternate between welfare and work, or combine both in a bewildering and rapidly shifting pattern. Of currently active AFDC recipients in 1973, Williams found that almost one third had worked thirteen months or more in the past three years, and only one third were dependent solely on welfare over the entire thirty-seven-month interval.[34] Like the ex-convict, the ex-welfare recipient is "at risk"; consigned by prejudice, discrimination, and institutional constraints to a narrow range of opportunities to "get a living" by combining or alternating work and welfare. Put more graphically, the third stage of welfare can be described as a "workhouse without walls."

A Workhouse Without Walls

What are some of the elements that underpin the development of welfare as a "workhouse without walls"? Without trying to exhaust all possibilities, we will devote the remainder of this paper to a brief discussion of several of these elements: (1) the increase in labor-force experience of welfare recipients, (2) the change in welfare rules related to income disregarding, (3) the effects of the Work Incentive (WIN) program, (4) the skill levels and occupational status of welfare recipients, and (5) indirect effects of welfare/single mother status.

As with most mothers, the labor-force participation rate of welfare mothers was low in the past, but today over 90 percent have worked at some time, and fully three fourths of AFDC recipients worked full-time at a regular job at some time in the past. Most began regular work early, almost half starting their first regular job by the time they were seventeen, including 18 percent who began regular work when they were fifteen years old or younger.[35] Together with the figures cited above, it is clear that the typical woman on welfare is, or has been, a worker. If instead of viewing welfare recipients as single mothers who have "lost" their (male) source of economic support, one views welfare recipients as disadvantaged workers who are unemployed, then welfare takes on a different character. Essentially, welfare viewed this way is a kind of poor woman's Unemployment Compensation, but with a difference. Although serving the same economic function as Unemployment Compensation, that of temporarily supporting workers who have become involuntarily unemployed and thereby easing for both the individual and the economy the stress of being out of work, welfare is a privilege (however dubious) and not a right. This has important consequences for both recipient and the prospective employer; welfare supports a low-wage, predominantly female, labor pool that is so stigmatized, harassed, and degraded, that many eagerly seek to exchange welfare poverty for wage poverty.

Making the transition permanently from welfare recipient to worker is becoming increasingly difficult because of the way in which income disregards work. In 1967 Congress required that states not tax the recipient's earned income at 100 percent, but rather that they disregard one third of all earned income plus employment-related expenses. While this reduced the effective tax rate to about 40 percent, the rest of the population does not face this steep rate until their income is above $40,000.[36] Even so, the tax rate forces recipients into a position whereby it is almost impossible for them to work their way off welfare. It does this in two ways: first, the combined value of welfare's cash benefits, food stamps, and medical benefits, plus the income disregards, make it necessary for recipients to earn quite a bit more than the maximum allowable amount to achieve an equivalent standard of living; second, the tax rate subsidizes and rationalizes the payment of poverty-level wages. Appel estimated that in Michigan, where one may earn up to $669 per month and sustain welfare eligibility, it would take $904 per month to buy the equivalent of welfare-subsidized food, child care, and medical care.[37] Likewise, there is a "notch" in terms of getting on welfare; it frequently is advantageous to quit work because one's earned income is too high to get on welfare, and then return to work at the same wage. Even with the high tax rate, the total welfare benefit package is higher than low- or poverty-level wages without the nonmonetary benefits.[38] This should not be taken to mean that income disregards are not an improvement but rather that they widen the group who work but do not earn enough to escape from welfare or poverty. As we shall see, few women on AFDC have the skills and education to earn their way to independence.

In addition to incentives to go on or stay on welfare while working, welfare systems offer incentives to work while on welfare simply by giving recipients less than the state has declared that they need. About half the states do not pay the full standard of need, resulting in over 62 percent of AFDC families having budgets that recognize unmet needs;[39] any amount earned up to the level of need is usually totally disregarded.

Altogether, the income disregards and notches that push welfare recipients to work, and low-wage workers to go on welfare, could potentially be the modern equivalent of the Speenhamland Plan.[40] That is, employers have no reason to raise wages, for there is no scarcity of low-wage workers and much incentive for those who are on welfare to seek employment. But there is much incentive to lower wages below subsistence level, since the worker will be paid the difference, at least minimally, by welfare. Thus the creation of low-wage jobs is subsidized by welfare, making profitable manufacture and services that would otherwise be too costly to produce. This thus creates a class of workers who are forced onto welfare because their work pays too little, and welfare recipients who are forced to work because welfare is inadequate.

The Work Incentive Program (WIN)

Since the days of the Poor Laws, welfare has sought to force people to work. This has been done not only by stigmatizing the poor, as when seventeenth-century Pennsylvanians had to wear a "P" on their sleeves (for Pauper), and by inadequacy of benefits as in the principle of "less eligibility" wherein no recipient receives more than the lowliest worker. It has also been done by coercion. The workhouse and poorhouse were the nineteenth-century means; today's poor are coerced through forced registration in the WIN program.

Although WIN does not force all recipients to work, its implied promise of a route out of poverty is, for many, a cruel hoax. WIN contributes to the poverty of women in several ways, each of which is a variation on the theme of reinforcing rather than removing the handicaps that women face in the labor market.

First, WIN has promised much but delivers little for most women. Although many women on welfare are required to register for WIN, there are a number of stages between registering for WIN and obtaining employment: certification, determination of need for services, training, job placement, etc. Thus while there were 1,175,800 ongoing mandatory registrants in November, 1975, there were only 6,900 who left WIN that month for employment (including those who became employed on their own and not through or because of WIN).[41]

Second, once in training, WIN enrollees find that the jobs that they are being trained for are ones that will not remove them from poverty. As can be seen from Table 2, almost half the training slots are for jobs which are in sectors that have very high poverty rates for women who head families.[42]

Third, in addition to placing small numbers of women, and providing them with occupations that frequently do not pay a living wage, WIN has been moving towards direct job placement (sometimes with on-the-job training), in spite of the fact that women in particular benefit from even minimal skill upgrading.[43] Most job training under WIN was classified as minimum—less than six weeks—or moderate—up to several months.

The bottom line in assessing WIN, however, is its ability to

Table 2
Comparison of Occupational Distribution of AFDC Female Family Heads and WIN Institutional Training Positions

	Ever employed AFDC mothers	Female family heads with work experience	Percent in occupational group in poverty	WIN training positions
Professional, technical, managerial, official	2	17	9	10
Clerical and sales	14	33	12	41
Craftsman and operatives	12	12	46	22*
Private household workers	20	8	56	
Other service workers	28	22	34	23

S. Levitan, M. Rein, and D. Marwich, Work and Welfare Go Together *(Baltimore: Johns Hopkins University Press, 1972); U.S., Department of Commerce, Bureau of the Census, "A Statistical Portrait of Women in the U.S.,"* Current Population Reports, *special study, Series P-23, no. 58 (Washington, D.C.: Government Printing Office, 1976).*

**Listed separately in occupational training distribution as "processing, machine trades, bench work, structural work."*

prepare participants to earn a living wage; in that it has failed. Those recipients who are able to find employment do not usually earn even a poverty-level wage.[44] Smith reported that the average salary was $5,572 for women and $6,306 for men; perhaps even more discouraging was the fact that the net average increase in earnings for all program participants was $676 per year for women with little or no recent work experience and $41 for women with recent work experience.[45]

Since WIN does not train women for jobs that provide the means to economic self-sufficiency, it is not surprising that one of its outcomes is increased case loads and/or an increase in working welfare recipients. The study by Smith et al. of Chicago found that two thirds of the ex-WIN female participants who were working received supplementary welfare grants, but only one third of the male recipients did.[46] About a year and a half after completing the WIN program, a majority were working or had worked, yet a majority were also still on welfare.

The WIN program, whatever its phase, is thus a cornerstone of the "workhouse without walls." By taking a group of women who are already handicapped by low educational levels, low skill, and occupational status, and giving them either no training or minimal training in fields that do not pay a living wage, and forcing them to work, WIN has created for many women a "no-win" situation. They cannot use welfare training programs to get decently paid employment, nor can they use paid employment to get off of welfare.

Conclusions and Implications for Policy

The problem of women in poverty has many aspects that should be mentioned. First, many of the disadvantages suffered by poor women are exacerbated by racism and prejudice for minority women. Such effects, however, are complex and uneven. Second, many of the economic problems of women are reinforced or increased by the indirect effects of being female and/or a single mother; for example, housing discrimination forces many women to live in "ghettoes," which are far away from the better-paying jobs in the new suburban industrial parks.

Even without having explored the added handicaps of minority status or the additional indirect effects of gender, it is clear that the relative economic status of women is declining. This is true regardless of the income source. In spite of increased labor-force participation, the occupational ghettoization and discrimination has prevented any improvement in women's earnings relative to men. Child support, which rapidly increasing divorce and illegitimacy rates make more important, is so minimal in reality that even the one- or two-child family runs a high risk of becoming poor if the father leaves. And welfare, although it supports more of the eligible population than ever before, does so at an even more penurious level than in the past (relative to the current incomes of American families in general).

Welfare's role in women's poverty is much more than simply one of penny pinching in payment levels, for it plays an important part in perpetuating women's poverty. I have maintained here that the Work Incentive program and income-disregard programs are creating a "workhouse without walls," from which escape is increasingly more difficult. The welfare system has not only "bureaucratized" inequality,[47] it has institutionalized it. By uniting inequality in the labor market with the pauperization that is endemic to public welfare, the American system is creating a set of forces that oppress all women, as well as those that are already in poverty. For the same work incentives that "encourage" women on welfare to work at poverty-level wages are also the means of subsidization of a low-wage labor force enabling entire industries to pay poverty-level wages. By "training" and/or placing AFDC women in traditional, low-paying, predominantly female, occupational ghettoes, WIN programs not only perpetuate their poverty but reinforce the barriers that many women face as they try to get jobs that pay a living wage but are traditionally male.

The major implication for policy for both the feminization of poverty and the increasing labor-force participation of welfare mothers is that gender cannot be ignored. That is, the poverty of men and the poverty of women are different problems, requiring different solutions. For men, the problem is more one of a high-dependency burden: in the New Jersey income experiment, the average number of children per family was 4.0,[48] while nationally the AFDC-UP family averaged 4.4 persons. In contrast, an average AFDC female-headed family was 3.1 persons.[49] Male poverty is thus more often a welfare problem, that is supplementing wages with some kind of family allowance for those with heavy dependency burdens. For women, however, the problem lies more with the labor market. Going to work, even full-time, is not likely to be the means of escape out of poverty for most welfare women.[50] Once welfare policy begins to treat female welfare recipients as disadvantaged workers, then it can begin to develop appropriate programs of intervention at the individual level (for example, training in traditionally male blue-collar occupations) and at the institutional level (aggressive action by the federal government against sex segregation of enterprises and even entire industries). Without such changes, we will continue to build a "workhouse without walls," and its inhabitants will become even more predominantly women who are trapped in a life of poverty by welfare penuriousness and institutionalized work force marginality.

SHORTCHANGED
The Political Economy of Women's Poverty

Elaine Donovan and Mary Huff Stevenson

For the past decade one of the most staggering trends in the United States has been the growth of female-headed households. From 1972 to 1982 alone the number rose by 57 percent, so that by now one out of every six American families is maintained by a woman. And, as the number of female-headed households has changed, so, too, has the proportion living in poverty. As has been stated elsewhere in this volume, one third of all women supporting families live below the poverty level, and for black and Latina women the figure is one out of every 1.67.[1]

Such figures count only the "official" poor, based on calculations of the federal government's statisticians about the numbers of people below the "poverty level." This may sound cut and dried. In fact, the poverty line is the subject of controversy and has historically represented a subbasement measure of poverty. It reflects assumptions about food budgets and nutritional adequacy long criticized as reflecting unreasonable expectations regarding the economic needs of poor families and the differences between urban and rural poverty.[2] Indeed, if the poverty line were just 125 percent of the official measure, thus including families often called the "near poor," then the number of Americans counted as poor would jump from 13 percent to 18 percent of the population.

Despite the problems defining the poverty line, however, there is no doubt that female-headed families constitute an ever growing proportion of all poor families. The common wisdom would suggest that the most effective way to pull women and their families out of poverty would simply be a year-round job at a living wage. Yet, any careful analysis of women's limited potential as wage earners in the current economy—coupled with a recognition of the negative effects of racism and the restrictions of public assistance programs—shows the limits of "common sense" in providing useful solutions to women's poverty.

Here we do not repeat the depressing figures. Instead, we present the differing explanations of the same facts about women's poverty provided by the three major economic perspectives. The neoclassical, institutional, and Marxist economic perspectives are each roughly tied to a separate political philosophy and differ in their basic assumptions, their choice of key issues, and the scenarios they offer to explain women's poverty. Each view offers different remedies to women seeking a road out of poverty. The neoclassical economists would suggest that women choose another, existing, road, while the institutionalists recommend clearing the present road to make the journey less obstructed. And the Marxists demand that new roads be built, since none of the available ones lead women out of poverty. In order to choose knowledgeably among the spectrum of proposed solutions, poor women and their advocates need to understand the differing economic arguments used to justify or oppose particular policy alternatives.

Free to Choose: Neoclassical Economics

Neoclassical economics stresses individual choice within a competitive, free market. With a bustling free-for-all market, full of large numbers of buyers and sellers, producers must compete against one another. In theory, this competition will lead to consumers obtaining the best-quality goods at the lowest price.

Thus, in perfect competition, according to neoclassical economists such as Milton Friedman, each producer pursues his or her own self-interest, and the outcome automatically benefits society (this is Adam Smith's "invisible hand" of perfect competition). In this model, every individual decides his or her course. Choices are unlimited, except for the discipline imposed by a competitive marketplace. What's more, the market has a built-in check: if too much of a product is available, its price will fall and some producers will go out of business; if too little, prices rise, new firms spring up, and production increases. All this makes government intervention unnecessary—and undesirable.

The neoclassical approach, often called "the new home economics," applies the economic principles of the marketplace to non-market relationships at home . . . an area traditionally considered off limits for economists.[3]

This market model assumes that economic actors are all trying to maximize something: producers try to maximize profits, consumers try to maximize satisfaction. To reach these goals, consumers will seek a variety of goods and services, and producers will specialize, through division of labor, to produce more efficiently (and therefore more profitably). Output for society as a whole will be maximized, giving consumers the widest array of choice and the largest amount of the goods they want.

Similarly, neoclassical economists explain the marriage marketplace by assuming that each partner seeks to obtain the most satisfaction, with the household maximizing its "output" (which includes the income from paid work as well as the production of goods and services within the household) through specialization. Though many clergy and marriage counselors refer to marriage as a "partnership," the neoclassical economists mean it quite literally. They see marriage creating a two-person firm, in which the goal is to maximize the household's well-being through specialization and division of labor.

This, of course, works best if the two individuals have different strengths and talents. If one spouse or partner should happen to command a high salary in the labor market but can't cook, while the other happens to be a gourmet who is a whiz at ironing and vacuuming but has few other marketable skills, each will be better off specializing in his or her strength and relying on the other to make up for his or her weakness.

Although this argument could be stated in sex-neutral terms (as we have just done), neoclassical economists are quick to point out that wives are more likely to be good cooks, while husbands are more likely to command higher pay (economists call this relative strength "comparative advantage"). Therefore, this difference quickly becomes not only a defense of the division of labor within the household but also a defense of traditional sex roles in marriage.

The neoclassical rationalization for women's home production (and men's comparative advantage in the labor market) revolves around women's traditional roles as wives and mothers. Men are assumed to spend all of their postschool years fully employed, picking up valuable skills, experience, and on-the-job training: women's labor-market experience is assumed to be intermittent, with some time spent completely out of the labor force and other periods of only marginal participation (temporary, part-time, part-year). Women acquire fewer new skills and less experience during these periods, presumed to be devoted to childbearing and child-rearing, and their existing skills may even deteriorate.

Critics point out that this approach is completely circular—women's roles within the household are explained by their labor-force status, but women's labor-force status is explained by their household roles. As University of Illinois economists Marianne Ferber and Bonnie Birnbaum put it in their critical analysis of the new home economics, "Women specialize in housework because they earn less in the labor market, and they earn less in the labor market because they specialize in housework."[4]

Neoclassical economists also have a theory of fertility. What is the economic value of a child? According to the new home economics, while it is acknowledged that children may be viewed as investment goods in agricultural societies (where, after a few years of nurturing they may repay their keep with productive labor), in industrial societies like our own, children have economic value primarily as consumer durables, i.e., for the satisfaction that may be derived from them over a period of years.

Given reliable methods of birth control, couples may decide whether to have children (and how many children to have), and in so doing will compare the costs and benefits of having a child with the costs and benefits of obtaining other consumer durables. Similar scenarios with their own cost-benefit analyses can be sketched out for the decision to marry or divorce. This emphasis on an individual's ability to choose, with little or no attention paid to the constraints that limit the range of choice, is an important basis for the criticism of the approach. Other criticisms address the assumption that the family can maximize its collective satisfaction, that family members' interests usually coincide and only conflict occasionally.

Neoclassical economists view women's poverty through this same lens of free choice. First, they argue that many people living below the poverty line in the contemporary United States are, nevertheless, far better off than people living in much of the Third World or even than wealthy people living centuries ago, before the advent of polio vaccinations, antiseptic surgery, refrigeration, and indoor plumbing. By measuring poverty on this sort of absolute scale, rather than on a relative scale, which would compare poor people with their nonpoor contemporaries, neoclassical economists avoid the most immediate issues of economic inequality. Second, they insist that a more generous level of welfare payments might interfere with recipients' incentives to work and thereby distort their choices. In order to preserve free choice and remove the distortions and disincentives that would accompany a higher level of support, they argue, income-maintenance programs must be pegged at a relatively low level.

Neoclassical economists take a rather sanguine view of women's earnings. If women are clustered into a relatively small number of low-paying occupations, neoclassical economists emphasize the role of freely chosen occupations in producing this outcome.[5]

Although neoclassical economists would not necessarily say that women choose to enter low-paying occupations in order to be poor, they might well argue that individuals weigh the advantages and disadvantages of various occupations, choosing the one with the largest net benefits to them. Consequently, women, anticipating that they will spend a large amount of time out of the labor force during their childbearing years, will avoid jobs that require lengthy training periods, since the payoff would come only with continuous labor-force experience. If women therefore choose to invest less in acquiring and augmenting their "stock of human capital"—things such as education and training that add to one's productivity on the job—and if that stock diminishes as a result of moving in and out of the labor force, then women's wages will necessarily be low. However, since this is the result of freely made choices, no intervention or corrective action would be necessary or desirable.

Neoclassical economists usually dismiss discrimination as an explanation for women's low wages. Discrimination represents an inefficient use of resources, and in a competitive market economy, inefficient producers will be driven from the marketplace. Thus, to neoclassical economists, women's poverty, though regrettable, is nevertheless the consequence of choices freely made. According to neoclassical economists, women wishing to avoid poverty should simply make different choices.

Beyond Choice: Institutional Economics

The institutional approach accepts the neat picture of the self-correcting market, in theory. But it also emphasizes the real-world constraints that interfere with the market's smooth operation. Institutionalists, such as John Kenneth Galbraith, point to noncompetitive elements in the economy, as for example, markets dominated by only one or just a few producers (also known as monopoly and oligopoly, respectively), and barriers to individual choice, such as racial discrimination in housing or race and sex discrimination in employment, as sources of problems. Institutionalists view economic actors not just as free-standing buyers and sellers but also as members of institutions (unions, corporations, families) that exert their own influence on the marketplace. According to the institutionalist perspective, the competitive market framework may work adequately in some limited areas. But there is the clear implication that in important respects the market mechanism has broken down. For example, high unemployment indicates a poorly functioning labor market; issues of availability and affordability plague the markets for housing and health-care and day-care services. Institutionalists propose government intervention to correct the abuses of a competitive market mechanism that often malfunctions.

Two key issues for institutionalists concerned with women and families are (1) how public policy often discriminates against nontraditional families and (2) the perverse outcomes of social legislation based on the premise of a traditional family structure (breadwinning husband, stay-at-home wife).

Institutionalists argue that eligibility for income-maintenance programs should be based on economic need, regardless of family structure. Therefore, they say, two equally needy families should be entitled to receive the same aid, despite the fact that they might live in households with different structures. This notion of equal treatment of equals—i.e., that individuals or households in similar economic circumstances should be treated the same—is called "horizontal equity." It is a primary criterion of fairness in government taxing and spending policy. Yet much income-maintenance policy, social-security policy, and income-tax policy violates horizontal equity.

There are numerous discrepancies in eligibility for Aid to Families with Dependent Children (AFDC). While needy single-parent families are eligible for aid through the "Regular" AFDC program (AFDC-R) in all states, similarly needy two-parent families are eligible for aid in about half the states, and then only under certain conditions. In those states that have adopted the "Unemployed Father" program (AFDC-UF), a needy two-parent family is eligible for aid if the father is unemployed, but not if he's working for low wages. This exclusion of two-parent, working poor families is one violation of horizontal equity; the availability of the AFDC-UF in only half the states is another. A third arises because AFDC-UF is available to families that are needy because of the father's unemployment, but not to families that are needy because of the mother's unemployment. Despite a U.S. district court finding that denial of aid to unemployed mothers when it is available to unemployed fathers constitutes sex discrimination, the Supreme Court initially stayed the lower court order because of the cost of extending coverage to unemployed mothers.[6]

The problems that arise when legislation presumes that all families are structured in the traditional manner are especially clear in the provisions of Social Security. This legislation, passed in the 1930s, is based on the assumption of a male breadwinner and a stay-at-home wife. The husband contributes to the system during his working hours; both spouses collect a pension based on his contributions during his retirement. If the husband dies, the wife is entitled to collect a pension as his surviving widow. Before some recent modifications, the Social Security system had the dubious distinction of being criticized for discriminating against men *and* working wives *and* nonworking wives.

The provisions presumed not just a traditional family but also a stable one. Originally, a woman divorced after less than twenty years of marriage was not entitled to any benefits based on her husband's earning record (this was recently changed to ten years, somewhat relieving the problem of the "displaced homemaker").

The system discriminated against men because a widow could collect a pension based on her husband's earnings record regardless of her own financial condition, but a widower could collect a pension based on his wife's earnings record only if he could prove that he had financially depended on her. This provision has also been changed.

One of the thorniest problems for the Social Security system to resolve is its treatment of working wives. In many instances a wife who works and contributes to the Social Security system during her working years may find, upon retirement, that she is no better off than she would have been if she'd never worked. A working wife must choose whether to collect benefits as a retired worker (based on her own contributions) or as a spouse (based on her husband's contributions); she is not entitled to both. Many women find that, given their own work histories of low wages and intermittent employment, it is more advantageous to receive benefits as a spouse rather than as a retiree. In such instances their own contributions to the system (which are, of course, mandatory) have brought them no additional retirement income. Proposals to correct this inequality while also assuring traditional families an adequate retirement income have been difficult to devise.

Similar problems arise in devising a fair income tax. Individuals earn income; but income is taxed according to households. Differences in household composition lead to horizontal inequity between married and unmarried working couples who may earn the same income but have different tax liabilities. Here again, a tax system based on the assumption of a traditional family leads to inequitable results for families that do not fit the mold.

This focus on public policy is also a key part of the institutionalist approach to women and poverty. Institutionalist economists look at the labor market, with its occupational segregation and the crowding of women into relatively few occupations, and argue that if women seem voluntarily to enter only a few traditional fields, it may well be because they perceive it as their only alternative, given the barriers and hostility they would be likely to face in trying to overcome employer or co-worker or customer prejudices in nontraditional employment. Thus, free choice plays a decidedly more limited role for institutionalist economists than for neoclassical economists. What's more, according to the institutionalists, access to training is not entirely within the individual's control; it is often controlled by employers and educational institutions. Therefore, institutionalists argue, acquisition of training should not be viewed solely as the outcome of unconstrained individual choice.

Institutionalists view women's occupational segregation as a fundamental cause of wage differences between the sexes. They emphasize discriminatory procedures that employers use in assigning jobs, given that employers may believe women to be less stable and therefore less desirable workers.

An important study by Isabelle Sawhill, an economist at the Urban Institute, shows the role of such a discriminatory labor market in perpetuating women's poverty.[7] Using survey data from 1968 covering several thousand individuals, Sawhill calculated what female AFDC recipients would be likely to earn if they had full-time jobs. To do this, she devised an equation to explain the earnings of a group of employed women using earnings-related characteristics such as age and education. The earnings-related characteristics of a nonworking woman may then be "plugged in" to the equation, telling us what that woman could expect to earn, given the way the labor market values those characteristics in women already at work. When Sawhill made that calculation, long before Ronald Reagan's welfare cuts of 1981, she found that even then half the AFDC recipients could not expect to earn as much working full-time as they received from AFDC. Only one quarter of the recipients could expect to increase their AFDC level of income by $1,000 or more.

But her most interesting results came when she went a step farther. Having also calculated an earnings equation for working men, Sawhill put the earnings-related characteristics of AFDC recipients into the *men's* equation and found that only 17 percent of the recipients would be better off staying on welfare. In other words, the low potential earning power of AFDC women was not so much a product of their own inadequate personal characteristics as it was a result of the low payoff to such characteristics in the *female* labor market compared with the *male* labor market. Sawhill concluded: "If women earned as much income in the job market as men, there would be less poverty and welfare dependency among women who head their own families."[8]

Sawhill's analysis, unlike the work of neoclassical economists, has clear public-policy implications. She takes job discrimination seriously, as well as the need for antidiscrimination, equal opportunity, and affirmative-action policies. She also seriously explores the role of government itself, with its built-in assumptions that shape public policy to penalize or reward different family structures. However, she and other institutionalist economists recognize that devising and implementing an appropriate set of remedial policies will not be easy.

Choice for Whom: Marxist Economics

Marxist economists question whether a nation with an economy based on markets and the profit motive can provide for the basic needs of all its citizens. If it is more profitable to build yachts for the wealthy than housing for the poor, there will be many yacht producers and few builders of low-income housing. What's more, since a competitive market economy is likely to produce losers as well as winners, the degree of income inequality in such a society is likely to be high.

The Marxist framework, unlike the more static neoclassical or institutional approaches, is more explicitly concerned with understanding the dynamics of a capitalist system and the relationships of classes within that system. Marxists also emphasize the importance of economic and political power, including the power to influence government activity. In the Marxist perspective, the role of the marketplace should, at the very least, be modified if not supplanted by economic planning at the national level and by work-place democracy within the firm.

Many Marxists argue that women's low status in the labor market grows directly from sexual inequality in the family. This inequality can be understood by focusing on the historical development of the family and how class relations determine women's position in the family.

Historically, the development of the family as an institution is based on a system of patriarchy, where men are the primary beneficiaries of women's production. A complex set of legal, social, and political arrangements developed over time and led to a division of labor based on sex. While the development of capitalism reshaped the form of these arrangements, it left their basic nature intact. For instance, while the site and control of production moved from the home to the factory, a family's share of production, whether goods made at home or wages earned in factories, remained firmly controlled by husbands and fathers.

This situation has led many Marxists to argue that the position of women who worked in the home deteriorated with the development of capitalism. In capitalist societies, housework was no longer considered "valuable," that is, paid work. Therefore, housework, and housewives, lost status. For many women this loss meant the double, some might say triple, burden of unpaid housework, unpaid child care, and low-wage market work. In fact, even with the significant increase in women's labor-force participation and the development of labor-saving devices, such as microwave ovens and washing machines, the number of hours spent on housework has remained remarkably constant.[9]

To explain the relationship between the family and capitalism, Marxists start with a historical analysis of family relations before capitalism, then look at how capitalist development has affected women's position within the traditional family.

In a capitalist economy, two distinct classes can be identified: the capitalist class, who own and control the means of production, and the working class, who must sell their labor to the capitalist class in order to survive. Both Marx and Engels predicted that with the development of capitalism, men and women alike would be increasingly forced to sell their labor for a wage, leading to the demise of the working-class family. They argue that before capitalism, the family served as a unit of production, providing a material basis for its existence. But under capitalism, most production takes place outside the home, which eliminates any material basis for the family's continued existence.

Many of the subsequent Marxist analyses have focused on why Marx's and Engels' prediction has failed to come true—and what that has meant for women. Here, two opposing views have emerged: one, functionalism, maintains that the traditional family continues to exist because it serves the needs of the capitalist class;

the other view is that the persistence of the working-class family serves as a defense against capitalist encroachment into all spheres of life.

The functionalist view maintains that the capitalist class, although not always unified in its interests, stands to gain both economically and politically from the sexual division of labor (and the resulting subordination of women).[10] First and foremost, women's work at home—child rearing, cleaning, cooking—serves the capitalist class by maintaining and reproducing wage laborers. This makes the traditional division of labor profitable for the capitalists. If it weren't, according to the functionalists, other forms would arise to replace it. But, women as household workers produce value above what is necessary to reproduce themselves (much in the same way the wageworkers produce value above what they need to subsist), which is then appropriated by capitalists in the form of a lower family wage and higher profits. For example, during recessions, when wages fall, women often attempt to maintain their families' standard of living by increasing their production at home, particularly by sewing clothes rather than buying ready-made clothing. This is, in a sense, an indirect form of speedup, where wages remain the same and the work pace becomes faster.

A second economic and political advantage that results from the traditional family structure occurs during an expansion. When a larger supply of labor is needed, women are courted into the work force, which keeps existing workers' wages down. What is more, capital segments the labor force by sex, which keeps women's wages low and dilutes the strength of the working class to fight against capitalist exploitation.

Finally, there are political advantages to the traditional family structure. While men must submit to capitalist control at work, they can dominate their families at home. This not only reinforces a system that is based on unequal distribution of power, it also provides a haven from the vicissitudes of the work place, contributing to a docile work force.

In contrast to the functionalist theory of the family, Jane Humphreys and others argue that the persistence of the working-class family in the face of capitalist development is a result of working-class struggle.[11] Proponents of this view argue that functionalism assumes an all-powerful capitalist class and a completely powerless working class. They maintain that the working-class family has always fought capitalist attempts to encroach into family life.

Humphreys argues that the surplus produced by women working at home, in whole or part, goes to the family rather than the capitalist class. In this model, men and women have a unified interest in maintaining the family structure. An undeniable outcome of that family structure has been the unequal status brought about by the traditional division of labor and the resulting low earnings for women whether or not they are part of a traditional family. However, to understand the family as an institution and to predict and/or prescribe changes take understanding what forces have led to its survival: that is, does the family continue to exist because it serves the needs of men, that is, capitalists, or of the family members themselves? What distinguishes these viewpoints from each is that each stresses a different group as the primary agent determining the persistence of the family in its traditional form. Both views, however, reach a consensus that eradicating a capitalist economy is a necessary, but not sufficient, condition for ending sexual inequality.

Conclusion

It is important to understand the diversity of economic approaches to the question of women's poverty. Especially in light of the federal government's retreat from enforcing laws to promote gender equality, activists need to know the economic theories underlying such action, if only to be able to offer cogent rebuttals. In our opinion, much of the neoclassical analysis does little more than provide a quasi-scientific veneer for justifying traditional male-female relationships. Although we may chuckle at a theory that enshrines traditional sex roles even as those roles crumble before the onslaught of rising divorce rates, smaller-size families, and rising female labor-force participation rates, we must recognize that such theories provide the basis for much of the current attack on women's rights. George Gilder, for example, is best known as Reagan's economic guru for his ultraconservative work justifying economic inequality. Few people remember that his earlier work was a defense of sexual inequality.

It is especially important for women activists to recognize that, for all its use of sophisticated mathematical and statistical techniques, economic analysis is neither wholly scientific nor value free. We must not allow ourselves to be bullied by victim blaming, even when it is dressed up as dispassionate economic analysis. For this reason it is vital that we understand the neoclassical analysis and the questionable assumptions on which it is based.

Some of the changes in federal policy of the 1960s and 1970s—antidiscrimination laws, liberalization of AFDC regulations—promised a period of genuine economic improvement for women. Consistent with the institutionalist approach, there was a concern for correcting the abuses of the unfettered market mechanism, as well as a concern for reducing inequality. The incomplete and fragile nature of these reforms, however, attests to the notion that economic policy is not formulated in a vacuum.

Recent moves to limit the rights of women may be seen as a means of buttressing the traditional family structure, read, "keeping women in their place." As we have seen, poverty is often the price paid by women choosing to live outside the traditional family. If, as many Marxists argue, maintaining the "family" is necessary for the smooth operation of capitalism, then meaningful improvements in women's economic position may well require altering traditional capitalist relations.

Clearly any changes made to improve women's status will require the vigilance and strength of a broad-based political movement, one that serves the interest of all women by interpreting and acting upon the policy of both government and business. As activists we hope that an understanding of the economic theories discussed here will help poor women and their advocates to play a central role in such a movement.

REEVALUATING FEMINIST ECONOMICS

"Feminization of Poverty" Ignores Key Issues

Pamela Sparr

The gender gap was a hot issue in the 1984 presidential campaign. The news that women hold different political values than men made headlines across the nation. Less widely debated is the economic gender gap, which has widened significantly over the past two decades.

Today, many more women than men are living below the poverty line (defined by the U.S. Census Bureau as $9,862 per year for a family of four). According to the most recent statistics available, in 1982, women constituted an estimated 61 percent of adults (people fifteen years and older) who were living in poverty. Nearly one half of all poor families were headed by single women.

Since 1978, when sociologist Diana Pearce first labeled this trend, the "feminization of poverty" has attracted growing public attention. Articles by feminists Barbara Ehrenreich, Karin Stallard, Holly Sklar, and others argue that the feminization of poverty deepened dramatically in the 1970s, when an increasing proportion of the poor came to be women, and more women became poor.

This essay appeared in *Dollars & Sense,* no. 99 (September 1984). Used by permission.

The issue has spurred a surge of academic research, popular articles, speeches, and organizing efforts focused on downward mobility for women. Women representing many shades of the political spectrum—from leftists to mainstream, grass-roots activists—have come to the same conclusion: poverty is a crucial issue around which women should be mobilized.

While poverty is an urgent organizing issue for women, the reasoning used to arrive at this conclusion can be misleading. Widespread recognition of the feminization of poverty may be a recent occurrence, but widespread poverty among women is not. By ignoring the historical picture and asserting that increased poverty among women is a recent phenomenon, proponents of the feminization-of-poverty theory minimize the enduring plight of millions of working-class women in the United States, particularly women of color. Such analyses also understate or ignore the significance of class and race in understanding women's poverty.

A danger of this narrow view is that political prescriptions that are based on it tend to be at best superficial and of limited effectiveness. Moreover, important allies in the struggle for change may be overlooked or antagonized, both within the women's movement and outside of it (working-class men, for example).

Marriage and Motherhood

Why are women and their children a large and growing proportion of the poor? Most discussions of the feminization of poverty are based on the assumption that women and men are poor for different reasons.

According to Ehrenreich and Stallard, one reason for women's poverty is the segregated nature of the labor market. They wrote in a 1982 article in *Ms.*, "The extreme occupational segregation of women in our society makes for a crucial difference between women's poverty and men's. For men, poverty is often a consequence of unemployment, and is curable by getting a job. But for women concentrated in the low-wage stratum of the workforce, a job may not be a solution to poverty."

However, women faced limited opportunities for employment and earnings long before the 1960s and 1970s. At least since the

Industrial Revolution, women have been in a more precarious economic state than men, confronting obstacles such as job segregation, lack of paid employment opportunities, wage differentials, and the lack of protection by unions. The authors cannot use a long-standing phenomenon to explain what they see as a relatively new trend.

Marital and maternity status are also commonly cited as major causes of the feminization of poverty. The National Advisory Council on Economic Opportunity (NCEO) report, for example, suggests that "women, especially minority women, may be poor for some of the same reasons as men, but few men become poor because of divorce, sex-role socialization, sexism, or of course, pregnancy."

Recognizing that sexism and motherhood are long-standing features of U.S. society, Ehrenreich, Stallard, and others wisely narrow their focus. They point to increasing divorce rates and single-parent births as the major social changes contributing to the feminization of poverty. "For many women . . . poverty begins with single parenthood—becoming single or becoming a parent, whichever comes first." Observing that the number of poor persons living in female-headed families has increased, they link that increase to the explosive growth in the proportion of households headed by women. The implication is that as more women head households alone, they will find themselves and their dependents in poverty.

Certainly, these two social changes seem to have contributed to the proportion of poor persons in female-headed households. But there are serious flaws in the argument put forth by Ehrenreich and Stallard. First of all, the proportion of poor persons in households headed by women grew most rapidly in the 1960s, although it continued to increase at a slower rate in the 1970s.

Moreover, divorce is not a cause of women's poverty per se. The economic disadvantages women face do not derive from their marital status. At the root of women's economic oppression are the more profound underlying problems of racism, sexism, and the capitalist economy. Marriage may lift a woman out of poverty, but it does not fundamentally alter the economic disadvantages she faces.

Finally, the argument that "poverty is just a divorce away" implies that such a threat somehow equalizes the vast majority of women. Yet this argument underplays the substantial class differences that persist among women. A significant number of women, most of whom are white, are economically comfortable in their own right. The most recent Commerce Department statistics estimate that nearly 1 million women have an annual income of $35,000 or more. Another 6 million women earn between $20,000 and $35,000. Together, the number of these women roughly matches the 7.5 million women who, as heads of households, are poor.

Race and Sex

Because the feminization-of-poverty analysis is cast along male-female lines, it ignores the importance of racism in shaping economic status. Feminists need to be aware of the great disparity in poverty rates among women of various races and ethnic origins. It is telling that hypothetically, if a black woman could change her race, she would have a better statistical chance of escaping poverty than if she were to change her gender.

Once we begin to pay closer attention to race, our analysis brings men into the picture in a new way. Although women have a higher incidence of poverty than men of their same race, this generalization does not hold across races. An example of this: the poverty rate for black men is nearly double that for white women.

A fuller analysis of race can be made for a more sophisticated and accurate understanding of the role gender plays in other ways as well. Marriage improves the tenuous economic position of women of color far less than it does that of white women. Black married couples, for example, are more than twice as likely to be poor today as white couples are.

The biases contained in the official poverty data may also understate the extent of poverty among men and persons of color. According to the Census Bureau, the undercounting of the poor that is inherent in the collection process primarily affects men and people of Third World origin. Undocumented workers trying to avoid deportation and homeless people tend to be missed by surveyors. Individuals who are incarcerated, a disproportionately large number of whom are poor males and people of color, are also excluded from census surveys.

Structural Factors

Because some commentators focus almost exclusively on the trend toward the feminization of poverty, they end by minimizing the extent of men's poverty in the United States. Some interpret the NCEO's prediction to mean that, within a generation, poverty among men will be eradicated.

Although the proportion of poor male adults declined during the 1960s, men continue to make up a major, and currently stable component of the poverty population. The apparent decline in the proportion of the poor who are male must be placed in its historical context.

Since 1959, when the U.S. Census Bureau began to publish poverty statistics regularly, women have been recorded as 50 percent of the poor or more. During the affluent 1960s, the government launched the War on Poverty to reduce the number of poor people. In retrospect, it appears that poor white males were the main beneficiaries of those programs, since their numbers declined sharply during that time. The number of poor white women and their dependents, meanwhile, remained fairly constant, and the number of women of Third World origin and their dependents in poverty rose. Consequently, the overall proportion of the poor who were women grew. By 1970, women made up 62 percent of poor adults.

That proportion has remained relatively constant ever since. During the 1970s, with the deepening of the economic crisis, the absolute numbers of both poor adult women and men increased. And between 1980 and 1982, comparable numbers of men and women fell below the poverty line.

What does all this mean? In addition to considering social factors such as rising divorce rates and more single-parent births, feminists who are concerned with poverty should also consider the structural characteristics of the U.S. economy, which affect both women and men. For example, the number of people who are poor, and the composition of the poverty population, may be different in long periods of growth compared to periods of crisis. In times when the U.S. economy experiences a long boom, as happened during World War II and the postwar period, men's experience of poverty may be more cyclical than women's, a short-term consequence of unemployment. But in periods like the current economic crisis, this pattern may change.

Evidence from recent years supports this view. As deindustrialization has proceeded, men's jobs have been the first to feel the impact. Men dominated the high-wage, unionized jobs in basic manufacturing that have been reduced by plant closings and relocation of production facilities overseas, union busting, and automation. For the first time in history, men's unemployment rates have risen above those of women.

Women, on the other hand, were shielded in the first phase of the crisis and only felt the crunch after the heavy industrial production workers did, if at all. While some women have also lost manufacturing jobs in the electronics and apparel industries, the majority of women work in less cyclically sensitive sectors, such as retailing, fast foods, or clerical work. And in some areas where women are concentrated, such as banking, financial services, health, and communications, the number of jobs has actually grown.

The feminization-of-poverty argument does recognize that capitalism has meant the loss of jobs for both men and women and the erosion of the middle class. But it does not explain how the current economic crisis, primarily the loss of men's jobs, fits into the picture. By stressing what is uniquely female, proponents of that argument may leave a mistaken impression that sexism is the fundamental problem. They fail to examine thoroughly the nature of the capitalist economy, which requires and maintains an impoverished class of people.

The NCEO's remedies, for example, emphasize eliminating sexism: "To alleviate women's poverty, social welfare policy must focus on two crucial areas: first, the services, particularly quality day care, that are essential for wage-earning mothers; and second, the structures and practices that bar women from jobs now held by men with similar education, skills, and experience in the labor force." If sexism were eliminated, there would still be poor women. The only difference is that women would then stand the same chance as men of being poor.

In educating and organizing women around bread-and-butter issues, feminists are forcing some sorely needed public attention to women's economic plight. They also are raising the consciousness of many women about the importance of economic struggles. A more comprehensive analysis of poverty can only strengthen women's role in the fight against economic oppression.

A LONG-RUN LOOK AT POVERTY

Total Number of Poor Persons (in millions)

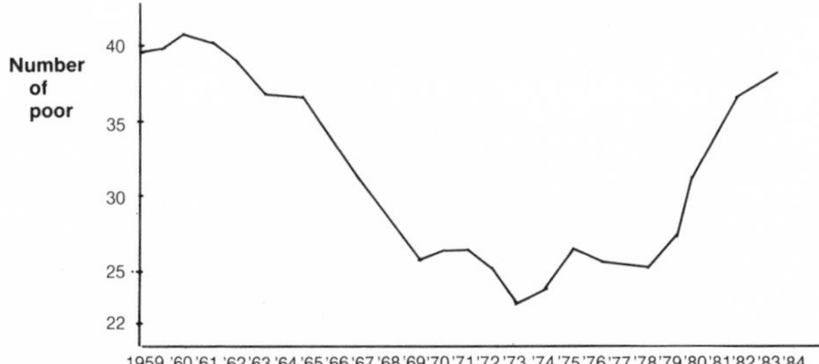

Peak year: 1960—39.85 million poor
Lowest point: 1973—22.97 million poor
1983 35.27 million poor

Note: *The number of poor persons has been rising steadily since 1978.*

Poor Persons by Family Status (in millions)

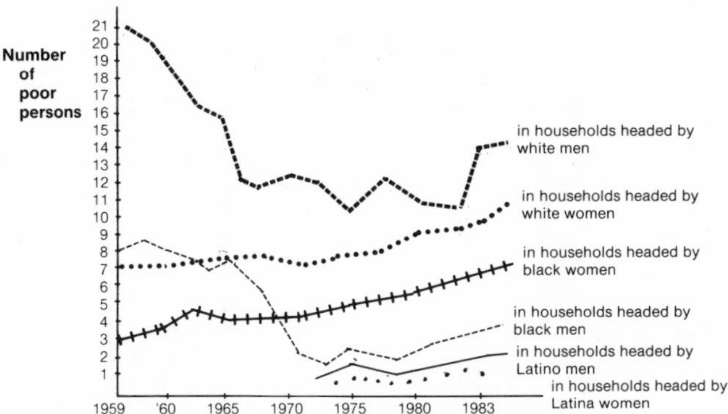

Chart by Pamela Sparr. Source: U.S., Department of Commerce, Bureau of the Census, "Characteristics of the Population Below the Poverty Level," Current Population Reports, *Series P-60 (Washington, D.C.: Government Printing Office, 1983).*

STANDARD OF LIVING—U.S.

Real Median Family Income by Race

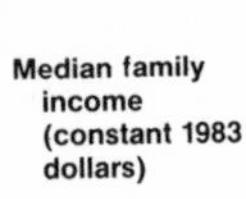

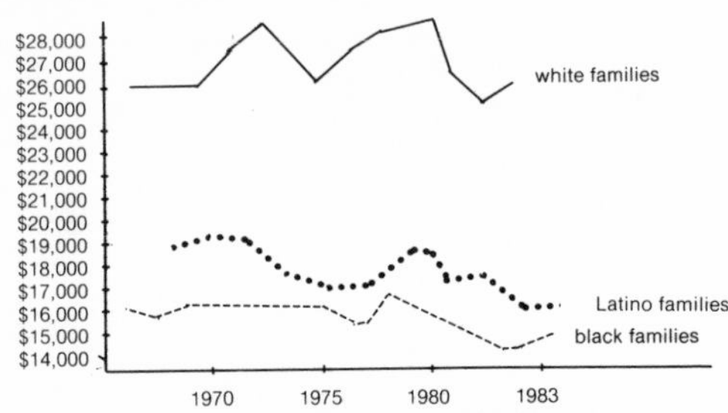

We see a declining standard of living for the average family regardless of race in the above graph.

The average Latino family's real income FELL by 13% between 1972 & 1983.
The average black family's real income FELL by 10% between 1970 & 1983.
The average white family's real income FELL by 2% between 1970 & 1983.

The Income Gap Comparing Real Median Family Income by Race

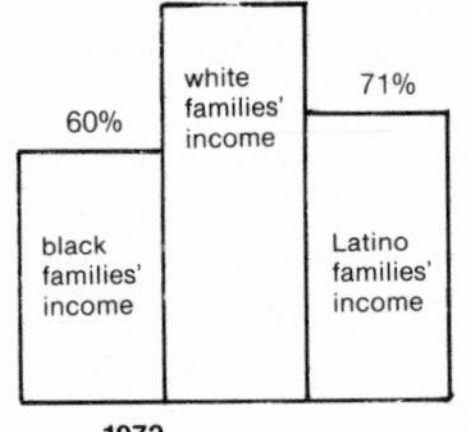

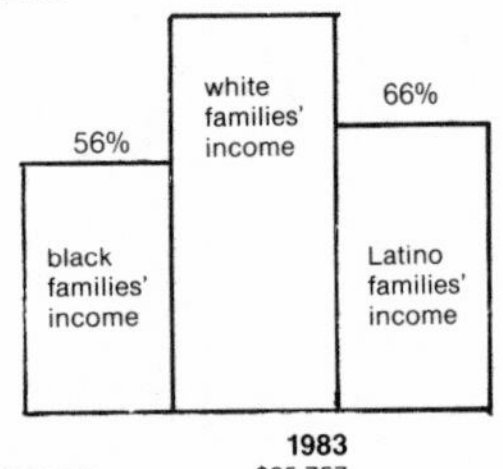

1972		1983
$27,504	white families' real median income	$25,757
$16,347	black families' real median income	$14,506
$19,488	Latino families' real median income	$16,956

Chart by Pamela Sparr. Source: U.S., Department of Commerce, Bureau of the Census, "Money Income and Poverty Status of Families and Persons in the U.S.," Current Population Reports, *Series P-60, no. 145 (Washington, D.C.: Government Printing Office, 1983).*

HAS POVERTY BEEN FEMINIZED IN BLACK AMERICA?

Linda Burnham

For the past several years, the declining economic status of women in the United States has been captured in the phrase the "feminization of poverty." The term was coined to call attention to the fact that women and their dependent children are making up an increasing proportion of the U.S. poor.

The phrase has been adopted by women's movement activists of nearly every political persuasion. And, on the broader political landscape, both liberals and leftists have come to speak of the feminization of poverty as the women's issue of the 1980s.

Its promoters see the feminization of poverty as the basis for an organizing strategy with the potential to mobilize millions of women and revive the women's movement in the 1980s. The following assessment is typical of its proponents: "A focus on the feminization of poverty is important for the women's movement . . . it offers a new bond which cuts across class, age, race and

---

A slightly longer version of this essay was first published in *The Black Scholar,* in a special issue on Black women, in 1985. Used by permission. *Black* is capitalized in accordance with the author's wishes.

sexual preference because women are in fact just a husband away from poverty."[1]

Vulnerability to impoverishment is seen as the common condition of all women and, thus, the issue to organize them into united political action. Even many social analysts and activists who are particularly concerned about the deteriorating conditions of Black women and their families have assumed the feminization-of-poverty analysis to be an explanation of their plight and a basis upon which to organize a counter attack.

To the extent that the "feminization of poverty" analysis has turned public attention to the accelerating impoverishment of a certain sector of women, it has served a useful purpose—especially in light of the devastating impact of Ronald Reagan's budget cuts on poor women and children. But, there are a number of grave pitfalls and blind spots inherent in the feminization-of-poverty analysis.

The idea that poverty is being "feminized" presents a highly distorted picture of the general dynamics that are at the source of poverty in the United States. These distortions are the inevitable result of a theory that abstracts women as a group out of the overall socioeconomic trends in U.S. capitalist development.

Distorting the Poverty Population by Using the Feminization-of-Poverty Analysis

It is especially important that those who seek to understand and change the conditions faced by the Black community be wary of uncritically adopting a feminization-of-poverty perspective. This theory is not simply an identification of demographic shifts in the poverty population; it also projects a reconceptualization of the social factors that generate and regenerate poverty and of the sectors of the population who are most vulnerable to impoverishment.

This reconceptualization incorrectly shifts the focal point of analysis from class and race to gender, betraying a superficial understanding of the relationship among the three social dynamics of women's oppression, class exploitation, and racism. The analytical difficulty of correctly expressing this relationship is a problem that impedes the full understanding not only of female poverty but of practically every other major social question as well.

In regard to the feminization of poverty, the factors contributing to the impoverishment of Black women are misconstrued; the vulnerability of white women to impoverishment is overstated; the impoverishment of Black men is ignored or underestimated; and the fundamental basis in working-class exploitation for the continual regeneration of poverty is abandoned for a focus on gender.

The purpose of this article is to identify the major problems with the feminization-of-poverty analysis and to elaborate how the intersecting dynamics of class, race, and sex combine to shape the socioeconomic conditions of Black women. We argue that Black women are disproportionately positioned in the lower strata of the working class; that this class position is an integral aspect of the racialized class stratification in the United States; that Black women's impoverishment is primarily a product of this intersection of class and race; and that, while women's oppression has affected the rate of impoverishment of working-class women and gives Black women's experience of poverty particular shape, it is not the determinant factor in their condition.

1. The first problem is that the fundamental social relations that create an impoverished sector of the population are misidentified. Essentially feminization-of-poverty advocates give the impression that poverty's determinant factor has become gender rather than class. This view is captured in the outlandish but often-repeated projection that: "All other things being equal, if the proportion of the poor in female-headed families were to continue to increase at the same rate as it did from 1967 to 1978, the poverty population would be composed solely of women and their children before the year 2000."[2]

As a mathematical projection this statement might be true in the narrowest sense of how the present trend might chart out on a graph, presenting a situation abstracted out all of social reality. But as a serious social forecast (or as scientific sociology) it is worse than useless since it seriously misleads people into thinking that poverty is fundamentally a female problem.

Poverty is a class condition, a permanent feature of U.S. capitalism that affects women, men, and children of the lower strata of the U.S. working class. Unemployed and underemployed workers and the low-wage sectors of the work force are an inherent feature of the capital-labor relation and not primarily a function of gender oppression. And the social condition of increasing misery is a characteristic of the bottom rungs of the working class in all capitalist societies.

Social differentiations within the working class—mainly those of race, nationality, sex, and age—play a major role in determining which sectors of the working class are more vulnerable to impoverishment and which are somewhat cushioned from the worst effects of capitalist exploitation. In effect, and in brief, competition within the class is weighed in favor of U.S.-born white males against racial and national minorities, women, and immigrants. This unequal competition results in the disproportionate representation of women and minorities in the impoverished strata of the working class. But this disproportionate representation does not mean that poverty is mainly a function of race or gender. It remains mainly a function of class relations, which, in the historically specific circumstances of advanced capitalism in the United States, create a poverty population with a particular social composition.

2. The second problem is that the feminization-of-poverty analysis obscures the class differentiation among women. Feminist analysis tends to minimize the enormous differences in social condition between women of different classes. The feminization of poverty is no exception. According to one characteristic statement, "Virtually all women are vulnerable—a divorce or widowhood is all it takes to throw many middle-class women into poverty."[3] In fact, one of the most politically compelling features of the feminization of poverty, particularly for those who translate the analysis of women's impoverishment into a political agenda for the women's movement, consists of its presumed ability to unite the traditionally poor, the "new poor," and the "potential poor." Thus, the idea that all women are in relatively equal and imminent danger of becoming poor enjoys an undeserved currency in the women's movement.

Women are represented in the *broad* social classes in roughly the same proportions as men. What has changed in the decades since World War II is the increasing rate of integration into the labor force of women who had been part of the working class by virtue of the social conditions of their household. Many of these women have now become a functional part of the working class in their own right. The combination of family instability and low female wages has made these women more vulnerable to impoverishment. This is to say that within the working class, women comprise disproportionate numbers of the poor.

But in no way has the process served to make *all* women vulnerable. In fact, together with the integration into the labor force of working-class women, there has occurred an increasing rate of women's representation in the professions and middle management, especially over the past decade. A few statistics highlight this trend. The proportion of women lawyers and judges rose from 5 percent in 1970 to 14 percent in 1980; of doctors from 9 percent in 1970 to 13.4 percent in 1980. And, between 1970 and 1981 women increased their share of masters degrees from 40 percent to 50 percent and of doctoral degrees from 13 percent to 31 percent.[4]

These and similar changes have brought into being what is known in the popular press as the two-career family, the family in which the woman is a fully functional part of the petit bourgeois or the professional strata and in which there is a large disposable income. Furthermore, women are an integral part of the U.S. bourgeoisie and own or control a considerable portion of bourgeois property even though they are not proportionally represented in the corporate board rooms.

The point here is that there is not a general trend toward women as a group sinking into the lower levels of the proletariat. The feminization-of-poverty analysis obscures the differentiation in social condition (and consciousness of women) and the class and racial privilege on which that differentiation rests.

3. The third problem is that the feminization-of-poverty analysis obscures the racialized stratification of the U.S. working class. Essentially, particular sectors of the population have been singled out to "specialize" in being poor. Historically and today the key determining factor as to who would so specialize has been race and nationality, not gender.

Thus, whites in the United States have a poverty rate of 12 percent while Hispanics have a rate of 29.9 percent, and 35.6 percent of Blacks fall within the government's definition of poverty. While whites make up more of the poor numerically because of their majority in the population, as a racial group they have been relatively shielded from having to experience the worst capitalism has to offer. In the Black, Mexican, Puerto Rican, and Native American communities, however, poverty is a generalized phenomenon experienced by the men, women, and children of a large and growing proportion of these populations.

The feminization-of-poverty analysis obscures the fact that whites, *both men and women,* are qualitatively less vulnerable to impoverishment than racial and national minorities.

4. The fourth problem is that the extent of poverty among black men is downplayed. The blindness of the feminization-of-poverty analysis to racial and national oppression is evidenced in its assertion that "there is a fundamental difference between male and female poverty. For men, poverty is often the consequence of unemployment and a job is generally an effective remedy. While female poverty often exists even when a woman works full-time."[5] However, the "effective remedy" of employment is absolutely unavailable to large numbers of men, those of racial and ethnic minorities in particular, whose unemployment rate remains at least two times higher than that of white men and women.

The deepening impoverishment of Black women has not been accompanied by a rise to affluence on the part of Black men. On the contrary, recent reports have indicated a very strong correlation between the rapidly rising numbers and increasing proportion of Black female-headed households and the declining labor-force participation of Black men. To quote the most relevant sections of the report:

> The plight of Black men is the other, virtually unnoticed, side of the troubling increase in the single-parent Black families. Simply put, the economic status of many Black men is deteriorating. . . .
>
> The combination of unemployment and labor force data more accurately reflects the status of Black men than either gauge taken alone. In 1960, nearly three-quarters of all Black men included in Census data were working; today, only 55 percent are working.
>
> The picture gets even worse. There are an estimated 925,000 working-age Black men whose labor-force status cannot be determined because they are missed in the Census. This "undercount" in the Census is most severe among Black men, amounting to more than 10 percent among working-age Black men, compared to less than 1 percent for working-age white men.
>
> The cumulative impact of these measures—unemployment, labor-force participation, and the "missing" Black men—is startling. For each Black man we count as unemployed, another two are out of the labor force . . . 4 million out of the 8.8 million working-age Black men, or 46 percent, are without jobs; i.e., they are either unemployed, out of the labor force, in correctional facilities, or unac-

counted for. These data are even more noteworthy when juxtaposed with comparable data for white men. In 1981, while 78 percent of all working-age white men were employed, only 54 percent of all working-age Black men had jobs. (Not to speak of the wage differential between those that did work.)

Looking at this another way, the percent of working-age Black men who are unemployed, discouraged workers, or unaccounted for is almost three times that for white men. Thirty percent of all working-age Black men are in these categories, compared to only 11 percent of working-age white men.[6]

Figures like these hardly give one reason to believe that poverty has become "feminized" for Black Americans.

What Has Changed for Women?

In spite of its profound distortions of social reality, the feminization-of-poverty concept has directed attention to phenomena and trends in women's conditions that must be accounted for. While poverty has not been "feminized," it is true that increasing numbers of working-class and minority women are sinking into impoverishment. This is a subtle but crucial distinction. On the one hand, gender has not become and will not become the determinant factor shaping the poverty population in the United States. On the other hand, the contemporary combination of women's low-wage status and the instability of the family has resulted in the phenomenon of working-class women and their dependent children making up a growing proportion of the poor.

At least since World War II there has been a steady trend toward the direct proletarianization of women. For the past decade, the entry of women into the labor force has been the chief factor in the growth and change of the labor force. Women employed or looking for work increased from 30.3 million in 1970 to 44.5 million in 1980, a 47 percent increase. Women accounted for 60 percent of the increase in the civilian labor force.

In 1981, 62 percent of women between eighteen and sixty-four were workers, with labor-force participation highest among younger women between the ages of twenty and twenty-four (7 percent). The number of working mothers has increased tenfold since the period immediately prior to World War II, and in March

1982, 59 percent of all mothers with children under eighteen were in the paid labor force (18.7 million mothers.)[7] In the poorer strata of the working class and among minority women in particular, the labor-force participation rate has traditionally been higher. But the influx of women from the more economically stable strata of the class in the 1970s has begun to equalize the women's labor-force participation rate. The 1981 rate for Black women was 53 percent, for white women 52 percent, and for Latinas 50 percent.[8]

The increased labor-force participation rate of women is, for all intents and purposes, irreversible. Women have been integrated into sectors of the economy from which they cannot be expelled without major disruption; there is no reason to expect that capital will retreat from the higher degree of exploitation it has imposed on the working class by pulling women into the work force; and the subjective expectations of the majority of working-class women, including increasingly women of the more economically secure section of the class, are to marry, raise a family, and work rather than to marry and become lifelong housewives.

But women's integration into the work force takes place on a discriminatory basis relative to men. While women's labor-force participation rate has steadily increased, the gap between men's and women's wages has not closed.

When working women are part of two-parent, dual-income families, their wage generally contributes to shoring up the household's positioning in the economically stable sector of the working class. Though Census Bureau statistics are obviously not broken down by class, much less by strata within classes, this form of family is clearly more economically secure than either the two-parent, single-income family or the single-parent family. The median income for families with both adults working was $29,065 in 1981. For whites in this category the median was $29,713; for Blacks it was $25,040.[9]

Women who are part of these types of families do not escape discrimination in the labor force relative to men, but that discrimination does not push their class status down into the lower reaches of the proletariat.

But, when the discrimination women face in the labor force intersects with the accelerating trend toward the destabilization of the nuclear family, the effects on working women can be devastating. Increasing numbers of women are rearing their children without the economic support of a husband or partner. The divorce rate more than doubled for all sectors of the population between 1970 and 1981. For white women the divorce rate was 118 divorces per 1,000 marriages in 1981 as compared to 56 per 1,000 in 1970. For Black women the ratio rose during the same period from 104 to 289 divorces per 1,000 and for Hispanic women the ratio rose from 81 to 146 divorced women per 1,000 active marriages.[10] These ratios do not include temporary or permanent separations, only legally finalized divorces. Thus the actual rate of functionally dissolved marriages is undoubtedly far higher.

During the same decade, the numbers of children born to unmarried women also rose significantly. As a consequence of these two trends, female-headed, single-parent families became a greater proportion of the total number of families (from 10.8 percent in 1970 to 15.4 percent in 1982). The overwhelming majority of single-parent families, 90 percent, are headed by women.[11]

The poverty rate for this form of family is extraordinarily high. For female-headed households taken as a group, the poverty rate was 34.6 percent. This compares to a 10.3 percent rate for male-headed households and a 6.8 percent rate for husband-wife families.[12] Men rarely take the main economic or broader parental responsibility for raising their children after divorce or separation. They also rarely provide their ex-partners with child-support payments.

Thus, increasing numbers of working-class women face the difficult prospect of providing for themselves and for their children on less than 60 percent of the wages earned by men. It is this situation that has made working-class women more vulnerable to impoverishment than men of the same class.

The Class and Racial Aspects of Poverty in the Black Community

Some of the early popular literature on the feminization of poverty focused primarily on the plight of white middle-class women who had been unexpectedly plunged into poverty for the first time.[13] In attempting to generate sympathy and influence social policy on behalf of these "new poor," those sectors of the population that have long borne the brunt of poverty were virtually ignored. Instead, emphasis was placed on the tribulations of previously married middle-class housewives who were having to cope with the frustrating and humiliating intricacies of the welfare and food stamp bureaucracies as novices.

Characteristically, minority women's particular condition was dealt with unsatisfactorily: "and all these trends are even worse for women of color." The situation of men of racial and ethnic minorities was left out of the picture altogether. Again, the essential problem stems from the difficulty of developing an integral analysis of class, sex, and race relations in the United States. Unfortunately, leftist and Marxist analyses are not immune to this problem.

Poverty is not becoming a female-only phenomenon in the Black community, and only a serious misreading of the trends and facts and complete unfamiliarity with the concrete realities of that community would lead one to suggest that such was true. Poverty is and has been a consistent feature of the U.S. Black community since its earliest development, affecting children, youth, adults, and the aged, men and women, across the board.

The conditions of the Black community in the United States are completely framed by the fact that the U.S. class structure is thoroughly racialized. The principal material expression of racial oppression is the near total exclusion of Blacks from the upper classes and their disproportionate representation among the most oppressed mass of the population.

The opposite side of this coin has been the dispersion of whites across the class spectrum; the exemption of the great majority of whites from the lowest social strata; or, for white immigrants especially, their mobility out of the lower depths within a generation or so. The reproduction of this basic dynamic has been an integral element of class exploitation and bourgeois political rule in the United States practically from its inception.

Within the modern working class, this racialized class formation is expressed in the varying proportions of each racial group to be found in the different strata of the working class. The great majority of whites are to be found in the broad, economically stable sectors of the working class; there is a quite small proportion in the impoverished layers. For Blacks, however, a quite large proportion is impoverished or near poor, and only a small proportion is able to achieve economic stability. Income data give a rough approximation of this differentiation.

The median income of Black families in 1981 was $13,266, only 56.4 percent of the $23,517 median income of whites.[14] This figure represents a net change of only one percentage point from 1960 when Black income stood at 55.4 percent that of whites. But an even more telling indication of the intersection between class stratification and racial differentiation is the spread across income levels. According to "A Dream Deferred," quoting 1981 figures:

> . . . Black family incomes have continuously been concentrated in the lower part of the income range in comparison to white family incomes . . . 16.7% of Black families had incomes below $5,000 per year while only 4.5% of white families had incomes below this level.
>
> At the upper end of the scale, the disparities were also wide. In 1981 46.5% of all white families had yearly incomes above $25,000 compared to only 23.1% of Black families. White families were more than four times as likely as Black families to have incomes at the very highest level, $50,000 per year and above. 9.7% of all white families had these high incomes compared to only 2.1% of Black families.[15]

A similar picture comes into focus when we look at 1981 poverty rates and unemployment rates. Thirty-four percent of Black individuals, 30.8 percent of Black families, and 44.9 percent of Black children under the age of eighteen lived below the government's poverty level in 1981. The comparable rates for whites below the poverty level were 11.1 percent of white individuals, 8.8 percent of white families, and 14.7 percent of white children under eighteen.[16]

Finally, the Black unemployment rate has consistently maintained at least a two-to-one ratio to that of whites for more than twenty years. In 1960 the Black unemployment rate was 10.2 percent while the white rate was 5.0 percent; by 1982 both these figures had risen considerably, but the differential remained more or less constant with Black unemployment at 17.3 percent and white at 8.6 percent.[17]

According to every other major social index—infant mortality rates, life expectancy, educational level, and literacy—the disparity between the situation of Blacks and that of whites is stark. And, for many of these indicators the gap has remained constant for decades or is widening rather than narrowing.[18]

These figures and all others like them are simply the mathematical abstraction and statistical expression of the devastated condition of the urban Black ghettoes and the lack of opportunity or resources of Blacks in the rural South.

Theoretically speaking they are an expression of the fact that the conditions faced by the majority of the Black community are simultaneously the material manifestation of racial oppression and a concentration of the class conditions of the lower strata of the proletariat. This represents, in the final analysis, an economic polarization between classes and an economic stratification within the working class that finds its expression in the historically specific and concrete situation in the United States, in a socioeconomic differentiation between the white and Black racial groups.

The Impoverishment of Black Women

This general framework may be applied to women and is the basis for understanding the particular conditions facing Black women. The situation of Black women is absolutely incomprehensible once class and race factors have been abstracted out. A key shortcoming of the feminization-of-poverty analysis is that it views poverty as a female problem that is *quantitatively* intensified for Black women.

But, as part of a racial group that has been incorporated into the U.S. class structure in a way that is peculiarly weighted toward the lower end of the spectrum, the class configuration of Black women is qualitatively distinct from that of white women, just as is true for the broader racial groups. It is this that is reflected in the statistical disparity between white and Black women, not simply an additional measure of women's oppression. The numbers and proportions are a quantification of a qualitative differentiation.

Within the working class, this differentiation again takes the form of the pileup of Black women in the poorest sections of the working class and the dispersion of white women across the strata with the majority falling within the economically stable sector of the proletariat. But this is a general feature of the racial contradiction, shaping the class realities of both males and females.

What is more particular to women are the trends noted earlier regarding the specific dynamics of their discriminatory integration into the labor force and changes in family forms and child rearing. Black women's location in the bottom layers of the working class has meant that their social conditions are a concentrated manifestation of the economic and social factors that increasingly serve to undermine the stability and cohesion of the working-class family.

Marxists have long projected that, in the absence of the economic compulsions that tie the upper-class family together, the working class would begin to find other forms and modes of constructing personal love relations. The positive vision of love relations without the economic blackmail of a wife's complete dependence on her husband for bread and butter and of parental relations without manipulation based on the prospect of disinheritance was contrasted to the bourgeois family built around the cash nexus and private property.

But, of course, the working-class family of today is unraveling in the context of antagonistic class relations, and the sweet projection of unencumbered love is instead a bitter and wrenching process that has left whole sections of the class without adequate social, economic, or personal support. The devolution of the modern household from extended family to nuclear family to the more or less irreducible minimal unit of mother and dependent children is most advanced in the lower strata of the class.

Here there is no property to be inherited, the household does not function as a production unit, and the individuation of direct exploitation takes the form of the individuation of impoverishment. With such a tenuous and unstable hold on gaining a living wage, the nuclear family of the poorest sections of the working class no longer holds together as a unit of consumption.

The social conditions facing Black women are the concentrated manifestation of this dynamic affecting the working class. The divorce rate for Black women is much higher than that for whites and the remarriage rate is lower. Nearly three out of ten Black women are divorced. At the same time, there is a higher proportion of never-married women among Blacks and higher separation and desertion rates. Consequently, female-headed households represent a much larger proportion of the total Black families than of white families.

The vulnerability to poverty of female-headed households is extremely well documented. The median income of female-headed families is less than 40 percent that of husband-wife families. More than half (52.9 percent) of Black female householders lived in poverty in 1981 compared to 27.4 percent of white female householders.[19] And the numbers of poor Black female-headed households tripled, from 889,000 such families in 1960 to 2.7 million in 1982. Thus by 1982, two thirds of all poor Black families were headed by women.[20]

The impact of impoverishment of female-headed households on the economic status of children under the age of eighteen has, of course, been devastating. Of the Black children in female-headed households, 67.7 percent were poor in 1981. The comparable rate for white children in female-headed households was 42.8 percent.[21] But, since the proportion of female-headed households is so much lower among whites than among Blacks, these figures translate into an even more dramatic differential between Black and white children. Nearly one half of all Black children, 44.9 percent, live in poverty while "only" 14.7 percent of white children do.[22]

This differential brings back to the fore a point made earlier, the qualitatively distinct class configuration and social conditions of white women and Black women. This distinction is missed by feminist economists who note that the labor-force-participation rates of white and Black women are nearing equivalence and that there is only a six percentage point gap in their median incomes.

These figures mask the fact that the dissolution of the family is much more advanced in the lower strata of the class and *Black women are therefore much more likely to be the sole support of their families.* Among whites, though the number of female-headed households has grown significantly, they still represent only a relatively small proportion of the total. *Consequently, for the great majority of white women who work, their wages are a portion of shared household income and do not constitute the total resources of the family.*

There again, grasping the relation among class exploitation, women's oppression, and racial oppression is crucial. The number of white female poor has risen over the past two decades, but several million white women are not in the working class at all but part of the petite bourgeoisie and bourgeoisie and thus not vulnerable to impoverishment. This reality together with the fact that the majority of white working-class women are part of the economically stable strata of the class and members of households with a male wage earner means that "only" 12 percent of white women are considered poor.

By contrast, Black women's representation in the bourgeoisie and petite bourgeoisie is negligible, and within the working class they are predominantly part of the economically unstable social strata and highly likely to be the only support of their families. For this reason, the poverty rate among Black women, 35.8 percent, is three times higher than for white women.

Class and Race

In sum, class and race are more significant causative factors in Black women's impoverishment than is gender, and the female poor are disproportionately composed of women of racial and national minorities. Thus, the feminization-of-poverty analysis seriously misrepresents the dynamics shaping female poverty in the United States and misidentifies the sectors of the population most at risk of becoming poor.

Strategies that seek to unite women across the class spectrum while remaining oblivious both to the particularities of the conditions faced by minority and poor women and to the oppression suffered by minority and other working-class men have always doomed the women's movement to the perpetual hegemony of white middle-class women. The feminization-of-poverty analysis and stragegy promises to be a repeat performance.

An examination of female poverty, Black women's poverty in particular, must proceed from a vantage point that effectively integrates class, race, and sex as simultaneously operative social factors. The difficulty of such a synthesis is reflective of the complexity of reality, but in its absence, "theories" will continue to be concocted that fail to illuminate the dynamics behind observable social trends.

The feminization of poverty is one such perspective. Those of us who are urgently concerned about the devastated state of the Black community can ill afford to adopt a perspective that so seriously distorts both the reality faced by Black women, men, and children and the contemporary intricacies of U.S. social relations more broadly.

PART TWO

Sister Struggle: The Varieties of Women's Poverty

White women keep talking about how degrading it is to be on welfare, how they can't tell anyone. I can understand that, I guess, but I don't see it so much that way. They do treat you bad and you have to fight them and it does get you down. But it's not our fault, it's theirs, and we still need what we need for our babies. After all, as a black woman I have to take grief from almost everyone, almost all the time—so why should welfare be any different?

Different women are poor for different reasons and have different options for escaping poverty. When policy makers disregard this basic fact, they devise policies that do not fit the needs of most poor women and that serve to discredit the notion that any government intervention can help. When feminists forget the distinctions, they alienate themselves from poor women and transform themselves into another adversary, instead of an ally, in the eyes of different constituencies of poor women. In this section we attempt to avoid such pitfalls by highlighting some of the differing realities poor women face.

As editors this has been our difficult but central task. Sometimes our lists of all the topics we should cover filled pages—and terrified our publisher. We wanted to include every possible group with a separate article. After all, women in prison have special needs, as do Asian women, lesbians, Southern women, physically disabled women. We shrank from being yet one more book about women that denied, by omission at least, the concerns of so many—what about Native Americans, or Chicanas, or women who work as prostitutes?

As the catalogue grew we finally began to understand our task differently; it was not to include information on the specific needs of each possible group of women, important as their concerns were. Instead, it was to create a climate of understanding so that the particularities of any one group are mirrored in the particularities of another, the lesson being never to generalize without qualification, without recognizing that another woman might experience herself, her life, or her poverty very differently.

Roberta Praeger, a Boston-area welfare activist, aptly begins by reminding us that we can never underestimate the variety of histories and concerns that characterize any woman and any woman who is poor. Whether it be as a survivor of incest, a battered woman, an immigrant, or a displaced homemaker, "every picture tells a story," which must be heard before meaningful change can occur.

Next, Elizabeth Higginbotham elaborates on the crucial observation that poverty is not new for women of color, nor does it represent some new loss of status for them. Iris Zavala Martinez follows this argument with the recognition that cultural and psychological explanations blame *machismo* or historical "passivity" for Puerto Rican women's situation, rather than offering a more complex understanding of the effects of colonialism and economic discrimination. Both writers suggest the pressures on a woman of color to make it in the job market and to care for her children (and often her brothers, sisters, parents, and grandchildren as well).

We have not focused this book entirely on racial and cultural differences among poor women. For example, there are no Asian, Native American, or Chicana voices here. We hope, however, that readers will come away from this section with appreciation for the critical way in which cultural traditions, like those mentioned by Zavala Martinez may make different groups of women respond to their poverty differently. An experience that may lead to embarrassment for one woman may be a call to arms for another and force a retreat into extended family networks for a third. Such differences are not just "psychological" or "subjective"; they may have real effects on organizing strategies and goals. At the same time, false assumptions within the dominant society about an unyielding "culture of poverty" may serve to perpetuate and justify the economic and social oppression of women of color.

Age differences also influence how women experience poverty. Older women, as Kathleen Kautzer notes, are the fastest-growing age group in this country, and they are the group with the least ability to change their economic status through individual action. For most, "Prince Charming"—if there ever was one—is dead, and few well-paying jobs are in sight. So the organizing activity of the Older Women's League is linked with a discussion of the range of problems facing older women: age and sex discrimination in the job market and in pension and Social Security systems, lack of economic recognition for care-giving work in the home, as well as social and psychological isolation. And again, as Kautzer acknowledges, the differences within the group of older women—age, race, and class differences—create even further variety and prompt a complex organizing strategy.

At the other end of the age spectrum, teenagers are threatened with doom if they become pregnant, are denied birth control, and then are left alone to cope under the stigma of being labeled a "teenage mother." As Nancy Aries and two young Boston mothers explain, the best social support for a young pregnant girl is often yet another woman, her mother. Here again we see the ways that society depends on poor women to care for other poor women without adequate supports; mothers must take care of their daughters' children as well as their own aging mothers.

By focusing on the variety of women's poverty we are also forced to remember the women whose poverty has long been accepted as a "fact of life," rural women and women working in low-paid jobs. Here Eleanor Anstey and Janet Kuller show the quiet despair of many traditionally poor rural women, and Marion Graham reminds us of the invisible poverty of secretaries. Both groups have been somewhat removed from the stigma of being branded "welfare recipients" but at the cost of denying their economic and social needs.

The "poor but proud" label, often coupled with racial blinders, has served to keep farm women and women who work as clerical, domestic, retail, and service employees from seeing their common interests with women who use the welfare system to meet their economic needs. And, in turn, many advocates for welfare mothers have forgotten or disregarded the deep needs for income, housing, and medical supports among a far wider group of women than those labeled "poor" exactly because they receive such benefits. This section begins to bridge such gaps.

A WORLD WORTH LIVING IN

Roberta Praeger

As an impoverished woman I live with the exhaustion, the frustration, the deprivation of poverty. As a survivor of incest I struggle to overcome the emotional burden. One thing has led to another in my life as the causes of poverty, of incest, of so many issues have become increasingly clear. My need to personalize has given way to a realization of social injustice and a commitment to struggle for social change.

Living on Welfare

I live alone with my four-year-old child, Jamie. This state (Massachusetts) allocates $328 a month to a family of two living on Aid to Families with Dependent Children (AFDC). This sum places us, along with other social service recipients, at an income 40 percent below the federal poverty line. In today's economy, out of this sum of money, we are expected to pay for rent, utilities, clothing for two, child-care expenses, food not covered by food stamps, and any other expenses we may incur.

My food stamps have been cut to the point where they barely buy food for half the month. I have difficulty keeping up with the utility bills, and my furniture is falling apart. Furniture breaks, and there is no money to replace it. Things that others take for granted, such as sheets and towels, become irreplacable luxuries.

Chaos exists around everything, even the most important issues, like keeping a roof over one's head. How are people expected to pay rent for their families on the shameful amount of income provided by the Welfare Department? The answer, in many cases, is reflected in the living conditions of welfare recipients. Some of us live in apartments that should be considered uninhabitable. We live with roaches, mice, sometimes rats, and floors about to cave in. I live in subsidized housing. It's that or the street. My rent without the subsidy is $400 a month, $72 more than my entire monthly income. It took over a year of red tape between the time of my first application to the the time of final acceptance into the program, all the while watching the amount of my rent climb higher and higher. What becomes of the more than 80 percent of AFDC recipients who are not subsidized because there isn't enough of this housing available?

Emergencies are dealt with in the best way possible. One cold winter day, Jamie broke his ankle in the day-care center. It was the day my food stamps were due to arrive. With no food in the house, I had to take him, on public transportation, to the hospital emergency room and then walk to the supermarket with my shopping cart in a foot of snow. This was not an unusual event in my life. All AFDC mothers get caught up in situations like this, because we are alone, because we have few resources and little money.

Ronald Reagan's war on the poor has exacerbated an already intolerable situation. Human service programs have been slashed to the bone. Regulations governing the fuel assistance program have been changed in ways that now make many of the impoverished ineligible. Energy assistance no longer pays my utility bills. For some these changes have meant going without needed fuel, thereby forcing people to endure freezing temperatures.

The food stamp situation has gone from bad to worse. The amount of money allocated for the program has been drastically reduced. My situation reflects that of most welfare recipients. Last year, my food stamps were cut back from $108 to $76 a month, barely enough to buy food for two weeks. Reagan doesn't even allow us to work to supplement our meager income. His reforms resulted in a law, the Omnibus Budget Reconciliation Act, that, in one fell swoop, instituted a number of repressive work-related changes. Its main impact came when it considerably lowered the amount of money a recipient can earn before the termination of benefits. Under this new law even a low-paying, part-time job can make a person no longer eligible for assistance.

The complexity of our lives reaches beyond economic issues. Monday through Friday, I work as an undergraduate student at the University of Massachusetts. On weekends, when in two-parent families, one parent can sometimes shift the responsibility to the other, I provide the entertainment for my child. All the household chores are my responsibility, for I have no one to share them with. When Jamie is sick I spend nights awake with him. When I am sick, I have no one to help me. I can't do things others take for granted, such as spend an evening out at the movies, because I don't have enough money to pay both the admission fee and for child care. Even if I did, I would be too exhausted to get out the front door. Often I wind up caught in a circle of isolation.

What kind of recognition do I and other welfare mothers get for all this hard work? One popular image of welfare recipients pictures us as lazy, irresponsible women, sitting at home, having babies, and living off the government. Much of society treats us like lepers, degrading and humiliating us at every turn, treating us as if we were getting something for nothing. One day I walked into a small grocery store wearing a button that read "Stop Reagan's War on the Poor." The proprietor of the store looked at my button and said to me, "You know, all those people on welfare are rich." Most welfare recipients would say anything rather than admit to being on welfare because of the image it creates. My brother-in-law had the audacity to say to me in conversation one day, "People are poor because they're lazy. They don't want to work."

And the Welfare Department shares this image of the recipient with the general public. From the first moment of contact with the department, the client is treated with rudeness, impatience, mistrust, and scorn. She is intimidated by constant redeterminations, reviews, and threats of being cut off. Her life is controlled by a system wracked with ineptness and callous indifference. Two years ago, unable to pay my electric bill, I applied for emergency assistance. It took the Welfare Department so long to pay the bill that the electric company turned the power off. We lived for two days without electricity before my constant badgering of the Welfare Department and the utility company produced results.

The department gives out information that is misleading and/or incomplete. The recipient is made to feel stupid, guilty, and worthless, a "problem" rather than a person. When I first applied I had to answer all sorts of questions about my personal life time and again. Many of my replies were met with disbelief. I sat there for hours at a time, nine months pregnant, waiting to be interviewed. And that was just the beginning of hours and hours of waiting, of filling in forms for the programs that keep us and our children alive.

The Personal Is Political

For most women in this situation, suffering is nothing new. Poverty is seldom an isolated issue. It's part of a whole picture. Other issues complicate our lives. For myself, as for many of us, suffering is complicated by memories, the results of trauma brought forward from childhood. Under frilly pink dresses and little blue sailor suits lay horror stories shared by many. The memories I bring with me from my childhood are not very pretty.

I was born in a Boston neighborhood in 1945. My father was a linoleum installer, my mother a homemaker. I want to say that my childhood was colored by the fact that I was an abused child. It's still difficult for me to talk about some things to this day.

My mother didn't give me a life of my own. When I was an infant she force-fed me. At age nine, she was still spoon-feeding me. Much of the time she didn't let me out of her sight. She must have seen school as a threat to her control, for she kept me home half the time. In me she saw not a separate person but an extension of herself. She felt free to do as she wished with my body. Her attempts to control my elimination process have had a lasting impact on my sexuality. The methods she used have been documented for their use in cases of mother-daughter incest. She had an obsessive-compulsive desire to control what went into me, to control elimination, to control everything about me. I had no control over anything. I couldn't get out from under what was happening to me psychologically. Powerlessness, frustration, and emotional insecurity breed a chain of abuse as men abuse women and children and women abuse children.

In the face of all the adverse, perverted attention received from my mother, I turned to my father for love and affection. We became close. In time, though, it became clear he knew as little about child rearing as my mother. His own deprived childhood had taught him only bitterness.

Throughout the years I knew him, he had gambled literally thousands of dollars away at the horse track. He left me alone outside the track gate at age five or six when the sign read "No children allowed." When I was twelve, he set fire to our house. He had run out of money for gambling purposes, and the house was insured against fire. When the insurance money arrived, my mother somehow managed to intercept it and bought new furniture. When my father found out what she had done, he went on a rampage. I had a knicknack shelf, charred from the fire. He threw it across the room, splinters of glass flying everywhere, and then he hit my mother. This was not an uncommon scene in my childhood.

By the time I reached eleven, my father was beginning to see me in a different light. At this point, the closeness that had developed between him and me still existed. And he proceeded to take advantage of it.

My mother belonged to a poker club, and once a week she would leave the house to go to these sessions. On these occasions my father would come over to me and remove both my clothes and his. He would then use my body to masturbate until he reached orgasm. He attempted to justify these actions by saying, "A man has to have sex and your mother won't." This occured a number of times when I was between the ages of eleven and thirteen. I cried the last time he did this and he stopped molesting me sexually. In incestuous situations there doesn't have to be any threat; very often there isn't, because parents are in a position of trust, because parents are in a position of power, and because the child needs love. Children are in a developmental stage where they have no choice.

I went to public school and did very well. When I was sixteen, the school authorities told me that no matter how well I did, no matter how high my grades were, they could not keep me in school if I appeared only half the time. So I dropped out. I just spent the whole time sitting in front of the television until my mother died.

I didn't understand the extent of my mother's sickness in her treatment of me. Fear that if my mother knew what my father was doing she would kill him seemed realistic to me at the time. And so, I kept silent. I looked at my parents, as all children do, as authority figures. Longing for a way out of the situation, I felt trapped. In the face of all this I felt overwhelmed, afraid, and isolated. I retreated from reality into a world of fantasy. For only through my imagination could I find any peace of mind or semblance of happiness. The abuse I had taken all these years began to manifest itself in psychosomatic symptoms. Periodically, I started suffering intense abdominal pain. Once I fainted and fell on the bathroom floor. There were three visits to the hospital emergency room. My doctor had misdiagnosed the symptoms as appendicitis.

When I was seventeen, my father, after a major argument with my mother, moved out. Without money to pay the rent, with no job training or other resources, we rented out a room. Ann, the young woman renting the room, was appalled at the situation she discovered. She began to teach me some basic skills such as how to wash my own clothes. For the first time in my life I related positively to someone. My father moved back two months later. For two years this is how the situation remained, my mother, father, Ann, and I all living together.

In 1965 my mother was diagnosed as having lung cancer. Three months later she was dead. I felt nothing, no sorrow, no anger, no emotion. I had long ago learned how to bury my emotions deep down inside of me. I packed by belongings and moved out with Ann, in the midst of my father's ranting and raving.

Living in an apartment with Ann made things seem to improve on the surface. My life was quieter. I held a steady job for the first time. There was a little money to spend. I could come and go as I pleased. It felt good, and I guess, at that point I thought my life had really changed. It took me a long time to realize what an adult who has had this kind of childhood must still go through. I had nightmares constantly. There were times when I went into deep depressions. I didn't know what was going on, what was happening to me, or why.

After holding my first job for three years, I went through a series of jobs in different fields: sales, hairdressing, and, after a period of training, nursing. It seemed I was not functioning well in any area. I fell apart in any situation where demands were made of me. I had no tolerance for hierarchy. I discovered that I performed best when I was acting as charge nurse. Unfortunately, in my role as a Licensed Practical Nurse, I usually wound up low person on the totem pole, generally having to answer to someone else. In time, it became clear to me, that control was a major factor in a variety of situations that I encountered.

My self-confidence and self-esteem were abysmally low. Every time something went wrong my first thought was, "There must be something wrong with me." I didn't know then, what I know now. Children never blame their parents for the wrong that is done. They blame themselves. This feeling carries on into adulthood until it is difficult not to blame oneself for everything that does not go right.

I was depressed, suicidal, frightened out of my wits, and completely overwhelmed by life. After a series of failed relationships and a broken marriage, I wound up alone, with a small child, living on welfare. The emotional burden I carried became complicated by the misery and exhaustion of poverty.

Why have I survived? Why am I not dead? Because I'm a survivor. Because I have Jamie and I love him more than words can say. In him I see the future, not the past.

A Major Change

I survived because in the midst of all this something happened, something that was to turn out to be the major guiding force in my life. In 1972 the owner of my building sent out notices threatening eviction if the tenants did not pay a huge rent increase. Everyone in the building was aghast at the prospect and so formed a tenant union to discuss alternatives. Through my activities with the union, I learned of an organization that did community work throughout the city. Cambridge Tenants Organizing Committee (CTOC) was a multifaceted organization involved in work around issues such as tenants' rights, welfare advocacy, antiracist work, and education concerning sexism in society. I began working with a group of people unlike any that I had been exposed to in the past. They treated me as a person capable of assuming responsibility and doing any job well. My work with CTOC included organizing tenant unions throughout the city, counseling unemployed workers, and attending countless demonstrations, marches, picketings, and hearings. As a group we organized and/or supported eviction blocking, we helped defend people against physical racist attacks, and we demonstrated at the state house for continuation of rent control. I wasn't paid for my work. What I earned was far more important than money. I learned respect for myself as a women. I learned the joys and pitfalls of working collectively and began assimilating more information that I had at any other time of my life.

And I flourished. I went to meeting after meeting until they consumed almost all of my nonwork time. Over the years I joined other groups. One of my major commitments was to a group that presented political films. My politics became the center of my life.

Through counseling and therapy groups with therapists who shared my political perspective, the guilt I had shouldered all these years began to lessen. Within a period of three years, through groups and conventions, I listened to and/or spoke with more than three hundred other survivors of incest. I heard stories that would make your hair stand on end. New learning led to making connections. Although the true extent of incest is not known, owing to the fact that sexual abuse within families usually goes unreported, various statistics estimate that 100,000 to 250,000 children are sexually molested each year in the United States. Other studies show that one out of every three to four women in this country is a victim of sexual abuse as child. Incest Resources, my primary resource for group counseling, believes these statistics heavily underestimate the extent of actual abuse. So do I. Although the guilt for the abuse lies with the abuser, the context of the problem reaches far beyond, beyond me or my parents, into society itself as power and inequality surround us.

Connections with other people have become part and parcel of my life as my life situation has led me into work surrounding the issue of poverty. Although I had known for years of the existence of the Coalition for Basic Human Needs (CBHN)—a progressive group composed almost totally of welfare recipients—my political work, reflecting my life situation, had led me in other directions.

Now I found myself alone with a toddler, living on AFDC. When Jamie was two, I returned to school to acquire additional skills. My academic work led me into issues concerning poverty as I became involved in months of activity, along with students and faculty and a variety of progressive women's groups, constructing a conference on the issue of women and poverty. Members of CBHN were involved in work on the conference, and we connected.

Social change through welfare-rights struggles became a major focus in my life as I began working with CBHN. Collectively, we sponsored legislative bills that would improve our lives financially while, at the same time, we taught others how we actually live. Public education became intertwined with legislative work as I spoke at hearings on the reality of living on AFDC. Political support became intertwined with public education as I spoke on the work of CBHN to progressive groups and their constituencies, indicting this country's political system for the impoverishment of its people.

CBHN is composed of chapters representing various cities and towns across Massachusetts. Grass-roots organizing of welfare recipients takes place within local chapters, while the organization as a whole works on statewide issues. We mail out newsletters, hold press conferences, and initiate campaigns. We are currently involved in our most ambitious effort. Whereas in the past our work has been directed toward winning small goals such as a clothing allowance or a small increase in benefits, this time we have set about to bring welfare benefits up to the poverty level, a massive effort involving all of our past strategies and more. We have filed a bill with the state legislature. Public education has become concentrated in the campaign as we plan actions involving the work of welfare-rights groups and individuals throughout the state.

The courage we share as impoverished women has been mirrored throughout this effort. At a press conference to announce the campaign a number of us gave truth to the statement that we and our children go without the basic necessities of life. One woman spoke of sending her child to school without lunch because there was no food in the house. Others had no money for winter jackets or shoes for their children. Sharing the reality of living at 40 percent below the poverty level brings mutual support as well as frustration and anger. In mid-April hundreds of welfare recipients—women carrying infants, the disabled, and the homeless—came from all over Massachusetts to rally in front of the state house along with our supporters and testify to the legislature in behalf of our "Up to the Poverty Level" bill. Courage and determination rang out in statements such as this:

> Take the cost of implementing this program and weigh it, if it must be weighed at all; then weigh it against the anguish suffered by the six-month-old twins who starved to death in a Springfield housing project.
>
> The day that the state legislature has to scrape the gilt off the dome of the state house and sell it for revenue is the day that this state can answer to us that there is not the means to do this.

The complexity of the situation comes home to me again and again as I sit in the CBHN office answering the telephone and doing welfare advocacy work. I've spoken with women on AFDC who have been battered to within an inch of their lives, some who are, like myself, survivors of child abuse, and others who are reeling from the effects of racism as well as poverty.

In this society so many of us internalize oppression. We internalize the guilt that belongs to the system that creates the conditions people live in. When we realize this and turn our anger outward in an effort to change society, then we begin to create a world worth living in.

The work isn't easy. Many of us become overwhelmed as well as overextended. It takes courage and fortitude to survive. For we live in a society laden with myths and an inequality that leads to human suffering. In order to alleviate the suffering and provide the equality each and every one of us deserves, we must effect social change. If we are to effect social change, then we must recognize social injustice and destroy the myths it creates. Little did I realize, years ago, when I first began this work how far it reached beyond my own survival. For those of us involved in creating a new society are doing the most important work that exists.

WE WERE NEVER ON A PEDESTAL
Women of Color Continue to Struggle With Poverty, Racism, and Sexism

Elizabeth Higginbotham

> *When I came out of high school, I thought I was going to get a good job. I tried looking in many places, but the big companies downtown just took my application and I never heard from them. I was able to get a job at a small office in the midtown area. I am the secretary for many people. At first, I was excited about making $120 per week. But I quickly discovered that after Social Security, taxes, and my health insurance were taken out, I was left with very little. It was hard to make it from one payday to the next. I've been there seven years now. I really cannot find another job. This place is sort of comfortable. They know me and they know my work. I even get small raises and occasional bonuses when we have a good season. They were very good about letting me work less when my daughter was first born. But I would really like to do the same type of work and just make more money.*

Anna Rivera has a high school diploma and works as a clerk-typist for a small firm in an Eastern city. When she began working, she felt lucky to find a job. Many of her female Puerto Rican friends

---

Black is capitalized in this essay in accordance with the author's wishes.

were less successful in their efforts and could not find clerical work. They followed their mothers into the garment factories. So there was much celebration in Anna's family when she got a white-collar job. She made more money than her father, who washed dishes for a major hotel in the city. And her job was far more regular than the garment factory work her mother did. Initially, her weekly wages sounded very good. She even got two weeks paid vacation each year and sick pay. Yet, over time, Anna and her family came to question the "goodness" of her job.

When she was twenty-two Anna married José, who works as an operative in a small factory. And when she was twenty-three, their daughter, Iris, was born. Both Anna and José are employed full-time and her sister, Nilsa, watches Iris. Anna gives her sister a little money for helping her with child care. She would like to give her more but cannot. She and José are perplexed by their persistent poverty. They have more education than their own parents. They have mastered English and hold regular jobs. Yet, they cannot save enough money to leave their tiny apartment. They have already given up the dream of owning their own home but would just like a little more room for their family. Limited job mobility plagues their lives. They, like many of their friends, are keenly aware that racism continues to be a major limit on their lives, just as it was for their parents, but the nature of the restrictions has changed.

There are many young women of color who share Anna's plight. Even though they have worked to make a "better life," they still find themselves well acquainted with inadequate housing, poor health-care facilities, and jobs that are not leading them anywhere. Afro-American, Latina, Asian American, and Native American women have never been on a pedestal. Thus, they are not suffering the shocks of the fall. Instead, they are choking on the bitterness of despair because their many efforts have not resulted in significant changes in their lives.

It is very common for Afro-American, Latina, Asian American, and Native American women to complete high school and to avoid adolescent pregnancy, single parenthood, and welfare. Yet these young women still find themselves either in poverty or near poverty. Gender, race, and class oppression make it particularly difficult for women of color who are raised in poor families to climb out of poverty. This essay focuses on work for women of color and briefly addresses three major issues, which are rarely given attention, but which contribute to the persistence of their poverty. First, is their history in the labor market. Women of color share a legacy of racial oppression with other members of their racial-ethnic group. Second, race and sex discrimination have kept women of color at the bottom of the occupational ladder. Therefore, their high rates of labor-force participation have been ineffective in bringing them out of poverty. And finally, the past few decades have seen women of color enter new occupations around the nation. This progress is celebrated in many spheres, but questions remain about the significance of employment shifts for the economic well-being of women of color.

A History of Exploitation

People of color were brought to the United States to work. There was little attention to other aspects of their lives, such as family life, education, culture, political rights, and so forth. Instead, the racism of the eighteenth and especially the nineteenth centuries denied them their rights and justified the exploitation of their labor. Therefore, while work in the nineteenth century was frequently organized in ways that jeopardized white working-class life, this was always true for working-class Afro-Americans, Chinese immigrants, Japanese immigrants, Mexican Americans, and Native American Indians.[1]

Concerned only with the labor power of people of color, white landowners and employers showed only a minimal interest in their lives outside the fields, factories, kitchens, mines, canneries, and railroad yards. Frequently the harsh working conditions made family and community life precarious. Women of color were forced into market work, along with their men. This employment complicated their tasks of caring for children and the home. Frequently, they could only tend to their own children after they had worked long hours in the labor market.[2]

This point is easily illustrated in the case of slavery, where creating profits for the owners took priority over the survival of any individual slave or slave family. Angela Davis identified what this meant for Black slave women. "The slave system defined Black people as chattel. Since women, no less than men, were viewed as profitable labor units, they might as well have been genderless as far as the slaveholders were concerned. In the words of scholar

Kenneth Stammp 'the slave woman was first a full-time worker, and only incidentally a wife, mother and homemaker.' "[3]

It was under such harsh conditions that Afro-American people had to persist in building and maintaining family life. Other people of color share a heritage of labor exploitation and the task of maintaining family life without institutional supports. For example, there was no "family wage" for Black, Latino, and Asian men, while this privilege was extended to native-born white males and many white immigrants. Such efforts, which supported patriarchial families and afforded white women a level of protection, were routinely denied to people of color.[4]

Chinese immigrants, who constructed railroad lines and developed agricultural areas in the late nineteenth century, also faced oppressive working conditions and low wages. Federal legislation prohibited these laborers from bringing their wives to join them. They were explicitly given the message that their families were not permitted to flourish on American soil.[5]

This legacy is also shared by Mexican Americans, who suffered horrible living and working conditions to open the mines of the Southwest. Their work necessitated either separation from their families or bringing them along to live in isolated mining communities.[6] In each instance, like slavery for Afro-Americans, men were either unavailable or unable to protect and provide for the family. This situation had a direct impact on the roles of females. Women not only had to bear and raise children and care for the home, they also had to contribute directly to the economic support of the family.

Like other working-class daughters in the nineteenth century, women of color frequently had to take paid employment to bring wages into the household. Yet, they entered a labor market where they faced both gender and racial restrictions. For example, when the structure of Southern agriculture in the late nineteenth century jeopardized the survival of sharecropping Black families, it was the women, frequently daughters, who were released from farm work to sell their labor. The only positions open to them were in household work, which paid low wages.[7] Regardless of whether they stayed in the South or migrated to the North, they were routinely denied factory work and had to do domestic work to supplement their families' income.[8] These women discovered through their personal experiences that the labor market was a limited one for women and a more restrictive one for women of color.

The same discovery was made by nineteenth-century Mexican American women in California, who watched their husbands' livelihoods disappear. Like their Afro-American counterparts, they sought paid employment but could find work only in laundries, canneries, other people's houses, and in the fields as migrant laborers.[9] The small population of Chinese immigrant women found new employment options outside of the "Chinatowns" around the nation, but they were able to find employment only in garment factories and other low-wage manufacturing jobs. A high percentage of Japanese immigrant women, who entered this country in the early twentieth century, were household workers.[10]

Women of color learned that race and sex discrimination were to be parts of their lives. Industrialization in the late nineteenth and early twentieth centuries created new employment opportunities for women. But these jobs were limited to native-born white women. Later clerical, sales, teaching, and social work positions would be expanded to incorporate the daughters of white immigrant families. Meanwhile, women of color were still overwhelmingly found in private household work, farm labor, laundries, canneries, and the lowest of manufacturing jobs.

Job ceilings and various types of racial barriers operated well into the twentieth century to keep Afro-American, Latina, Asian American, and Native American Indian women out of "traditional white women's jobs." Prior to the 1960s, it frequently took a college education to make significant gains in the labor market. And few families had the resources to enable their daughters to attain higher education.[11] Women of color with various levels of high school education found that many segments of the labor market were still hostile to them. It would take more than their own individual efforts at improvement to challenge the blatant discrimination in the labor market. Their wages were essential to the economic survival of their families, but even with both spouses employed full-time, people of color in working-class occupations had difficulties escaping poverty.

The Contemporary Scene

In the last decade, each racial or ethnic community has become more stratified. Blacks, Latinos, Asian Americans, and Native

Americans with college and advanced degrees have been able to move into the middle class, but other members of their communities have been untouched by these advancements.[12] After major campaigns to encourage racial and ethnic youth to stay in school and get a high school diploma, the labor market has not fulfilled its end of the bargain.[13] Racial discrimination is still quite pronounced, and at this time of dramatic economic shifts, race is a key factor in the process of who stays middle class, who becomes middle class, who remains stably employed in the working class, who falls through the cracks, and who is not able to get out of poverty.

As deindustrialization proceeds in the Northwest and Midwest, and the nonunionized industrialization of the Sun Belt and Third World nations continues, it is evident that the working class suffers. But just as in the past, people of color are particularly jeopardized. After decades of struggle, Black and Latino men and women had made real employment gains in heavy, unionized industries, and their families were beginning to appreciate a margin of security. But these sectors are currently in decline, especially steel, automobiles, and rubber. Families that have crawled out of poverty on unionized wages are now losing their edge as their jobs disappear.

Women of color, who traditionally have been called upon to enter paid employment on behalf of their families, continue to do so. In the last two decades, many have found new areas of employment, especially clerical and sales positions, but many of their sisters are still found in private household work, factory work, and the service industries. All of these jobs are only minimally rewarding financially. Thus, families who have lost the security of employment in heavy industry have watched their economic positions deteriorate. The contributions of women employed in low-wage sectors have become even more critical to the survival of their families. This is the scenario that is enacted weekly around the nation. Too often scholars only focus on the difficulties of deindustrialization for white working-class families, but Black and Latino working-class families who had just begun to "make it" are also now living on the "edge" again.

The persistence of poverty or near poverty for people of color is illustrated in Table 1, "Earnings for Year-Round, Full-Time Workers by Sex, Race, and Hispanic Origin." A total of 9.9 percent of Black

Table 1
Earnings of Year-round Full-time Workers by Sex, Race, and Hispanic Origin, 1982

	Male				Female			
Earnings of:	**Total**	**White**	**Black**	**Hispanic**	**Total**	**White**	**Black**	**Hispanic**
Under $6,700	5.8	5.5	6.4	5.9	9.9	9.9	9.9	12.1
$ 6,700–$ 9,999	6.3	5.7	13.6	15.3	17.7	17.3	20.8	28.0
$10,000–$14,999	16.3	15.3	27.4	27.0	32.7	32.5	34.9	35.4
$15,000–$19,999	17.4	17.1	21.1	8.0	20.7	20.8	20.1	12.5
$20,000–$24,999	16.6	16.6	15.7	13.5	11.0	11.2	8.9	7.0
$25,000 +	37.8	39.7	15.7	20.2	8.0	8.3	5.4	4.9
Total	100.0	99.9	99.9	99.9	100.0	100.0	100.0	99.9

Columns may total less than 100 owing to rounding.

Table compiled from U.S., Department of Labor, Bureau of Statistics, Linking Employment Problems to Economic Status, *Bulletin 2201 (Washington, D.C.: Government Printing Office, June 1984), p. 19, tab. 9.*

and white women who work full-time, all year earn under $6,700. Fully, 12.1 percent of full-time employed Hispanic women earn less than $6,700. In contrast, only 5.8 percent of males who are employed full-time make below $6,700. These data support the contention that men are poor as a result of unemployment, while women are poor because of the type of work they do.[14]

A high percentage of women, 17.7 in all racial groups, are found in near poverty (between $6,700 and $9,999). Many are caught in nonunionized work settings and forced to exist on minimum wage; thus their earnings push them just over the poverty line. While a significant number of women are clustered in this wage bracket, there are clear ethnic differences. Hispanic women are more likely to be found at this wage level than are Black or white women. Poverty is even more exaggerated for working Hispanic women than the figures reflect. Many Latinas work in the garment industry and other factories where work is seasonal. Thus, annually they face periods of unemployment. These women's earnings are not included in the table here, because they do not work all year. Instead, the data represent the earnings of women like Anna Rivera, who do clerical work, and other Latinas employed in service industries, especially hospitals, hotels, and restaurants.

The largest percentages of employed women earn between $10,000 and $14,999 per year. They represent a wide range of occupations, which have enabled women either to escape poverty or to stabilize their positions in the working class. But if these women are not attached to a man, in all likelihood they live on tight budgets. This income bracket is also the modal category for Black and Hispanic males, indicating that many of them are in positions that keep them out of poverty but probably fail to deliver a high quality of life. This is in sharp contrast to white males, only 15.3 percent of whom earn between $10,000 and $14,999. Instead white male earnings reflect centuries of advantage, with 39.7 percent earning $25,000 or more.

In summary, being employed full-time, year-round is not a guarantee that you will not be poor, if you are a Black or Hispanic male or a woman of any color. The data show that only 11.2 percent of white males who are employed year-round in full-time positions make under $10,000 per year, leaving them either in poverty or near poverty. Yet, 20 percent of Black males, 21.2 percent of Hispanic males, 27 percent of white females, 30.7 percent of Black females, and 40.1 percent of Hispanic females do not earn more than $10,000 per year for their labor.[15]

The earnings reflected in Table 1 are directly tied to the occupational positions of white people and people of color. Table 2, "Occupation of Year-Round, Full-Time Workers by Sex, Race, and Hispanic Origin," indicates that women are still heavily represented in clerical jobs (along with other administrative support positions) and sales jobs, and people of color are still more likely to be found in certain occupations. Increasingly, women are entering professions. In 1982, 15.9 percent of employed white women and 12.6 percent of employed Black women were in professional specialities. Yet, the majority of professional Black women are found in traditionally female occupations, especially teaching, library work, nursing, and social work, and they are overwhelmingly employed in the public sector.[16] Hispanic women have made fewer gains in this area. What is troubling with respect to this occupational distribution is the large numbers of women of color in service and factory work.

Julianne Malveaux suggests that Black women have moved out of private household work into occupations that offer only a slightly better standard of living. Table 2 shows low percentages of household workers but higher percentages of women of color in service and factory work. Further examination of Table 2 indicates that service and factory work are also significant sectors of employment for Black and Hispanic males.

We know that operative positions are jeopardized by the economy. Service work tends to be paid either a minimum wage or slightly above it. This includes service work organized in traditional ways, like hospital and hotel work and occupations influenced by technology, particularly in the fast-food industries. While these are growing sectors they provide barely livable wages and do not foster full participation in the mainstream. The tight economy and discriminatory barriers have operated to keep people of color in this tiny corner of the labor market, where they continue to struggle against the odds to make a living and raise their families.

An examination of current employment for women of color reveals a decline in private household workers and an increase in women of color entering traditionally white female occupations. Today, Afro-American women who could only clean and cook for affluent white families watch their grandchildren while their

Table 2
Occupation of Year-round Full-time Workers by Sex, Race, and Hispanic Origin, 1982

	Male				Female			
	Total	White	Black	Hispanic	Total	White	Black	Hispanic
Executive, administrative, and managerial	15.9	16.6	8.5	8.9	11.1	11.9	5.8	7.3
Professional specialty occupations	13.8	14.1	7.8	5.2	15.5	15.9	12.6	8.5
Technicians and related support	3.2	3.2	2.4	2.1	3.9	3.8	3.6	2.4
Sales	11.6	12.3	3.8	6.8	9.7	10.5	4.4	9.6
Administrative support, including clerical	6.2	5.9	10.4	7.0	34.9	35.8	30.3	34.4
Private household service	—*	—	—	—	0.6	0.4	2.0	1.1
Protective service	2.7	2.6	4.6	2.8	0.4	0.4	0.8	0.4
Service, excluding household and protective	4.7	3.9	11.8	11.1	10.9	9.2	22.4	12.1
Farming, forestry, and fishing occupations	4.4	4.5	3.5	5.4	0.7	0.7	0.3	0.6
Precision production, craft, and repair occupations	19.7	20.3	14.6	20.7	2.3	2.2	2.6	3.9

Table 2 (continued)

	Male				Female			
	Total	White	Black	Hispanic	Total	White	Black	Hispanic
Operatives, except transport	7.5	7.1	11.6	14.3	8.2	7.4	12.9	16.6
Transport operatives	6.2	5.9	11.1	7.8	0.5	0.4	0.8	0.4
Laborers, except farm and mine	4.0	3.6	9.9	7.8	1.3	1.4	1.4	2.5
	99.9	100.0	100.0	99.9	100.0	100.0	99.9	99.9

Column totals may equal less than 100 owing to rounding.

*"—" *indicates less than 0.05%.*

Table compiled from U.S., Department of Commerce, Bureau of the Census, "Money Income of Households, Families, and Persons in the United States, 1982," Current Population Reports, *Series P-60, no. 142, (Washington, D.C.: Government Printing Office, February 1984), p. 184, tab. 52.*

daughters go to work in clean offices. Puerto Rican women who could find jobs only in the low-wage garment industry, are proud of their daughters, who now work in fashionable department stores. People can see the progress, but they are also aware of the ways that racism, class, and gender continue to limit employment options.

A history of labor exploitation and limited access to jobs continue to hamper the efforts of women of color to improve their occupational positions. Economic circumstances still force them into the labor market to assist their families. As daughters, wives, or mothers, their wages are critical to the economic well-being of their families. People of color find many aspects of the new poverty to be familiar to them. Their experiences indicate the need systematically to address the nature of racial discrimination in current educational and employment settings. Without an agenda that acknowledges these factors, there will be few significant changes in the lives of people of color. Anna's daughter and the daughters of other working women of color are likely to find that the labor market is also hostile to them. They are destined to face barriers in schools and on the job, which steer them toward low wages and dead-end jobs. Thus, the contemporary attention to poverty must seriously address differences in women's situations that are rooted in race and class and also examine the factors that persist in keeping certain segments of the male population in or near poverty.

EN LA LUCHA
Economic and Socioemotional Struggles of Puerto Rican Women in the United States

Iris Zavala Martinez

When a Puerto Rican woman is asked how she is, how things are going, she often responds with *"Pues, ahi, en la Lucha"* ("Well, struggling," or "in the struggle"). Although I have not discovered the origins of this phrase, it epitomizes reality for many Puerto Rican women. We are struggling; we are in the struggle. In fact, this brief term encapsulates the broader history, as well as the daily struggles to survive—to deal with and overcome a multitude of social, economic, and personal factors—that is reflected in the lives and experiences of Puerto Rican women. It is a statement of survival, a comment on economic and social circumstances, a means of coping and perserverance; and, finally, the phrase contains the seeds of a commitment to be involved, to be engaged, to be in struggle no matter what the odds.

Puerto Rican women in the United States have been portrayed in many ways. Often, there are the statistics: numbers of single heads of households, numbers on welfare, level of educational attainment, percentages using public services. The factual data, however, only draw an outline; they cannot present the complexity of the lives embodied in the numbers. Another picture is painted from descriptions of functional style, descriptions that frequently draw upon negative stereotypes. For example, Puerto Rican women, along with Latin women in general, are often portrayed as passive, submissive, and all-suffering, or the opposite, as loud with a "hot temper." Such simplifications distort the varied lives of Puerto Rican women, taking their behavior out of context, making it seem that there is some peculiar and "cultural" reason for behaviors, which, in fact, may exist for other women too, if they are valid descriptions at all.

Finally, both the statistics and the stereotypes treat Puerto Rican women as if they were all one homogenous group. Such treatment fosters a myth that ignores class differences, racial variations, and differences in places of birth and cultural background, as well as in educational process or language preference. Only when the portrayal becomes richer, more sensitive to the multitude of such interacting characteristics, will the dynamic, complex, and changing world of the Puerto Rican women come fully into view.

Fortunately, the literature and research on Puerto Rican women has been growing in the last decade. This developing literature begins to address the misconceptions and caricatures, as well as to examine critically the social and historical role of Puerto Rican women. In essence, through it Puerto Rican women have begun to give voice to their *Lucha,* to their "struggles."

This essay contributes to that growing body of literature by summarizing the impact of economic struggles on the socioemotional lives of Puerto Rican women in the United States. It does not analyze the complex economic and political forces because that has been done well by others,[1] but it does refer to these forces and builds upon them from a critical perspective. It attempts to "set the record straight" by reappropriating our history and its emotional interface.

This essay attempts to show how the interaction of social, economic, and historical pressures affects the changing lives of Puerto Rican women, thereby questioning and challenging some of the "cultural" attributes, the mental-health labels, and the myths that are used to undermine the liberating commitment to be *en la lucha.* Further this essay is directed to a vast multilevel collective of sisters, Puerto Rican and non-Puerto Rican, who seek legitimate sources of study and dialogue regarding the particular experiences of women. Ultimately it is an effort dedicated to the sisterhood of struggle.

A Brief Historical Detour

To understand the struggles of Puerto Rican women in the United States, it is necessary to point out four key historical processes that directly influence our reality:

1. the political and economic relationship between Puerto Rico and the United States, i.e., colonialism
2. the development of capitalism in Puerto Rico and the economic transformation from an agricultural to an industrial society
3. the role and social status of women in Puerto Rico and in a class society
4. the emerging forms of consciousness and struggle among Puerto Ricans regarding the political relationship with the United States and among women as part of the women's movement in Puerto Rico, the United States, and elsewhere

Numerous writers have analyzed the impact of colonialism and capitalism on the history, family systems, and present status of Puerto Ricans.[2] Suffice it to say here that the systematic development of capitalism in Puerto Rico not only propelled abrupt industrialization but also insured economic control of the island as an expanding market and a source of cheap labor for U.S. interests. Such complex developments meant vast changes in the fabric of life for the Puerto Rican people.

One such consequence was massive migration, especially in the 1950s and 1960s. Another was the incorporation of masses of Puerto Rican women into lower-paying and sexually segregated jobs in the labor market.[3] In the United States, immigrant Puerto Rican women increasingly did piecework in factories or unskilled work or had jobs as factory operatives, cigar makers, domestic or service workers. The resulting "proletarianization" of women in the first thirty years of this century meant involvement in labor struggles and a changing consciousness regarding sex-role relations.[4]

There has been a progressive decline, however, from the high point of 38.9 percent female involvement in the labor force set in 1950, when Puerto Rican women found employment more readily than men. By 1970 the percentage of Puerto Rican women employed was the lowest among ethnic-group women, a fact that has been attributed to "unfavorable labor-market conditions and large declines in central city industries."[5]

In fact, the sociological and mental-health literature documents the disruption to family life prompted by immigration and by the differential labor-force participation of women and men and by the increase in female-headed households. The traditional role definitions and identities of Puerto Rican men have been abruptly challenged without there being a productive way to come to grips with the changes. Women have been forced to develop themselves in the public sphere of work while maintaining subordinate roles at home or to carry on "independently" by depending on welfare.[6]

Yet, while such tensions are perhaps heightened in the United States, they also exist in Puerto Rico and elsewhere. What is perplexing, however, is the way in which traditional roles are seen as the problem for Puerto Rican women rather than the changing nature of class and gender relations resulting from changing economic and historical forces. In the face of the evidence of objective pressures on Puerto Rican women and men in regard to finding jobs in a discriminatory market, several questions must be asked:

1. Why has so much attention been paid to "cultural" factors and to "traditional" roles as the barriers to Puerto Pican women's success?
2. To what degree have cultural descriptions of Puerto Rican women obscured the source of their oppression within the social relations of capitalist production?
3. Have Puerto Rican women internalized a "false consciousness" about the cause of their woes being attributed to *hombres machistas* ("male chauvinists"), instead of understanding how males and females compete for scarce jobs and how these attitudes are part of a social process?

Questions like these lead us to wonder whether we have not too quickly labeled as "traditional," with negative antifeminist implications, roles and functions that may, in fact, have been useful, productive, and generative of positive human qualities in Puerto Rican women and men at a given historical point. We need to be careful about embracing an overly "feminist" prescription for modern women's roles before we understand those features of "traditional" roles that help women cope with changing economic and social conditions. As Puerto Rican men have become increasingly displaced from jobs, Puerto Rican women have had to adjust to the changing situation in the home. This essay suggests that only by gaining a complex understanding of changing roles in the context of changing socioeconomic structures can we make reasonable judgments about what is "traditional" and what is "progressive" behavior for Puerto Rican women.

Another result of the stereotypes about Puerto Rican women has been that feminism and the women's movement have been erroneously viewed as something that came to us from the outside, from the United States or other parts of the world. Surely, Puerto Rican women in the United States and in Puerto Rico have been affected by the new analysis of both private life and community activism that has come from modern feminism, but feminist liberating consciousness had its own history in Puerto Rico prior to the contemporary women's movement. To highlight this history and our concept of *en la Lucha* it is necessary to pay tribute to the important participation of women in Puerto Rican political and labor struggles.

In the days of the Spanish colonizers, Taino women were in struggle by resisting their conquerors' sexual and imperialist advances, both individually and as part of the collective opposition. Much less documented, black slave women in the haciendas participated in the antislavery uprisings of the 1800s.[8] And, in the heroic but unsuccessful 1868 uprising against the Spaniards known as *el Grito de Lares*, Marianna Bracetti and other revolutionary women engaged in varied organizing tasks. Lola Rodriguez de Tio was a nineteenth-century poet whose beliefs in independence twice led to her deportation, and she was the author of the Puerto Rican national anthem, "La Borinqueña."

We know more about the numerous women in this century who engaged in the political, working-class, and feminist struggles of their day. The early suffragettes included such women as Ana Roque de Duprey, Mercedes Solá, and Isabel Abreu de Aguilar. Well educated, they defended women's rights in writing and through the first feminist organization on the island. Within the working-class movement Concha Torres was the first woman on the island to speak at a political rally. Juana Colon was an organizer of tobacco strippers and a militant socialist; Luisa Capetillo wrote manifestos from 1904 to 1916, which promoted a new ideology that was both antipatriarchal and pro working class.

Women such as Blanca Canales, Doris Torrescola, and Lolita Lebron are well known for their leadership particularly during the nationalist struggles from the 1930s through the 1950s. Currently a number of Puerto Rican women political prisoners are held in U.S. prisons, on account of their anticolonialist activities. And, to a different degree, numbers of women participate in community and governmental affairs. Certainly all these women have been part of a long history of liberating consciousness. So Puerto Rican women, indeed, have been *en la Lucha* against colonialism and different forms of oppression for many years.[9] To struggle, in fact, has become a necessary daily fact for political, economic, and socioemotional survival.

Present-Day Reality

The political and social factors described above result in a set of statistics that show all too well the structural outcome of oppression. Taken together, the statistics and the historical analysis form an essential background for understanding the daily efforts of Puerto Rican women to survive, as well as for explaining the need for collective struggle.

According to a 1978 statistical portrait of women in the United States, Puerto Rican women comprise 16 percent of all women of Spanish origin, have a median age of 22.4 years, and have the highest unemployment rate, 12.2 percent. In the 1980 census, the total Puerto Rican population was 1,823,000, of whom 985,000 were women. The median income for Puerto Ricans overall was $9,855, the lowest of all Latino groups and significantly lower than that of non-Latino families, which is $19,965. By 1983, 28.4 percent of all Latinos were living in poverty, in comparison to 12.1 percent of whites. Only 51 percent of adult Puerto Ricans were in the labor force in 1982, with Puerto Rican women's participation rate at 37 percent, in comparison to a 50 percent rate for Chicana and Cuban women.[10]

It is not surprising, therefore, that Puerto Ricans have a high rate of people on welfare. They have been increasingly forced—by high unemployment, low education, and invisible factors of institutionalization—to survive within the welfare system.

The family constellation has also changed. In 1960, 15.3 percent of Puerto Rican families were headed by women; by 1970 this figure increased to 24.1 percent. By 1982 40 percent of families were headed by women. These figures must be compared to shifts from 6 percent to 13.9 percent of white female-headed households during the same period.[11]

This brief statistical profile shows that Puerto Ricans are in a very disadvantageous situation, and Puerto Rican women even more so, particularly in comparison to both the white population and to other Latino groups. Certainly such a stark profile has implications for the overall well-being of the Puerto Rican community and for the socioemotional status of women.

The Socioemotional Profile

The mental health of women has received increased scrutiny over the past fifteen years. Many generalizations have been made about women's social roles and emotional worlds. When we look briefly at some of the major findings we find highly distressing implications for Puerto Rican women, if not for all women:

1. The experience as housewives and mothers has been found to be stressful and associated with emotional difficulties.
2. Depression in working-class women has been associated with the social situation.
3. Lack of power over one's life has been associated with psychological problems, and low social status and powerlessness are seen as making women increasing vulnerable to emotional stress.
4. Environmental factors have been found to affect adversely lower-class women's physical and mental health.[12]

The combined effects of these statements could present a highly distressing socioemotional picture of Puerto Rican women.[13] Given the historical and statistical realities as well as the theoretical assumptions, then, what does a socioemotional profile of Puerto Rican women in the United States look like?

Before analyzing the complex interaction of various stresses on the lives on Puerto Rican women, a few examples may make the picture more concrete.[14]

Carmen is a nineteen-year-old working-class woman who came to the United States to live with an aunt, for a change of environment *(cambias de ambiente),* and in hopes of learning to "do something" to earn a living and support herself. She was fleeing a very strict father, who entrusted her to his sister. Carmen was ambitious and very idealistic. She began English classes and enrolled in a vocational-training program in the community. Nine months after her arrival she had gained some ability to communicate in English and laughingly, with a heavy accent, would demonstrate her new skill.

At this time her aunt became quite ill and Carmen had to quit some of her activities and care for her. Although the aunt had teenage children who had been raised in the United States and who spoke English, they felt less obligation than Carmen to look after her. Carmen felt obliged because she depended on her aunt for housing and because she felt indebted to her. She also felt that it was "expected" that she would take care of her aunt.

Two months later Carmen came into an out-patient mental-health department complaining of tension headaches, of feelings of wanting to yell and throw things, and of sudden crying spells. She made self-deprecatory remarks about how she would not amount to anything in life, how she had no skills, was not intelligent, and was selfish.

Maria is a divorced women with three children who has been in the United States for ten years. Her husband has been gone for three years and she has been struggling to make ends meet and to raise her children. She knows enough English to *defenderse,* or "get along," but she has limited vocational skills and works in a shoe factory. She works from 8:30 to 4:30, but her children get out of school at 2:30, which means that they are left alone in the afternoons, supervised by her eleven-year-old son.

The sexual overtones of comments from a fellow worker have made her feel increasingly anxious, while at home she has grown more tense about household demands. She has been growing increasingly irritated with the children, scolding them more and more often. She has not been sleeping well and has begun to calm her nerves with a *traguito,* a drink. The children have grown increasingly hard to control. When the oldest disappeared for over five hours Maria became quite agitated, lost control, and experienced an *ataque de nervios,* an anxiety attack.

Ana is a twenty-eight-year-old woman who has been raised in the United States since she was three. For two and a half years she has been married to an island-born Puerto Rican, Ernesto, who has been in the United States for the past five years. She and her spouse have been fighting increasingly over the past six months, often with the result that he storms out of the house and does not return for hours or even until the next day. Ana's familiy is in New York, and her husband's family is in Puerto Rico. Ernesto feels little support, is antagonistic to the "Americanos," and has difficulty holding a job.

Ana went to trade school and is a medical assistant in an area hospital. As she is bilingual, her skills are well used and she feels good about working. Ernesto constantly berates Ana and is critical of any and all of her activities, often to the point of being verbally abusive. She has been overwhelmed by his attitudes and has begun to doubt herself. Ana has become increasingly depressed and withdrawn. While suppressing intense anger at her husband she has felt helpless and upset.

While obviously not a statistical sample, Carmen, Maria, and Ana help to highlight important areas for consideration in understanding the socioemotional needs of Puerto Rican women.

All three women described here have been exposed to the general stresses on women that were mentioned earlier. In addition, they face particular problems as Puerto Rican women. First, they encounter different forms of discrimination—ethnic, class, and race—in work and community life. Second, they face the psychosocial pressures of immigration, such as loss of homeland and dislocation. Third, they must deal with mastery of the English language, issues of cultural identity, and other stresses associated with acculturation. Fourth they are subject to the particular sex-role expectations of their culture. The interaction of these factors can tax the coping ability of any woman—as it has the abilities of Carmen, Maria, and Ana—and result in emotional difficulties.[15]

Of particular importance is the tension between learned, "traditional" role behaviors and the woman's own developing needs, strivings that are often in conflict with cultural and sex-role expectations. Women are to be self-sacrificing wives and mothers, subordinate to men. This is the demand of dominant elements in U.S. society, as well as of traditional Puerto Rican culture. Puerto Rican women are to accept this "reality" and not to show signs of anger, aggression, or independence. But at the same time they are to be strong and in control. Therefore, Puerto Rican women experience two forms of oppression. They are oppressed by the external, dominant Anglo system and by the socialization process and expectations of their own culture. In the words of S. Urdang, "the key to the perpetuation of such oppression is the ability of the oppressor to persuade the oppressed to cooperate in their servitude."[16]

This situation of Puerto Rican women in the United States embodies just such "double discrimination." The Puerto Rican woman is on the one hand, "entrapped within the bleak economic and political powerlessness affecting the Puerto Rican population in general. . . . On the other hand, she suffers from the socialization of sex roles that cause her to have guilt feelings about the fulfillment of her potential."[17] Along with the stress of adverse environmental and socioemotional factors, this tension and eventual conflict has various psychological symptoms. They include such problems as somatic ailings, nervousness *(los nervios alterados),* depression, fear of losing control, inability to handle children, and persistent feelings of inadequacy, powerlessness, and frustration *(no puedo hace nada, no valgo, estoy agobiada, aborrecida).*

Before returning to a brief discussion of how to understand the situations facing Carmen, Maria, and Ana, however, it is important to note that these difficulties do *not* mean that Puerto Rican women are overrepresented in mental health or medical facilities. In many ways Puerto Rican women are manifesting the general tensions pressing down on all women. It is important to reaffirm Puerto Rican women's relationship to all women so that their stresses are not used to victimize them once more by means of discriminating and biased profiles. Without constant reminders as to the broader context within which Puerto Rican women find themselves, misinformation and distortion of their reality can occur once again, this time in the context of the "helping professions."

Some, for instance, would focus only on the ways in which the three examples demonstrate the individual difficulties that Puerto

Rican women experience in coping with their circumstances. Instead, a more liberating approach means trying to understand their emotions and behaviors in the light of the complex pressures and struggles that define reality for Puerto Rican women.

Viewed in this way, Carmen can be seen as a young woman trying to develop herself within the limits and possibilities of cultural family expectations. She has turned against herself because of her own strivings. Her frustrated attempts make her angry, but she cannot show her anger, lest she be seen as *ingrata,* or "ungrateful," by her aunt. The conflict between her striving and other people's perceived expectations of her leads to distress and to difficulty in negotiating change.

Maria presents the struggle of a woman attempting to survive without a support system. She manifests the cultural concept of *hembrismo,* which dictates that women be perservering and strong. Underlying this concept is the goal of being a *supermadre,* or great mom, a do-it-all concept probably akin to the popular idea of "superwoman" as an unrealistic goal for working women.[19] Maria struggles to provide for her children, as she has been socialized to do, and thereby enters into conflict with the extreme demands of the outside world as well as those she places on herself. Although Maria has lived for some years in the United State, she has not developed supports for herself and fears failure and resorting to Aid to Families with Dependent Children, seen by her a a symbol of defeat.

Maria has experienced both sexual and class discrimination, but she ignored their psychological effects on her. She has been so intent on providing economically for her children that she has neglected their and her own emotional needs, becoming irritated and guilty; and, finally, she has taken to soothing her frayed nerves with drink. Plagued by feelings of inadequacy, of not being educated enough to seek help, she has circumscribed her world to work and home, instead of seeing how forces outside her world affected her options.

In addition to concerns similiar to those of Carmen and Maria, Ana reflects the conflict of "success." Her achievement of biculturality, economic status, and autonomy came at the expense of confusion and marital strife. At the same time, Ernesto is an example of the privatized reactions to economic displacement experienced by minority men. Neither Ernesto nor Ana can see the social context of their marital strife, nor how different cultural and educational experiences underlie their disagreements. They personalize a conflict that is rooted in the reality of differential experiences, of economic injustice, of colonialist history—a conflict that represents, in some ways, the struggle of a divided nation.

These examples show that life for the Puerto Rican woman can be a vulnerable one. Given this fact, the follow-up questions are: How have women coped? What have they done to overcome adversities, attitudinal limitations, and structural barriers?

Coping and Surviving

The unifying theme of the history, social status, and psychological processes mentioned previously is that, through them all, Puerto Rican women are struggling to survive. The examples of the Taina, the slave, the revolutionaries, and the militants create a rich heritage to follow. In addition, contemporary Puerto Rican women have internalized ways of resistance, some passive, some active, with which to survive. These can be counterposed to some of the more self-defeating patterns just described.

Puerto Rican women have mastered many "passive" methods of coping. For example, a common adage states that women know how to *salirse con la suya,* or get "what they want." The implication is that by using unassuming, indirect, passive, or covert methods, a Puerto Rican woman can obtain what she needs and wants. The value placed on this ability implies that a direct approach would not be successful. Thus, within existing social norms, some Puerto Rican women may learn manipulative approaches to counter oppressive familial and male attitudes and situations.[20] Such approaches respond to and emerge from a context in which assertiveness and direct expression are not allowed or valued. In fact it has often been said that Puerto Ricans have a tendency to avoid direct expressions or confrontations and to deny hostile thoughts and feelings. Given their island's history of domination by an outside force, these manifestations are not surprising. They suggest seemingly little hope for change. However, the price paid is accumulated emotions, which will seek some outlet, in somatic complaints, for example, or in an *ataque*. Coping attempts such as these, then, extort a high personal price. They are private, individual efforts to deal with forces rooted elsewhere.

Puerto Rican women have also used more active, socially sanctioned strategies to seek self-esteem, survive, obtain power, and promote change. Through education, for example, individual women have tried to improve their chances of coping and surviving. Given all the forces working against her, if a Puerto Rican woman can become educated she is more employable, more economically independent, and more able to participate as a competent individual—not as the extension of some man or her children—in the community. Carmen, for example, was especially frustrated because her route to power, education, was thwarted by her aunt's illness.

Hembrismo is another overt way to cope. Through it, a woman adheres to the cultural script of motherhood, but by being exceptionally strong and powerful in linking various roles she gains power and recognition. This strategy can give a determined woman a certain adaptive strength, although it can also establish ideals that conflict with her own development and strivings. As was seen with Maria, when the objective pressures increase, the very strategy that gave strength in the past can become a barrier to flexibility.

The kinship system is most often identified as the source of support for Puerto Rican women. It can often be a first resort in times of trouble without which a woman's life is harder, as was noted for Ana. But the expectations of kin—both real and assumed—can also be a source of stress, as Carmen's distress shows.

For Puerto Rican women the reliance on extended family is culturally encouraged and often socioeconomically necessary. But extended family systems go through their own growth and conflicts and are not always the best support. In the United States kin may not be close by. While for some their absence may create a sense of isolation and loss, for others it may motivate development of networks that are not kin, such as folk healers, religious groups, and neighborhood and community groups. Suh extrafamilial support systems may benefit women who are single parents or are experiencing serious emotional difficulties.[21]

Many of the increasing numbers of Puerto Rican women who are heads of their households have learned the mixed blessing of welfare as a coping strategy. While public assistance can provide women with the chance to become somewhat independent of family or men, that "freedom" may be illusive because of the ways in which it forces them to go against the dominant and respected values of the culture without really providing economic autonomy in return. The female-headed family is less a cultural phenomenon than a "functional adaptation to a specific economic situation; a situation which leaves the lower class male unable to provide long term maintenance for a family."[22] Puerto Rican women, then, have little choice but to develop their own resources and networks of support in order to survive.

Indeed, varied groups of Puerto Rican women have been developing in some communities.[23] These may both help women cope with their personal and emotional needs and become an organizing base for community change. When women come together to discuss anything from parenting to a rent strike, they transform passive, self-defeating responses into an active participatory way of dealing with their personal difficulties, their social concerns, and their educational and political needs. In such a group Carmen, Maria, and Ana could begin to talk with others about problems, opportunities, and ways to make change. Such groups provide a forum for transforming privatized emotional experiences into a collective social process of healing. They can allow Puerto Rican women to resist the fragmentation of our people, whether by place of birth, by skin color, by dominant language, or by gender. They help women discover new ways of negotiating change with or without the participation of a "professional helper"—although some may still require clinical intervention. But this coming together of women continues and legitimizes an important Puerto Rican tradition: to struggle, to be *en la Lucha*.

TEENAGE MOTHERS
Seduced and Abandoned

Nancy Aries

Vera is fifteen. Two months ago, she gave birth to Daryl, who weighed slightly over five pounds. Vera and her son live with Vera's mother, who is thirty-seven, Vera's twelve-year-old brother, and her sisters, who are ten and seven.

Since his birth, Daryl has been the center of attention. But things are about to change. Vera's first attempts to arrange day care, so she could complete high school, began to make dropping out look like the easiest solution. That will put Vera at a disadvantage compared to her friends. Without a high school diploma, she will be qualified only for low-paying jobs. Meanwhile, the added expense of her child may force her to apply for public assistance to help her mother support the family. As the tension at home mounts, Vera may decide to apply for public housing and move out of her mother's house altogether. If she does, not only will she find herself among the poor, but over time it will be increasing difficult to improve her situation. It is also possible that Vera will become pregnant again and have another child.

Vera is just one of more than half a million American women under the age of twenty who have children they plan to raise themselves. In the last few years, over 20 percent of all births in the

United States (one in five) were to teenagers.[1] Although each young woman will shape her own life, to a large extent her social script is already written. Being an adolescent and a mother creates conflicts that are not easily resolved. Adolescence is a time to achieve independence. In contrast, the first years of motherhood have been defined as a time of selfless giving. There is no easy reconciliation. What's more, given the way the society in which these contradictions are played out treats teenage mothers, these conflicts result in most of them, and their children, facing a life of poverty.

It is not surprising, therefore, that so much attention has been focused on preventing the consequences of teenage pregnancy. Prevention, however, can have many dimensions. Services can be directed at preventing unwanted pregnancies. Or they can be aimed at preventing the problems related to adolescent pregnancy. Or they can be structured to prevent young mothers from falling behind so quickly and so painfully.

These days, the tendency is to emphasize the former. Teenagers are directly and indirectly told that they should not become pregnant. But the message is mixed. With teenage unemployment already more than 50 percent, adolescents, particularly those from poor homes, find that they have few options in the labor market. For these young women, childbearing appears to be one of the few positive alternatives.[2]

A growing number of programs have been organized to assist this group of more than 500,000 young women offset the problems related to pregnancy. Such services, though, are not enough. Adolescents who are trying to raise children and achieve adulthood need support for the stresses of their dual roles. But services to help with these kinds of problems are not forthcoming.

Consider what happened to Vera. When the school nurse realized Vera was pregnant, she helped her enroll in a special program. Instead of continuing at the local high school, Vera was driven each day to the Adolescent Pregnancy Project, which was located in a large, rambling house on the outskirts of town. The program included a school, group rap sessions, individual counseling, and medical services. Vera was actively involved at the center until she gave birth to her son. She returned a few times after she came home from the hospital, so that she could see her friends and show off her baby. But once her son was born, she was considered a "graduate."

The program's intent was to help teenagers cope with pregnancy and the difficulties they might encounter because of their decision to keep and raise a child. The teacher who ran the school organized lesson plans on an individual basis. She was trying to keep Vera and the others in the program at the same level as their classmates back at school. In addition, there were special group sessions on pregnancy, childbirth, and child care.

For the most part, this information was all new to Vera. She had younger siblings, but babysitting seemed less complicated than caring for a baby. While some of the meetings were educational, there were also rap sessions. Vera found these particularly helpful because she realized she was not alone. Everyone's back ached; everyone's boyfriend was excited about becoming a father but did not help make plans for the baby; no one seemed to be getting along with her mother. Vera also had weekly meetings with one of the social workers. While they talked about many of the same issues, Vera had a chance to explore what was unique in her situation, for example, how her mother's arthritis might make it hard for her to help Vera handle the baby.

Finally, the program emphasized nutrition and personal health. In order to prevent undesirable medical results such as low birth weight, the program served two meals a day. A light breakfast was available when Vera arrived each morning. At noon, the program provided hot lunch. The staff talked about personal habits to the point where it had become a joke. However, many of Vera's friends at the center stopped drinking and smoking. They all exercised, since that was part of the schedule. Once a month at the beginning of the pregnancy and once a week by the ninth month, each mother-to-be saw a doctor, who weighed and examined her. Vera enjoyed these appointments because the doctor had an instrument that he placed on her belly so that she could hear her baby's heart beat.

But delivery marked the end of the program. It was expected that a few weeks after her child was born, Vera would return to school and her regular activities. Yet eight weeks after Vera came home from the hospital, she was exhausted and she felt pulled in every direction. The baby's habits were erratic. Daryl slept off and on during the day and then was wide awake at eleven when Vera and the rest of the family were ready for bed. Nights became long and trying as Vera and her mother tried to cajole Daryl to sleep and catch some sleep themselves.

The baby quickly became less of a novelty. Vera began to feel torn between her desire to take care of the small infant and her desire to hang out with her friends. All of a sudden, nothing was working out as she had planned. Her mother seemed rigid when it came to the baby; she expected that Vera would assume most of the responsibility for Daryl's care. Vera's boyfriend and school friends seemed uninterested in accommodating her or her baby boy. They preferred drinking and partying to watching television while the baby slept. Even her brother and sisters did not help feed, change, or play with Daryl very often.

Vera was not certain how her world had so suddenly unraveled. As long as she attended the program, she felt sure of herself and about becoming a mother. Since she came home with Daryl, she had lost that sense of certainty. Although Vera had officially stopped seeing her social worker after Daryl's birth, she now felt in need of support. She knew the baby would require constant attention, but it never seemed to let up. The baby made silent demands on her day and night. All of the preparation in the world did not seem enough for the reality Vera was facing.

To the program, though, the birth of Vera's son was the sign that Vera was now an "adult" and expected to cope in the adult world. One social worker would no longer coordinate services for her in one setting. If Vera wanted to obtain comparable services to those the program offered, the burden would fall on her. For her own health care, she would have to travel to one of the family-planning clinics or the outpatient department of the public hospital. She would have to take her baby for monthly visits to the well-child clinic on the other side of town. In addition, she would have to go to still another building to register for Women, Infants, and Children (WIC), which would provide food supplements for her and the baby. When Vera applies for public assistance, she will find that social services are coordinated by yet another office. Vera will wait long hours at the welfare office to see the social worker, and that will be just the beginning. So many offices, so many lines, and no guarantee of services. Didn't they realize that just getting through the day with a small baby was hard enough?

Teenage Mothers and Poverty

Vera's experiences are, unfortunately, typical. By and large, teenage mothers are poor. They find themselves in jeopardy because they are single, have left school early, and have limited work experience. Over the last decade, teenage mothers have increasingly chosen to remain single. In addition, there is a higher probability that those who marry will become separated or divorced. Even as these young women are chosing to be single, almost 50 percent of female-headed households live below the poverty line as compared to 10 percent of two-parent households. For black adolescent mothers the situation is even worse. Very few black teenagers marry. Of black women below twenty-five who are heads of households, 85 percent live in poverty.[3]

Welfare statistics provide even more evidence that teenage mothers make up a disproportionate proportion of the poor and near poor. Generally, women who receive public assistance are more likely to have been teenage mothers than are other women in the United States. In 1975, 71 percent of the women under thirty who received Aid to Families with Dependent Children (AFDC) had been teenage mothers. In the general population only a third of first births are to women under twenty.[4]

The poverty of teenage mothers also stems from the disruption of their education. Pregnancy and child bearing are among the most common reasons given by adolescent women for leaving school. As of 1982, 83 percent of seventeen-year-old mothers had no high school diploma. As candidates for poverty, the youngest mothers are at greatest risk. They have the least education and work experience and the highest probability of eventually having large families to support.[5] Although these young women often intend to complete high school, their educational aspirations come into conflict with child rearing. Teenage mothers report that it is difficult to make arrangements for services such as child care and transportation.[6] At some point, dropping out of school becomes the easiest solution. While the comprehensive programs have been successful in keeping a slightly larger percent of teenagers in school preceding and immediately following the birth of their children, their disadvantage relative to other women is not significantly changed because the average length of schooling has increased for all women.[7]

Having completed fewer years of schooling than their classmates, teenage mothers find it difficult to compete in the job market. Those who find jobs typically find low-status ones. They are cashiers, waitresses, salegirls, and stockgirls. These are minimum-wage jobs which do not offer steady employment, good benefit packages, or the possibility of advancement.[8] Given the cost of housing, food, and support services, such dead-end service jobs often trap teenagers in a cycle from which it is hard to escape. They are poor because they do not have the education to find better jobs. They do not have the education because they dropped out of school. They dropped out of school because they had children to support and care for.

Buffers Against Poverty

Although the odds are stacked against teenage mothers, not all of them become poor. Family networks and social services protect some teenage mothers from the necessity of making it alone with their children. Families can often provide the support these young mothers need to continue their own development while raising a young child. Rather than being forced into adult roles, the mothers who remain with their own families are allowed to continue to make the transition from adolescence into adulthood. At times they must be responsible for their children, and at times they can be independent. Where personal networks are inadequate, public and private agencies hold out the promise of providing a wide variety of support services. Many teenagers are eligible for health and other services that enable them to achieve both emotional and financial independence.

Family networks and human services, however, both have limits. Teenagers need to see themselves as separate from their parents, and yet as mothers, they need their parents' support.[9] While it is accepted that teenagers may not be prepared for parenting, their mothers, the new grandmothers, may be no more prepared to go back and raise another child. There may be younger children still at home. Or this may be just the point where these women planned to end their child-rearing days and begin school or work outside the home. These conflicts can cause even the best arrangements to collapse.

Similarly, the social service system is not set up to provide a broad range of services to these young mothers. With rare exceptions, more effort is made to prevent the birth of a teenager's child than to assist her to raise a child. Where they were considered needy children before the birth, immediately afterwards teenage mothers are looked upon as self-sufficient adults. At that time, responsibility is shifted from the system to the young mothers to coordinate available services.

While birth is a significant event, it is a biological, not a developmental, one. Teenagers' capabilities to care for themselves and their children can only develop incrementally. It is the failure of both the informal and formal service systems to accommodate this reality that makes the problems of teenage mothers virtually inevitable.

Family Networks

A child's birth puts pressure on any family as its members have to cope with new roles and responsibilities. Becoming a mother requires reorganizing one's time. Babies and small children need constant attention. That means that less time is available for work, school, relationships, and oneself. For teenage mothers, the problems of parenting are even more complex. During adolescence, it is important to establish one's own identity as separate from one's family. Having a baby, however, means that young mothers become more dependent on those from whom they are trying to separate.[10] Adolescence and parenting are both difficult. The opposing demands that each can place on a young woman makes the situation exceptionally stressful.

Those teenage mothers who live with their parents do better than those who choose or are forced to establish independent households.[11] Living arrangements are important because they affect the amount of support young mothers will receive. Indeed, social networks are one of the main ways for which most poor and near poor families survive, given their limited financial resources. Through the process of exchange, they obtain necessary goods and services.[12] For teenage mothers this is often true. Those who live with their parents or kin tend to receive greater financial assistance and support services than those who live alone or with the baby's father. In this way, the household arrangement makes it easier for these young women to negotiate the dual roles of adolescent and mother.

Yet a teenage mother's decision to remain at home creates another set of problems. Adding an infant to a household that already has fixed patterns often creates conflicts for which no one is prepared. New grandmothers and mothers both must become accustomed to their new status. Some young mothers may no longer think of themselves as children and claim a new-found independence in regard to their family and infant. Others may decide to cling to their adolescent status and deny responsibility for their children. The issues for the new grandmothers are the reverse. They may expect either too much or too little from their own daughters in the way of child care. The tension between them inevitably becomes focused on specific child-rearing issues such as feeding and responding to an infant's tears. This tension ultimately leads many young mothers to establish their own households or find other living arrangements.

Not all young mothers live at home. At present, a little over half of teenage mothers marry. While this number has been declining over the last several years because teenagers are chosing to remain single, teenage mothers who marry also get along better than those who live alone. Marriage is another way for young mothers to become part of a family network. Two responsible adults in the home means that young mothers do not have to bear sole responsibility for their new families. Tasks can be shared by two.

But, teenage marriages do not tend to be stable. The stress of marrying so young and raising children usually leads to separation and divorce. Young fathers are no more ready than young mothers to take on the responsibilities of a family. What's more, with only two black teenage males in ten employed, marriage does not offer financial stability to young black single mothers and their children.[13] The result is that teenagers are twice as likely to dissolve their marriages as are women who marry in their twenties.[14] Once separated, young mothers are far less likely to obtain child-support payments than older mothers. Only one in ten mothers age fourteen to twenty-four receives child-support payments as contrasted to four in ten for older women. Child-support payments for these mothers are less than $1,500 per year.[15]

While social networks may potentially buffer teenage mothers from the problems of raising children so early in their lives, these systems are usually not capable of handling the problems alone. The pressure resulting from small children can disrupt even the best arrangements. Grandmothers, mothers, fathers, and infants all have needs, but these needs are often contradictory. Sadly, these conflicts are usually not resolved in favor of the mothers and children. After a period of time, they move out of their parents' home and attempt to manage alone. In effect, social networks have put off, not prevented, the problems these young women encounter as single, teenage mothers.

Social Services

In theory, the social service system should be available when informal networks fail. The system, however, also fails teenage mothers because it denies the full scope of the problem.[16] Discomfort with the idea that adolescents can be both mothers and children causes the principal service problem to be defined as primary prevention. Even when it is recognized that teenage pregnancy and child bearing cannot be prevented, only transitional services are provided. Within the comprehensive service programs for pregnant adolescents, the young women lose their status as children once they give birth. They are then expected to fend for themselves in the incomplete and fragmented adult service system. Giving birth, however, does not transform fifteen-year-olds into mature adults. The lack of emphasis on teenage *child rearing* as distinct from *child bearing* means that help for young mothers is virtually nil.

The differences between liberal and conservative programs lie in the attitude of the care givers. The primary concern of the Reagan administration in the 1980s has been to discourage adolescents from becoming sexually active or from raising their own children. The approach is punitive. The highly touted Family Life Programs try to reach teenagers before they become sexually active and teach them about the responsibility of sexuality and parenting. For teenagers who become pregnant, the programs offer information and counseling services focused on adoption. Family-planning programs have been cut back because they are seen as encouraging inappropriate sexual activity among unmarried teenagers. If successful, this approach would reduce the number of teenage pregnancies and the number of teens raising children by discouraging teenage sexuality.

Programs initiated in the 1970s took a less judgmental approach. Their goals, however, were ultimately the same. Research on adolescent sexuality recognized that the proportion of teenagers who are sexually active increased each year. In addition, teenagers seemed to have limited knowledge about reproduction and the risk of unwanted pregnancy.[17] Assuming that those who provide services could not change people's sexual practices, it was argued that programs were responsible for helping teenagers avoid unwanted pregnancies. Therefore, sex education and birth control were deemed the essential components of an adolescent pregnancy program. Using the existing network of family-planning clinics, programs were developed that sought to decrease the number of teenage pregnancies.

Although no longer supported by federal funds, abortion is also an essential back-up service for pregnant adolescents. When all else fails, the women's movement has been the strongest proponent of the position that these young women must have the right to terminate unwanted pregnancies. At the present time, over 60 percent of teenage pregnancies are terminated by abortion.[18] The argument is made that chastity programs cannot prevent all (or even most) teenage sexual activity. Therefore, they do not provide a perfect solution to the problem of unwanted teenage pregnancies. Likewise, even if all sexually active adolescents effectively used birth control, there would still be instances of contraceptive failure and therefore, a number of unwanted pregnancies. Thus the only way to assure that every child is a wanted child is to assure the accessibility of abortion services. Women should not be forced by unjust policies to have children they do not want. Because it is assumed that most teenage pregnancies are unintended, the accessibility of abortion services is seen as the ultimate means of preventing the problems associated with teenage child bearing.

These programs' basic assumption is that children should not bear children. For those teenagers who become pregnant, comprehensive programs for the duration of their pregnancies have been organized by a variety of agencies. While such services are necessary, they are not sufficient because they do not last long enough. Many programs are aware of this problem. However, they find themselves in a difficult position. The population of teenage mothers is continually expanding, and agency capacity is limited. Agencies resolve their dilemma through a narrow definition of the problem. The argument is made that it is better to assist a large number of young women for a short time than to maintain a small number as part of an on-going case load. It is hoped that the skills taught during the course of the program will enable the mothers to manage on their own following their infants' birth. These programs judge themselves successful if they can eliminate some of the negative physical and psychological consequences of adolescent pregnancy.

Some agencies that recognize the problem of offering comprehensive services during pregnancy and then leaving young mothers to negotiate the adult services system, are making a social worker available to the young mothers for the first years of their child's life.[19] This approach attempts to compensate for the time-limited services provided by the comprehensive programs but continues to emphasize pregnancy as the critical point for delivery of service. By accepting the predominant perception of teenage childbearing, these programs fail to recognize the need of young mothers for separately identifiable services such as day care and health care. In order to maintain their independence, teenage mothers must find adequate support services so that they can go back to school or find jobs. Many also express the need for additional financial support.[20]

The need to arrange for support services does not end for many years. All mothers must make arrangements so that their children are not left unsupervised in a society where the work day and the school day start and end at different times. While all mothers need services, for adolescents the barriers can seem insurmountable. The frustration of finding adequate day care gives some indication of why so many young mothers may ultimately despair. Whether a mother uses an organized center, a day-care mother, a baby-sitter, or her own relatives, every option has shortcomings. Purchased day care is exceedingly expensive. In 1985, the cost of full-time care ran as high as $10,000 a year. While some centers are subsidized, the number they can serve is limited and the subsidy is often made on a sliding fee schedule. It is also difficult to determine the quality of care. Mothers do not actually know what happens with their children during the day. They must depend on their own judgment, the feedback of teachers, and the assessment of state agencies. Cost and quality aside, there is the fragility of the arrangements. Sick children cannot go to day-care centers. If babysitters become sick, there is no one to take care of the children at home. Almost no mother of any age has networks that can provide backup.

Very few programs address these issues. A small number of high schools have day-care centers on the premises so that teenage mothers can continue their education, knowing that their children are being cared for in the same building. These programs have integrated the needs of adolescent mothers for support services into the school's educational program. Courses on child development, for example, use the day-care center as a field site. By working at the center, students gain experience with small children and may also derive a more realistic notion of what parenting involves. Thus the programs serve multiple functions. They are oriented toward prevention of teenage pregnancy, education of new parents, and maintenance of mothers who need services so that they can move ahead with their lives. Unfortunately, there are not enough of these programs.

As matters now stand, teenage mothers are set up to fail. Adolescents are encouraged through all existing service mechanisms to avoid pregnancy. If they become pregnant, they are encouraged either to terminate the pregnancy or put the baby up for adoption. The young women who choose to keep their babies receive intense services during their pregnancies. The programs, however, do not address the reality of teenage child rearing. Services cannot end with the postpartum period if the goal is to create independent and self-supporting adults. Since neither the social service nor education system is prepared to follow up on the problems of teenage mothers, they are dropped from the system. Teenagers are held responsible and punished for their personal situations. They are expected to cope with only minimal support because they do not conform to social expectations.

Toward a Model of Support for Teenage Mothers

The problems of teenage mothers are both unique and ordinary. They are unique because teenage mothers become responsible adults before they have completed their own development and are prepared to participate in an adult world. They are ordinary because many of the supports that teenage mothers require are no different from those required by all mothers. As a result, the services these young women and their children need cover a broad spectrum. At a minimum, it is important that the mothers continue their education, since education is one of the best predictors of an individual's potential to earn a living wage. If they drop out of school, the gap between them and their peers cannot be closed. But it is not enough simply to encourage young mothers to stay in school. In order to complete their education, they need a full range of support services. Comprehensive day care must be readily available. But day care is just the beginning. Teenage mothers also need support in terms of household maintenance and their own personal development. Food must be bought, laundry washed, and doctors' appointments scheduled—all as they struggle to become adults and responsible parents. For teenage mothers to overcome the problems of early childbearing, there must be a commitment to provide them with all of the support that they will need to succeed in both roles.

In the best of all possible worlds, Vera would not find herself so isolated. Schools would be prepared to welcome young mothers like Vera back into the classroom. Daryl would be enrolled in a day-care center affiliated with Vera's school. As part of the school day, Vera would learn about child care with other young mothers. In addition to the school program, Vera would continue to meet with her social worker, who in turn, would take on responsibility for coordinating other service needs such as family counseling and financial assistance. While Vera's mother supports her daughter and grandson, she may also receive support to see Vera through the transition from adolescence to adulthood. Only when young mothers like Vera are seen as young people with problems, rather than as scapegoats for society's sexual discomfort, will they and their children have a chance for a fuller and richer life.

WHAT DO THEY WANT US TO DO?

Michele Credo and Kim Jones

Aswalos House is Boston's YWCA in the black community. In coordination with local high schools and community programs it provides a Comprehensive Adolescent Parenting Program to almost one hundred pregnant and parent teenagers. The program offers each girl a personal counselor, supports for completing her high school education, job training, and placement services as well as pre- and postnatal medical care. It also helps pregnant teenagers plan for day care and transportation needs and makes referrals about legal advice, adoption, or foster care. As if in answer to the suggestions made by Nancy Aries in the previous essay, the program also offers support and training for teachers, parents, partners of pregnant teenagers, and new teenage mothers.[1]

The editors interviewed two participants in this program in order to let them speak for themselves about what it is like to be a teenage mother.

Michele Credo

I am nineteen years old and I grew up in Boston. I have two brothers and two more sisters—I'm the youngest of the girls—with one younger brother. I will be a senior in high school and I am seven months pregnant. I have one more year of school before I graduate.

I loved elementary school, only in junior high it got kind of rough. But once I got used to school again it was all right. I didn't make the honor roll or nothing, but I did make perfect attendance. By the eighth grade I was popular and I didn't want to leave. It was hard to go to the high school and not know anybody and have everybody be bigger than me. So the first year I used to skip a lot of days. Then I got kept back in the ninth grade. I got kept back again in the tenth. But then I went on and finished the tenth and stayed on in the eleventh.

When I got pregnant this year, in the eleventh grade, all my friends asked, "What are you going to do about it?" I said that I was going to go ahead and finish school and get my education. So I stayed in school all year. I just decided to stay in school, maybe even to go on to college.

I wasn't really upset when I got pregnant. I figured if I was having sex I would get caught one day. It just happened before I thought it would happen. My mother didn't believe in birth control, so it was hard to bring it in the house. I snuck it in the house and was hiding the pills, afraid that she might find them. But later she told me it would have been all right; she would rather have had me take the pills than get pregnant. But it was too late anyway. I started using the pills when I was a month pregnant, but I didn't know.

When I found out I was pregnant, my mother asked me and my boyfriend what we were going to do. He said he preferred to keep the baby, rather than kill the baby. My mother figured that if he was that much of a man to come with me and talk about it, then we should be able to keep the baby if we wanted to. So we decided to keep it. My boyfriend is seventeen and goes to a different school. He realized that he had to be responsible for bringing another life into the world, so he went out and got a job to help me out. My mother helped him get a job at the same place where she worked.

I live with my mother, and my boyfriend lives with his, a few blocks away. At first my mother was pretty skeptical about the situation, but afterwards she accepted it because there was nothing she could do about it. His parents were very understanding, maybe because since he was a boy he wasn't bringing a baby home to their house.

When I got pregnant I found out who my real friends were. There was a couple of people talking, complaining about all the pregnant girls in school, making remarks about how it was turning into a "maternity school." But I told them, "Just because we are pregnant doesn't mean we don't want our education just like you want your education." Maybe I even want my education more now, because I have to raise a baby. I have a close friend who is real helpful; she talks with me a lot and is real glad for me.

Sometimes when I get on the bus, people make remarks and look at me as if they didn't like to see a young girl pregnant. But my mother told me, "Don't be ashamed that you are pregnant. Hold your head up high and you keep walking." My aunts and uncles also tried to give me trouble and asked me why I was having the baby. But my mother took care of that too. She said to them, "As long as you don't have to pay for the baby, or take care of the baby, or buy pampers and food, then don't worry about it. The baby will get taken care of." When my mother speaks her mind, people have to listen.

All the stuff about "What is she going to do with her life after having a baby?" really makes me mad. It makes me really want to go out and get my education and make something of myself, just to show them.

There was some jealousy from my sisters. I was the baby girl, the one who always stayed with my mother. They couldn't believe it at first. My older sister told me about how the first time she got pregnant she had an abortion and she felt bad about it for a long time. So when she got pregnant two years later, she didn't care what anybody said, she kept it. So she thought it was good that I was keeping the baby.

When the baby is born I will take the six weeks off that the school allows me, to be with the baby. Then when I go to school one of my girlfriends will baby-sit; she lives in the apartment next to mine. I want to get a part-time job after school, so I'll get home about 5:30 and feed the baby and be with the baby. And my homework . . . I guess I'll have to work it out. I know that it's not as easy as it sounds.

I like this program. I have been in it since my fourth month, and the counselor has really helped me. She helped me to understand some things about what to expect—she inspired me. I can tell her secrets because she really understands. I tell her things and she tells me things and we laugh about stuff. She has been pregnant herself and I can really trust her. In fact, I used to say I wanted to be a computer programmer, but now I say that I want to be a counselor with teenage pregnant girls, so I can help other girls like I have been helped. I want to go to school to do that later. When it happens to you, you realize that maybe you can help some other girl.

If I were a counselor I would tell girls to use birth control if they don't want to get pregnant, or if they are not yet ready for a baby. Most girls aren't really ready for a baby; they should live their lives. Teenage years are the best years of your life, after all, and you shouldn't waste them. Sometimes now I sit in my bed, at nineteen, and think about all the fun I had and all the things I did. Sweet sixteen, that's the prime of your life—you want to come and go as you wish, not ask someone to baby-sit before you go anywhere. So, if you are not ready, you shouldn't let anybody pressure you into having a baby.

Some girls think that if they have a baby they can keep their boyfriends, but it doesn't work. I might be with mine for two years, or he could be gone tomorrow. Sometimes having a baby can make them more likely to go. You never know.

I want to know what age they want us to have babies. At nineteen you are too young. At thirty you are too old. Twenty-two is too young. What's right, twenty-eight? Suppose you don't have it then, do you give up? Every age, they say, "You have to be married." I disagree with that 100 percent. Why should I get married just because I'm pregnant? It's not a good time to make that choice. Being married doesn't mean he can't leave. My uncle said, "Get married." I asked him if he was still married, and he had to say no. Being married doesn't solve anything.

There are a lot of girls out there that want to get pregnant and are scared to admit it, so they just don't use anything. They are scared of what people will think. I would tell them that if they really want a baby, they should have it and not be ashamed. I would tell them not to knock themselves because they are pregnant. They should get counseling to decide whether to get an abortion, or give the baby up for adoption, or keep the baby. I would try to let them see that they don't have to bring a baby into the world if they are not ready for it, because they might hurt the baby. They should do what is best for them.

I want everything for my baby. I want it to have everything it needs, not everything it wants. I think I was too spoiled. I want my baby to want things, but I don't want it to need things.

I hope my baby is a girl. If it's a girl I hope that she will be like me when she's my age—not pregnant, maybe—but like me. I would hope she would be out of school, but I wouldn't put pressure on her to go to college. I want to have a really nice relationship with her, like a sister or an aunt or something. I want her to tell me things, be the friend I never had.

In order to finish my education I will need a car and my own place. And I'll need friends to help, and my mother, of course. It will be important to have a good baby-sitter, someone I can depend on, I know that.

I am on welfare now and I hate it. All my life I heard people say how much they hated welfare. I never understood it. I thought, "You are getting free money, be thankful." Now I understand. They give you so much aggravation that you feel bad. Every three months you have to go down there and sign papers and fill out more papers. And they talk to you like you really desperately need them. They should treat me like I am a human being, not like a piece of garbage. Actually, my caseworker now seems nice, but that is probably because I never see her. I try not to go down there except when I really have to.

I do need the Medicaid especially. Right now I take natural childbirth classes, and I try not to hear about how bad it is going to be. My first four months were rough. Every day I used to get what I call "all-day sickness," not morning sickness. I felt so bad. I'll be so glad to have that baby out that I can take the pain now.

The most important thing to have when you're pregnant is your mother. I feel real bad for girls that are alone. It is good to have everybody else, even the father, but as long as you've got your mother's support you are all right. She may get on your nerves sometimes, sure, but if she's there you feel like you can take on the world, no matter what nobody says. You can just forget everybody else.

If I was going to talk to somebody who says teenage mothers are bad, I would ask them, how they can blame everything on us? Before we were here there was poverty, there were teenage mothers. The problems of poverty are not our fault. You look at some people out there, they should be thankful we are just getting pregnant. I would rather be pregnant than out there selling drugs or downtown working the corner. I guess they would rather see us downtown doing that, so they can get more, instead of having babies so that we get a little too. If I had to talk to those people who blame teenage mothers for everything I would be so mad at them, because they are so unfair and don't really know anything about how things really are. What do they want us to do?

Kim Jones

I am from Dorchester, Massachusetts. There are eleven children in my family, with me being the youngest except for a set of twins. My mother is divorced and has always worked. I just graduated from high school. I had my son, Robert, when I was in the ninth grade, so I went through my whole four years of high school with a child. I also have a two-year-old daughter.

I was fifteen when I got pregnant with Robert. I was pretty upset because I didn't really know what was going on or anything. My mother had never really talked to me about sex or birth control or anything like that. I was always real quiet—they always say it happens to the good girls, and it was true with me. And Robert's father was only fifteen too. He didn't even tell his mother about the baby until it was born.

I went to school then at a local home for pregnant girls. I just wanted to stay out of the house, because it was a tense situation there. That place was good because I found out I wasn't the only one. Some of the girls there were hiding out from their families, girls from New Jersey, the Cape, New Hampshire. They would just say they had run away and then put the baby up for adoption. There were girls even younger than me, so it helped me not get really depressed. Of course I was younger then and didn't want to talk to nobody. I was confused, but that was just like any new mother, I think. Nobody really knows what to do with a first baby.

I never really hung out or got high or anything. So having babies never really interfered with my life. Maybe if I hadn't had Robert I would have hung out in the streets, but I never had the chance. I was always good in school, even though in the seventh grade I stopped making honor roll, and I liked school. That's part of the reason I stayed in school. A lot of people may drop out after they have a baby, but it may be just because they never liked school. My sister dropped out in the ninth grade; she never had a baby, but she just didn't like school. Even now in my computer training program I do pretty well. It's an "earn while you learn" type program.

When I got pregnant with Robert, my mother didn't really say anything, she just gave me the silent treatment. But after he was born she was OK, and we lived in her house, which helped me out. Once she found out I was still going to school she was happy. After he was born I had to quit school for a little while, because of a baby-sitting problem, but I worked it out and started back the next year. My mother and sisters couldn't really help with the baby-sitting because they all work.

I found a lady to baby-sit who was on my way to the bus stop where I went to school. So I would drop Robert off and go to school. I worked in the summer at temporary jobs, through the local poverty program. The Department of Social Services would pay the baby-sitter, and I would make up the rest myself.

After that Roxanne came along. My mother was kind of upset about that. She was close to the father and started talking about marriage, but I had to put a stop to that. He didn't even have a good job and I wasn't even out of high school. It just didn't make sense. A lot of girls get married and then it doesn't work out, and they are not so happy down the line. I'm not going to get married until I am at least thirty.

It was better after I got both of them in day care. I would get up and dress Roxanne while my mother would dress Robert, and then I would put them both on the bus so I could get dressed. Then I was at school with my friends, so I had something to do. I could never just sit home with the kids; that would really get to me. When they came home they were mine, but I could send them downstairs to my mother or my sisters—she has a three-family house. That was a relief. I didn't always have to ask someone to baby-sit and then leave the house. All I had to do was ask somebody to watch them, and then I could go hide in the bathroom or in my room just to be by myself for a little while.

I moved from my mother's house this year. There weren't really problems there, but I had a Section 8 certificate, and I knew I wanted to live by myself when I could afford it. Now the girl upstairs often visits, and the company is good. Also I have girlfriends that live in the area, so we share. Like last week I took four kids to the movies—I'll never do that again—but when we got home, one of my friends took the kids for the night so I got some rest. By sharing that way nobody has to pay for baby-sitting.

I don't like welfare, but sometimes you have to deal with them. It was hard for me to get to the office, it was so far away. But now I do a lot of my business by mail. They didn't give me too much of a hassle because I didn't come in with an attitude, and they could talk to me. I always came there with all my papers. If you go in there with a straight face and are straight with them, then they are OK. And the programs they have there, the job and educational programs, they can really help if you let them. After all, the money they give you is not so much, anyway. I could honestly live off what I get, only I want more.

Some people think that getting on welfare and having kids is going to give them lots of money. But they don't understand how little it really is. Some people really think that they can make the guy stay with them if they have a baby, but it really doesn't work that way. They don't see that a lot of problems can come from being raised poor with no money.

If I was to give advice to young girls, I would tell them, first, that even if their mothers don't want them with pills, it is better to have them and take them. It's better to be fighting about the pills than to come home with a big stomach and have to fight about that. But some girls don't want to admit they are doing anything.

Five years from now I want a good job, like two hundred and something a week. But then again if I get a job they will take away my housing subsidy. My apartment now is free for me, but it rents for $450 a month. So if I was working I would have to pay that, and I wouldn't do so well. And then there is health insurance.

Next year I hope to go to college, with financial aid. I think I want to get into social services, but I'm not really sure right now. Some people say you should try out a lot of things, other people say that's wasting time. It is hard to make choices.

In lots of ways I find that I am more mature than a lot of girls my age. Like last year I worked and saved money and bought furniture for when I would have my own apartment. So when I moved I had everything I needed. I didn't have to take anything from my mother.

I hope my children's lives will be a lot different from mine. I want to be able to send them to a private school or something, but I hope I don't spoil them. If my mother can raise eleven kids without help, then I should be able to do it with two.

But now I don't have any problems with my mother. My mother loves me. She always calls me when my other brothers and sisters get on her nerves. In fact, she always uses me as an example with them, "Kim did all this with two kids."

GROWING NUMBERS, GROWING FORCE
Older Women Organize

Kathleen Kautzer

> *We have played the game according to rules you set down. Now the rules have changed and we're called out, but we have one half to one third of our lives still to go, and we will not be shelved.*
>
> ——Tish Sommers, "Epilogue"[1]

With these words, Tish Sommers, a self-described "free lance agitator," aptly summarized the spirit and message of the Older Women's movement that she labored to initiate and build over the past fifteen years. (Sommers died in the fall of 1985.)

Sommers described her generation of American women as "playing by the rules" because her cohorts, by and large, accepted traditional female roles in both the family and the labor market. This generation had very limited exposure to feminism because their youth and adolescence occurred between 1930 and 1950, when the first wave of the feminist movement had subsided, and the second wave had not yet coalesced. During World War II many

This essay is based on ongoing work for my dissertation on the Older Women's League (OWL). It could not have been written without the collaboration and support of Tish Sommers and Alice Quinlan.

had enjoyed brief stints of employment as "Rosie, the Riveter," recruited to replace male workers who entered military service. However, at the end of the war, many women were persuaded, with varying degrees of reluctance and resistance, to relinquish their lucrative and challenging jobs to returning soldiers, or as was often the situation, to continue to work at less well-paid "women's jobs." In order to achieve this transition, American producers and public officials subjected this generation to an intense propaganda campaign extolling the homemaker role as the most suitable and rewarding occupation available to women.

Now that Sommers' generation has reached late adulthood, many of her cohorts are discovering that "the rules have changed and we've been called out." In other words, contrary to their expectations, older women are encountering penalties rather than rewards for their lifelong service in female roles because of changing demographic and social trends and discriminatory social policies. Rising divorce rates and increasing gaps in the longevity rates of males and females have left today's generation of older women more likely than earlier generations to survive over an extended period without spousal companionship or support. After being socialized to view their husband as their provider, many older women find themselves lacking the resources needed to insure their own economic survival. As a result of the combined effects of age and sex discrimination in the labor market, older women are frequently unable to find employment or earn adequate wages. Equally important, older women find their retirement security jeopardized by both Social Security and pension programs, which penalize women for their lower lifetime earnings and/or their status as dependent spouses. Lastly, the passive, self-effacing, and subservient behavior women acquire during their lengthy playing of female roles inhibits their ability to assert their rights and protest the omnipresent discrimination they encounter.

Fortunately, Sommers' assertion that her generation of American women "will not be shelved" is being echoed by many of her cohorts, more than 13,000 of whom have become members of the Older Women's League (OWL), the first and only advocacy organization in the United States for mid-life and older women. Founded in 1981 by Tish Sommers and Laurie Shields, OWL is dedicated to the goal of "bridging the gap between the women's movement and aging activism."

This chapter presents an overview of both the problems and potentialities of older women that have been exposed and documented largely through the efforts of the Older Women's League. The chapter begins with a demographic portrait of the older female population, followed by an analysis of the disadvantages older women encounter in the family structure, labor market, and retirement income policies. The final section described the reform initiatives older women activists have undertaken to remedy their disadvantaged status.

A Demographic Portrait of Older Women

Describing the demographic characteristics of older women is complicated by the fact that the word older is a relative term, with variable meaning according to the social context and/or reference group to which it is applied. In fact, the term older is not even applied uniformly to persons of the same chronological age because of differences in appearance, social status, or occupation. (For example, age forty is considered "young" for a senator but "old" for a fashion model.) To complicate matters further, numerous studies have revealed that many persons over the age of sixty reject being labeled "old" or "older" in order to avoid being stigmatized by ageist stereotyping.[2]

As a result of demographic trends toward an aging populace and increasing longevity gaps between the sexes, the absolute and relative size of the older female population has increased dramatically over the past several decades; and these trends should persist beyond the turn of the century. In 1982 the U.S. Census Bureau estimated that women age forty-five and above numbered 39 million and comprised roughly 17 percent of the population. Elderly women numbered 16 million and represented 41 percent of the older women population.* Older women of color numbered 3.7 million and constituted 9.5 percent of women over the age of forty-five.[3]

* In the interests of clarity I use the term "older women" to refer to women age forty-five and above and the term "elderly women" to refer to women age sixty-five and above.

A comparison between the incomes of older men and women clearly reveals the disadvantaged status of older women relative to older men and a bleak economic future for women as they age. While income declines sharply with age for both genders, women face the higher risk of impoverishment because their incomes are consistently so much lower than men's. For example, in 1983 men age forty-five to forty-nine received a median annual income of $23,347 compared to $16,311 for men age sixty to sixty-four. In contrast, women age forty-five to forty-nine received a median annual income of $8,373 compared to $5,872 for women age sixty to sixty-four.[4]

Poverty rates among older women reach their highest level after age sixty-five: in 1983 the median annual income of elderly women was $5,600 or about $800 above the poverty level, and $4,000 below the income of elderly men. While women comprise 60 percent of the population over age sixty five, they comprise 71 percent of the elderly poor.[5]

The elderly women most likely to have incomes below the poverty level are women of color and unmarried women. High poverty rates among elderly women of color reflect broad patterns of racism in the labor market, patterns that subject women of color and their nonwhite spouses to frequent periods of unemployment and segregation in low-paying jobs. Consequently, women of color who reach retirement age have usually been unable to acquire adequate personal savings and/or pension income. Currently nearly one in two black women over the age of sixty-five lives in poverty. Black women comprise 8 percent of elderly women but 21 percent of elderly women with incomes below the poverty level. Likewise, Latina women, who comprise 2 percent of the elderly female population, also have higher poverty rates than their white cohorts: in 1983 the poverty rate for elderly Latina women was 23.7 percent compared to 14.7 percent for elderly white women.[6]

Unmarried elderly women, especially those living alone, also encounter high poverty rates in old age. In 1983 unmarried women (including single, divorced, and widowed women) constituted 80 percent of elderly women with incomes below the poverty level.[7] Of course, unmarried elderly persons of both genders have higher poverty rates than their married cohorts, quite simply because they are unable to partake of a spouse's income or share living expenses with a spouse. In addition, elderly women tend to outlive their husbands and are less likely to remarry than elderly men. At present 77 percent of men over age sixty-five are married and living with a spouse, while only 39 percent of women over age sixty-five are in similar circumstances. Nearly 80 percent of the 8 million elderly who live alone are women.[8] Unmarried women are also less likely than unmarried men to have adequate retirement incomes, particularly since widowed and divorced women are frequently denied benefits by their husband's pension plan or accorded only token settlements, and women who are never married are subject to all the inequities of lifelong job discrimination.

Older Women and the Family Structure

Traditional family mores and sex roles serve as the primary source of the structural inequalities encountered by older women in both the labor market and pension programs. So family structures represent an appropriate place to begin explaining older women's poverty.

In the United States (and indeed most of the Western world) traditional family structures have assigned women almost exclusive responsibility for unpaid domestic labor (including housekeeping and care of dependent family members), while men were expected to serve as the primary family breadwinner. The current women's movement has challenged these traditional roles by expanding employment opportunities for women, but it has made few inroads toward shifting housekeeping and care-giving responsibilities to men. Numerous recent studies have shown that women continue to serve as primary family care givers, and receive, at most, minimal assistance from male family members.[9]

Feminists' efforts to relieve women of the burdens of domestic labor have primarily focused on the areas of day care, maternity leave, and child support. For most older women, however, whose offspring have reached adulthood, the burden of unpaid domestic labor primarily takes the form of care for disabled spouses, parents, and other family members. Even single women without children do not escape care-giving responsibilities, since they have traditionally been expected to care for their parents if they become disabled, and the tasks involved in caring for disabled adults are usually more demanding and arduous than raising children. For example, care givers for severely disabled family members frequently become virtual prisoners in their homes because of the round-the-clock attention required.[10]

One of the tragedies women face as they age is that, despite their service as lifelong care givers for other family members, older women face the highest risk of institutionalization in old age. The fact that over 70 percent of nursing home residents are women is partly attributable to women's greater longevity but also to the fact that most elderly women have low incomes and hence may be unable to afford in-home services.[11] Currently both of the public health insurance programs for the elderly, Medicare and Medicaid, provide more extensive coverage of nursing home care than in-home services. In addition, elderly women today may be less able than earlier generations to rely on younger female relatives, who have become geographically dispersed and/or employed full-time.

A second and equally tragic irony resulting from the traditional family situation is revealed by the fate of displaced homemakers. In 1975 Tish Sommers coined the term "displaced homemaker" to refer to a woman who was dependent on her spouse for a substantial number of years while providing unpaid domestic service to her family but who loses spousal support as a result of death, divorce, abandonment, or the disability of her spouse. The fate of displaced homemakers exposes the reality underlying the societal myth that homemaking is a stable and secure occupation. Traditional family patterns have jeopardized rather than insured the economic security of full-time homemakers by designating a male wage earner as their sole source of support. When their husband dies or leaves, women quickly discover the economic insecurity that underlies their dependent status.

To begin with, the unpaid (or underpaid if they worked part-time in "women's jobs") nature of their work makes displaced homemakers ineligible for the unemployment compensation or disability coverage available to full-time wage earners. Second, many displaced homemakers find themselves without health insurance after losing coverage under their husband's plan: they may not have reached the age of eligibility for Medicare or Medicaid and may be unable to afford private coverage and/or denied coverage because of preexisting medical conditions.[12] Third, widowed displaced homemakers are unable to collect Social Security benefits during the period referred to as the "widow's gap," which extends from the time the widow's eldest child reaches eighteen until the widow reaches sixty.

Divorce settlements are another economic stumbling block. Displaced homemakers are frequently granted only nominal awards, with no compensation for the homemaker's contribution to family income or the opportunity for paid employment lost by filling the homemaker role. Divorce courts commonly justify their decision to grant displaced homemakers meager awards on the grounds that these women can quickly secure paid employment.

Older Women and the Labor Market

Obviously, younger and older women alike face restricted opportunities for paid employment as a result of the burdens involved in performing unpaid domestic labor: unlike men, they must choose jobs with schedules and workloads that can be integrated with care-giving duties. The employment prospects of women in all age groups are further restricted by patterns of sex segregation in the labor market, which channel 80 percent of women workers into traditionally female, low-paid jobs.

Yet while sex discrimination victimizes older and younger women alike, the employment problems of older women are further compounded by the combined effects of age and sex discrimination in the labor market. This "double discrimination" works in two ways. First, sex segregation in the labor market puts older women at a disadvantage relative to older men. While male occupations may protect and even reward older workers with job security and career ladder provisions, female occupations are noted for their unstable and dead-end nature. Consequently, in contrast to older men, older women experience more stagnant earning histories, as well as longer durations of joblessness, shorter job tenure, and higher representation among the unemployed.[13]

Second, older women are disadvantaged relative to younger women because of social norms that deny the attractiveness, vitality, and competence of older women. Generally speaking, older women are subject to earlier and more severe age discrimination than men. Many feminists have decried the "double standard of aging" in which physical evidence of aging (such as graying hair and facial lines) are viewed as a source of prestige and maturity for men but a source of decline and shame for women. The mass media reinforces negative stereotyping of older women by presenting them primarily in roles as shrews or matronly figures, while older men are assigned roles as statemen and high-level executives. In the words of an OWL leaflet: "Today's emphasis on youth leaves older women the task of promoting denture cream and regularity."

As a result of this double standard, many women encounter age discrimination even before reaching forty. In fact, before the passage of the Age Discrimination in Employment Act in 1967, many employers maintained age hiring limits ranging from twenty-one to thirty-five for female jobs.[14] Despite the fact that age discrimination is now illegal, many employers continue to express preference for young female applicants through more subtle but no less effective methods. For example, many older women report being passed over for employment in favor of younger women on the grounds that they were "overqualified."

Double discrimination affects both older women reentering the work force and also long-term female employees who are frequently passed over for raises and promotions in favor of male or young female applicants. Far from being rewarded for their long-term service, many older women workers find their skills and experience exploited by employers, who continually assign them added responsibility while denying raises and promotions. One example so commonplace it has become a stereotype is the indispensable older women secretary who is consistently passed over for promotions but is expected to train newly hired management recruits. Societal myths depicting women as becoming more irritable and domineering as they age have apparently persuaded many employers to exclude older women from management positions. For example, in 1969 (before age discrimination was outlawed), the U.S. Department of Health, Education and Welfare adopted a policy not to hire women over age thirty-five for higher-level jobs in the department (and later raised the hiring limit to age fifty).[15]

It is difficult to overestimate the devastating psychological consequences older women endure as victims of this double discrimination. The experience of being labeled "old" or "unattractive" is particularly damaging to the self-esteem and self-image of many women precisely because American society tends to grant recognition and rewards to women primarily on the basis of their physical appearance. Moreover, many women have this first encounter with double discrimination during a period of intense personal stress: many mid-life and older women reenter the labor market after becoming widowed or divorced or encountering the "empty nest syndrome" (when offspring leave home or reach adulthood). Consequently many women are coping with depression and high anxiety levels when they undertake the intimidating task of job hunting. Predictably the experience of being repeatedly rejected by employers inflicts further blows on flagging morale and deflated egos. Likewise, the older women who are long-term employees may become depressed when forced to confront the likelihood of remaining stuck in their present jobs. Striking evidence of the psychological damage endured by older women was uncovered by several recent studies, in which older women vividly described their ongoing battle to maintain their dignity and sanity in a society that demeans and degrades them.[16]

The interaction between age and sex discrimination has gone largely unrecognized and unchallenged by state and federal antidiscrimination agencies. To begin with, older women are unlikely to file either age or sex discrimination suits because they are frequently unfamiliar with federal legislation, unable to finance a private attorney, and reluctant to assert personal rights. Furthermore, since there is no legislation specifically prohibiting combined forms of age and sex discrimination, antidiscrimination agencies choose to handle age and sex discrimination separately. Consequenty, such agencies routinely advise older women to file complaints on only one charge; even if both charges are filed, they are usually litigated separately. Employers have therefore been able to avoid persecution for discrimination against older women since they can point to younger female employees and older male employees to disprove claims of sex and age discrimination, respectively.[17]

Existing antidiscrimination laws not only fail to protect older women against overt discrimination based on age and sex, they also fail to protect them against the subtle discrimination encompassed in the employer's evaluation of the homemaker role. Displaced homemakers report that "lack of recent job experience" is the most frequent reason employers give for rejecting their job application. "Lack of recent job experience" is a legally acceptable camouflage for age and sex discrimination that reflects lack of respect for homemakers' prior work as community volunteers and unpaid family care givers. Ironically, displaced homemakers usually seek employment in traditionally female service occupations that require the same nurturing, housekeeping, and organizing skills they acquired as homemakers. Nevertheless, there is little reason to believe that employers consider homemaking as a viable qualification for such paid employment, as uncovered in a 1979 Florida survey, which revealed that "a large majority of firms do not accept homemaking skills as having market value."[18]

Obviously, then, the unequal status of older women in the labor market reflects and reinforces the inequalities they encounter in the family structure: women are assigned primarily to housekeeping and care-giving labor in both spheres, and the unpaid status of their labor in the home contributes to its devalued status in the labor market.

Older Women and Pension Policies

Not surprisingly, the same patterns of discrimination that women encounter in the family structure and labor market are repeated in both Social Security and employee pension plans, both of which are designed primarily for male wage earners with continuous histories of paid employment. The accelerating risks of impoverishment women encounter as they age are an inevitable by-product of retirement-income policies that penalize women for intermittent work histories and confinement to low-paying, sex-segregated jobs.

The most glaring inequity women encounter in the Social Security system stems from the fact that United States, unlike many European countries, provides no coverage to homemakers for years spent performing unpaid labor in the home. While homemakers are entitled to benefits as "dependents" of retired spouses, they may collect these benefits only by forfeiting any benefits accrued based on earnings from paid employment. Consequently, both benefit options put women at a disadvantage relative to male wage earner, because the earnings-based benefit reflects women's lower salaries and intermittent work histories, while the dependent spousal benefit is calculated at a rate equivalent to only 50 percent of the benefit awarded to the wage-earning spouse.

The discriminatory policies women encounter under Social Security are particularly detrimental to retirement security. First, as a result of their greater longevity, women are dependent on Social Security income for a more extended period than men. Second, women are more likely than men to rely on Social Security as their sole or primary source of retirement income since they have less access to pensions benefits, income from earnings, and/or personal savings.[19]

To an even greater extent than Social Security, employee pension programs penalize women for their lower lifetime earnings. Pension benefits are generally based solely on earnings, while Social Security benefits include both an earnings component and a mild bias toward low-income beneficiaries. The contrast between the pension benefits of male and female workers clearly demonstrates the negative impact of women's lower lifetime earnings: in 1983 the median monthly pension income for men was $473, compared to $243 for women.[20]

Not only do women receive lower pension benefits, but they are also substantially less likely than men to enjoy pension coverage. Currently only 20.4 percent of women over age sixty-five receive pension income, compared with 42.6 percent of men.[21] Women workers tend to have less access to pensions both because traditionally female occupations are less likely to provide pension coverage and also because women workers are frequently unable to meet the vesting requirements of most pension plans (which grant eligibility only after ten years of continuous employment).

Women need, then, to challenge the increasingly popular theory that predicts that the retirement incomes of men and women will equalize over time simply as a result of increased labor-force participation by women. On the contrary, as long as women are delegated responsibility for unpaid domestic labor and remain confined to sex-segregated jobs, their lower lifetime earnings will result in inadequate and inequitable retirement incomes.

Emergence and Growth of the Older Women's Movement

With the rallying slogan of "Don't Agonize, Organize," Tish Sommers attained wide recognition among both feminist and aging activists for her keen political instincts, her witty and captivating speaking style, her energetic and persistent leadership, and her path-breaking insights regarding the problems and potentialities of older women.

The origins of Sommers' interest in social justice and political activism can be traced to her experience when, as a young, foreign, exchange dance student residing with a Jewish family during the 1930s, she witnessed Hitler's rise to power. Following this early encounter with the horrors of racism and militarism in Nazi Germany, Sommers pursued a lifelong career as a volunteer community organizer supporting poverty programs and the Civil Rights Movement. Sommers' organizing talents reached their most complete expression when her own encounters with discriminatory treatment sparked her interest in launching a collective protest movement of older women.

When Sommers became divorced at age fifty-seven she experienced many of the problems of other displaced homemakers: she had difficulty getting credit in her own name and was unable to purchase medical insurance because of medical history. She also found that her background as a former homemaker and community organizer commanded little respect from employers and society as a whole. As an experienced political activist, Sommers quickly recognized herself to be the victim of structural inequities that negatively affected many women of her generation. Shortly thereafter she concluded that her peers were clearly "ripe" for political mobilization based on their overwhelmingly positive response to her public appeals for collective protest by and for older women.

Sommers' formal career as an advocate for older women began in 1973 when she convinced the National Organization for Women (NOW) to form a Task Force on Older Women. As coordinator of this task force, Sommers attracted a dedicated group of older women activists. Although Sommers and her colleagues maintained an ongoing dialogue with organizations representing women and the elderly, they eventually recognized the need to build their own advocacy organization focused exclusively on the unique problems of older women that remained largely ignored or misunderstood, even by feminist and aging activists.

Sommers' first attempt at organization building focused on displaced homemakers. In 1974 she formed a partnership with Laurie Shields, a former advertising executive and recently widowed displaced homemaker, and together they founded the Alliance for Displaced Homemakers (ADH). At present the ADH has been supplanted by the Displaced Homemaker Network (DHN), with headquarters in Washington, which serves as an information clearinghouse and national advocacy organization for displaced homemakers.

The women who became participants in the displaced-homemaker movement represented a wide range of backgrounds including middle- and upper-income women who entered the ranks of the "new poor" upon loss of spousal support; (2) welfare mothers who lost Aid to Families with Dependent Children benefits when their eldest child turned eighteen; (3) homemakers with graduate degrees whose credentials were considered "outdated" by employers; and (4) women of color who remained "underemployed" as a result of their dual burdens as a family wage earner and care giver.

In spite of its limited resources and small membership base, ADH compiled an impressive list of legislative victories: by 1980, thirty states had passed displaced-homemaker legislation, and the U.S. Congress had officially recognized displaced homemakers as a "disadvantaged group" eligible for priority services under the 1978 Comprehensive Employment and Training Act (CETA) Reauthorization Act. ADH achieved these victories relatively easily and quickly by designing strategies that appealed to the political incentives of legislators. By emphasizing that displaced homemakers embodied the American virtues of "motherhood and apple pie," ADH skillfully deflected opposition from right-wing forces. In order to win the support of legislators, ADH emphasized that displaced-homemaker centers were inexpensive programs designed to enable a disadvantaged group to avoid welfare by securing gainful employment.

Obviously there were trade-offs involved in ADH's efforts to make displaced-homemaker centers politically viable. In order to control costs, displaced-homemaker centers are designed to operate on a shoe-string budget and usually offer employment counseling and referral rather than on-the-job training. Despite these limitations, however, displaced-homemaker centers serve as a lifeline for many older women who are rejected or bypassed by other employment agencies. One noteworthy feature of displaced-homemaker centers is their emphasis on peer counseling and self-help: most displaced-homemaker centers are staffed by older women, and clients are organized into support groups that assist each member in identifying career goals and coping with the pressures and pitfalls of job hunting.

Shields and Sommers always viewed the displaced-homemaker movement as a first step toward their long-term goal of building a mass membership organization for older women. In 1978 they laid the groundwork for realizing this goal by establishing the Older Women's League Education Fund (OWLEF), to engage in public education and consciousness raising regarding the problems shared by today's generation of older women.

Documenting the problems of older women proved to be a challenging task for OWLEF because of the lack of prior research. Feminist researchers had focused primarily on issues of concern to younger women (child care, reproductive rights, hiring policies) and had barely tapped issues of concern to women during the latter stages of the life cycle (retirement policies, health insurance, tending disabled family members, nursing home care, age-sex discrimination). Gerontological research was even more disappointing. For example, in the field of retirement research, inclusion of female subjects was "almost unheard of" before 1975. Many gerontologists justified their preoccupation with male retirees by arguing that retirement was primarily a "male" problem because of the role discontinuity men experience when forced to abandon their lifelong role as family wage earner. Even when women were included as research subjects, gerontologists usually failed to explain or highlight the high rates of unemployment, poverty, and institutionalization encountered by older women.[22] Lastly, government statistics are organized into categorical schemes that disguise the disadvantaged status of older women. For example, the Department of Labor does not cross-classify their employment statistics by age and sex, thereby making it impossible to pinpoint how older women fare relative to other employee groups. Similarly, homemakers are not recognized as an occupational category, thereby making it impossible to identify the number of older women who are full-time homemakers or displaced homemakers.

Shields and Sommers recognized that as long as the problems of older women remain undocumented and unpublicized, they would remain invisible. After all, the very existence of displaced homemakers had escaped public attention and concern until the displaced-homemaker's movement emerged and provided them with an official label and evidence of their disadvantaged status. Consequently OWLEF prepared a series of policy papers outlining inequities in divorce settlements, Social Security, pension plans, the labor market, and health insurance. These papers—the OWLEF Gray Papers—received favorable reviews from policymakers in the field of the aging. In turn, this heightened awareness and receptivity to OWL issues on the part of professionals concerned with aging greatly enhanced efforts to solicit funds and find prestigious sponsors for OWLEF activities from organizations that serve the elderly.

In 1980 Sommers served as convenor of the Mini-Conference on Older Women (funded by the U.S. Administration on Aging) and invited delegates to remain an extra day at the close of the conference to participate in the launching of the Older Women's League. Three hundred of the four hundred conference delegates responded to the appeal, and the Older Women's League (OWL) was born.

To date OWL has attracted more than 13,000 members and has established ninety-five local chapters. The composition of OWL's membership is not, however, truly representative of the older female population. According to a recent membership survey, only 4 percent of OWL members are ethnic minorities and only 8 percent are full-time homemakers. A majority of OWL members have college degrees, are currently employed, and are between the ages of fifty and sixty-five. In the interest of building a more representative organization, OWL leaders are currently experimenting with a variety of strategies for increasing the number of members who have low incomes and/or belong to minority groups.

Shields and Sommers take pride in OWL's expanding capacity to engage in organizing and advocacy activities. For example, OWL's staff currently includes a government-relations specialist and several field organizers. Grants from private and public foundations enable OWL to provide grants and leadership training to local chapters and to publish an extensive range of consciousness-raising and educational material. OWL also receives pro-bono services from a prestigous media consulting firm, which designs public-service ads that cleverly dramatize OWL's mission. (One popular ad features a picture of a weeping Statue of Liberty with a caption that reads: "When it comes to older women, this country takes a lot of liberties.")

In discussing OWL's political objectives, OWL leaders consistently emphasize that genuine and enduring equity for older women can be accomplished only by eliminating structural inequities that are responsible for the multiple forms of discrimination they presently encounter. Reforms viewed necessary to achieve this long-range goal include the following:

- Social Security coverage for homemakers to eliminate the penalties imposed on them as a result of their "dependent" status
- full employment and expanded employment training programs to ensure employment to displaced homemakers and other older women who are subject to widespread discrimination in the current labor market
- comparable pay legislation to establish more equitable pay scales in traditionally female occupations

It should be noted that none of these reforms can be characterized as exclusively older women's issues; instead they would eliminate inequities encountered by women of all age groups. A variety of feminist organizations consequently include such proposals on their reform agendas. Needless to say, however, OWL leaders recognize that reforms of this magnitude can be achieved only as a result of an intensive and protracted struggle, led by a broad-based coalition of organizations representing women, the elderly, and their allies.

In the meantime, OWL has devised an interim strategy to foster self-organization and political mobilization among older women and to alleviate some of the most pressing problems they face today. OWL selects its own reform priorities on the basis of the following four criteria:

- Does the proposed reform have a reasonable likelihood of being passed under existing political conditions?
- Does the reform raise consciousness by exposing the structural inequities that create the need for reform?
- Does the reform lay the groundwork for ongoing reform by moving in the direction of long-range goals?
- Does the reform present a problem and proposed solution that will move older women to action?

In accordance with these criteria and the policy preferences voiced by its own membership, OWL has selected six primary agenda items:

1. *Social Security.* OWL's advocacy activity in this area has been directed toward protecting current benefit levels and promoting earning-sharing legislation, which would replace the dependent-spousal benefit with a new benefit formula granting more equitable benefits to both spouses.
2. *Pension Rights.* OWL participated in successful campaigns on behalf of the Retirement Equity Act, the Civil Service Spouse Retirement Equity Act, and amendments to the 1982 Former (Military) Spouse Protection Act, all of which passed Congress in 1984. These pension-reform bills eliminated a variety of loopholes and provisions that previously denied pension coverage to many widowed and divorced women. OWL continues to work toward greater pension equity by pointing to remaining inequities in existing plans, conducting a pension literacy campaign, and arguing on behalf of a comprehensive national retirement policy.
3. *Access to Health Insurance.* OWL is currently sponsoring legislation at both the federal and state level that would require employee health insurance plans to permit dependents to remain in the plan in the event of death, divorce, or retirement of the wage earner.
4. *Support Services for Care Givers.* A variety of OWL chapters nationwide are currently working at the state level for respite-care legislation, that would provide publicly funded relief services to care givers of severely disabled family members.
5. *Jobs for Older Women.* OWL chapters throughout the country conduct workshops and conferences focused on the employment problems and opportunities of older women. OWL also supports the advocacy efforts of the Displaced Homemaker Network to secure public funding for employment training and job counseling services for displaced homemakers.
6. *Budget Cuts.* OWL works in coalition with other women's and elderly person's organizations to resist budget cuts in

human service and entitlement programs, and documents in the detrimental impact proposed cuts would impose on older women.

Sommers' own words best describe the guiding principles of the older women's movement:

> One way we have worked in OWL is to take our experience, some of it bitter, and turn it into good energy to make this a better society for ourselves and those who will follow us. "We build a new road to aging and the road to aging builds us." Facing death and planning for it, squeezing the sweet juice out of adversity, is part of what OWL is all about.[23]

WORKING YOUR FINGERS TO THE BONE

Marion Graham

I was born in Boston, the youngest of a four-girl family. When I was thirteen my father's firm went bankrupt and he found himself out of a job. My family were so ashamed they wouldn't tell their friends that they had to move from the suburbs to a three decker in Boston, even though they weren't really poor. Now I know a lot of people who would love to move out of the projects into a three decker.

In 1960 I got married. I left my good job with the telephone company when I was pregnant with my first child, in 1961. I really looked forward to being home with my children. Nobody worked that I knew. During the Sixties I was always pregnant when everybody was out rebelling against everything. I was too pregnant to rebel, so I have to rebel now! I have five kids. They are now twenty-four, twenty-two, twenty, nineteen, and sixteen.

When I saw how my marriage was disintegrating, I did work at

Marion Graham was originally interviewed for *We Need a Change,* a collection of interviews produced for the University of Massachussetts/Boston Conference on Women and Poverty, held in April 1984. Jean Humez and Melissa Shook conducted the original interview. In July 1985, Ann Withorn updated, edited, and expanded the interview.

home for marketing research companies, and I did typing for college students, just to try to make money. I had planned for two or three years to get a divorce before I did. But I never had the money to do it. I knew I had to have a job in order to save the money to go to a lawyer. I couldn't leave the kids; there was no day care. Finally, I had to go on welfare because my husband did not pay enough support, and sometimes he did not pay at all.

When I started working full-time again, I thought it was going to be wonderful, that I wasn't going to be poor anymore. I was going to be away from the bureaucracy; they couldn't call me in anytime they wanted to. Even then, though, I still earned so little that I was eligible for a housing subsidy, Medicaid, and food stamps. I remember at the time being ashamed to let people where I worked know that I was poor enough for food stamps. And I hated that.

About three years ago they came out with some new "poverty line," that's what they called it, and they decided I earned too much for most of those other benefits. I only grossed something like $8,600 at the time, but it was still too much for them, so they cut me off. I still had the same needs I had before, but suddenly I was no longer poor. I guess I was supposed to be proud.

Since then I got a raise, so I thought things would be OK, but then I lost my housing subsidy because I earned too much. I ended up having to take an apartment that cost exactly seven times what I had paid with a subsidy. My rent came to half of my net pay. Just the rent. After that sometimes I would get to work but not be able to pay for lunch. I had my subway tokens, but no money to eat. Every week they take something different out of my salary. Life insurance, disability insurance, union dues, retirement benefits are all good, but you don't get much to live on. Now, finally, I can buy *Woman's Day* and *Family Circle* magazines—that used to be my dream.

How you dress for work, the hours and flexibility, transportation, whether you can bring a lunch—all these nitty gritty things make a big difference in how you can live on a low salary. You just cannot afford to take some jobs even if they sound interesting because you have to spend too much money on clothes or transportation. It's sad. I couldn't afford to work at a place where I had to dress up, for instance. You can't "dress for success" on a secretarial salary. It's an invisible poverty.

You think you're not poor because you are working, so you don't even ask for the information about benefits you need. And nobody tells you that you might be eligible, because they think you are working and all set. Also, it is even harder to ask for things from your family, because if you are working you should have the money. I feel bad, though, that I don't have more chance to help my family. I can't afford it, even though I'm working.

The average pay in my union of clerical and hospital workers is $11,000. That's not much—it is poverty for a woman who is trying to raise a family. When people need child care they have to pay for it, and they can't afford it. I don't need child care, but the health insurance, which I had to wait two years for, costs a lot. And I couldn't get it for my son, who is twenty and has juvenile diabetes.

Not having money affects everything about how you feel. I used to feel lousy about myself. I thought I was supposed to be set, to have slice of the American pie. Now I was a big person and I worked and everything and I was supposed to get there. But instead I found myself just with a job and no money. When I reached forty I was so depressed.

Now I have learned that I am not alone, that it is not my fault. The average secretary around here makes $14,000. So we are just over the line for many benefits, but we still have expenses we can't meet. That makes some women, who don't understand how it works, take it out on women on welfare. They blame them for getting something they can't have, instead of blaming the rules, which keep them from getting anything. Some secretaries may think, "I am better off than they are," instead of seeing how we have similar problems. But they are afraid of the label that would be put on them if they identify with welfare. I don't do that because I have been there and I know both, and I know that none of it is good. It's bad to be on welfare, and it is bad to be working and have no money.

As secretaries here we have worked hard to do things together so that we can know each other as people, because at work we are all separated in our individual little offices. We go on picnics together, or to dinner, just to get to know each other. Although they don't pay us much, they act like we can never be absent or the world will fall apart, so we have to cover for each other, and we can't do that if we don't know each other. I keep saying, if we are so important why don't they pay us more? But they don't, so we have to help each other.

Marion Graham

The hardest thing about being a secretary is that people think there is something wrong with being a secretary. You are an extension of your typewriter, you are a piece of furniture, you aren't really important. They always say, "You are overqualified," but many people with degrees still can't do the job; it's hard and important. We don't have money or status. For instance, my job now is strictly administrative work, detail and organizing. I don't even have a typewriter any more, but I am still listed on a secretarial line because it's cheaper to keep me that way. I hope the comparable-worth stuff will help us some, even though they will fiddle around with it forever.

They act like all secretaries are young girls waiting to get married who don't need much money. But that is not how it is. Besides that, young girls, like my daughter, want money too, to save, to do what they want. So nobody deserves bad wages.

It's also frustrating that so many people, like my family, think unions are "low class" and are afraid of them, even when they need them. My mother told me not to "upset management" when I became a steward. I told her that was the whole point.

I think our union should invite women on welfare to come talk about what they get and don't get. And to let people know about benefits. That would be a help and could bridge the gap and keep working women from looking down on welfare mothers, or say they aren't working. We need to make alliances; it is sad that we haven't done it.

I have to admit that I am thrilled that my income has doubled in the past six years. It took a lot of hard work and I am proud. But I still don't have enough money, and that's the bottom line.

AND SUNDAY LASTS TOO LONG
Rural Women and Intergenerational Poverty*

B. Eleanor Anstey and
Janet Paige Kuller

Out Here

Sunday drags on into the afternoon
while Jim's out somewhere
at the tavern, watching a game.
It's not that I want to go.
I get tired of people.

I don't know how he can stand
going down there, the same men, same stories.
At least the kids are big enough
to play outside alone. I'm not
an unlucky woman. But somehow
I feel too old these days.

Oh sure, I could call Louise
and listen as she goes on about her husband,
or the neighbors or the new minister.
But sometimes I wonder why she stays where

The authors were born on farms in the Midwest and lived there. The reflections and stories used in this essay are based on transcripts of the authors' interviews and conversations with women living in rural areas of the Midwest over the last seven years.

she is. You'd think she hated life.
Of course, she don't know this,
I can't say anything.
Maybe none of us can.

Things aren't so bad these days
as some of them would say.
Out here you can breathe fresh air.
We have each other. I'm just tired
and Sunday lasts too long.

Women in rural America are included in the statistics of poverty but only in a one-dimensional way. Their feelings about being poor never leak out. Yet a look at the richness of their personal histories discloses a special complexity within the general pattern of rural poverty.

In today's rural America there is both "new" and "traditional" poverty. The "new poor" are persons who, after days of planting, plowing, and fertilizing crops, find themselves victims of drought, unseasonal flooding, or early frost. They are also trapped by high interests rates, unavailable financing or credit, farm foreclosures, and bankruptcy reenforced by dwindling markets at home and abroad. Their poverty arises from debts impossible to satisfy in a current time of economic farm instability. The husband accepts a job welding; the wife cooks at a neighboring country club to earn grocery money. The teenage children shoulder major responsibilities for doing farm chores and attend school at the same time. Death in the family, disease in herds of animals, impossible bank loans—conditions often beyond their control—have changed the life-style familiar to them and have made them the "new poor" of America's heartland.[1]

They are caught in the same dilemma that confronted the "new poor" of the 1930s depression and drought. Like them, many will probably find employment off the land. Far fewer will somehow manage to survive on their farms and, often with the aid of outside jobs, gradually achieve a greater independence. The "new poor" of rural populations have not ordinarily become the "traditional poor" of their own areas. Instead they have migrated to cities or, to some degree, to other rural areas. The "traditional poor," however, are still in rural areas and still relatively untouched by all the current attention paid to the "new poor." The "traditional poor" retain today the sense of isolation that has become such a dominant factor in their lives. These people have seldom known any way of life other than intergenerational poverty. They are much more mobile than their more affluent fellows who also live in the country. Sometimes, they find temporary employment in small towns or on farms. Often their jobs are seasonal; always, they lack seniority and are the first to be laid off. They are always renters, subject to every vicissitude in the landlord's life or in the local economy. Their destitute life-style is their heritage; it is who they are. They seldom feel a part of the communities where they reside, and they in turn feel threatened by outsiders. They spend long periods of time alone or with their immediate families. They grow increasingly aware that no one cares for their opinions. Those who do have a sense of the worth of their talents find that the opportunity for fulfillment almost never comes.

Before listening to the voices of "traditional poor" rural women it is important to remember that 58 percent of the rural population is solvent and living in some degree of affluence. The other 42 percent is either the growing group of "new poor," whose homes are lost to foreclosures, or the long-term poor. This essay will focus on rural poverty by looking at the "traditional poor"; it will not discuss rural living—which would demand concern with the nonpoor and many of the "new poor" as well.

Hearing the Voices of the "Traditional Poor"

The children of the "traditional poor" often have bad teeth and swollen bellies brought on by malnutrition. Poor health and the lack of proper clothing often contribute to their poor attendance at school. Growing up with the same limitations and the same myopic view of their parents, they complete the vicious circle: the "hollow-eyed syndrome."

The stories recorded in this essay come from women who are products and perpetuators of that syndrome. Living in the Midwest on farms or in small towns of less than 2,500 population, these women bear witness to the isolation, loneliness, and lack of education and marketable skills that characterize the "traditional poor" in rural America today. They speak of their personal relationships with grandparents, parents, spouses and in-laws, children and babies, friends, adversaries, and lovers. They share their experiences with domestic violence, alcoholism, high prices, and poor housing.

We Got Something Special

I was a little hellraiser from the start from what Mom says. She got divorced when I was three. She married my stepdad then and we moved to a house where we had no plumbing. There was an outhouse and we had to pump our own water. We didn't have no bathtub and we used to have to take baths inside a sink.

I knew my real dad since I was eight or nine. I get in touch with him once in a while now. I've got one real sister and one real brother and a stepbrother and a stepsister. I'm the oldest.

My stepdad didn't treat us really like we were his own. We liked to work on the farm and there was a big yard. I didn't get along with my stepbrother especially. He would pick on me and I'd get in trouble and spanked and sent to bed without any supper and he'd get off scot free.

My stepdad beat us all the time. Like with my real brother. He'd take him and just beat him. He tried to run away quite a few times. I just left a lot. Once the folks did send the police after me to bring me home.

Gramma is the main one who really took care of me a lot. I really care a lot about her. If it wasn't for her and my real dad I don't think we'd know half the things we do. That's how we learned to butcher chickens and cut up hogs.

We have a lot of aunts and uncles that have farms. Every once in a while they'd get together and butcher like fifty roosters and we'd have a great big party and everybody gets drunk and has fun. You'd have to make sure you got everything done first. Sometimes they'd get a little pie-eyed wild. You'd get an extra leg or gizzard later on because they didn't know what they was doing.

Mom's getting to the point where she is drinking pretty heavily. She started that when I was in ninth or tenth grade. She'd stand there and watch him beat me. I didn't like to go home. He'd just feel like doing it. Mom, she wasn't very faithful. He'd beat her up and then he'd beat us up. I knew it was illegal and a lot of people tried to do something but he'd go and threaten 'em. He always used to tell everybody I was pregnant when I was fifteen. I feel sorry for him. I really think he belongs in an insane asylum. I think they should put both him and my mom there.

His father, he used to beat his wife. His oldest sister is in an insane asylum 'cause she's kooky. His father used to take advantage of her and it drove her crazy. My dad's proud of it. The boys got away with everything and the girls got beat.

Now I got somebody who loves me and doesn't beat me. I've known Ronnie since fifth grade. He moved away though. I didn't see him again until last May. He was going out with somebody else then. Then in January, it was January 4th, we ran into each other again. We got married February 17th. We started going together January 16th and he asked me to marry him January 24th. I thought he was kind of dingy, but I guess it was love at first sight. I loved him right away. It was kind of scary because something usually happens when I love someone. But we got something special.

It's my mom that's hurting us. I want my boy to know his gramma. But if I keep thinking about how she treated us and how she didn't care if her husband raped me, then it don't hurt so much.

They Say the First Hundred Years Are Worst

I was born on the farm June 13, 1921, and I was a farm girl. I lost my mother when I was five years old. I was never adopted because my dad would never sign papers, but I drifted here and there, whoever would have me. Dad left me with strangers he knew because he used to work for them. He was a wood chopper. I stayed with them 'til I was fourteen years old, worked for my board and room. They didn't send me to school. They kept me home to work instead. I cooked breakfast and packed my own dinner before I left and lots of time I was there alone just with the dog. I carried in the wood and water and had the cows to milk.

Then my sister got married and took me in with her. I baby-sat for her until I was sixteen years old and then I went out on my own. I got married when I was seventeen and had two children. But I lost my first guy in the air force and I stayed single and by myself for a long, long time. He was shot down in a plane and never seen the baby. I had dates but I never had the urge to marry again for a long time; I don't know why. I had bad luck the first time; I thought I probably would again. I was a waitress for a while but I didn't like that because I never liked being around too many strangers. They say you get used to it, but I didn't stay long enough to find out. I felt lost, lost. My brother adopted and took care of my little boy for me, until he was old enough to go out on his own. When he started high school, he was on his own and went to war, got married, and had his own family.

I wasn't much of a traveler. I would have liked to be, but I didn't have no one to go with me. But now that I'm older I don't even care; I don't have the money still.

I feel more at home in a small town, but they're not as friendly as they are supposed to be. If you need a helping hand or anything, they're more independent. My husband died from the lungs closed up and when I worked in the nursing home up here to pay off the funeral bills, I seen lots of people die when their lungs fill up. That's it and they're gone. You put the blanket over them. It was so soon after losing my own husband so I couldn't take it any more.

I'm used to being alone again now after six more years of it. It seems like part of you is gone, though. I still miss this one. It's been six years looking around and no one to talk to. No one's there to see.

I just can't find no one in this town. This is a family town. I'm too old for marriage now anyway. This town is all husbands and wives. If I had a car I could take off but nothing in this town. You got to know it can't be happiness all the time. A person's never really ready to be alone. But I'll survive; they say the first hundred years are the worst.

You Got a Breeze up Here

The folks had a farm first, and then they had ten acres in town. I suppose there was one hundred people lived in the town. I was the only child. Mom's about seventy now and my dad was older. They didn't get along, fought like cats and dogs. They got divorced and then they got remarried again. They were both stubborn.

I was a loner. I didn't finish high school. I quit. I finished up in night school. I was about eighteen when I first got married. He drank a lot. We was only married about two or three years. Long enough. We had two children. I didn't get along with my parents too good and they didn't give me any sympathy. Then after the baby was born they got real possessive, like he was theirs. Well, he was mine, but I didn't have nothing to say about it.

Joe was eight years older than I was. It was all right when he was sober. He was a real nice guy. But when he got to drinking and got after me it made it pretty rough and he got mean. You'd wonder when they come home from work or something, well are they gonna be drunk or are they gonna be sober? We only had one car and he had to take it.

Any woman getting beat up by her husband, I'd say, "Don't take it; leave." After Joe would sober up he'd say, "I'm sorry, I won't do it anymore," but then it would be the same thing. It was most usually just one a week. I don't bruise that easy anyway. He hit me in the back I think. He tried to choke me a few times. The worst part of it was, he was really a nice guy when he was sober. But he'd get in trouble and we'd have to pay a fine. It cut down on groceries.

I got my divorce and got married maybe five or six years later. I moved away. That time I didn't have any friends. I just kept going. If you can't make it any different then you might as well just live with it.

Now that I'm out here I'm just as happy to stay here on the farm. Well, I like to go to the mission church. Outside of going to town, I'd just as soon stay here.

Out here it's peaceful. You got a breeze up here. I've got my garden and I had pigs and chickens. I had pigs last summer. Three. I sold 'em. One was gave to me; she was real skinny. They were crippled. We butchered one. We got an old junky freezer for thirty-five dollars. The lid won't stay shut; you got to put something on top of it. But as long as it runs and keeps cold, that's all I care about. I've got five or six chickens left now. We had seventeen and the mink came around and killed 'em. We've got four dogs. They keep your strangers away.

If you work your food stamps right, you got enough. We had a lot of beef hearts at eighty-nine cents a pound and turkey legs too. We didn't have enough money for Christmas presents and I got worried but the church, they come through.

Now that I'm out here I don't care if I work or not. You can do your gardening and you got your house to do. I like being alone. That's the only way.

It's Just Amazing How He Works

. . . Come to find out, he was another one. We never got married. We lived together, which is bad, but he put me in a brand new three-bedroom double-wide trailer and went to work every day from nine to five. He got fired for taking money. Finally I got mad. We got kicked out of the trailer on Christmas Eve. He was a very smooth talker.

About that time the authorities decided that my son should be put where he'd get help. He was hyper. They carted him off to a research hospital, which is a wonderful institution if you are retarded. Glen had a very high I.Q. He was just overactive. He'd get to the point where he had so much energy he was uncontrollable. The first thing they did was put him on drugs. If he was good, he'd earn a pass.

One day I went to pick him up and he was naturally excited. They gave him a sleeping shot because he got too excited. When I got there I had to carry him out to the car. I carried him into the house and he slept all the time he was there. I carried him back out to the car and carried him back in and put him to bed. If he didn't have a pass, we'd stay there. But I know how I'd feel if I was put in a place like that.

Then I was going with this other fellow and I thought I was in love with him, but the feeling wasn't that much mutual. I had a girlfriend told me to go to a psychiatrist and they put me on drugs right away. One day I was very upset and I went and got the prescription filled and on my way back took the whole bottle. They pumped my stomach and put me in the mental hospital. I couldn't understand how some people are just absolutely filthy rich and here I'm struggling to get food on the table. If I have to buy a dress I feel guilty about it because I'm taking food out of their mouths.

Then I met my present husband. He had been through two tours in Vietnam, was wounded, and the government was not giving him a fair shake. He was explosive. He wouldn't really beat up on me, but he'd make shambles of the house. He'd have flashbacks.

We met some people from a spirit-filled church. He asked Jesus into his heart and got help. It'll be three years June 7th since he's had a drink. The Lord is dealing with him about his patience because sometimes he'll fly off. It's not directed at me, but it's because of financial pressure.

Jesus keeps us going, period. if we ask, He'll give it to us. If we have financial problems, we'll say, "Jesus, we need your help paying this bill." He'll tell us where to go and get the help. It's just amazing how He works. He don't ask how, why, or when. We just watch and see when He does it. He won't give you any more burdens than you can handle. We'll go down to the last cracker in the house, but He's not gonna let us go hungry. I know He's always here, right in the heart.

The Isolation of the Rural Poor

Most of the definitions of "rural" come from outside observations based on size of farm, agricultural production, occupation, population, or cultural content.[2] The advantage of the above stories is that they define a mentality. Speaking out of an island in the midst of their communities, these women give voice to the special isolation imposed by their rural environment.

A two-car family is most unusual for them. "If I had a car I could take off but nothing in this town." "We only had one car and he had to take it." Because of this mobility, the men have a social structure that allows them to have friends in the work force. The mores of the small town make no room for women in local taverns, but they struggle with alcoholism, "Mom's getting to the point where she's drinking pretty heavily." But men do gather in taverns for recreation. "Jim's out somewhere at the tavern. . . . I don't know how he can stand going down there. The same men, same stories." However, most of the women's social clubs in rural communities are composed of lifelong members and their married daughters. Little effort is made to recruit new members in these clubs, and newcomers soon learn that their sex is an inadequate qualification for membership. "Small towns are not as friendly as they are supposed to be."

Rural women are also isolated by an old cultural practice that keeps women separated from each other: competition for men's attention. One woman who moved into a small town a few years ago said she had made many male friends but no female friends because a single woman is seen as a threat to existing marriages. Women's main ties with other women tend to be within extended families.

Little opportunity for employment outside the home exists in communities where any attractive jobs will be given to residents of long standing. Even if jobs are available, women often feel awkward about accepting them. As one woman remarked, "I feel a woman's place is in the home. Sometimes she has to go out because of financial reasons. Out here most of the women don't work; there aren't many jobs for women." Any special contacts that might develop from friendships established at work are denied them. Lacking this kind of outlet, their world becomes increasingly monotonous, and the friends they have may only reenforce that monotony. "I could call Louise and listen as she goes on about her husband or the neighbors. . . . You'd think she hated life. of course she don't know this. I can't say anything. Maybe none of us can." Obviously monotony is the mother of withdrawal and lack of communication, which results in loneliness as a constant companion. Time hangs heavily. Drugs may be a passive way to swallow a "solution." "For loneliness, I take two Excedrin and go to bed." Or "I'm used to being alone. . . . It's been six years looking around and no one to talk to. No one's there to see." "That time I didn't have any friends. I just kept going." "I just can't find no one in this town." "I wasn't much of a traveler. . . . I didn't have no one to go with me." "I was a loner." "A person's never really ready to be alone."

The traditional antidote to loneliness is viewed as marriage or remarriage. Being single seems to be very frightening to rural poor women because it is against the norm and generally unacceptable. Many remarry soon after a breakup or a death. "This is a family town . . . This town is all husbands and wives."

Alcoholism and family violence go together. Few towns in rural America can claim a movie theater, but almost every town has several busy taverns. Drinking in these cultural centers starts in the morning among the old and unemployed. Particularly among the unemployed, the frustrations of poverty breed violence. A recurring theme is the belief that it is a man's prerogative to beat his wife.

This, combined with the hard facts of women's financial dependence on men, results in the women's belief that they have no alternative other than to "take it."

Child abuse is also a very evident part of the above pattern. "My stepdad beat us all the time. . . . His father, he used to beat his wife." "He was a real nice guy. But when he got to drinking and got after me, it made it pretty rough and he got mean." "He was explosive. He wouldn't really beat me up, but he'd make a shambles of the house. . . . he'll fly off. Usually it's not directed at me but it's because of financial pressure."

Sources of Help

While urban women may turn to medical, legal, or domestic-violence centers for help in times of family trouble, any organizational help a rural woman receives is apt to come from her church. Although not all churches fill these needs, some few have made notable strides in providing support for women threatened with physical violence and a sense of isolation. One of these, referred to as the "mission church" by a number of women interviewed, has become a gathering place for poor people from the surrounding five counties. This church is an island of matriarchal power in a very traditional patriarchal culture. Staffed by female volunteers, it provides a natural support system especially for the women of the area.

> I hope that my work at the Mission church will fill another void in my life. Okay, here I go a wishin'. I'd like to go into nursing or some kind of social work, but here again it's the financial situation. CETA was helping me in the division of vocational rehabilitation, but when we moved here they wouldn't help me anymore because I'm not "bananas" anymore [i.e. no longer classified as a mental patient]. I'm an unskilled person. I was working in a store a year ago and hurt my hip so now I'm stuck.

Even those churches that do not provide such specific support systems may be avenues of spiritual strength for women in disruptive situations. "We go to church. I think that helps a lot. When a person gets depressed you can pray and believe it's going to work."

Not all contacts of the rural poor with religious organizations are comforting. When a church established an outreach project in a back room of a church center where food and clothing were sold at reduced prices on Wednesday, the church experienced an exodus of many of its prominent members moving to the other "more respectable" church. Even in relatively successful situations involving natural helpers there are limits. Often personnel are not adequately trained in such specific areas as mental health to help the poor who come for assistance. As in any form of "residual welfare," decisions are made on an inside basis as to who is and is not deserving of help. Affluence and particular concepts of poverty go hand in hand with hostility and prejudice directed towards low-income people by their more fortunate fellow citizens. Often family size is an issue for judgment. "It's your own fault if you are poor; you are a freeloader." "The Lord is punishing you and has a lesson in store."

Natural helpers, churches, schools, and formal agencies that have successful intervention records are usually those that are aware of the cultural characteristics of the rural poor. Rural areas have serious shortages of adequate transportation, too little and substandard housing, scarce medical and mental-health services, and not enough professional staff. Distance and cost present difficulties for urban-based services to provide relevant outreach in rural areas. Few resources, both financial and staff, are available to focus on the problems. Stigmas exist in rural areas against people receiving formal help or letting their problems be known. Extreme self-reliance characterizes many rural residents. Middle-class intervention techniques are often meaningless to people who have problems created by long-term poverty and cultural attitudes. Since many of the rural poor do not have telephones and cannot afford subscriptions to newspapers, they have little knowledge of available services. Even when such knowledge is available, a woman whose time is primarily spent on survival tasks and seldom has a car at her disposal can hardly take advantage of those services.

Recently, these cultural difficulties have been compounded by the systematic reduction of funding of social services that were just beginning to be successful in their attempts to bring help to rural areas. In spite of such budgetary cutbacks, the heroic efforts of members of formal agencies have continued to sustain those whose daily existence calls out for attention. Home health care brings help into the home rather than expecting the ill and elderly to find an agency office in an urban setting. Hospices are emerging in rural as well as metropolitan centers to ease the physical, mental, and financial burdens of the terminally ill. Social workers now reside in rural areas, becoming members of the community, interacting with rural women as friends rather than clients whom they visit once a week in clinical settings. Domestic shelters and programs for women alcoholics in rural areas are pinpoints of light in a world characterized by darkness.

Ironically, the depressed economy has had a positive effect in the increased acceptance of women as workers outside the home. As relief agencies cut back and men lose jobs and farms, women who have had no real work experience and little formal education are finding jobs. Many of these jobs are menial, monotonous, and physically demanding. One farm woman cleans the lobbies of banks and business buildings; another works in a small factory producing medical supplies; and a third has found employment in a small factory producing farm machinery locally. Although the work is arduous, these women are making contacts outside the home and at least one of them has returned to school.

Perhaps the pressures of the economy are becoming a positive factor in breaking down the isolation and sense of low self esteem that have been so much a part of the rural life. In spite of such demeaning and demanding tasks, rural women still retain a certain resiliency—"I got something special." Perhaps one day they can have more than a breeze and a garden to be thankful for, and Sundays will not seem so long.

PART THREE

The Ties That Bind: The Social Reality of Poverty

Pay the gas bill and they'll shut off the phone. Do the laundry and the carfare for the dentist's gone. Buy the baby's diapers— and tell your older girl she'll have to skip her class trip because you can't give her bus or lunch money.

For poor women, life is a series of small Sophie's Choices, a painful, bitter, humiliating juggling act. To be poor in the United States today is to live between a rock and a hard place, day in and day out.

But if that isn't hard enough, society seems to insist on adding insult to injury. A fly on the wall in an unemployment line or social security office would hear very different tones and topics than one in a welfare department. For every woman whose survival is tied to government benefits and services but who must endure the snide barbs about her sex life, who must grit her teeth and smile when told how to raise her children, who must push and plead to obtain what she's entitled to receive by law, there's an aching question: Why do they hate me so?

Each essay in this section is an attempt to answer this question, to explore why we Americans seem to as a society have some sadistic streak, some deep-seated need to torment and punish poor people. While the previous section broke down the broad category of poor women into the diverse individuals who come to the end of the line from different places, the purpose of this section is to regroup them—but with a difference. The essays that follow probe beyond the varieties of poverty to uncover its deep similiarities and to expose the underlying tension that makes being poor in the United States such an awful burden.

The authors describe the price poor women pay for being living proof of the limits of the American dream. This is, after all, the nation where real life never quite measures up to its image. Long before television, immigrants heard that America was paved with gold, but instead they found teeming tenements, sweatshops, and prejudice. For every Horatio Alger, hundreds were left behind in the old neighborhood, wondering what they had done wrong. Today, if you're not a yuppie, you're left to wonder where you failed. Indeed, in a society that ties success to self-worth, self-hatred is one of poverty's most bitter burdens.

Another burden is being invisible. Today, from "Dallas" to "Dynasty," most Americans are fascinated with what life's like for the rich. Millions of us are glued to the screen to find out what they wear, drive, drink, and do everyday. Yet we walk quickly past the homeless woman curled around her shopping bags on a subway bench and look away; we drive past housing projects hoping the light will stay green.

These essays and accounts will focus on the ties that bind poor women, some that chafe, others that are lifelines. First, Janet Diamond, a former welfare mother, looks at poverty through her experience. If you're poor, says society, you'd best be the right mix of meek and proud, and you'd certainly best not laugh too much. In her wry style, Diamond dares to challenge this taboo, and with just the opposite mix of dignity and humor, to expose the complex feelings that poverty provokes and the role of laughter and other survival gear.

Next, Betty Mandell traces the history and underpinnings of welfare, to expose a system that was set up to fail its intended beneficiaries. In digging deep into the roots of proletarianism (which actually means "their wealth is their children") she unearths the elements of control that make the current U.S. welfare system totalitarian at its core.

In the next essay a group of women on welfare who together attended the College of Public and Community Service at the University of Massashusetts/Boston offer their "Report from the Front." The Advocacy for Resources for Modern Survival (ARMS) collective offers a firsthand glimpse of the pain of poverty at close range—from the literal anguish of going to a dentist where Medicaid doesn't cover anesthesia to what it's like to pull a shopping cart through a snowstorm because you've "squandered" the carfare taking your child to the hospital emergency room. Hardly a bleak tale of despair, each story is a powerful portrait of a survivor.

Anyone who spends ten minutes in a welfare office can testify as to who's there—women, on both sides of the desk. Ann Withorn takes a hard look at the relationship between these women who are locked in a duel with no winners and reveals the contradictory nature of human services—their punitive downside as well as their potential for forging a powerful, progressive alliance truly to support poor women, financially and emotionally.

Stephanie Golden then walks up to the homeless women whom so many others rush past with averted eyes. She reveals that far from a breed apart, many homeless women she came to know while working in a New York City shelter had simply "lost their jobs." In this essay, Golden makes a convincing case that what's normal for a grown woman becomes a self-destructive dependence when women are forced by circumstance to function alone in the world.

Finally, Margaret Cerullo and Marla Erlien probe beyond just economics to the deeper cultural subconscious core of the New Right's challenge to the welfare state. They explore why women are punished for daring to live beyond the pale, especially those who decide, for a complex set of reasons, to live without men. And they expose the roots of the judgments we make on those whom we cast outside the mainstream because they don't play by the rules.

"AND THE SKIES ARE NOT CLOUDY ALL DAY"
Confessions of a Welfare Mother Poster Girl

Janet Diamond

I'm in the welfare biz. Have been for twenty years. You might say poverty is my beat. And I love it. I love everything about it: love the people; love the work; love the anger and the laughter; love the game, the winning, and sometimes even the losing.

So this article is a valentine of sorts to those who have provided warmth, affection, and often inspiration as well as frustration, anger, and pain. It is an arena in which nothing is unimportant. The smallest triumphs are cause for celebration.

I am a bureaucrat. There, I've said it out loud and in public. Announcing you are a bureaucrat is a bit like confessing you never use dental floss. Many people do it, but few would admit it publicly. Before I was a bureaucrat, I was a welfare-rights organizer. Before that, I was a welfare mother. Of my three welfare careers, I spent the most time pursuing welfare eligibility. Of course, I still pursue a "welfare check." The difference is that now I get a lot more money and respect for my efforts, but I can't say I work any harder for it.

When I was on welfare, I thought of myself as a person, an individual in a particular circumstance: the mother of Christine, a Cambridge resident, the daughter of Bob and Mary, a student at

U.Mass/Boston. It was not until I began community organizing and political confrontation that I began to realize that I was a part of a statistical constellation: a point on a linear regression chart, a standard deviation. Imagine my consternation to discover that I was not a person at all but a coefficient!

When I would speak with my cohorts, my fellow y^2 variables, I would wonder how our rich complex lives could be so easily reduced to sets of A B. It seemed that everywhere we looked, someone was quantifying us. Budget analysts were cost-projecting us ("a 7 percent benefit increase will require a $6 million budget increase"). Sociologists were categorizing us ("43 percent have less than 2.3 children"). Politicians were analyzing our voting behaviors ("of the 42 percent who are registered voters, 83 percent are Democrats"). Even feminists were counting our numbers ("95 percent are single mothers living 43 percent below the poverty level").*

I decided to go to graduate school so that I could learn to play the game too. If I was going to be counted, then I wanted to count. Having penetrated the mystery of statistics, I feel qualified to announce that what I suspected is true—the emperor has no clothes on. Now he may be a perfectly good emperor, but nonetheless, he has no clothes on.

What do I mean by this riddle? Simply this. Statistical analysis has a valid place in the discussion and design of public policy. Decisions affecting millions of people and involving millions of dollars do require highly distilled data. Decisions based on numbers alone, however, will not respond to the moral imperative embodied in welfare policy and will not reflect the experience of one mother beholding her baby's first smile.

The reason over-reliance on numbers is dangerous is that we can lose sight of the reason we have a welfare system. Quantified data drains the life out of our mission. And the language of bureaucracy builds a comfortable wall between those who design policy and those affected by it. Lives are flexible and creative. Policy is rigid. People live in families. Policy describes assistance units.

If you had to tell someone you were terminating her only source of income, whom would you rather tell, a head of a household or a mother? This is perhaps a radical notion, but I believe bureaucrats

* Some of the statistics in this essay are real and some I made up, but I am not going to tell you which is which.

have a responsibility to feel a bit of the joy and pain felt by their clients. All the statistical back flips and linguistic sommersaults in the world will not change reality. Bureaucrats, administrators, and policy makers must choose between deadened, disassociated emotions and risky but rewarding involvement.

What are the benefits of stepping beyond the safe (but boring!) confines of statistical analysis? The answer is that you might get to know some wonderful people. You might have the time of your life.

When I was a welfare-rights organizer, we spent a lot of time developing a media image. To that end, we created a file of "horror stories," which we called Central Casting, a card catalogue of individuals listing demographic details and specific welfare experiences. When a reporter would call us looking for an Hispanic family of three in western Massachusetts who had recently had its food stamps cut off, we would place a few calls and produce an interview subject. The system represented equal parts of cynicism, exploitation, and hard necessity. We were very good and received a lot of press coverage.

At times, when we would think about what we were doing, we would look guiltily over our shoulders and giggle. We were amazed at our own audacity and stunned at the ease with which a small group of welfare mothers such as ourselves could reach and affect public opinion. Were the horror stories true? Yes they were. Did they reflect the totality of that person's life? Of course not.

The secret we hid so carefully from the public eye was that we often had fun, that sometimes we were frivolous, silly, and occasionally even extravagant. That was why we felt guilty when we giggled. After all, lives were at stake. People could starve to death. Welfare policy is a lot of things to a lot of people, but no one thought it was funny.

So when we would return from the State House, having won a round in the long legislative process toward passage of a bill to improve benefits, we might chip in our laundry money to buy a bottle of champagne. Later that week, of course, we knew we would all be washing clothes by hand. The kids needed clean clothes so the wash would get done. Frivolity did not include irresponsibility. But for that one day we could be just like everyone else. We could have some fun.

It's interesting that even as I write this, as a genuine tax-paying, self-supporting citizen, I feel the old twinges of guilt. I can still see the frowning faces and stern wagging fingers of disapproval. Have I blown the cover on current and future welfare moms? Have I exposed the unworthiness of an entire population and single handedly proven Charles Murray right?†

Life on welfare is hard, but it is not miserable all day every day. Welfare recipients do not go around thinking of themselves as "Welfare Recipients" except when they have to call or visit the welfare office or when they read about their statistical selves in the newspaper. Welfare recipients are defined in very specific ways, but recipients do not define themselves by welfare criteria. They are mothers, students, waitresses, lovers, softball pitchers, aunts, and much much more.

It seems, however, that there are only two public responses to welfare: outrage and pity. Liberals and conservatives alike romanticize welfare recipients. One is either the object of scorn or sympathy. The ugly undercurrent of both responses is contempt.

Once, a group of us were interviewed for "60 Minutes" on the subject of welfare fraud. We groomed ourselves very carefully for the taping session. We wore what we called our State House uniforms—clean, ironed, plain cotton blouses and skirts, no jewelry, clean hair simply styled, no visible makeup. We knew that we had to walk a thin line between too shabby ("they're slobs") and too well dressed ("they're queens"). The week after the piece aired, three viewer letters were read. One speculated we must be actresses, not real welfare mothers. The other two expressed outrage at my "designer" eyeglasses. We all were amazed and I was distraught.

It had never occurred to me that my eyeglasses would be the subject of public debate. My glasses are extensions of my cornea. I look through them, not at them. What about our statements? We had expected disagreement with our positions but not with our appearances. I have come to understand what had happened. We were guilty of making an attractive presentation. We had let our wit and humor surface. We were intelligent, articulate, and animated. We had attached real personalities to the flat and despised term, "welfare mother."

Because we defied the stereotypes, neither frail, sad urchins nor

† Charles Murray is the author of *Losing Ground* (New York: Basic Books, 1984).

boozy, stupid child neglectors, we had somehow jeopardized the thin wall between us and them, and the public was ready to beat us back to our proper place. The crime we had committed was that while our situations were difficult, we clearly did not see ourselves as suitable material for pity or contempt.

For years, in all my various welfare careers, I have heard it said that "We have a right to be treated with dignity." There is something wrong with this expression. Dignity is a personal quality, not a gift. It cannot be a right because it is not dependent upon someone else allowing it. We do have a right to walk in the rain with smiles on our faces without having someone else walk up and say, "Get that smile off your face. You don't deserve to be happy." A thing like that can ruin your whole day. Enough of them can ruin your whole life, and no one has the right to ruin your life just because he or she thinks your happiness is inappropriate.

I've had a lot of good times with welfare mothers. I am proud to be an alumna and permanent member of the sorority. I can't think of another group of people with whom I'd rather be associated. Recently I attended a conference on welfare and education at a very prestigious university. Educators, congressmen, economists, and welfare administrators, and assorted academicians presented carefully researched papers in mahogany-paneled rooms. Toward the end of the second day I heard a voice in the back of the room, a student asking a question. The cutting edge under the gentle, hesitant tones struck a familiar note. I strained to catch a glimpse and saw a young blond woman, intense, leaning forward on the edge of her chair. My pulse quickened and I smiled—a welfare mother in our midst!

As soon as the session broke, I left my seat and beckoned her to follow me out of the room. She and I and a fellow student welfare mother we picked up along the way adjourned to a cafeteria and for two hours held an animated, sometimes heated, seminar on welfare policy. We exchanged war stories as veterans often do and told secrets about ourselves. On my way home thinking about the conference, I realized that my sense of fulfillment was almost entirely the result of those two hours.

All three of us had felt a bit like ants at a picnic hating to disturb delicate hypotheses with rude personal experience. After two days of listening to the hushed awe in the voices of speaker after speaker as they pronounced "these people" to be heroes, we needed to touch base with reality lest we start believing in our sainthood. After a few minutes together we had remembered that, after all, "girls just wanna have fun"—and to earn as much money as men.

The burden of welfare is far more than the burden of poverty. It is the burden of being a special case, of feeling that special rules apply to your life. Welfare mothers are very conscious of being made to feel that the price of that measly check is forfeiture of the pursuit of happiness. It is not enough, it seems, to be in poverty. You must also be miserable. If you are not miserable, then you are not deserving. So we learn to hide our laughter, ambition, intelligence, and dreams in basement cafeterias and present only our downtrodden faces to the public.

In spite of public censure, welfare mothers graduate from school, get decent jobs, watch their children achieve, make good lives for themselves, and marry men they love. I feel that I am now in a position to make that process a little bit less of an uphill struggle. But what I now give is small compared to what I receive in return. Welfare mothers continue to be my inspiration, not because they survive, but because they dare to dream. Because when you're a welfare recipient laughter is an act of rebellion, and I can sometimes catch those faces smiling in the rain.

WELFARE
Death by Exhaustion

Betty Reid Mandell

To most American newspaper readers, Aid to Families with Dependent Children (AFDC) is a "problem." Readers of liberal papers may conclude that AFDC grants are too low; conservative papers suggest that welfare recipients are lazy parasites and AFDC should be drastically cut or eliminated. If radical papers mention AFDC at all, they are often confused and vacillating about the "correct" position.

In Europe, on the other hand, a variety of newspapers, including the French daily *Le Monde,* yield a very different picture. There are occasional references to the family allowance—a government benefit families receive regardless of income—and debates about whether to increase it, which the Mitterand government did in France, or decrease it, which the Thatcher government did in Britain.

Why is AFDC so uniquely American? Why doesn't the United States have a family allowance like most other industrialized nations? Why don't American trade unions adopt AFDC as their

Thanks to Diane Dujon for this title.

cause, the way trade unionists and socialists in Europe and Canada defend the family allowance against government cuts?

At least part of the answer lies in the different historical development of the European and American welfare states. In general, the European labor movement has been stronger and demanded more comprehensive and universal social welfare benefits. What's more, the European labor movement demanded these from government through labor-oriented political parties, while American unions more often bargained for benefits from employers, through individual unions.

Means-Tested vs. Universal Programs

Typically, there are two kinds of transfer programs. One is called "universal," the other "means-tested." Universal programs such as Social Security support people with a certain status, regardless of their income. Thus, all people who paid into the program, rich and poor alike, are entitled to receive Social Security payments when they retire, become disabled, or become dependents of deceased, retired, or disabled workers. Social Security covers more than 90 percent of U.S. citizens.

Means-tested programs are only for people whose income and assets fall below a certain low, official "standard of need." Because these programs are only for the poor, they carry a stigma. While universal payments were never meant to provide a full income or even a comfortable living, they pay more than means-tested grants.

Two other terms often used to distinguish between social welfare programs are "institutional" and "residual." Institutional programs recognize certain human needs such as illness, disability, pregnancy, child care, old age, and death as a predictable part of life and make provisions to meet those needs. For example:

> Paid maternity leaves range from three months in Denmark to nine months in Sweden to three years in Hungary. In Sweden, both the father and mother are eligible, and benefits can be prorated to cover full- or part-time leaves. . . . As for substitute child-care arrangements, most children between three and six years of age in European

> nations attend all-day preschool programs associated with the regular educational system. This is true whether or not mothers are employed, since Europeans consider such experience beneficial and healthful for children. . . .[1]

Residual programs, on the other hand, are built on the assumption that certain needs are unpredictable and temporary. The Aid to Dependent Children (ADC)* program, for example, was shaped by policy makers who assumed that the population it served was small and marginal and would gradually wither away. State-sponsored General Relief programs for unemployed people without dependent children carry the assumption that unemployment is a temporary, unpredictable, and undesirable condition, which should not be encouraged by overly generous transfer payments.

Other industrialized nations have larger institutionalized programs and smaller residual programs than the United States does, which they pay for out of more steeply graduated taxes. It is particularly to women's advantage to expand institutionalized social welfare programs, since women depend upon transfer income much more than men do. Consider the statistics:

- In 1982, more than one half of U.S. families headed by women received AFDC.[2]
- Before they are eighteen, one third of children today are likely to live in homes headed by women receiving welfare benefits.
- Four to six million displaced homemakers fall between AFDC and Social Security.
- One of every two women can expect to be widowed by sixty-five, and one third of all widows live below the poverty line. In 1982, women over age sixty-five had median incomes of $5,365, about $700 above the poverty level, while men's median income was $9,188.[3]

* The program was not called AFDC until 1962, when states were given the option of including unemployed parents. Today, only twenty-four states have the AFDC-UP (Unemployed Parent) program.

The Shaky Foundations of ADC

The framers of the ADC programs were badly mistaken in their belief that it would be a temporary program. It did not wither away as they had hoped; rather it grew, and since its beginnings it humiliated women and children, kept them poor, and never included all those who were eligible. Policy makers' conceptual blindness about women and children prevented them from planning an adequate and dignified program for them. Income transfers for families were constructed according to a male view of the proper place of women and children. Deanne Bonnar calls this the "Genesis paradigm" for women[4], the assumption in the biblical Book of Genesis that women are weak and easily tempted to do evil and, as a consequence, are to be ruled over by men and are to bring forth children "in sorrow." In regard to children, I would add another paradigm—the "prole paradigm." The Latin root meaning of "proletariat" is "people who have no other wealth than their children." In ancient Rome, "prole" meant offspring. When children's labor was valuable as apprentices or wage workers, they were their fathers' property. As immigration to the United States increased the available work force and the number of farms declined, children were no longer as valuable for cheap or unpaid labor. Then it became cheaper to maintain them in their own homes than to pay for their care in institutions or foster homes.

It is probably no coincidence that agitation against child labor occurred at about the same time as agitation for a Mothers' Pension, the state-sponsored income-maintenance program for poor women and children on which ADC was modeled. Some historians argue that once children were excluded from the work force and became financial liabilities, they were increasingly awarded to their mothers.[5] Until the beginning of the twentieth century, mothers had no legal right to custody of their children, and by 1930, nine states had still not granted mothers guardianship rights.[6] At the point when mothers began to gain ownership of their children, the state began to take grudging and limited responsibility for supporting children whose fathers were absent.

The framers of ADC could not see women as independent of men, and so they shaped income-transfer programs according to their conception of women's proper relationship to men. Women, they believed, should be married to men and caring for their husbands and children, without wages. Men, in turn, were expected to earn wages to support their wives and children. Since the beginnings of relief in the seventeenth-century English Poor Law, various moralistic criteria have been used to divide the poor into the "worthy" and the "unworthy." Men's worthiness was heavily influenced by their relationship to the work force, while a woman's worth was more likely to be determined by her relationship to a man as well as her relationship to the work force. A woman could hardly be blamed if her husband died, but if the husband deserted her or she got divorced, a censorious finger was likely to point at her, and it most certainly would point at her if she had a child without being married.

Therefore, the more dignified income-transfer program was provided for widows of deceased wage earners. Title II of the Social Security Act was for widows and dependents of retired or deceased workers in covered employment. The amount of the benefit was related to the amount of money the husband had earned. In 1950, divorced mothers who had been married twenty years were entitled to benefits, and still later the twenty-year requirement was reduced to six years. Although survivor's benefits are not ample enough to lift one third of their recipients out of poverty,[7] the benefits are larger than AFDC and the program carries no stigma. Recipients are given benefits as a right, and no attention is paid to their "worthiness." Yet, despite the fact that there are more women and children in this program than in AFDC (35,000 more in 1960), the program receives little public attention.[8]

So strongly were the planners of ADC convinced that women should not be divorced or give birth to babies out of wedlock that they did not carefully examine the population that ADC was designed to serve. If they had, they would have realized that ADC would not be a small and temporary program.

> The 1930 census showed that more than two million children lived in female-headed households—six percent of the population. . . . Seventy-one percent of female heads were widowed, and 29 percent were divorced, deserted, separated, or never married. More critical than this, however, is that for female-headed households with children under 10 years only 52 percent were widowed and 48 percent were divorced, separated, or never married. This dramatic difference represents, in part, the increasing likelihood of death of the father as

> his family grows older. Such figures should have indicated to planners which group of women would have the greatest need for assistance. Had policy makers looked at female-based families carefully they might have seen that ADC over time would be increasingly composed of the divorced and separated mothers simply because their period of need was longer.[9]

The planners also did not attempt to project future trends, ignoring the implications of rising divorce rates. More recently, planners of AFDC have also ignored the implications of rising numbers of out-of-wedlock births. These conceptual blinders, however, were not due to ignorance of the facts. The data were available. The neglect of women was due partly to their lack of political clout. During the 1930s, there were large organized groups, including unions and the Townsend movement, fighting for old age pensions. At that time, single mothers had no organized voice and no group willing to fight for them.

The story of Title IV of the Social Security Act (ADC) is quite different from the story of Title II. It is a saga of unending official harassment and humiliation of recipients and unending poverty. Policy makers seem to have used the sexual double standard, dividing women into "pure mother" and "loose prostitute." Social Security beneficiaries were the "pure mothers," while ADC recipients were the "loose women."

> Thus, when the State entered the role of partner with a husbandless mother, it entered as if standing in for the husband, and it exacted from her the same behavior that men could exact from their wives. Support was exchanged for clean homes, careful supervision of children, and sexual monogamy. Concerns about sexual behavior were so strong that mothers were denied aid if they took in male boarders. Taking male boarders was one way widows with children could stay in their own homes but mere suspicion of wrong doing was all that was required to deny aid.[10]

That sexual harassment, begun with the Mothers' Pension programs, continued unabated in the ADC and AFDC programs, the most notable example being the "midnight raids" of the 1950s and 1960s when welfare investigators would burst into a mother's home to try to catch her living with a man. Only when welfare recipients organized were they able to check this practice, which was struck down by the Supreme Court.

Finally, the framers of the ADC program assumed that women

should always be available to do the dirty work. Often this involved domestic work, but it also involved other kinds of low-paid service, factory, and farm work. The early Mothers' Pension programs traditionally expected women to do family laundry in exchange for their support.[11] Bell notes:

> The gilt-edged widows, therefore, worked as domestics or took in washings to supplement their meager grants. . . . One early pamphlet describing the program (Mothers' Aid) has a cover illustration of a fatigued washerwoman with three scrawny children pulling at her skirts.[12]

The ADC and AFDC programs continued the tradition of keeping recipients in low-wage labor. Decades after the picture of that exhausted laundress appeared, what a shock of recognition we got when, in response to welfare recipients' activism, U. S. Senator Russell Long complained that he could no longer find a maid to iron his shirts!

Mothers' Aid, the Mother of ADC

The current AFDC program was built on a shaky foundation of Victorian moralism, laid in place in the states' Mothers' Aid (or Mothers' Pension) programs. The Mothers' Pension movement† was spearheaded by the Progressive Party in the early twentieth century. This movement led the first White House Conference on the Care of Dependent Children to recommend in 1909 that no child be removed from home because of poverty. Until then, and even to a lesser degree for several decades after, pauper children were put in almshouses, indentured out to work, sold to families, or placed in institutions that often put them in "free boarding homes" where they worked for their keep—boys usually doing farm work, and girls always doing domestic work. Although most child-welfare officials would deny that children today are taken from their homes because of poverty, a recent study showed that

† The women who wanted the program were eager to have it called a Mothers' Pension rather than Mothers' Aid, as "pension" carried less stigma and more a feeling of entitlement. (Abbott, p. 231)

the Reagan administration's AFDC cuts have forced some parents to place their children in foster care:

> The ultimate dilemma facing families is between family stability and economic survival. Some parents in this state have actually surrendered their children to the Department of Social Services in hopes of ensuring their physical survival. In fact, some parents have had to choose which of their children to put in foster care because welfare benefits are insufficient to maintain the entire family. They are forced to make a "Sophie's Choice" of the 1980s.[13]

Indeed, there is still a strong link between poverty and foster care. Most children in foster care are poor, and there is some evidence that the higher a state's AFDC family grant, the fewer children there are in foster care.[14]

New Jersey was the first state to establish Mothers' Aid in 1910. Other states joined in gradually until by 1934, all states except Georgia and South Carolina had some kind of Mothers' Aid law. It claimed to avoid the stigma of the poor laws. Some states even passed laws barring recipients from being considered paupers. Yet the stigma that poor laws embedded into poor people like asbestos fibers went on from Mothers' Aid to the present AFDC. State legislators who passed Mothers' Aid played the age-old game: "Who are the deserving poor?" Widows were considered the most deserving of all mothers; women with disabled husbands were a close second. But women whose husbands had deserted or were in prison scored very high on the stigma scale; unmarried mothers were excluded altogether. By 1934, only ten states and the District of Columbia had Mothers' Aid laws including all categories of mothers.[15]

Back then, many professional social workers displayed moralistic bias toward the "deserving" poor. Homer Folks, secretary of the New York Charities Aid Association, thought only widows could regard public charity as a right.[16]

Mary Richmond, renowned pioneer of social work theory, opposed the entire program, shocked at the idea of "public funds not to widows only, mark you, but to private families, funds to the families of those who have deserted and are going to desert!"[17]

Even some of Mothers' Aid's proponents doubted poor people's ability to run their own lives without professional help. Concern for the poor's needs became fused with mistrusting them and—

viola!—a program run by professionals. Grace Abbott deplored the fact that "In many counties, the need of a professional staff had not been appreciated." She did not hestitate to call for investigations to establish "the need of the mother and her moral and physical fitness to maintain the home" and recommended social services to help mothers obtain resources.[18]

Just as with AFDC today, grants were almost always below an adequate subsistence level and varied greatly among localities and states—from an average family grant of $69.31 a month in Massachusetts in 1931 to $4.33 in Arkansas.[19] Yet Mothers' Aid was higher than relief under the Poor Law, just as AFDC today, though inadequate, is higher than General Relief. Still, its opponents argued, it would break the state, and some feared it would weaken poor people's characters to have so much money to spend. One 1912 social-agency director protested; "Where an average of $23.28 per month is provided for each family, temptations come to spend money recklessly or foolishly, even in some of the better families."[20]

Social Security Act

Massive discontent and protest movements during the Depression led to the first large-scale federal income-maintenance programs; first, through direct relief under the Federal Emergency Relief Act of 1933, then through the Social Security Act of 1935. It contained a mix of universal and means-tested programs. What is popularly called "Social Security" was the universal portion—Old Age Insurance, a pension plan for people sixty-two or over, financed by payroll tax and employer contributions.[21] This part of the Social Security Act never carried the stigma of the means-tested portions. Although it is not strictly insurance, calling it so removes the stigma. People also feel that it is their right since they pay for it directly from their paychecks. While one's salary helps to determine one's Social Security check, no one receives less than $122 a month,[22] and most people receive back a lot more than they paid in.

Women's average benefit is lower than men's, though, because of women's lower wages. Still, widows receive more from Social Security than from AFDC. In 1978, widows with two children received average Social Security benefits of $582.80. Contrast this with the AFDC program, in which

> in January 1981, the monthly maximum payment to a family of three persons with no other income was $96 in Mississippi, $117.81 in wealthy Texas, $263 in Ohio, $425 in neighboring Michigan, and $463 in California. . . .Except in California, no cost-of-living adjustments are required. . . . Between 1970 and mid-1981, in constant dollars, average benefits declined over the nation by almost 20 per cent and the rate of decline increased dramatically toward the end of the decade. Even with food stamp bonuses added, benefits dropped by 9 per cent.[23]

The means-tested portions of the Social Security Act included public assistance for four different categories:

1. *Aid to Dependent Children (ADC)* for dependent children whose fathers were absent, dead, disabled, deserted, imprisoned, or not married to their mothers. (Mothers were not included in the grant until 1950. Evidently officials agreed with Apollo in Aeschylus' play *The Eumenides*, who argues that Orestes was not guilty of killing his parent because "mothers" are only incubators—"the parent is he who mounts.")
2. *Old Age Assistance (OAA)* for retirees sixty-five and over who were not covered by Old Age Insurance or who received lower OAI benefits than the OAA grant.
3. *Aid to the Blind (AB)* for legally blind persons of any age.
4. *Aid to the Permanently and Totally Disabled (APTD),* for people of any age unable to work due to disability.

In 1974, all these categories, except AFDC, were federalized, under the Social Security Administration, and named Supplemental Security Income (SSI). The federal government pays states a uniform amount, which states may supplement.

Like the cheese that stands alone in the children's game of "Farmer in the Dell," AFDC now stands alone like an unprotected orphan, the sole remaining means-tested public assistance program with federal-state matching funds. (General Relief, the welfare program for so-called able-bodied people without dependent children, is entirely state and/or locally funded.)

The federal government only partially sheltered poor women and their children with ADC. While it gave states matching funds, it left administration to the states with only the loosest guidelines.

From the start, states had vastly different grant sizes and administrative methods.

While ADC was an improvement over Mothers' Aid, progress moved at a snail's pace—and with a snail's slime. The contradictions built into Mothers' Aid continued, and the sources were the same: devaluing women and children; stigmatizing the poor; confusion about the place of women in the work force; moralism; the constant push of state and business interests to cut social costs and to discipline the work force; the powerlessness of the poor, particularly women and children; and racism.

Mistrust of the Poor

When ADC began, there was much debate about whether mothers should simply be given money without social services, like Social Security checks, or whether social workers should administer the program. Social workers urged that they should be involved, some of them arguing that the poor could not be trusted to spend their money wisely. Some observers thought social workers, part of a middle class hard hit by the Depression, wanted to be involved because they needed jobs.

Another 1930s debate still continues: can the poor be trusted with cash, or should they be given vouchers for food, shelter, clothing, household furnishings, and utilities? For the most part, proponents of cash won out; women receive grants in the form of semimonthly checks, mailed to their homes.

Yet, although recipients receive basic grants in cash, they receive many other benefits in kind. Most emergency help comes as vouchers or authorization to purchase food stamps, rather than as cash. Food stamps supplement the grant, and before food stamps there was surplus food. Giving food stamps rather than cash reflects some mistrust of poor people's ability to shop wisely, but food stamps also aid farmers by assuring a market for food and help grocery stores and banks, whom the government pays to process them.

Many states had required Mothers' Aid recipients to come to a welfare office to pick up their check. A Massachusetts Department of Welfare report on 1933 to 1934 described the overwhelming press of applicants for relief, which led to mailing the checks. But the victory was only partial. Uneasy at the idea of simply mailing checks, welfare officials decided to "check up on the mothers in their homes."[24] Workers regularly investigated recipients to determine continuing eligibility. Today, in states like Massachusetts, "redeterminations" are conducted every three months. Many welfare workers were called "investigators." While some workers interpret regulations flexibly, others, holier than the Pope, submit applicants to unending harassment, often egged on by the federal government. Recent "sex questionnaires" probed women's intimate sex lives, ostensibly to determine their children's paternity. In Massachusetts, AFDC recipients and their allies were strong enough to stop this practice. Some states have recently devised Monthly Income Reporting, a long form that recipients must fill out and return every month to remain eligible. In every state with this form, AFDC rolls have gone down. That is one function of such elaborate requirements, to make receiving welfare so difficult and uncomfortable that people don't apply or get off welfare in disgust and fear.

When large numbers of recipients make concerted, insistent demands, though, welfare bureaucracies, like all others, make some concessions to their constituencies. During the Depression, officials no longer insisted that women pick up their checks in person. Likewise, militant Welfare Rights activists of the late 1960s often got cumbersome regulations lightened. For example, a liberal New York City welfare director did away with investigations and substituted a simple "declaration of need," an experiment that ended about the same time that militancy did.

Investigations, including home visits, began under Mothers' Aid. At that time, the main purpose was to determine whether mothers were fit to care for their children. In 1911, the Mothers' Aid law in Illinois said that if a probation officer established a parent as unfit, the children should be put in "some suitable State institution," training or industrial school, or private charitable institution. Only "fit" mothers could receive Mothers' Aid. A 1932 New Jersey Mothers' Aid law had similar provisions.[25]

Besides establishing eligibility, home investigations maintained the pervasive threat that the state could remove children if a worker accused the mother of neglect. States often wrote "suitable home" regulations into Mothers' Aid and ADC-AFDC laws, making welfare contingent on being a "fit" mother. These "suitable home" laws were often used to force women off welfare rolls into the low-wage labor market, particularly in Southern and other agricultural states, and to force unmarried and black mothers off the rolls.[26]

Recipients of Mothers' Aid, ADC, and AFDC can never forget the state's control over their lives, nor are they allowed to feel that the money is theirs by right. Although early Mothers' Aid laws in some states clearly distinguished Mothers' Aid from Poor Relief, giving Mothers' Aid higher status, anyone who suggested mothers had a constitutional right to money was quickly disabused of that notion by the courts. A Mrs. Rose Snyder of Washington sued that state in 1916, claiming that the equal protection clauses of both state and federal constitutions made it illegal to refuse her Mothers' Aid because her husband had abandoned her. The court countered unequivocally that

> the state may care for its indigent and poor in any manner it pleases. . . . Indeed, the state is under no legal obligation to care for its poor at all. While it undoubtedly has a moral obligation to do so, there is no such obligation as can be enforced in law. Such relief as it does provide is legally in the nature of a largess or bounty, which may be discontinued at the legislative will.[24]

Ever since, the state has continued to insist that it has no legal responsibility to honor any contract but a business contract involving private property. The social wage that the state gives women to reproduce the work force is very grudging indeed.

Part of mistrusting recipients includes declaring some recipients incompetent to run their own affairs and appointing a trustee to manage their welfare grant. Federal regulations specify the percentage of recipients for whom this is allowed. While still relatively small, this percentage was increased by the Reagan administration.

This message is not lost on applicants and recipients. They understand that they are not being welcomed to relief rolls. The stigma thus communicated keeps many who are entitled to relief from applying. This, of course, is that the government wants. The stigma is compounded by unattractive and crowded waiting rooms, and underfunded, understaffed, and overworked welfare departments, conditions that almost guarantee that a recipient will not receive dignified, thoughtful treatment. In Massachusetts recently, 180 AFDC cases was a "normal" case load. Officials tried to undercut even that limit by changing the "caseload" to a "workload" system, where workers handle who ever appears when they are on duty. Union bargaining has recently led to a return of the case-load system.

The stigma is best reinforced by the media's massive brainwashing job about welfare and welfare recipients. AFDC has drawn the nation's prejudices, about both the poor and women, like a lightning rod. Stories of lazy, cheating, promiscuous welfare moms proliferate like mosquitoes in a swamp. They help to keep workers slaving at any dirty job they can find rather than be called "a lazy welfare bum," and they help keep women sexually passive. This prejudice has been so successful that recipients themselves often share myths and develop an agonizing self-hatred about being on welfare. The welfare-rights movement of the late 1960s and early 1970s countered this atmosphere by declaring that families had a right to welfare. While the stigma continued, that movement helped many women to feel more confident about applying for and demanding their rights from welfare. The AFDC rolls increased dramatically during this period.[28]

The 1960s saw what the sociologist Herbert Gans called the "equality revolution."[29] Women, minorities, homosexuals, handicapped people, old people, and children began to believe they had entitlements and consequently to break out of their oppressed state. Reagan's former director of the Office of Management and Budget, David Stockman, told us, "There are no entitlements, period!" The Reagan administration can more easily dismantle the welfare state if people do not feel they are entitled to benefits. Social Security has been more resistant to the Reagan administration's tampering because people believe it's their right. The poor and oppressed must develop that sense before they can break out of their oppression.

The Stingy State

When the state agrees to care for the poor, it not only declares that it has no legal obligation to do so, but it also declares that it need not provide an adequate livelihood. A low grant helps to keep people in the low-paid labor market. This is what welfare scholars call the "principle of less eligibility." The grant shall be kept lower than the lowest paid job so that *any* job will pay better than welfare. The first ADC law specified that the amount of the grant must be "a reasonable subsistence compatible with decency and health." That clause was later deleted because the South feared that northern standards "would be forced on the South in providing for Negro and white tenant families."[30]

States use various devices to keep grants low. They set maximum amounts, set a low standard of need, give only a certain percentage of their "standard of need," cut down on what they will pay for, give no cost-of-living allowance or give low ones infrequently, cut back on child-care allowance and work expenses, and cut back on education and training programs.

The federal government uses some of the same devices. Reagan's 1981 Omnibus Reconciliation Act cut back child-care and work expense allowances, cut back on children's age of eligibility (teenagers must now work rather than attend college), set a limit on the eligibility levels, cut back the Work Incentive program, and made more stringent work requirements. These cuts, along with cuts in food stamps, housing subsidy, and Medicaid, terminated or reduced hundreds of thousands of families' benefits. The national May 1982 AFDC caseload was 8 percent smaller than the 1981 case load.[31] In Massachusetts, where a conservative state governor and welfare administrator were only too happy to cooperate with Reagan administration cuts, there was a 22 percent reduction in the AFDC case load.[32]

When ADC began, it combined services with income maintenance. Social workers were expected to counsel recipients and help them locate needed resources. In 1962, amendments funded "rehabilitation" services. Predictably, these did not have the sought-for result; they did not remove large numbers of recipients from the rolls. Follow-up studies of demonstration projects showed that expanded job opportunities, not services, reduced welfare rolls. Yet the assumption is that the poor are to blame for their poverty and need "rehabilitation." Child care is generally paid to help the mother work, not to give her some relief from household chores or to benefit the child.

Understandably, many recipients have mixed feelings about the services their social workers offer, often seeing them as merely disguised forms of social control. Many welfare activists during the 1960s and 1970s called for separation of services and income, which was done in 1974. The victory was bitter—there were precious few services to separate, and assistance-payments workers were given still heavier work loads, which increased the likelihood of their making errors. But rather than reduce their work load, the federal government stepped up an efficiency/accountability binge, threatening to cut off funds to states that did not reduce their "error rate." This "error rate" battle continues; if workers and states are inclined to be more humane, the federal government will punish them.

The state's stinginess is sometimes eroded a bit by grass-roots protest movements. In the 1930s and 1960s, grants and benefits increased in response to protest. When it subsided, cuts in benefits and increase in work programs resulted.[33] During the protests of the 1960s and 1970s, the welfare rolls increased dramatically; during the Reagan administration, the rolls decreased, and more stringent work programs were introduced.

Welfare and Work

People on the bottom rung of welfare are the so-called able-bodied unemployed. If they receive anything at all, it's General Relief, the last remnant of the old Poor Law. In the nineteenth century, they were called paupers. Officials have always been ambivalent about whether "able-bodied" mothers should stay home or enter the work force. As more women take jobs, pressure on AFDC mothers to work has increased. During the Depression, many people urged women to stay home so that men could have the available jobs. Some, including government officials, accused women of helping *cause* the Depression by working. In such a climate of opinion, the newly created ADC program did not require mothers to work. However, poor women did work during the Depression; 16 percent of heads of families involved in the WPA (Works Progress Administration) were women. Most took care of other people's children, and some early framers of ADC policy, including Grace Abbott, thought that was misguided; those women should instead be paid to care for their own children.[34]

"Able-bodied" unemployed men were excluded from ADC; the

state did not want a cushion that might save them from doing society's less desirable jobs. This led to an unresolvable contradiction. Officials were forced to concede that this exclusion contributes to breaking up families, since many men left home to make their families eligible for ADC. But, in 1962, when the federal government allowed states to include an unemployed parent in the grant, they built in such tight restrictions that relatively few unemployed parents qualified.

One reason for moralism about mothers with deserting husbands was that these men were assumed to be able-bodied workers who had eluded the state's control, and their families were not to benefit from their desertion. Welfare policy has come full circle: the Reagan administration now proposes that "children who are deprived of parental support or care because a parent has left home to seek or retain employment would no longer be eligible for AFDC."[35]

Although federal regulations did not require AFDC mothers to work until the Work Incentive (WIN) program of 1967, states and localities often refused them welfare in order to force women into the labor market, using "suitable home" laws. At first the WIN program gave sufficient leeway to states so that WIN could help recipients get a college education. That changed during the Nixon administration, when the 1971 Talmadge amendment to the Social Security Act tightened the program to include more mandatory recipients and limited the training to one year.

Under the Reagan administration, work requirements have become still more draconian, looking very much like slave labor. The 1981 amendments to AFDC gave states the right to set up "workfare" programs for recipients to work off their grants, or as an alternative to AFDC. These programs provide little or no job training, no sick leave or vacations, no fringe benefits, and no right to unionize or strike.[36] The WIN program was virtually eliminated.

The myth of the dead-beat, lazy-loafer welfare recipient helps keep people off the rolls by making them too ashamed to apply. In fact, welfare recipients are an exceptionally hard-working group of people. In 1980, approximately 45 percent of AFDC recipients also had earned income during the year. Most AFDC recipients are in and out of the low-paid work force. Nationally, half of all AFDC families leave the program within two years. Of those not in the labor force in 1979, three out of four fathers and three out of five mothers were either incapacitated or caring for a child under age six.[37]

Sexism, Racism, and Classism in AFDC

Prejudice against sex, race, and class come together under AFDC in a kind of worst-case scenario. Recipients are at the bottom of the labor pool and are meant to be kept there. Prejudice and discrimination force a disproportionate number of minorities onto AFDC. In 1979, nationwide, women headed four fifths of all AFDC households (as compared to less than 15 percent of all families in the United States that were headed by women in March 1979). That same year, 89 percent of the AFDC children received aid because their fathers did not live with them and provided little or no support.

Since its beginning, the AFDC program has combined sexual oppression with economic oppression. Prejudice and myths abound about AFDC women's assumed promiscuity and lesser competence as parents. Officials and the general public seem preoccupied with recipients' lives. The "suitable home" requirements were usually of a sexual nature. During the 1950s, more than 5,000 children were removed from the rolls in Florida because of promiscuous conduct of the mother (having a male friend was considered promiscuous). Only seventy-three children were removed because of abuse or neglect. When they were dropped from the rolls, no other provision was made for the children.[38]

All single AFDC mothers threaten the patriarchy because they prove their ability to live without a man. That is one reason so much scorn and rage is heaped upon them. Never-married mothers are the greatest threat since they have made a conscious choice, *from the start,* to raise a child alone.

Some welfare recipients have been sterilized without their permission, or with permission obtained under duress. Sterilizations have been reimbursed more easily by Medicaid than abortions.[39] Senator Russell Long (D-La.) once called AFDC recipients "brood mares," as he complained about his difficulty in finding someone to iron his shirts. His perverted fantasies about the connections between sexuality, reproduction, and work well illustrate the reactionary right's ideology, which is played out most heavily against AFDC recipients.

In his writings about the authoritarian character structure, Wilhelm Reich argued that sexual oppression and repression, which are perpetrated by parents and the institutions of society, serve the function of sapping people's self-confidence and making them more obedient workers and more passive people, more easily controlled by authorities. A sexually healthy person, he claimed, is less likely to submit blindly to authority than is someone who is sexually repressed.

> Psychic disturbances are the results of the sexual chaos brought about by the nature of our society. This chaos has, for thousands of years, served the function of making people submissive to existing conditions, in other words, of internalizing the external mechanization of life. It serves the purpose of bringing about the psychic anchoring of a mechanized and authoritarian civilization by way of making people lack self-confidence.[40]

The repressive male chauvinistic ideology of the Reagan administration was peddled earlier by George Gilder in his book *The Naked Nomad*. There he argued that civilization depends on men submitting their short-term sexual urges to the long-term maternal ambitions of women.[41] In other words, men should get married and work hard rather than playing around with a lot of women, and women should stay home and raise children. State programs that help women and children such as welfare, child nutrition, and food stamps, undermine this vision of "woman's place." Women who raise children without a man, wives who work, women with independent means—all these threaten this reactionary nineteenth-century scenario. The meaning of Reagan's "pro-family" policy, in the final analysis, is that women should stay home and take care of the children, the aged parents, and the handicapped relatives, rather than go to work and use social services such as day care, homemakers, special schools, or nursing care. Woman's role would become what it was in the nineteenth century—that of a person who subordinates her own needs and wishes in order to look after other people.

At least that is the Reagan administration's proposed program for middle-class women. For the very poor, those women at the level of AFDC eligibility, the proposal is to force them off the rolls and into society's undesirable jobs.

Welfare and Totalitarianism

Welfare is administered by a rigid and hierarchical bureaucracy. Fully to understand the welfare system takes an appreciation of how such bureaucracies function. They carry out the dictates of state and business leaders, but they also develop an autonomous life of their own. The bureaucracy that administers AFDC has taken on many totalitarian features because it has the mission of controlling the poor and disciplining the work force.

The philosopher Hannah Arendt's insights on totalitarianism[42] shed a great deal of light on the workings of the welfare bureaucracy. Many features of totalitarianism that she describes are also features of the current U.S. public-assistance system. For example, totalitarian rulers withhold information from people and mystify them by the information they do give out—as do welfare officials. Welfare regulations are byzantine in their ambiguity, complexity, length, and the frequency and unpredictability with which they change. One reason there is a high error rate in administering public-assistance programs is that welfare workers cannot understand the regulations and generally receive little help from the Welfare Department. Inefficient and arbitrary bureaucracy obfuscates the issues, diffuses accountability, and evades personal responsibility. Arendt speaks of the "administrator who ruled by reports and decrees in more hostile secrecy than any oriental despot."[43] She says bureaucrats must feel safe from control (both praise and blame) by institutions. They shun stable laws that could establish a permanent community where no one could be a god because all would have to obey a law. Thus they handle each matter separately and by decree. The essence of this system is aimless process; the two key figures are the bureaucrat and the secret agent.

Arendt discusses the state's intrusion into private thought and behavior as a hallmark of modern totalitarianism. This intrusion kills inner spontaneity along with the desire for social and political activities. The welfare system perpetuates chronic anxiety in recipients not only about their sex lives but also about their competence as parents. Recipients are under the triple burden of insufficient money, an outdated Puritan sex ethic, and child-rearing codes that are never clearly spelled out and lack the authority of scientific knowledge because child rearing is still more an art than a science.

Totalitarian rulers dehumanize, degrade, and stigmatize the people they rule—as do welfare officials. Totalitarian rulers resist spontaneity in their subjects; so do welfare officials. That vital spark of the unexpected in people makes them hard to predict and control. Totalitarian rulers behave like robots themselves and seek to reduce other people also to automatons. The attempt to control the poor and force them into a stultifying, conforming life-style is one sign of the effort to abolish the richness of diversity.

Totalitarian rulers isolate people to prevent them from sharing experiences and thoughts that might lead to resistance. Welfare officials seldom treat recipients like people with a *community* of interests. Each case is dealt with separately. People are not encouraged to discuss their common interests or complaints. When recipients do organize, as they did in the 1960s, welfare officials resist. As Hannah Arendt explains:

> . . . terror can rule absolutely only over men who are isolated against each other . . . therefore, one of the primary concerns of all tyrannical governments is to bring this isolation about. Isolation may be the beginning of terror; it certainly is its most fertile ground; it always is its result . . . power always comes from men acting together . . . isolated men are powerless by definition.[44]

The concentration camp, says Arendt, is the final step in uprooting and dehumanizing people. In concentration camps, moral choices cease to exist for most people. There are some similarities between the concentration camp and migrant labor camps, charity shelters, charity wards of hospitals, prisons, housing projects, state mental hospitals, or county homes. All depersonalize people, take away their privacy, remove them from significant ties, reduce their spontaneity and creativity, and make them easier to control.

Mechanization and depersonalization of life have become pervasive social problems. As Arendt says, "Political, social, and economic events everywhere are in a silent conspiracy with totalitarian instruments devised for making men superfluous."[45] If we can help welfare recipients find a sense of community, we will be working toward a society in which people care about what happens to one another.

REPORTS FROM THE FRONT
Welfare Mothers up in Arms

Diane Dujon, Judy Gradford,
and Dottie Stevens

Women on welfare know they are in constant battle to provide for themselves and their children. Their "enemies" are multiple, often including husbands, the welfare bureaucracy, and the attitudes of the general public. In this essay representatives from a group of welfare recipients in the Boston area who have organized into a welfare-rights group called ARMS (Advocacy for Resources for Modern Survival) describe some of the skirmishes they face every day.*

Our Lives No Longer Belong to Us

One of my sons was diagnosed as having a high lead level in his blood. The Welfare Department placed my son under protective

In addition to the three authors, several other members of the ARMS collective should be mentioned for their contributions to the larger unpublished paper from which this essay is taken, "Welfare Mothers up in Arms." They are Angela Hannon, Marion Graham, Jeannie MacKenzie, Carolyn Turner, and Hope Habtemarian. The cited quotations in this essay are taken from interviews with various ARMS members.

> services and told me that I would have to find another place to live or they would put my son into a foster home. With six children on a welfare budget, it's not easy to find an apartment. And I had to find one within thirty days! To keep the state from taking my son, I was forced to move into the first available housing I could find.
>
> Since I was an emergency case and eligible for a housing subsidy, my name was placed at the top of the list. I had to take the first available unit offered by the Housing Authority. The offer: a brand new town-house-type apartment *fifty miles away* in a white, middle-class suburb!
>
> I knew this move would devastate my family because we would be so far away from our relatives and friends. When you're poor, you have to depend on your family and friends to help you through when you don't have the money to help yourself. At least two or three times every month I take my children to my mother's house to eat. How would we ever be able to get to her house from fifty miles away?
>
> I also knew that my neighbors would not welcome me and my children: a black single woman with six children. I imagined the sneers of the merchants as I paid for my groceries with food stamps and the grunts of the doctors as I pulled out my Medicaid card.
>
> I thought about the problems of transportation that were sure to crop up. How would I get my children to school? What if they got sick; how far was the nearest hospital? I envisioned the seven of us walking for miles with grocery bags. In short, I felt no relief at having found a nice clean apartment within the allotted time, but my back was against the wall. I could not refuse or my son would be put into foster care.
>
> We now live in a totally hostile environment severed from our family and friends. And although we live in a physically beautiful development, life for us is hard. A poor family with no transportation is lost in the suburbs. We are as isolated as if we lived on a remote island in the Pacific.

Situations like the one described by this woman show how our lives no longer belong to us. We have, in effect, married the state. To comply with the conditions of our recipient status, we cannot make any personal decisions ourselves. We must consult the Welfare Department first, and the final decision is theirs. The state is a domineering, chauvinistic spouse.

Politicians often boast or complain about the many services and benefits welfare recipients receive. For us, these services and benefits are the bait that the predatory department uses to entrap us and our families. Like the wiley fox, we are driven by hunger to the trap. We must carefully trip the trap, retrieve the bait, and escape, hopefully unscathed. Also similar to the fox, our incompetence can lead to starvation, disease, and death for ourselves and our families.

This may seem an unlikely analogy to some; but the Welfare Department, in its *eagerness* to help us constantly adopts policies that put us in catch-22 situations. We are continuously in a dilemma over whether we should seek the help we desperately need or not. The purportedly "free" social services that are available to us extort a usurer's fee in mental and physical anguish. So, although there are several services available, we are often unable or reluctant to receive them. Below we describe some of the catch-22's that constitute mental cruelty for us.

Catch-22: A Low Budget

The first catch-22 we encounter is living under the conditions set up by the state for recipients. Under penalty of law we are required adequately to house, clothe, feed, and otherwise care for our children on a budget that is two thirds of the amount considered to be at the poverty line. If we fail to fulfill our obligation in the opinion of friends, strangers, neighbors, relatives, enemies, or representatives of the Welfare Department, the state can and *will* take our children from our homes. Anyone can call the department anonymously and report that we are neglecting or abusing our children. With no further questions, the state initiates an investigation, which further jeopardizes our family stability. While it is necessary for the state to protect children from abuse and neglect, a large portion of the investigations are based on unfounded allegations for which no one can be held accountable. It is no easy task to fulfill the basic obligation of surviving on welfare, because we often pay as much as 85 to 95 percent of our income for rent and utilities.

On the other hand, there is no reward for a job well done. If we manage to clothe, feed, and house our children, the risk is the same: at the least, biting remarks from people in public, and at the most, an investigation of fraud.

We are constantly under public scrutiny. We are made to feel uncomfortable if we wear jewelry, or buy a nice blouse, or own a warm coat. It's as if we're not supposed to have families or friends who love us and might give us a birthday or Christmas present. Absolutely no thought is given to the fact that we may have had a life before welfare! Heaven forbid that anyone should honor the great job we must do as shoppers!

There are a few legal ways in which welfare mothers can supplement their monthly grant. Some of these supports are available upon eligibility for Aid to Families with Dependent Children (AFDC); others, termed "social services," have additional individual eligibility requirements. Each has its quota of catch-22's:

Catch-22: Emergency Assistance

I was $300 in arrears with my electric bill. The electric company sent me several reminders, but I didn't have the money to pay my bill. It made me very nervous. It was winter, and although I had oil, if my electricity were turned off, my pilot light would go out and my children would be cold.

I took my bill and the warning notices to my social worker at the Welfare Department. She told me that I could receive up to $500 of Emergency Assistance per year, but that only one such grant could be made in any twelve-month period. However, I could not receive any Emergency Assistance until I received a 'shut-off' notice. She further explained that I should wait because if I received the $300 EA grant, I could not get the additional $200 to which I was entitled that year. I would have to wait twelve months before I could be eligible for another grant. I really wasn't interested in getting all I could, I just wanted to be able to sleep at night; but since I didn't have a shut-off notice, I had no choice but to wait.

I received a shut-off notice when my bill was about $400. I applied for, and received, the EA grant.

The very next year, I was in a similar situation. I again attempted to wait for the shut-off notice. One day I received a notice from the electric company stating that I was scheduled for a "field collection." My social worker reminded me that EA can only be awarded upon receipt of a shut-off notice. Even though the notice stated that my service would be "interrupted" if I failed to honor the collector, it did not have the specific words *shut off* and, therefore, I was ineligible for EA. I couldn't believe what she was telling me! To become eligible, I had to go to the electric company to ask them to stamp "shut off" on my bill. I was angry that I was being forced to humiliate myself by revealing my personal business to the electric company representative.

Catch-22: Medicaid

Medicaid is the most treasured benefit to families who must depend on AFDC, but it, too, falls short of the expectations of beneficiaries. Doctors, hospitals, druggists, and other health providers often refuse to accept Medicaid patients. The amount of paper work that is required for each and every patient is tedious and time-consuming. Medicaid also sets limits on the type and amount of treatments it will cover.

Every trip to the doctor is a grueling, costly, and time-consuming event. First, we must search for a doctor or medical facility that will accept Medicaid. If we are lucky enough to have a neighborhood health center nearby, we will often go to the clinic. In either situation, we usually have to wait for hours to receive the medical attention we need. Doctors often remark about the amount of paperwork that is required by the state and the fact that they often have to wait six to eight months to obtain their fees from the state. It is exceedingly distressing to be sick and have to hear about the doctor's problems!

> I had periodontal disease once. The dentist explained that an infection had settled under my gums and he would have to cut my gums and scrape the infection away. Since I was on Medicaid, I was required to wait until Medicaid approved the dental procedure.
>
> After several weeks, the approval arrived. My dentist informed me that although Medicaid approved the procedure, the amount approved was too low to allow him to use gas as was customary. I had a choice: either I could pay him the difference, and *enjoy* a painless procedure; or I could have the procedure done for the cost Medicaid allotted and he could use novocaine, which would be at least moderately painful.
>
> I didn't have the money to pay the difference, but I knew that if I delayed the operation I stood a good chance of losing my teeth. I decided to brave the novocaine.
>
> The dentist had to cut deep into my gums and the novocaine did nothing for the pain below the surface. I tried hard to be still and keep my mouth open wide, but I was in agony with the pain. The procedure took four hours and required sixty-four stitches and forty-seven injections of novocaine!

Catch-22: Food Stamps

Food Stamps are a symbol of the government's benevolence. Rather than increase the amount of the welfare budget so that we can afford to buy more food, the government *supplements* our budgets with food stamps. As the name suggests, food is all that can be purchased with them. And not much food at that. Households receiving the maximum amount of food stamps receive an average of forty cents per meal per person. All other commodities, such as soap, detergent, toilet paper, diapers, etc., must be separated at the time of purchase. Food, by anyone's definition, is a necessity for sustaining life. Why, then, do we feel as if food is a luxury?

Contrary to public opinion, we pay for these food stamps at a cost significantly higher than a cup of coffee per meal. We pay with the anguish of wondering how we are going to maintain healthy children on $1.20 per day. Food stamps last an average of ten days, depending on the supply of staples (flour, sugar, cereal, salt, spaghetti, etc.) we have on hand; the rest of the month we struggle to keep up with the milk, eggs, juice, fruits, vegetables, and bread so vital to good health. The last two weeks we are challenged to use our imaginations to ensure that our children receive the best nutrition possible. For those of us who are lucky enough to be able to commit "fraud" through friends and relatives, it's a little easier; but for many of us it's often an impossible task!

> The way the food stamp budget is calculated, it's as if our diet is supposed to shrink in the summer. Our fuel costs are counted as an expense in the winter, so we receive more food stamps in the winter and less in the summer. This budget policy is ludicrous because most of our fuel costs in the winter are paid with Fuel Assistance.
>
> I had trouble one time receiving my food stamps. Every month I would have to commute to the next town where my welfare office was located to report that I had not received my food stamps. Each time I was interrogated by the food stamps worker about whether I had cashed my food stamps and was trying to get some more under false pretenses. I had to sign a sworn statement to the effect that I had not received my food stamps before they could issue replacement stamps.
>
> I finally decided that rather than go through the hassle and expense of picking up my food stamps from the welfare office each month, I would purchase a post office box. When I went to inform my worker of my box number, I was told that food stamps could not be sent to a post office box. This policy was supposed to deter fraud. I was forced to continue to pick up my food stamps from the welfare office each month.

Food stamp redemption centers are generally located in areas that are virtually inaccessible to those of us without cars. Much of the money we are supposed to be saving with food stamps is spent on transportation to the centers.

> My food stamps usually come on the due date, but my welfare check is often late. This creates a problem for me because I always need the food, but with no cash money it is almost impossible to do the shopping I need to do the first time. I have to make at least two trips to the supermarket: the first trip for food only with the food stamps and the second, when my check comes, to buy soap, cleaning products, etc. Two trips to the store doubles the amount of transportation expenses, too.

Catch-22: Welfare Fraud

Fraud within the welfare system might also be called "devising a way to survive." The federal and state laws call it fraud if a welfare recipient uses up her allotment for any reason and seeks assistance from a friend, relative, or acquaintance (be it ten cents or $10). If she does not report this money to the welfare office, she is technically considered to be defrauding the Welfare Department. Such unrealistic definitions leave all of us vulnerable to fraud and make it difficult to separate honest need from intentional deception.

According to the narrow, unrealistic guidelines of the state and federal government, most or all welfare recipients could be accused of having committed fraud at some time during their ordeal with the welfare system, even though they would not have meant to defraud anyone. We are stuck in a system that inadequately provides for us and that even the social workers know, depends upon our having a "little help from our friends." However, if we are caught doing what we all have to do to survive, we may even be made into an "example" and used to discredit the difficulties faced by women on welfare.

We are poor because we do not receive enough money from the Welfare Department to live decently. If we lack family or friends, we may feel forced to find ways to get a little extra money for our families. Many who have been discovered working to buy Christmas presents, for example, have been brought to court by the Welfare Department and either fined, jailed, or made to pay back all monies received while working.

Although there seems to be large-scale vendor fraud among those who supply Medicaid services, it is seldom investigated or taken to court. While we are hounded for minor infractions, little is done to the unscrupulous doctors, dentists, druggists, nursing-home operators, and others in the health field who blatantly commit welfare fraud as a regular practice. Because of their "respectability" in the community, these providers are in a position to bill Medicaid for services never rendered, and they do so with some regularity. When these abuses are publicized, public outcry is minimal and fleeting at best. It is so much easier to blame "those people."

Even in the event of discovery by a Medicaid "fraud squad," the welfare recipient, rather than the health professional suspected of illegally using the system, often becomes the target of their investigation.

> I was ordered by our Medicaid fraud squad to appear at my local welfare office within the week. A dentist who had done surgery on my mouth for a periodontal disease was under suspicion of committing fraud.
>
> I arrived at the office not knowing what to expect. Two men who resembled G-Men arrived and hustled me into a cubicle and began interrogating me. Not being satisfied with my answers, they proceeded to look into my mouth at every tooth in my head to prove I had fillings where they were not supposed to be, according to the computer printout they were studying. They also wanted me to account for every filling, extraction, check-up, and cleaning of my three children, which had been done by the same dentist. This took me another week.
>
> I was treated as if I was guilty of something. When you are on welfare, no one cares about your feelings—they don't count.

The welfare system, in reality, has been set up to promote fraud as a means of survival. They *know* we can't live on budgets "below the poverty line." With a more reasonable system of providing financial assistance, there would be less "fraud" because people on welfare would be less desperate. But as it is, women are punished for being on welfare and pushed into impossible binds.

Enough Already

Families who must rely on the welfare system to survive are constantly torn to pieces by the bureaucratic policies that supply the services they need. Each benefit comes with its own rules and regulations, which must be followed if recipients are to remain eligible. The policies are designed separately, with little regard to policies of other agencies, so we are continuously in compromising positions.

Welfare policies are written in "still life." Like the prepackaged vegetables in the supermarkets, they look fine on the surface; but turn them over and look beneath the surface and you may see rotten spots. Living, breathing people need policies that allow for individuality and flexibility. No two families are alike or have the same needs. We should not be lumped together and threatened with extinction if we complain. Women who are already in crises do not need the added stress of conflicting policies among the services that are ours by right. We are strong, capable, and often wise beyond our years. We demand that we be allowed to have some control over our own lives. No governor, president, general, or legislator should be able to dictate to us where we live, what we eat, or where, or even, whether we should work outside the home when we are already taking care of our children.

FOR BETTER AND FOR WORSE
Women Against Women in the Welfare State

Ann Withorn

I would rather have a man worker any day. They, at least, are more likely to listen to you and seem sympathetic. The women are meaner. They act like it's their money and you should work hard like they do.

———Boston welfare recipient

Our office was all women, including the director, and I'll tell you, it was enough to make you hate women. Everybody fought among themselves and hated the director, who was

The basis for this essay is a series of ongoing discussions with feminist and other service workers in the Boston area. I teach adult human service workers at the University of Massachusetts, Boston, and have been formally and informally interviewing them about their activity for years. Some of the material used here has been published in my books *The Circle Game: Services for the Poor in Massachusetts* (Amherst, Mass.: University of Massachusetts Press, 1982) and *Serving the People: Social Services and Social Change* (New York: Columbia University Press, 1984). I have recently interviewed progressive human service unionists for the summer 1985 issue on labor and human services of *Catalyst: A Socialist Journal of Social Services*. I am also involved in doing advocacy support work with welfare recipient groups in the Boston area and have discussed these ideas with many of them. I am especially grateful to *Radical America* editor Gail Sullivan for help with this essay.

> *horrible. Then they brought in this nice young man and now everything is much better.*
>
> ———Suburban service worker

> *What makes our clinic so wonderful is that it's for women, by women. There is none of that male medical bullshit. We all struggle together to work out better ways to do things. It's not easy, but it is so much nicer not to have men around, laying their ego trips on everybody.*
>
> ———Feminist health clinic nurse

Most social services are provided to women clients by women service workers. Clients discuss "problems" identified with women's traditional roles: family difficulties; child care; "personal" problems with relatives or lovers or with the lack of health care, housing, and income. The help that women workers usually offer is traditional female "nurturing": listening, some general and specific suggestions, sympathy, and, sometimes money and other resources. Both workers and recipients suffer from the low status of being involved with society's "dirty work." In such an environment, complex relationships usually divide women but could, instead, teach important lessons and foster powerful new alliances.

As a teacher of human service workers and welfare recipients I meet many women frustrated by the gap between their hopes for the human service work place as a base for good relations among a variety of women and the reality of hostility and distrust among most women in the welfare state. In this article I examine the relationships among women in human service agencies in order to understand better why they are frequently so destructive and to determine what hope exists for the welfare state as an arena for struggle and change.

The Nature of Human Service Work

Human service work takes place in a variety of settings, which together constitute much of the welfare state. There are the large state bureaucracies—welfare departments, child welfare agencies, state institutions for the mentally ill and retarded—where public employees act like what Michael Lipsky has called "street-level bureaucrats" by providing such essentials as money, public housing, medical and mental health services, or "protective" services to people who are usually poor—and are primarily women and their children.[1] Women clients often come unwillingly to such settings because they have few other "private" options.

Many other agencies also provide human services. Most are labelled "private" even though much of their funding comes from government contracts. They offer such programs as day care, counseling, homemaker and adult education services, residential care for retarded and mentally ill people, and rehabilitation services for the physically disabled, to name a few. Finally, some alternative, even explicitly feminist, programs such as rape crisis centers or battered-women's shelters still offer services as a means for making social change. All these services, whether or not they are directly funded by public money, can be considered part of an expansive understanding of the "welfare state."[2]

It is difficult to generalize about so much activity. On the one hand, the agencies differ in their degree of bureaucratization, the professionalization of their staff, and the punitiveness of their function. Both clients and workers probably view their environment differently across the spectrum from big bureaucracy to smaller agency.

On the other hand, human encounters within most agencies are quite similar, with the possibilities for positive *and* negative relations present almost everywhere. Even in the most punitive welfare setting, a woman client can appreciate a service worker who "treats her like a human being"; and the most feminist battered-women's shelter can foster hostile, untrusting relationships. And, surely, most services simultaneously offer women relief from some aspects of their traditional roles, while also stigmatizing and punishing them for their "neediness."

Recently, feminists and Marxists have paid new attention to the welfare state. Many have found it a "public patriarchy" deserving women's distrust and avoidance. For such critics the overriding purpose of all human service activity is to continue women's dependence outside of the patriarchal family, while dividing workers and races from one another.[3] Yet this focus on one side of the contradictory nature of the capitalist welfare state denies that women can receive needed help from services or from their relationships with service workers.

Instead I suggest that sometimes the negative impact of the

welfare state can be thwarted. It is possible for women to emerge from human service encounters more able to cope with their lives, perhaps even to understand their personal and social needs. The crucial dimension for the successful delivery of almost all human services is the establishment of a relationship between service workers and clients. Because of the broader social functions of human service agencies, this relationship usually reinforces and solidifies class, race, and cultural conflicts in society. But, because of the real nature of the needs women bring to agencies (and despite state efforts to disregard them), sometimes it is still possible for astute women service workers to help women clients obtain what they need *and* make new, political, alliances—if they are neither naive about the difficulties nor cynical about the possibilities.

Workers v. Clients

When service workers first develop an analysis of the potential of human service work, they often decide it should be easy to "correct" things through their own behavior. The basic feminist insight that women can identify with and support one another, as women, seems overpowering. One young radical was typical in her hopes:

> I started out really naive. I thought that since I understood how we were all oppressed as women, and how the Welfare Department was out to screw us all, then it would be easy for me to work with clients, and with my fellow women unionists. Very quickly I found out that *no one* trusted me because of these ideas and, worse, that I was reproducing some of the very patterns of insensitivity that I criticized.

Most service workers don't even enter the work place trying to alter things. Instead, they come with class backgrounds and/or professional training that already distance them from women clients. They are likely to be influenced by all the stereotypes that abound in this society about their separateness from "people in need of service."[4]

Powerful pressures, then, create a complex dynamic, which limits the potential for positive relationships between women clients and women service workers. First, we cannot assume a simple gender identification between women workers and clients. In almost all service encounters, even in agencies less punitive than welfare departments, the direct-service worker is the "gatekeeper," the person who can deny or provide needed resources, lessen or intensify state harassment, and in myriad ways affect the quality of life for her clients. The power relationships are direct. Clients always recognize them, even as some service workers may try to deny them.

Second, the class and race of many women service workers, as well as their functional roles, pose further objective barriers to solidarity with most clients. The classic image of "white, middle-class social workers," removed from their clients' lives and issues, is all too accurate. When built-in role conflicts interact with class and race differences, the results can be devastating, even in "alternative agencies":

> With us it's intense. All our staff are women of color. The women who come here sometimes expect us to be "sisters," and they get angry when we push them. And sometimes we may expect too much of them. It's better than other places, but the problems sure aren't solved.

Such basic tensions often seem to overshadow any hope for a "contradictory" nature to human service work; the power to hurt seems so much greater than the ability to help. Yet for women service workers honestly to assist other women, much less to build alliances based on recognition of mutual needs and common oppression, the powerful bureaucratic barriers, coupled with class and race differences, must be recognized, examined, and understood.

Besides the material factors of power, class, and racial conflicts, however, there is a central *ideology* by which both women service workers and clients defeat themselves: "woman hating." By this I mean the many mechanisms by which women of all backgrounds distrust and disassociate themselves from other women. Woman hating allows women service workers to reject any identification with women clients and thereby to reinforce client distrust. The cumulative effect leads workers either consciously to reject equal relationships with clients or to act in ways that make such connections impossible, even when workers think they are desirable.

Personally, women service workers face the same structural and psychological constraints of so many other women workers. They are usually working two jobs—one unpaid as primary family care giver, the other underpaid. And, while the woman service worker may have chosen her "second job" partly because it builds upon skills learned in her first, that very similarity can be overwhelming. As one child advocate observed:

> I love my work but sometimes it is too much. When my own kids are in trouble I often think, "What am I doing here helping someone else's children? I should be home with my own."

This "overdose of nurturance" can be extremely difficult to handle and may lead women service workers, like this counselor, to seem cold toward clients:

> Since I had my baby I just don't have as much to give. I used to listen to everyone and be really understanding. Now it's not just the time, although that's part of it. It is also that I don't have the same emotional energy to spare. I see myself getting more structured and bureaucratic, and it makes me sad, but I don't know how to stop.

Such comments are common even though many service workers also feel that, as women, they are more sensitive to the problems women clients face. Without an overly clinical discussion of the psychological needs service workers project on their clients (called "counter-transference" in the professional jargon), I suggest that there may be "a lot going on" in relationships between women service workers and clients. Exactly because of the intensity of the issues and problems facing all women, then, it can be difficult for women service workers to accept differences in women's ways and means of coping.

I call the negative side of this the "who do you think you are?" phenomenon—the tendency of women service workers to judge their women clients more harshly than they would men. These judgments may be based on a sense of what's "realistic" for a woman to do in U.S. society and a fear of the repercussions for any woman who tries to break the rules. They may allow service workers to deny clients options that raise questions about the worker's own life choices. According to one feminist welfare recipient:

> I think many of my women workers are threatened by my choice to be on welfare, but they cannot admit it. I am saying that I don't want to work at a bad job in order to support my children in poverty, and that I don't want to live with a man to give me legitimacy. Many social workers are in bad, low-paying jobs or bad marriages, or both. I represent a threat to them and they can't admit it.[5]

Sexual dynamics may also be at play. If service relationships become too equal, the potential for more intensely personal, even sexual, interaction arises. While some male service workers may welcome this for sexist reasons, many women service workers may not want to acknowledge their own sexual feelings toward any women, much less women clients. Yet almost any good human service encounter involves highly personal sharing, even if only to determine "eligibility for service." As many feminist service workers have discovered, once the barriers to mutuality are discarded, then sexual feelings can emerge, in both directions. In our homophobic society, this becomes another reason for women in a human service relationship to fear each other.

All told, many service workers share a strong moral sense about women's proper role. The assumption that women should care for themselves and their families in certain prescribed ways runs very deep in social work—and may even stem from the profession's ninteenth-century feminist roots.[6] Since most service relationships consider questions of how a woman should perform her basic roles, women service workers may experience constant challenges to their own values. Says one child-welfare worker:

> I know I should be nonjudgmental and I try. But I also care about the kids (that's why I do the job) and the effects on them of troubled mothers. I don't know how to be sympathetic to both mother and kids, even though I am a mother too and know how hard it is for me. So I often act strange with the mother because I feel guilty for her and I don't know what to do about it.

Women service workers are under great personal pressure to deny the very commonality essential to feminist consciousness. In addition, it can be difficult for them to achieve professional legitimacy unless they put extreme distance between themselves and their clients; the management books for women promote a version of this by advising ambitious women to "avoid friendships with secretaries at all cost."

> Oh, my last worker was nice enough, but she had no power. So why should I talk with her? If I'm going to have to deal with any of them, I would rather have it be someone who can do something for me.

When I talked with a group of politically active welfare recipients about their reactions to such feelings, they were torn, just as I was. All felt that women service workers had treated them badly. "They are even less likely to treat me like a person than most of the men are" was the unanimous complaint. Yet all felt somewhat uncomfortable with their bias against women workers. One member of the group expressed the issue quite self-consciously:

> I know it's like the old woman-hating stuff, where women don't trust other women. Sometimes I know I want a man worker so I can manipulate him in traditional sexist ways. But I haven't got much power here and I have to use what I've got. Having a woman worker may get in the way. Besides, many women workers seem to resent us, like we're not suffering hard the way they do.
>
> It's confusing. Sometimes I *am* prejudiced against them or have unreal expectations of them. And then again sometimes they *are* more difficult to deal with. One thing is true, though. When you get a good woman worker, that's usually the very best. She can really make you feel supported and able to get what you need.

Both clients and service workers bring bad habits and attitudes as well as reasonable evaluations of power to the human service relationship. Creating a different dynamic may require altered expectations of how women should behave as clients. Just as there is no obligation to accept racism among white clients toward minority service workers, so clients' antiwomen attitudes need to be challenged, even within the confines of the welfare state.

Relationships Among Women Service Workers

> How can you expect us to be concerned about how bad things are for the patients when we are so understaffed that it's dangerous for us? In conditions like these, all I want is to give them enough medications so they don't beat me up.

For women service workers to make alliances with women clients, they must have more power over their work. Otherwise, clients' needs to obtain what they can from a system within which service workers have little power will dissolve any underlying similarities and prevent potential coalitions. This situation, then, implies that another set of relationships must be examined and changed, those among women service workers.

Many of the same pressures that make it difficult for women social workers to relate well to clients also impede their ability to align themselves with one another. The overload of nurturance, which they give both to family and to clients, makes sympathy and support for other service workers hard to muster. Add the pressures stemming from low pay and low status and it becomes difficult for service workers even to pay attention to one another without irritation, much less to form alliances for change. In addition, the varied and complicated reasons why women may become social workers can create very different job expectations among the women in a work place. One activist in a large private agency summed up the dynamics well:

> Here we have a real mix of women. There are a few of the "old guard," unmarried middle-class professionals who see saving kids as their life work and moral duty. Although they are dying out, their spirit judges the rest of us. Then there are the "new breed" of assertive women who see themselves on the way up into successful management positions. They seem almost embarrassed to admit that they are really still social workers. There are also a good many working- and middle-class women who see this as a good job that doesn't threaten their home and family life. And there are a few of us radicals, feminists, who want to talk about unions, or abortion, or alliances with clients, and we threaten *everybody* else.

Feminists in social welfare agencies have a particulary difficult time coming to terms with the lack of easy solidarity among service workers. They are often able to understand (and seek to change) the power and class divisions between service workers and clients. But they find themselves just impatient and judgmental about similar tensions in the work place among different levels of staff or among staff of different ages or races.

The double standards for men in human services are especially hard to take. Women service workers, for example, may criticize female co-workers if they are unprofessionally "soft" and concerned about their clients and co-workers, while male workers are praised if they are ever warm and nurturing. Yet when men do play traditional authoritarian roles, they are seldom criticized, as women are, for being too "hard" or "difficult to work with."

Before women service workers as a group can expect much trust from clients, they must come to terms with differences among themselves. And, before they can hope to work together, in unions or in other ways just to improve their own work lives, they must also examine the power relationships, woman hating, and other pressures that seem to divide them as deeply from one another as they are divided from clients.

Can This Contradiction Be Saved?

More often than not politicized service workers and clients within the American welfare state wonder whether they should try to do anything but bring the system down. The need for unity among service workers and between clients and service workers seemes obvious, but the possibility of achieving it seems utopian. Even worse, the daily struggle to improve things can lead to a deep "burnout" of creative energy and political purpose.

One way to cope with the tensions is to remember that change is not supposed to be easy. As capitalist creations to control and reproduce existing social relations, agencies quite naturally deliver services that continue oppressive patterns. Services *have* served to reinforce dependence on men as well as to solidify women's role as society's primary nurturer. Given this situation, we cannot expect easy change.

At the same time, the welfare state has also, historically, helped women to break away slightly from traditional roles, by providing subsistence benefits for a life without men. And, poor and punitive as they may be, its services offer institutional alternatives to some of the nurturing roles demanded of women. One woman expressed the tension with a powerful question:

> Why do they make it so hard? Lord knows I need the money and the services I get and I would like to be happier with them. But what I have to go through to get the little they give me makes me wish, most of the time, that I never heard of any of it.

Statements like this remind us how important it is to change, not simply abolish, the welfare state.

For women service workers the complexity comes around full circle. As the nurturers hired, at inadequate pay, to provide the care that other women have "failed" to provide, they wonder: should they reject such roles and become male-identified managers? Should they do their job with the self-sacrifice always demanded of women? Or can they foist some nurturing back on women clients? The problem becomes especially complex because, in my experience at least, most service workers and clients to not want to abandon their care-giving roles, on the job or in the home, but they do want recognition and support for performing them. And both need options besides nurturing in their lives, as well as relief from being seen only as care givers. Again, while this mutual conundrum theoretically unites service workers and clients, it does not suggest the basis for any easy alliance.

Yet a few experiences begin to suggest alternatives to this grim scenario.

The first and most fully developed source of hope comes from the wide range of explicitly feminist services that have grown out of the contemporary women's movement. Time and Reaganism have, not coincidentally, limited the growth and the political clarity of battered-women's shelters, rape crisis centers, and other feminist services. They still, however, offer hope that powerful models can be conceived.[9]

No matter what their current problems, feminist services have demonstrated that women can provide effective services from a base of shared experience and feminist analysis. All suggest that fighting the hierarchy among service workers, and between service workers and clients, is worthwhile, however difficult. Most important, feminist services provide a model that shows how services can be something valuable in themselves, not merely as organizing tools or as palliatives to an unfair society. One feminist health activist put it this way:

> By working at the clinic I understand better both how bad things are and that there is hope for change. I see how women are hurt in so many ways by doctors, husbands, and lovers who don't understand their needs. I also see that, when we do things differently, when we act differently toward each other and toward women wanting service, things *feel* different. Maybe we don't have the new answers yet about

> what to do, but at least it feels like a more equal, more honest way to try.

Second, many radicals have moved into small social service agencies or some of the bigger state bureaucracies. Here they struggle to "act like feminists," to change the dynamics mentioned above. Often this effort has meant building a union or engaging in advocacy with clients.

There are also many "progressives" in human service unions, even in leadership positions. Some have tried to reduce the stresses on service workers so that they can be more sensitive to clients. One social workers' union in Massachusetts has established a "women's committee" for women service workers to discuss their work with one another and provide the support that work-place structures deny. A leader of this committee acknowledged that members had not been able to discuss relations with women clients yet, but that they were beginning to address common experiences and to fight some of the individualism and elitism fostered by professionalism:

> At first, except for a concern about day care and abortion rights, we have not focused on client issues. It seemed important to build trust among ourselves and to become a force within the union. But, if the union leadership stays progressive, so that we don't have to go back to fighting internally, then there is a chance for us to do more internal education about "women's issues" that affect our work with clients. It won't be easy but we are almost ready to try.

Other women union leaders mention the same goal and the same caution. All speak of the need to raise consciousness among women service workers before better relations can reasonably be expected with clients.

A few client groups seem to be edging toward a parallel strategy, as one shelter worker explains:

> Now we are trying to suggest that welfare mothers push women workers to see their problems as broader women's problems. We want to "call the question," so to speak, by making a direct appeal to women workers to see us as having common interests.

Another welfare-rights group, in collaboration with the social workers' union, wrote a stern memo to the welfare commissioner asking for policy changes that would allow service workers not to be hostile toward clients. This is a far cry from the days when recipient groups simply demanded that a particular bad worker be fired.

Of course, the nature of much social service work means that welfare-rights groups will remain frustrated with women service workers. But alliances with the progressive unions may sow the seeds of new relationships, as one advocate hopes:

> When we marched together to fight the office closing, workers and welfare mothers were walking along together, laughing and joking about the department, the governor, and our lives. After that it will be a lot harder for workers to treat us like "cases," and for us to see all of them as "the enemy."

It will take such a two-pronged strategy to enable women service workers and clients to understand their intertwined situation. Women service workers will need to overcome their fear of identification with clients, as women, while women clients will need to begin demanding such identification as the starting point for a relationship.

For better *and* for worse, then, the human service agency is a setting that is centrally defined by women's roles and women's issues. Whether women come willingly as clients or not, whether they come seeking help to perform traditional roles or because they are being psychologically and materially punished for rejecting such roles, the special nature of women's place in society is the fundamental context for human service activity, for both service workers and clients. As long as the women there are unable to recognize and consider the implications of this shared reality, then women remain divided from one another, and "human services" remain associated with punitive, demeaning tasks. If they are able to acknowledge their shared situation, however, then whole new areas for feminist activity may open up. As one woman commented, when asked what she thought of my topic:

> I don't know what it means but it's got to matter that we're all women here, and we're always talking about women's problems. If we can figure this out, we may be able to change the way we think about what we ought to do.

DADDY'S GOOD GIRLS

Homeless Women and "Mental Illness"

Stephanie Golden

From 1977 to 1981 I was a volunteer at the Dwelling Place, a shelter for homeless women near Manhattan's Port Authority bus terminal run by a group of Franciscan sisters. We offered food, showers, clothing, emotional support, and a few nights' rest while helping those who wished to apply for welfare or disability obtain medical care and find a place to live. Many women passed through; quite a few returned periodically. By the end of the first year, a fair-size group had been placed at a nearby single-room-occupancy (SRO) hotel, and the shelter staff instituted a series of activities there to try to create some kind of community among these very isolated women. As part of this program I ran a weekly coffee hour at which I encouraged discussions of whatever subjects I could think of.

This experience, together with my research on female homelessness both historical and contemporary, led me to conclude that—contrary to common fantasies about "bag ladies"—such homelessness results not from special qualities in individual women but from their general condition *as women.* The homeless women I knew were neither unusually defective nor especially superior. Most believed in and had lived out conventional female roles. As a rule, they were homeless more because of the same economic and social factors that create women's poverty than because of whatever individual psychological problems (or virtues) they had.

A third to a half of the homeless have been estimated to be former inmates of mental hospitals who have been deinstitutionalized.[1] Their "mental illness" is therefore often taken as an explanation of their homelessness. But what does it mean in our society to say that a woman is "mentally ill"? In fact the social norms that define women's roles interact with a rather arbitrary concept of "mental illness" in a context where men hold the power to create and enforce those norms. Therefore I treat "mental illness" here not as a disease that exists entirely inside the ill person but as at least equally an attribute applied to her by someone else who has the power to make the diagnosis stick.

This account is impressionistic in that it is not based on any specialized methodology: partly because I am not a social scientist, and partly because the nature of the Dwelling Place made it impossible to gather data systematically. Not only did the constant pressure of extreme need militate against the impulse to collect information for its own sake; but also the homeless women have learned to beware of friends who come asking questions.

Mental Illness and Social Health

A well-known study of sex role stereotypes has suggested that most professionals consider healthy adults and healthy men to have the same attributes but healthy women to differ in several ways.[2] Two traits of the "mentally healthy woman" that were identified by this study, passivity and dependence, were constant themes in the lives of the homeless women I knew. Alice is a good example of such passivity "in action." She had lost her apartment, but continued to return to her old block on the first of the month to wait for the mailman, who knew her and would hand her her Supplemental Security Income (SSI) check. Finally, he said she had to file a change of address, and she did, but only with the post office, not with Social Security. The next month her check did not come to the new address. Alice went to the SSI office, and I called them. Speaking to different caseworkers, we heard different stories, which I tried to reconcile by calling a third, who gave me still another version of the necessary procedure. The upshot was that there would be no check for another two weeks. Meanwhile, Alice needed a place to stay; she had been on the street for several months. She talked and worried a great deal about not having a place, but it was very hard to get her to do anything. Because I was standing over her she finally called Mary House (a shelter run by the Catholic Worker) and was told they had no bed.

At this point, Alice's mind stopped working. If I said, "Alice, you have to decide to do something because if not you'll wind up spending the next weeks in Penn Station" (where she had been), she answered, "Oh no, I'll die before I spend the night in a station." However she wouldn't make any positive choice. Her mind simply hopped around all sides of the problem refusing to land *on* it. In her I sensed an emptiness that is hard to put into words. She could also have gone to SSI and obtained certification of a missing check, which at that time would have enabled her to go to welfare and ask for emergency money. She said she would do that, but she didn't. Her sense of purpose evaporated; it didn't last past the moment when you spoke to her. She was very grateful for my caring and wanting to help but quite unable to take the action that the help required. For women like Alice, when I or someone else took their problems in hand we became—like a husband—the filler of the void with our will and purpose. They could act for us or for one another (all were eager to help out in the shelter and quick to give one another advice on how to deal with welfare) but not for themselves.

The new address Alice wanted her check sent to was that of a man in Brooklyn whom she had met "in the park." Who was he? She didn't know him well but kept saying he had a good job, a nice apartment, so he must be honest, because how could he risk losing all that? She assumed that bad people didn't have good jobs—that is, they lost them because they were bad. Alice had been married for years and had a teenage daughter (who was staying with a friend), but whatever experience this had given her had not dented her extraordinary naiveté. I had to assume that marriage had totally protected her from ever having to act in the world. Now she acted almost as if she resented the fact that some external force was no longer setting her life in order.

This same feeling, I suspect, also lay behind an odd breakdown suffered by another woman, Lydia, who became incontinent and incoherent and did not recognize people or know where she was. She lay in her hotel room while volunteers came and babied her. Very shortly she recovered completely. Now Lydia was not unable to act in the world; she had worked all her life and had told me she always liked to work hard and therefore had trouble adjusting when arthritis had compelled her to stop. Her breakdown had to do with the fact that her husband had deserted her two months before, something he did periodically, each episode (we heard) being followed by a similar breakdown on her part. Thus at issue here was not so much a physical requirement of action or work as the psychological stance required to be alone or live for oneself. More than merely being the caretaker, the man functions as the *image* of the caretaker and especially as the locus of primary existence. To Alice for example, the stranger in the park *was* the man who should receive her money—that is, he was not himself, whoever he was; he was the MAN who takes care of you.

The fact is, women like Alice and Lydia have gotten a raw deal—or, to be precise, suffered a breach of contract. They had (implicitly) agreed to settle for passivity in return for being taken care of. After years of carrying out their end of the agreement, for which they gave up their capacity for autonomy, they were suddenly left with no caretaker and to add insult to injury found themselves expected (by social service agencies for example) to be able to function on their own. Naturally enough, they resented this—and resisted, in their way. So although it was irritating to sit and coax Lydia to sip some orange juice as though she were a child, I could hardly blame her for acting like one.

This image of the man as caretaker is not just an image; it is embedded in expectations and norms that shape the objective conditions of women's lives. As one researcher noted, "In middle class America, at least, it is easier to tolerate and carry a poor housewife and mother and an inadequate wife than a sick breadwinner."[3]

More is involved, however, than just being sheltered. The reason the female role can act as a mask is that the role itself is so close to the aberrant behavior that to some degree they overlap. If normal ("healthy") women are supposed to be dependent, where do you draw the line beyond which dependency is pathological?

Consider, in this respect, the meaning of schizophrenia. Most of the Dwelling Place women whose psychiatric histories we knew had been diagnosed as schizophrenic, somewhere along the line. I recall too a conversation I had with a young intern who, based on his experience in a hospital emergency room, airily dismissed all the bag women as "burnt-out schizophrenics." It seems clear that this condition has some congruency with the condition of homelessness, although the exact nature of the connection is clouded by the fact that no one really knows what schizophrenia is, let alone what causes it. Broadly speaking, though, schizophrenia is a failure to perceive and relate adequately to reality—including other people—so that one is unable to satisfy one's own needs or to fulfill others' expectations.[4] Even though the schizophrenic's behavior may constitute an accurate perception and logical response to some underlying reality of her life, she tends to apply that behavior indiscriminately in all circumstances.

Of the many theorists who have attempted to explain schizophrenia, one, Theodore Lidz, set forth a dynamic of family interaction based on dependency and passivity. He describes how pathological relationships within a family prevent a child from being able to develop an autonomous adult personality. The parallels between Lidz's portrait of the distorted and disrupted schizophrenic personality and the characteristics of the "mentally healthy woman" mentioned above are striking.

According to Lidz, the essence of the problem is that the child's self is not her own but is channeled into giving meaning to the parent's life. To do this, the child must repress not only her perception of the actual reality but also the awareness of her own feelings that is the foundation of a sense of self. The effect is to "distort the child's meanings and reasoning"—that is, her thinking becomes flawed. She never learns—or learns inadequately—to distinguish what is real from what is not. Lacking even the confidence that something dependably real exists, she lacks as well the firm sense of what place in the world she herself occupies. For someone with no sense of her self as a separate entity, the need to become independent of parents and begin to live her own life that arises in late adolescence is overwhelming and impossible to fulfill.[6]

This description of the type of setting that creates schizophrenia overlaps remarkably with the conventional picture of the setting in which all women are supposed to live. For them, living life for another person is the *norm,* while the list of traits of the "mentally healthy woman" seems to constitute a fair description of the damaged personality produced by the "schizophrenogenic" family. Here too lies an explanation of the abrupt disintegration even of women with no psychiatric history when they lose their husbands. A wife just divorced or widowed who suddenly must function on her own is in the same position as an adolescent never allowed to develop an autonomous self who must suddenly launch herself into the world. Especially in the past, many women evaded this necessity by getting married, thus entering a second adolescence that lasted at least as long as the marriage. The idea, so prevalent in the nineteenth century and not unusual today, that women are basically childish and have no ability to think both enforced this arrangement and accurately described its results. The childish female personality filled a social need that parallels the parents' need for the preschizophrenic child to accept their false version of reality. If the child-woman suddenly turned into an adult, it would upset the equilibrium not just of the standard husband-wife relationship but of the family as a whole and (by implication) of the entire society.

Further, both wifehood and schizophrenia are conditions based on dependence, for both wife and schizophrenic are considered to be impaired, unable to care for themselves. Thomas Szasz, in fact, sees schizophrenia as a contemporary *solution* to the social problem of what to do with such people, which, in regard to women, generally means those who do not marry. Until recently—and, even then, only in a few rather special realms—women were not supposed to live alone. They were required to be subject to some male figure—if not father or husband, then Christ—so in past centuries a standard solution for such women was commitment to religious life. In the modern period this was replaced by commitment to a "permanent-care facility," as madness largely replaced religious life as an alternative "career" for women who did not marry (as well as for men who threatened to be perpetually dependent).[7] We have come to take this solution so much for granted that now, as deinstitutionalization effectively cancels it and increasing numbers of solitary women appear on the street, we are shocked and horrified to discover that they even exist.

Homelessness among women, then, is created by a complex set of causes in which economic factors (such as the real estate market) and social values interact with individual psychology. It is true that most women do not develop behavior bizarre enough to make others decide they are schizophrenic. Neither are women who have disabling emotional problems indistinguishable from those who do not. Individual factors do contribute to such problems. There are many previously sheltered women who after losing their husbands go out and successfully fend for themselves, as well as homeless women who manage to get back into society. But these—in my opinion—are the heroes, and I do not believe society should be set up so that only heroes can survive. I do believe that if the social or economic pressures I have described did not exist, there would be almost no homelessness. That is why it is important to understand that "mental illness" is not an individual phenomenon—a disease—so much as a social one. And *that* is why the sight of the single, uncared-for woman provokes such concern and rightfully does so. The contemporary breakdown of our two systems of permanent care—marriage and the state hospital system—by creating such numbers of visibly homeless women, reflects real structural flaws in a society where childish dependency of women has its complement in the parental authority of men.

Their Father's Daughters

According to popular legend, St. Dymphna, who lived sometime before the thirteenth century, was the daughter of a pagan (probably Irish) king and a Christian mother, who died when Dymphna was very young, though not before she had been taught Christianity and baptized. As the girl grew older, her father developed an illicit passion for her because she closely resembled her dead mother, whom he had adored. On her confessor's advice Dymphna fled, but her father pursued her and caught her at Gheel, in what is now Belgium. When she persisted in refusing to submit to him, he murdered her. In the thirteenth century her relics were discovered and said to have cured "a number of epileptics, lunatics and persons under malign influence."[8]

The legend does not make any particular connection between the events of Dymphna's martyrdom and curing the insane, but I can offer one. A suggestion comes from the Dwelling Place woman who informed me one day at lunch that in a former life she had been St. Barbara, whose story remarkably resembles Dymphna's. St. Barbara, daughter of a rich Roman pagan, was martyred in the third century by her father. To prevent her from marrying and being taken away from him (or, in another version, to hide her so no man would see her great beauty), he built a luxurious tower and shut her up in it. Nevertheless, she became interested in Christianity and was secretly baptized. When she confessed her faith to her father, his fury at having lost her, despite his precautions, to another man (since her conversion meant accepting the superior authority of Jesus), led him to denouce her to the authorities. As was customary, he carried out her execution himself.[9]

Both these saint's tales address the position of women in a society in which men hold power. Those in power define who is mad, and St. Dymphna's legend reflects some sense of how this dynamic operates when a woman defies paternal authority. Since the legend is essentially a folktale, this perception is not highly developed but rather resembles the general tendency for someone who bucks a clearly defined power structure to be perceived as "crazy" by those whose own instinct is to obey authority. True, the story exalts Dymphna's rejection of her father; but that is only the Christian overlay. Sexual morality is not the issue here; power is. For both these stories are told from the perspective of the winning side in the struggle between the pagan and Christian fathers for the daughters' allegiance. These daughters chose the right side; thus they appear as saints instead of women possessed by the devil. Their stories make clear how vital the control of women was felt to be and what powerful social weapons were marshaled against those who showed reluctance to stay in line.

My lunch companion's choice of St. Barbara as her previous incarnation reflects a similar, unconscious perception of this same dynamic, which persists today, between people (but especially women) labeled insane and the structures of authority, still overwhelmingly male. There are two ways to look at this dynamic: as an objective reality consisting of courts and judges, hospitals and doctors, who define, dispose of, and treat people; or as the subjective reality of the women's own perceptions and images of the objective situation. It is this second reality that I want to use. I am less interested in the individual psychology behind these images (which are often shared by men and can be analyzed in terms of clinical diagnoses that are not sex-related) than in how they reveal a specifically female version of the dynamic in which passivity becomes necessary, suffering is required, and action interdicted.

It is perfectly logical that most homeless women are obsessed by images of all kinds of powerful men, images that are reflected back and forth between the women's own psychology and the society that surrounds them; for in this country the authority of government is conceptualized as male and represented by male images, from the local policeman to the black-robed judge to the President to the male deity to whose ultimate authority the whole operation supposedly subordinates itself. Thus during coffee-hour discussions of celebrities, the women talked about female movie stars, but the men they brought up tended more often to be politicians, whom they discussed as if they had been movie stars.

Nelson Rockefeller was one who evoked this kind of response. When he died in February 1979, there was a scandal over his relationship with his young secretary, a scandal played up to the hilt by the *New York Post.* At one coffee hour the women, passing the newspaper around, agreed that it was a shame, he was such a good man; he left someone $45,000, let Kissinger and others borrow money and never asked for it back, and on and on. At length I had had enough. "Rockefeller was a *bad man,*" I exclaimed. "Why are you wasting all this sympathy on him?" Astonished silence greeted me, until one woman said wonderingly, "I always thought he was terrific." I began to explain that Rockefeller represented the rich and cared nothing for poor people like themselves, but no one really heard. They were all swept away by sentimentality, as though Rockefeller were someone in a bad movie.

The feelings behind this sentimentality became clearer to me another day when one of the same women ventured a criticism of the mayor of New York and of President Carter. They had both done a bad job, she said, and wouldn't be reelected. Politicians say anything before the election but then break their promises. Several of us agreed with her, but she was evidently uncomfortable and, to my surprise, kept justifying herself, not hearing what we said. But whereas I took saying negative things about politicians for granted, doing so made her anxious and therefore defensive, although she never thought twice about criticizing the sisters or the volunteers or the other women in the Dwelling Place. Similarly she was very proud of her relationship with the manager of the hotel and always took his side when someone else complained about him. In fact her self-righteousness on these occasions inevitably brought out my own tendency to want to feel like Daddy's good girl, and each time I had to fight down the automatic assumption that the man in authority was right and the woman in conflict was wrong.

To some degree the government controls all of us; but homeless women, who depend on its checks, are interned in its hospitals, pushed around by its policemen, and disposed of by its judges, have a far more immediate experience of its power over their lives. Thus certain power relationships that in the lives of women inside society are discretely veiled by social gratuities, operate stark naked in the world of the homeless. This blatant force is, perhaps, the source of the menacing imaginings of some women, fantasies of violence and persecution by powerful impersonal authorities possessing secret knowledge. Certain institutions in particular turn into shadowy figures that inhabit many women's minds. Thus, for example, Fran, who claimed to be followed by an entourage of "intelligence," informed me that the men she went out with had always turned out to be CIA or FBI.

The opposite of these malevolent authorities is a male figure perceived as not destructive at all but benevolent, paternalistic, and often romantic. Nelson Rockefeller, as we saw, was such a figure for a number of women, quite in defiance of reality. What made him so was not only his glamorous personal life but his connection to the fabled Rockefeller millions: for money, both symbolically and really, is power, and men are the ones who have it.

While most women I knew employed one or two or three of these images to express their perceptions of male-female and social power relationships, Mimi used almost every one of them. While it was clear that Mimi's ideas were delusional, they were also quite meaningful—and not only as metaphor. Mimi was a black woman with very light skin who always wore a blond wig. Her father had been white, she said, her mother black; and her system of ideas was a composite of dualities, based on this condition of being two contradictory things at once. She was obsessed by the figure of the transvestite, a good emblem of such a problematic state of being. Whereas to Fran all men were CIA, to Mimi they were all gay. A gay man she had found in the women's room at her hotel threatened to rape her and throw her out the window. She talked of a husband who was "a gay" and had an operation to make himself a woman. She identified him with Satan and the "gays" with the demons who were taking over America. One day, however, she announced triumphantly that her husband had died—"the bad one." She claimed she never wanted to get married again but told me in the next breath that she was engaged to Rockefeller. (After Rockefeller died she became engaged to his brother.) Another time she came in saying she had been to court, and it had gone very well; she had had a woman judge who agreed with her and said it didn't matter if they were black or white, they were all gays.

Mimi evidently had organized a whole set of issues into dualities expressed through the one of gay/straight: good/bad, black/white, man/woman. And, in fact, all of Mimi's dualities boiled down to a single fundamental one, which I discovered on the day in 1979 that the Israel-Egypt peace treaty was signed. Waving the *Daily News* with its front-page photo of Anwar Sadat and Menachim Begin, Mimi announced that she was going to Egypt to make a business investment with Sadat. However he wanted her only as a blonde because that was the way he saw her, although it wasn't her true self. Her husband, who was a millionaire, did want her as her true self; and she had no intention of losing her true self but was going to appear to Sadat the way he wanted her, for a time, because of this investment, by dyeing her hair.

Mimi thus put in a nutshell the whole traditional power dynamic between individual men and women, as well as the more general dynamic that lies behind the elaborate delusions of spying, secrecy, and privileged information: the central duality of true self and false self. Like Mimi, most of the homeless women no longer know which is which; for after years of hiding the true self from the intelligence operatives, they have lost sight of it themselves. But this is the secret that the CIA seeks, the judges pass judgment on, and the Rockefellers want to buy. For as the study of sex-role stereotypes, Lidz's theory of schizophrenia, and the two saint's tales all suggest, the true self is not wanted: a woman who acted according to its dictates would step outside the power structure and be free, and therefore dangerous.

Mimi's images also had a literal meaning, however: one day she actually was attacked by a man in her hotel. Unlike an earlier occasion when she claimed to have been hit by a bus but had no bruises, this time she had two black eyes and a broken arm. The "gay" man's threat to rape her, which had seemed to us a fantasy, now appeared to be an actual incident that had been incorporated into her fantasy system. Similarly her earlier stories about a judge melted into what sounded like the real story of the rapist being brought to trial; she said he had pleaded guilty and would be sentenced (though we never found out what happened, because we knew little about Mimi's daily life).

We see, then, how subtly the homeless women's images of powerful male figures are related to the reality of their lives. While the images may symbolize a larger power dynamic in society, they also derive directly from experience and on that level are not symbolic at all. Thus the essential ambiguity of the male figure as both punisher and lover (perfectly expressed by Mimi's alternation, from one sentence to the next, from her gay husband to her rich Rockefeller fiancé) reflects a real-life double bind: the person who punishes the homeless woman is also the only source of what she needs. As a result, not only does she accept the punishment, but it becomes intertwined with gratification: a situation that constitutes the essence of powerlessness because it prevents her from seeing the possibility of other modes of being, such as strength or self-reliance. The idea of being strong herself is frightening—less because it invites more punishment, which after all she is used to, than because it threatens the loss of whatever she has been getting, little as that may be. So she devalues whatever real strengths she may have in order to avoid even approaching this conflict.

The results of such a training were demonstrated in the fall of 1981 when, as a result of Reagan administration cutbacks, the food stamps of the women in the hotel were cut by as much as 60 percent (from $38 a month to $17). One could request a hearing with a reasonable chance of having the cut restored, since real need was easy to demonstrate (aside from the food stamps the women had only $3.00 a day to spend on *all* their needs after paying rent). But very few could be persuaded to go for the hearing, even with a volunteer advocate. They were afraid that everything would be taken away. While men on welfare or SSI are treated as badly as women, they at least have generally not been trained up to the automatic expectation or assumption of punishment, an assumption that makes so many women unable to take action for themselves and explains why they so often actively punish themselves: they feel safer if they can get there first, as it were.[10]

If elements of this power dynamic seem familiar, that is because it does not operate only among the homeless, or even only among the poor. Out in the street, homeless women appear to be alien creatures, so it is easy to assume that they are responsible for their fate because of who they are, that is, because they are in some way different. But in fact the extremeness of their condition results from the conventional definition of "woman" being taken to the limit. Where the essence of woman is considered to be contingency and dependence, homelessness becomes a natural complement of marriage.

BEYOND THE "NORMAL FAMILY"
A Cultural Critique of Women's Poverty

Margaret Cerullo and Marla Erlien

We live in and with a bourgeois society, its history, its traditions and prejudices, its confrontations and wicked laughter. Anyone who tries to behave well and play by what seem for the moment to be the rules of the game passes judgment on others who are outside the mainstream because they break the rules or don't bother to acknowledge them.
———Hans Mayer, Outsiders[1]

In order to think critically about the causes of poverty and to respond politically to it, a perspective is needed that includes, but goes beyond, an economic understanding of the welfare state. Poverty, welfare, and "dependency," are never simple social facts or economic realities. Consciousness, culture, and politics play a crucial role in defining their meanings—for poor people and their friends as well as their antagonists.

Poor people's movements in the 1960s achieved two related goals. First, they increased benefit levels. But, second, and as a

The authors developed many of the ideas in this essay in conversation with Paulla Ebron, Fran White, and Ann Withorn. Ann Holder and Ann Withorn provided moral support and made the essay more readable.

crucial part of the first process, they also transformed the meaning of poverty from a personal shame to a national responsibility; they shifted welfare from an insult to a right. And it is poor people's expanded sense of entitlement and dignity that the New Right has targeted, as much as benefits and services. In its cultural war on the poor, the Right is attempting to reestablish poverty as a mark of sin, a character flaw.

Cultural assumptions, as well as political-economic structures, block the poor from claiming their rights and their humanity. The battle for poor women's empowerment, then, must also take place on the uncharted terrain of culture, as well as on the more familiar ground of economic policy analysis.

Culture and Poverty

The focus here is on women and how cultural norms of womanhood are used to explain the causes and meaning of women's poverty, as well as to dehumanize poor women and push them to the margins of society.

When the authors speak of "culture" in this essay we refer to habits of mind and feeling, "ways of seeing," that underlie the way people impart meaning to daily life and to the social world they inhabit. We are interested in the consciousness and ideology that surround questions of poverty and the welfare state. For us "consciousness" includes not only the explicit beliefs and values that people hold but also the psychological dimension: the unconscious commitments that affect how people act, that determine what disturbs, paralyzes, or mobilizes them.

A dominant culture (such as that of the contemporary United States) is a set of prescriptions and norms for living that anchor existing social and economic arrangements. It is important to expose and challenge the dominant culture. Whether one embraces it or not, this culture undermines alternative ways of living, loving, and seeing. Cultural norms accomplish this opposition, however, not only when they succeed in determining behavior. More deeply, their power comes from establishing the meaning attached to "deviating," or living outside the norms of society.

During the 1930s, for example, many mothers worked while

unemployed fathers stayed home. Children reared in such families did not experience this departure from prescribed sex roles as an alternative to dominant values but as a shame or stigma. As parents themselves in the 1950s, such children were quick to reestablish "normal families."[2] Today the "traditional" family of father as breadwinner, mother as homemaker, and the children is no longer an empirical norm. Yet its power as a model of right living haunts and often punishes those who live outside it.

The women's movement has exposed the ways in which cultural norms—definitions of "proper" family, "appropriate" sex roles, "normal" sexuality, "good" mothering—circumscribe women's lives. When women try to claim power over their lives, they must confront all the power of these cultural expectations, within themselves as well as in the broader society. But poor women must also confront the state's power to enforce those norms at will.

As black feminists have insisted, questions of racial identity have been crucial to the construction of gender in the United States. For example, the rules that separate "good women" from "bad women" have had a racial dimension.[3] Black women must prove themselves to be good; white women are always in danger of being seen as bad. In order to understand current welfare policy and the popular hostility to the welfare state, then, concerned citizens need to consider the ways in which poor women both challenge and embody cultural and racial norms.

Politics and Poverty

Feminists and other advocates for the poor have concentrated on proving the existence and extent of women's poverty. They have stressed the numbers and the hard data on benefits, as though ignorance of "facts" were the obstacle to women's poverty being recognized and addressed. The Right has provided most of the recent discussion of the cultural aspects of poverty, in order to reinforce and rigidify the dominant culture, not to challenge it.

On the one hand, conservative analysts invoke the dominant culture against those outside the mainstream. They locate the causes of poverty in poor people themselves, blaming them for their "inadequacies," lack of initiative, or "acceptance of dependency." Poverty is treated as a scourge, poor people as parasites on the majority. Poverty becomes not a circumstance but an attribute of a type of person.[4] The poor are presented as culturally different from the majority, a "pathological" subculture or, more recently, a permanent "underclass" prone to illegitimacy, crime, and debasement of the community. When poverty can be viewed as a function of race, the danger of cultural isolation for the poor becomes even greater.

On the other hand, liberals are willing to say that the culture of poverty is not immutable. Yet, in their failure to question the dominant culture, they link themselves to conservative critiques, even though their policy recommendations differ. While conservatives move to diminish welfare or deepen the stigma attached to it, liberals would keep economic supports but attempt to instill the work ethic and middle-class values in the poor. Both agree on the superiority of middle-class values, as well as on the assumption that lack of them causes poverty. They simply disagree about how best to force them on the poor—by threats and punishments or by "retraining" and "clinical intervention."

A quote from Hans Mayer begins this essay because he provides an alternative framework to that of liberals and conservatives. Mayer asks how it is that those designated as "outsiders" become dehumanized, objects of contempt for those who "play by the rules." For the purposes of this essay the question becomes: How is it that those who bear the burden of poverty are blamed for their situation and seen as undeserving of genuine social support?

To answer this question, Mayer shifts the usual explanations. Rather than focus on deviance, the culture of the poor, he views adherence to the dominant culture as the problem. He reminds us how difficult it is to behave according to the rules. The spectre of "outsider" status (or the effort to overcome it) strengthens the power of the rules; it keeps people behaving well. Moreover, the difficulty of adhering to the rules provokes resentment towards those who don't or can't.

Mayer's framework is especially illuminating today, when people perceive themselves to be losing ground. A television talk show that explored feelings about Medicaid abortions produced a telling response from one woman: "Why should we have to pay for someone else's pleasure?" This reaction, a familiar one, points up how economic realities become fused with moral issues to shape a potentially authoritarian response against welfare recipients.

The present economy makes personal sacrifice less meaningful as a means of guaranteeing present or future rewards. Such a situation allows people to turn against alternatives that seem to allow others the right to relief from the constraints and vulnerabilities of the marketplace. Only when people understand the fragile dignity that comes from playing by the rules, even if they lose, can they understand the popular passions that envelop the hopes of poor women.

When advocates of welfare rights sidestep a confrontation with cultural judgments about "proper" families, approved sexuality, and norms of right living, they eliminate the question of why it is so difficult to mobilize a movement in defense of an expanded welfare state. It is not enough, for example, to show how lack of decent jobs, not lack of husbands or "proper" values, creates women's poverty. Popular attitudes, as well as policy makers, have shown themselves to be remarkably resistant to such "rational" interpretations. Nor have appeals to self-interest succeeded in winning support for welfare rights: the logic of spending money on poor children in order to prevent more expensive social costs later is simply not convincing to those who want to punish teenage mothers, for example.

Such narrow, "common sense" analyses neglect the power of the morality and values that regulate private life and sustain the structure of work and family life. When self-interest is invoked to win popular support for the defense of welfare rights, we forget that self-interest can't be reduced to economics, that people's sense of worth is bound up with behaving well. When other people fail to "live by the rules" and go unpunished, then the sacrifices involved in "behaving well" are rendered meaningless.

Opposition to Medicaid-funded abortions is a good example of the failure of appeals to self-interest as a means of changing popular attitudes. In defense of Medicaid abortion, liberals argued that it was cheaper to fund them than to pay for expanding Aid to Families with Dependent Children (AFDC) rolls. Indeed, it does seem logical that conservatives who oppose the expansion of AFDC should be willing to pay the smaller cost of Medicaid-funded abortions. However, another logic, a cultural logic not addressed in the liberal defense, ties these two positions together.

Punishing both poor women who want abortions and AFDC mothers preserves the meaningfulness of the distinction between "good" and "bad" women, a distinction in which the racial dimension is seldom absent. "Good" women don't have abortions (not at least without feeling bad about them), and they don't have babies "out of wedlock." "Normal" women have breadwinners to support them, so it is more difficult to control their behavior from outside the family. Thus society punishes "bad" poor women who become pregnant without wanting a baby; it eliminates state funding for abortion. At the same time, it must also punish single mothers for failing to keep a man, so welfare benefits must be low enough to deny a dignified livelihood.

Following this argument, if the cultural assumptions about female sexuality, "normal" families, proper relations between men and women, and "good" mothering are not challenged, any defense of welfare rights will be inadequate. It will fail to break into the liberal-conservative continuum that requires punishing or pitying those outside the norms of "proper" living. Yet, in the current climate, so haunted by the New Right, this challenge is seldom raised.

Even those who most ardently advocate the welfare state are not immune from the impact of the New Right. When the Right moved in to reestablish its standards regarding relations between men and women, female sexuality, definitions of the family, and homosexuality, it put liberals, progressives, and even feminists on the defensive. Those who advocate abortion, aid for teenage mothers, or gay rights fear they will be cast as antifamily, in favor of promiscuity, i.e., that they will also be labeled "deviant." Many responded by trying to defuse these issues. They consider abortion and gay rights, for example, as "privacy issues," backing off from a defense of sexual freedom and female autonomy. Yet, such defenses deny what people know is at stake.

All the Women Are White, All the Blacks Are Men.

The dangers of avoiding deeper cultural challenges can be illustrated by turning to two recent efforts to rethink poverty. First we examine the renewed discussion within the black community in response to the seeming intractability, and worsening, of poverty among black people. Second, we turn to feminists who have developed an analysis of poverty as a women's issue. We want to show how the absence of a critical perspective on the interaction of race and gender limits both analyses. The result is that both discussions treat as marginal the experience, needs, and insights of black women and other women of color. There is a particularly cruel irony here, since women of color have borne so much of the burden of poverty and of popular hostility to the poor.

The devastating impact of the Reagan years and the emergence of black conservative analyses proposing "self-help" rather than public programs, have provoked a reexamination of the causes of poverty.[5] While black liberals continue to call for public programs, they have joined black conservatives in linking the persistence of poverty among blacks to the "crisis" of the black family.

"The 'disintegrating' African-American family is the most important and alarming demographic development in our time," according to Pierre Devise of the Chicago Urban League.[6] And Salim Muakkill, a black journalist writing in a socialist newspaper, gives the following as evidence of the deep crisis confronting the African-American community: "Black children are five times as likely [as white children] to be murdered as teenagers, four times as likely to be incarcerated between 15 and 19 and four times as likely to live in a female-headed household."[7] The casual equation of incarceration and murder with growing up in female-headed families is remarkable. The horror of such families and the exclusive concern with the fate of black males recalls the 1965 Moynihan Report, which many thought was dead and buried. Some blacks now argue that Moynihan should be reconsidered, that his analysis was too quickly and too defensively discarded. We think it is important to recall in some detail the assertions of the document and contemporary responses to it so that its revival will not turn the argument against black women.

Moynihan Revisited

In his notorious 1965 article, "The Negro Family: The Case for National Action," Daniel Moynihan tried to explain the persistence of poverty and unemployment in black America at a time when liberals thought systemic poverty would be cured through Keynesian economic policies.[8] In effect, Moynihan reduced racism and structural unemployment to a cultural failing of the black underclass. The "legacy of slavery" he argued, had resulted in a black American (male) population with structurally unemployable *attributes* and underclass *values,* such as lack of work orientation or interest in acquiring education and job skills.

"At the heart of the deterioration of the Negro community," he wrote in his most quoted line, "is the deterioration of the Negro family." According to Moynihan, slavery had left black people with a "matriarchal" pattern in which boys raised by mothers lacked the proper character structure to compete in the economic marketplace. Delinquency, poor educational achievement, the inability to delay gratification—all were presented as the products of "fatherless homes."

All this is well enough known. What is important is that the Moynihan report generated extensive controversy and opposition that have implications for today, in terms of what was and was not debated.

The black community and its allies vehemently denounced the Moynihan Report.[9] Indeed, it became the generative example for "blaming the victim"—for naming a black "culture of poverty," instead of racism as the cause of poverty. Lest we forget, it appeared at a time when the black liberation movement was exposing the structures of institutional racism as the barriers to black advancement. The Moynihan Report was a response to black demands, an argument for an expanded welfare state, a key document of the liberal "war on poverty." Yet by steering the discussion away from basic social and economic structures, Moynihan could call for reforming the poor rather than transforming society. It is worth looking at the contested issues since they reappear in the current discussion as well.

Moynihan's arguments about the "broken" Negro family were countered by historians and sociologists who showed the existence of more complex, extended-family patterns within the black community.[10] The assumption of a white middle-class norm of what a "proper" family is, they argued, blocked Moynihan and other writers from seeing these alternative traditions. Against the assumption that nuclear families provided an ideal setting for child rearing, African-American culture was seen as embodying a tradition in which, as the novelist Toni Morrison expressed it, "It takes a village to raise a child, not one parent or two, but a whole village."[11]

What is striking, though, after fifteen years of black feminist analysis, is how this early criticism responded, and did not respond, to the sexist character of the Moynihan Report, to its interpretation of the role of women in African-American history and its prescriptions for black women's future.

While some of Moynihan's critics recognized the attack on black women, they responded by defending the women's strengths in resisting a history of racist assaults on the community. Although this perspective has been and remains crucial, it stopped short of exposing or challenging the underlying assumptions about proper relationships between men and women that led Moynihan to blame black women in the first place.

A closer look reveals that Moynihan was concerned not about poverty in the black community but about the poverty of black men. Moreover, his evidence for black men's weakness in income, employment, and education was not primarily in comparison with whites (men or women) but with black women. The implication throughout is that the employment and education of black women is denigrating to black men, perpetuating the "reversed" roles of husband and wife, which Moynihan said characterized the black family.

Moynihan's assumption that black women's education and employment status make them powerful, indeed too powerful, in relation to black men is key. It is an assumption that, as early black feminists pointed out, was often shared by black men (and women), indeed one that became embodied in the sexual politics of black cultural nationalism. Thus the racist aspects of Moynihan's "black matriarchy" thesis were underlined, but its sexist implications were unrecognized.

To take a striking example, when Moynihan proposed the army as an alternative source of discipline and character building for black men, the racist character of using blacks as cannon fodder in Viet Nam was immediately obvious. Less emphasized was Moynihan's elegy to the army as a world of men, a world away from black women, a relief from "the strains of the disorganized and matrifocal family life in which so many Negro youth come of age."

More generally, the model of "traditional" family structure was upheld as the goal for the black community, as the solution to black poverty. It was not only a white middle-class model but, crucially for Moynihan, a male-dominated one. As he wrote: "Ours is a society which presumes male leadership in private and public affairs. The arrangements of society facilitate such leadership and reward it. A subculture, such as that of the Negro-American, in which this is not the pattern is placed at a distinct disadvantage." The defense against Moynihan was to accept the presumption of male leadership, and argue that it was intact in the black community.

Twenty years later the failure to challenge Moynihan's sexism comes back to haunt black women—indeed, all women. Now there are "legitimate" black as well as white conservatives to take up the call to reassert male authority. Now both black and white liberals are reviving the notion that it is female-headed black families that somehow cause poverty. And once again the concern is for the (male) children who must be "abnormally" socialized in female-dominated worlds.

At least this time black women have entered the debate to turn the emphasis around, by focusing on the burden that unsupported female-headed families place upon women and not on the "problem" of female-headed families for males. As Eleanor Holmes Norton puts it, "It is simply too much to ask what amounts to an increasing number of black women to raise the children of the black nation."[12] For Dorothy Height, writing in *Ebony,* the problem is the increasing isolation of teenage female-headed families from the once stronger extended family network, which "has fallen victim to the hardships of urban community life and the anti-family policies of public assistance agencies."[13] In her view, it's not the fact that families are female-headed that is the problem, rather that such families are "breaking down into smaller poorer units."

If the needs of poor black women are to avoid being pushed to the margins of society by the new debate about poverty, the sexism voiced by Moynihan must be exposed. Today, black women have begun to draw on traditions within the black experience to challenge the "normal," white, nuclear-family model, which is being posed as a backlash against the women's movements. As Moynihan realized, "normal" presumes male leadership, and "proper" socialization requires a child-centered, self-denying mother. By posing alternative models of family life, drawn from black history, black women are making the dominant culture itself contested terrain.

Good Women and Bad Women

It is in this context that the most popularized "feminization of poverty" discussion is disappointing.[14] The writings of Barbara Ehrenreich, Karin Stallard, and Holly Sklar attempt to debunk the myth that a "culture of dependence," attributed to women of color, is the root cause of poverty. They try to show how unpredictable poverty is by highlighting the experience of Avis Parke, "with her handsome New England features and hearty outgoing manner, . . . not the kind of person you would expect to catch paying for her groceries with food stamps." Her story—she was "a virgin when she married thirty years ago"—is presented as typical of the "new poor" and as a means of breaking the traditional isolation of poor women. By exposing how poverty haunts all women, the authors hope to dislodge divisive stereotypes of poor women. Middle-class women can see themselves in Avis Parke; thus such examples help build cross-class identification among women.

Yet the very device intended to create unity serves to reinforce cultural stereotypes of who poor women are: promiscuous women, women of color, and unwed teenage mothers. For many readers, Avis Parke is simply presented as not "one of them." In fact, the term "displaced homemaker" used to characterize women like Avis Parke who "played by the rules" comes to rescue such women from the stigma attached to being on welfare. By highlighting the "fall" of middle-class, white, once-married women into poverty, the historical poverty among women of color and young women is taken as a norm.

The dominant U.S. culture often views black women's poverty as due to promiscuity, having children "out of wedlock." The poor black woman is a type of person, whereas the poverty of a good woman, such as Avis Parke, is situational. By casting the new female poor as good women who have fallen on hard times, the authors appeal to, rather than challenge, the good woman-bad woman dichotomy. Black feminists have shown how casting black women as immoral is crucial to the construction of white womanhood, how the purity of white women is a mark of racial superiority.[15] When Ehrenreich et al. root for poor (white) women's claim to recognition in their "goodness," they leave black women undefended. They also reinforce the values of self-sacrifice and sexual purity that imprison "good" women. They evoke sympathy for poor women as victims, blocking the ways in which rebellion against dependence on individual men may also be part of the reason for women's poverty.

What would have been the effect if Avis Parke had kicked out her husband, perhaps in order to come out as a lesbian? In choosing to build bridges to white women by avoiding racial issues, instead of reaching out to black women by addressing them, feminists will fail to create the alliances needed to protect all poor women from increasing stigmatization.

Beyond the Nuclear Family

While we were writing this essay, a series of developments occurred in our home state, "liberal" Massachusetts, that provide a dramatic "case study" for examining how these central issues related to cultural norms play themselves out in the making of social policy.

In May of 1985, the liberal governor of Massachusetts reacted to press accounts decrying the placement of two young boys in the home of a gay couple for foster care. Although the Department of Social Services had spent a year investigating the two men, the governor removed the children from their care.

This precipitous move created a climate of permission for legislative New Rightists, who quickly introduced a resolution that would bar gays from foster care, guardianship, adoption, and family day care—because of the "physical and psychological danger" represents their sexual preference to the well-being of children. The resolution passed overwhelmingly, 112 to 28.

Two weeks after the removal of the boys from the home a new policy was issued. The new regulations invoked the "traditional" family structure—working father, mother at home with children of their own—as the model child-rearing situation for foster-care placement. Except for relatives of the foster children, the policy makes it very difficult for any "nontraditional" family to be considered for giving foster care. If society truly considers the well-being of children from already disrupted families, the policy makers argued, then it should not further "burden" them by placing them in nontraditional settings.

The *Boston Globe* editorial that anticipated the policy announcement made the stakes clear. Entitled "A Normal Setting," the editorial upheld what some called the "Ozzie and Harriet" or "Father Knows Best" image of family life. Families with working mothers, single parents, or gay or lesbian couples were clearly deviant, undesirable, and abnormal. Nowhere was there mention of the decreasing numbers of "normal" families, much less that such families have been the site of most battering and sexual abuse of women and children. And, of course, nothing was said about the inequality between men and women that lies at the core of what is "normal" about traditional families—just as Moynihan noted twenty years ago.

Amazingly, many of the liberal centers of power—even those that support women's and gay rights—showed strong commitment to this myth of the happy, traditional family. The *Globe* and most politicians gave consistent support to the governor's stance. One New Right state representative exposed the profound conservative-liberal continuum that is operating here when he proclaimed that he was delighted to see the liberal governor taking time away from Reagan-bashing to uphold the value of the traditional family. Only the liberal social work and psychological professionals broke ranks and questioned the logic.

More importantly, the blatant way in which the policy attempted to enforce cultural norms of right living through welfare policies was recognized and opposed by a wide variety of groups. The primary target of the foster care policy was lesbians and gay men, who have continued to lead the fight against it. However, the policy also triggered the historical memories of other constituencies. For some it recalled the Nazi separation of Jew from non-Jew. For others, it recalled Moynihan's punitive hierarchy of normal and deviant families. Leaders of the progressive black community denounced the racist implications of upholding the model of "traditional" family life. One black activist noted: "The traditional family enslaved my ancestors," thereby giving one more rejoinder to those who forget how central notions of proper family life are to white racial superiority in the United States.

Finally, opponents of the policy have emphasized how it does more than "regulate" the behavior of the poor and others directly subject to state control. It forces social workers into being "culture cops." Like so many other welfare-state policies, it is also about establishing *a* way of life, consistent with existing social and economic arrangements. The suppression of alternatives is integral to its goals.

This is an essay whose political conclusion is still in the making. The authors cannot end with "solutions" to women's poverty or even with specific social-policy recommendations. Rather we have tried to explore the cultural environment within which social policy is formulated. As the discussion proceeds about the pervasiveness and seeming intractability of women's poverty, we suggest that substantive change will not occur without dislodging the cultural norms that keep some people behaving "well" and that force others to the margins of society.

Reforms that obviously helped to relieve the burden of poverty have been dismantled. Efforts to reassert them have been blocked, or never even started. Even as homelessness and hunger show the situation of the poor to be even more desperate, hostility to them intensifies, assuming ever more "irrational" overtones. We suggest that such hostility cannot be countered with appeals to economic self interest. Instead poor women and their advocates must find ways to counter the moral authority of cultural norms that both create blindness to growing impoverishment and provide a rationale for turning against the poor, the deviant, the "outsider."

PART FOUR
And Still I Rise: Visions of Change

What's a poor girl to do?

The deep, abiding problems of women's poverty often lead to a frustrating, circular fatalism. Standard explanations view the poor woman as passive. Either she is a classic victim—needing the "charity" of individual men and of government—or she is somehow responsible for her fate—the "fallen woman" who has "made her bed," through sexual promiscuity or bad marriage, and "must lie in it."

Policy makers, at their best, only tackle a piece of the problem—here a job program, there an educational incentive, everywhere a too-small amount of money. Such responses fail both because they are inadequate to the depths of the need and because they ignore underlying problems. And by failing, they teach the incorrect lesson that nothing can be done to end the "cycle of poverty" for most poor women after all.

In this section the authors attempt to go beyond traditional solutions that are inadequate or that will help only one group of poor women, often at the expense of another. Together they address the major underlying problems that create and maintain women's poverty: the undervaluing in the home and in the job market of care giving; the need to expand and radically improve public programs, instead of abandoning them; and the need to develop models for empowerment and political organizing that will allow women to exert leadership without abandoning men of color or other male allies. Although each writer offers some concrete suggestions, none attempts to be narrowly "realistic." All exhibit an unspoken, but shared sense that what is realistic for many men and governmental policy makers has little or nothing to do with the real needs of poor women.

Comparable worth, or pay equity, is a tactic for highlighting and changing the ways in which women's work is economically valued. As discussed by Teresa Amott and Julie Matthaei, it returns to a theme that is sometimes lost in the focus on the woes of poor women within the welfare state: the notion that without a breadwinner's wage, and the benefits that go with that wage, women will stay poor.

But, as Deanne Bonnar and Frances Piven both argue, women cannot rely on regulation of the capitalist marketplace alone to cure poverty. Real pay equity will be a long time coming, and even then it will not address the fundamental class inequities within the society. When a secretary and a maintenance man earn the same wages, together they will still earn half what a lawyer makes and one fifth of what a big executive makes, and they will still not be able to send their children to elite colleges, even if they stay married. Class and racial discrimination will remain.

In addition, most women make less because so much of their care-giving work in the family is totally unpaid, except in the puny salary scale of the so-called social wage of welfare benefits. Their hard work holding home and family together is unacknowledged, either as an additional drain on them when they work outside the home or as an essential job that must be done for society to continue. When poor women are heads of households they need many supports that are practically unavailable outside the welfare system. So in the short run certainly, many poor women will need expanded and more appropriate benefits, not just jobs, in order to live decently—and with a sliding fee scale, instead of the arbitrary cutoffs that pit some poor women against others.

Even in the long run, it is not clear that full employment would solve all the needs of poor women or of society. Perhaps part of being "unrealistic" is to question whether the goal of U.S. society is to employ every person outside the home or whether it is to organize all the activities of society so that people can live well, if they work outside the home or within it. Here Deanne Bonnar's speculations about the need for a "redefinition of work" are critical. She suggests that only when we, as a society, reevaluate the meaning and economic value of care-giving work will we be able truly to understand, and redistribute, our real "gross national product." In fact we might see her arguments as calling for a kind of "pay equity" between labor in the job market and nurturing labor in the home.

And, finally, there is political action and political education. Twenty years ago a welfare-rights movement spurred policy makers into expanding welfare benefits and gave the world a picture of the collective power of poor women. Today welfare mothers are grouped by politicians and journalists into an "underclass" with ex-convicts, drug addicts, and alcoholics. Meanwhile politics 1980s style puts a right-wing woman on the Supreme Court, while another rich white woman runs for Vice President and then proclaims that motherhood is the only thing she never regrets—in a Pepsi Cola ad, no less.

It is time for a change, and perhaps, again, time for a change led by poor women. Rochelle Lefkowitz discusses the value of voter registration for poor women. Her question is whether there is a broad base for new tactics and strategies for building new movements and new coalitions and forming new political agendas. Her hope, and the hope of this volume, is that poor women can avoid conciliation with either conservatives who want women to settle back into "normal" families (and "normal" poverty?) or with experts who will once again produce policies irrelevant to their needs. In order to accomplish this, all women may need the "community education" for political and economic literacy that Pat Jerabek and Teresa Amott describe.

In the poem that gives the title to this section Maya Angelou speaks of black women's ability to "rise" in the face of hate, doubt, and lies. We begin here with the voices of women who have made powerful personal changes through attending an educational program that gives the lie to the methods and assumptions of traditional "job training" programs. Their hopes and their dreams demand change and demand that it be the dramatic change poor women need, not the "feasible" change others with more privilege, power, and resources might choose.

WEAVING NEW HOPES

Delores Rainey, Theresa Goings, Denise Martin, Florence Dumont, Bertha Franklin, Roslyn David, and Rosalie Johnson

Women Inc. is a nonprofit community service agency in Boston. It provides innovative treatment programs to meet the special needs of urban women who have difficulties with drug and alcohol abuse. It is an alternative-treatment program administered by women for women and their children. The staff is a group of racially and culturally mixed women from various professional and nonprofessional backgrounds.

Women's Educational and Vocational Enrichment (WEAVE) is one of the projects of Women Inc. It was designed to address the specific educational, prevocational, and employment needs of women in the treatment program. WEAVE has also served many women from Boston's poorer communities who have not experienced drug and alcohol abuse. WEAVE has grown into a model school that provides an intensive, problem-centered, self-development curriculum to build analytical and conceptual skills. In addition, classes in reading, writing, and math prepare students for a high school diploma.

---

* For further information about Women Inc. and WEAVE, write or call the Director, Katie Portis, 570 Warren Street, Roxbury, MA 02119.

WEAVE provides a supportive atmosphere that inspires self-awareness and offers a social and cultural understanding of the conditions under which women must survive in U.S. society. A major goal is to explore how social and personal life events have a major influence on people and their behavior. Staff assume that they cannot examine and help clarify the interpersonal experiences of people without giving equal consideration to the community and the social and cultural aspects of the society in which they live.[1] [In this way the program embodies many of the principles discussed next by Amott and Jerabek. Ed.]

Here some of the graduates of WEAVE's class of 1985 discuss their hopes and accomplishments in the program.

Delores Rainey

I see WEAVE as one big family—women struggling through life helping each other as one community. We learn how to deal with the outside world better. Here at WEAVE we, as a community, help each other build our self-esteem. I have had my share of struggles and at WEAVE I have learned to deal with them.

I was born September 30, 1954, in a small town called Waynesboro in Georgia. I dropped out of school at the age of fifteen and left home due to family difficulties. I was never able to return to school. There I was out in the world struggling, a fifteen-year-old black girl, not afraid, just taking life as it came.

My first job after leaving home was homemaking. I got myself a studio apartment and earned enough money to support myself and pay my rent. Then I had my first child when I was eighteeeen. I gave up my apartment and went back home to live with my father, who gave me a helping hand with my son.

I left Georgia in 1974. I had heard that I would have a better opportunity here in Boston to support myself and my son. So I came here and lived with my father's sister for nine months. She was very kind to me. She helped me find my first apartment here. I first worked at Sears and Roebuck, and then my second son was born. Then I did volunteer work at the Lindsey Shattuck Hospital as a way of learning new skills. Then I set out again and found my current job as a mental-health worker, where I have stayed for the last six and a half years. The people I work with have been very understanding and supportive while I have been in school.

It has not been easy for me at WEAVE because I have had to work at my job and attend school. Plus I have a family to support and raise. My boys, Daniel and Seneca, whom I love very much, have been patient and very understanding. I've also got a lot of support from the staff at WEAVE and from my classmates.

Theresa Goings

I was born in Boston with the given name Theresa Tess McCarthy. At the time of my birth, my biological mother was seventeeen years old, and she felt that she wasn't ready to deal with the responsibility of a child. She put me up for adoption, and five years later, I was adopted. It wasn't until years later that I met my real mother.

I was sixteen years old when I quit school. My biological mother was found murdered in the Columbia Point Project, and this hurt me so much that I couldn't deal with her death and going back to school too. So I dropped out.

Later, I decided to go back to school, but I felt it would be hard to return to public school. I asked around until I was told about the WEAVE program.

Since I have been at WEAVE, I have learned a lot about my feelings as a woman and the feelings of other women. I've learned how to express my feelings to others instead of hiding them all inside until one day I just burst out in tears.

I believe that we as women have the right to come together and stand and fight. And when the fighting's all done, we'll come together and unite as one.

Denise Martin

I grew up in Boston with my mother and four brothers. Growing up in the [housing] projects was typical for a black woman without a husband. My father abandoned my mother when we were very small. She had to work and raise us by herself. Her job wasn't easy, but I respect her because she gave us all the love she had. Her life was hard in Boston, but she did her best.

I am a thirty-one-year-old woman, who quit school when I was seventeen. The reason I dropped out of school was because I became pregnant. A year later I got married and began to raise a family. Marriage wasn't what I expected it to be, but I am still married. As my children got older, I went to work at factories and at odd jobs I could find.

One day while I was at work, I began to think about who I was, where I was, and where I was going. I knew I was not educated and that there was not much I could do without an eduation. This started to bother me. I had always thought that I couldn't learn, and, to tell the truth, I thought I really didn't need to. But my life was changing, and my kids needed help with their homework. I wasn't even able to help them.

A friend of mine told me about WEAVE and how it was a good program for women. By coming to WEAVE, I have learned about different women and that the struggles of other women's lives are not that different from my own. I really needed confidence in myself. I have never believed in me, but the class that I'm in—the reading of black women's literature, the writing of essays, and the self-esteem we gained—made me aware that I can reach my goal with a little effort and a lot of love—love of the other women in my class, the staff at WEAVE, and most of all love of myself.

Florence Dumont

My grandparents were born in Canada. They had twelve children, five girls and seven boys. They had a farm in Maine with animals and acres of land to harvest crops. I was born when my mother was twenty-one years old. When my brothers and sisters came along, my mother had to go to work in the shoe factory. We were taken care of during the week by a lady who had eight children of her own. I couldn't wait for Friday to come so I could go home to my mother's homemade breads, cakes, jams, and jellies. Everything was made from scratch, and we ate it as soon as it came out of the oven. My mother never had to worry about leftovers. At

Christmas my grandmother took our toys, did them over, and gave them to us again. We didn't know at the time these were the same toys we had broken up, because our grandmother had repaired them like new.

My mother wanted very much for us to get an education so we wouldn't have to spend our lives on a farm or working in a shoe factory like she had done. Unfortunately, times became even harder. At the age of sixteen I had to quit school and go to work. I came to Boston when I was seventeen. I worked most of my life until I got sick. Three years ago the doctors told me I would no longer be able to do any type of work that required me to stand on my feet for any length of time. It was then that I decided to further my education and get back to work as soon as possible. I wanted to better myself and to be able to help my son with his future.

During my sixteen weeks at WEAVE, my classmates and I became very close. There were times when we all had bad days, and sometimes there was confusion among the class. Some students even thought of dropping out, but we worked hard to understand each other by sharing our common struggles. From this experience we all became better women to ourselves and to each other. We are lucky to have a program like WEAVE to help women help themselves. The staff at WEAVE is devoted to helping women realize their potential. It is a school that is greatly needed in our community.

Bertha Franklin

I was born August 14, 1952, in Greenville, Mississippi. I started school when I was six years old, and the next year my mother died. I was raised by my father, who worked hard to keep us together. I had my first child when I was fifteen years old, and when he was eleven months old my sister sent for me to come up here to Boston. As the years went by I had two more children and worked at different factories. After searching for a job for a long time, I had to get on welfare but I hope someday soon to get off of it.

I came to WEAVE because I was tired of going to different places looking for a job. I have really learned a lot here. I've learned how to write essays and many things about myself and other women.

One of the short stories we read was about a young black girl named Frankie Mae growing up in Mississippi. It was written by Jean Wheeler Smith.

Frankie Mae was a lively and happy child who was determined to learn. She had to take care of the house and the younger children, and when the man came to repossess the stove, she knew how to put him off. When the white boss insisted that she quit school and work in the fields, she still took advantage of every opportunity to learn. She kept a book with figures in it for her father and revealed that the white bossman had been cheating her father out of money for years. But when she told the bossman he was wrong, he put her down by calling her a "nigger." None of the black folks around said a word in her defense.

After that Frankie Mae lost interest in learning. She thought if no one else cared about her learning why should she. So she then went to school only occasionally to get out of chores, but mostly she stayed at home and got fat. She no longer dressed in clean cotton dresses but wore any old thing that was around. Frankie Mae died giving birth to her fifth child when she was nineteen years old.

Frankie Mae's death got her father and the other black sharecroppers involved with the civil-rights movement. It was a time when black people stood up for their rights—their right to education, their right to vote, and their right to stop working for so little money. This is how Frankie Mae's death helped change the times.

The life of Frankie Mae made me think of many things that happened to me in my life. She grew up having to take care of her sisters and brothers, keeping house, and working in the fields as I had done as a child. Like Frankie Mae I was fifteen when I had my first child. Also I lived through the civil-rights movement. But most of all I can understand how Frankie Mae felt when the white bossman told her that as long as she lived he would be right and she would be wrong. I can relate to her life as if it were my own story.

Roslyn David

I am a country girl from a beautiful island in the West Indies called Trinidad. My grandmother was a stout and beautiful lady with long silk hair. She lived in a little dirt house on the bank of a ravine between two annoying neighbors. One was a drunken old man, and the other was a woman my grandmother had an argument with almost every day for allowing her pigs to run through our yard. My mother didn't have a job because in those days women only worked at home and in the gardens. So my mother washed and ironed people's clothes to support her three children. I loved my grandmother. The last time I saw her she was waving goodbye to me as I was leaving for New York. I am sorry I was not there when she died. She left me with memories of love, warmth, and hard but good times.

Today I am a thirty-six-year-old woman with five children. Now that my children are old enough to take care of themselves, I have decided to return to school and pursue a career. When I was a little girl in Trinidad, I was fascinated by the way my elders used herbs and tree bark, among other things, to cure the sick. Trained medical personnel were not available in Trinidad back then. As I got older, my curiosity about medicine grew into a real desire to help the sick. That is why I have decided to become a nurse.

I came to WEAVE to get my high school diploma. As a foreigner I had very little knowledge of black Americans. Studying the civil rights movement was the highlight of my sixteen weeks at WEAVE. I was inspired by the courage of those involved with the civil-rights movement, and this has made me more determined than ever to attain my goal of becoming a nurse. I am now in the process of completing my five tasks in the External Diploma program and have applied for entrance to nursing school.

The staff at WEAVE is beautiful. There is always a listening ear to any problem you might have and always an outstretched hand to guide you along the way. After I walk across the graduation stage I'll walk out of the doors of WEAVE, but it will always be a very big part of my life.

Rosalie Johnson

I was born and raised in Boston. My parents were strict with their children because they loved us. If we did something bad, boy did we get it! My mother always had to work in order for us to survive. I remember her leaving out really early in the morning and coming home late at night. Life back then was just as hard as it is today.

I married at age sixteen and had eight children: Louis, Douglas, Jr., William, Ian, Tran, Natrina, Juanita, and Hazel, my baby. We have always lived in the ghetto part of town. I had to go on welfare to be able to survive with all my children. I didn't have any help until my oldest son, Louis, who is thirteen, found a job to help me out. I have worked in a nursing home, as a cashier, and even at a paper box company. Boy did I hate that, always cutting up my finger. My son Louis works at Brigham's. I believe they must know how old he is but just want to give him a break.

I had to go to my social worker at the welfare office one day, and she said now that my youngest daughter was seven, I must go to work. I told her what I would really like to do was to go back to school and get an education so that I could get a good job that would support my family. So she sent me to see an Education and Training program worker, who told me about WEAVE.

I have found that the staff at WEAVE is friendly and always willing to help me accomplish my goals. Everyone in my class tries to pull together as one. I sure hope that we will continue to see each other like we did in school and will remain friends. The going's a lot easier when you're not alone.

LEARNING FOR A CHANGE

The Role of Critical Economics Education

Teresa Amott and Pat Jerabek

Education has always played an integral role in the American dream of upward mobility. Generations of poor people have sacrificed so that their children could receive an education and rise above their parents' standard of living. Today, poor women are still told that their lack of education is the reason they are at the bottom of the economic and social hierarchy.

But education in America serves differing purposes. On one level, it legitimates and justifies the room at the top of the hierarchy reserved for the few and preserves the illusion that society is meritocratic and democratic. This is the role education plays in the Right's vision of an "Opportunity Society." On another, it trains workers in the skills needed to participate in the labor market, ranging from the empowering skills—such as literacy and certain technical knowledge—to the accommodating skills—such as learned docility and punctuality. Educators committed to social change need to thread their way carefully among these conflicting functions. Like social workers, they have an ambivalent relationship to popular movements for economic justice, a relationship that must be understood before its positive potential can be realized.

We believe that the solutions for poverty, joblessness, oppressive job structures, and the economy's failure to meet basic human needs lie in profound economic and social change. Conceptualizing that change, organizing it, and implementing it require a different kind of education at all levels of society from that provided by traditional institutions of learning.

The education capable of producing transformation must be radical, critical education, which allows people to make their own judgments on the goals, purposes, and effects of American economic institutions. This type of education is fundamentally different from the job-skills programs usually promoted for the poor, programs that prepare people for low-wage, dead-end jobs. Such training programs preserve a hierarchy of economic status by allowing individuals to move up one rung on the ladder: critical education fundamentally challenges hierarchical economic institutions. In that sense, it does not prepare people for jobs in the system but rather enables them to take part in movements to change the system.

One such experiment in grass-roots critical education for women was launched by a collective of radical women economists based in a Boston community group called Women for Economic Justice. The project came out of a desire to inform the women's movement about the economic basis of women's oppression and to build economic literacy among women's advocates so that they could articulate their arguments more effectively and build a stronger movement.

In the early stages of the project, the participants, including the authors, identified a constituency of women open to the possibility of learning more about economics and a group of women with economics training who were open to the possibility of developing new ways of teaching economics. We began by calling progressive women economists in the Boston area and brainstorming about strategies.

Early on, it became clear that the traditional way of teaching economics was inappropriate for our purposes. Generally, academic learning about the economy begins with the theory of a perfectly functioning, free-enterprise economy. Material on problems in the economy such as poverty or the monopoly of power is introduced late in the course, if ever. We decided to work with a different framework, beginning with what participants perceived to be problems in the economy, moving to theories and explanations, and concluding with strategies for change. The format would be small-group discussion in informal settings.

Our kickoff event was a set of workshops one Saturday morning at a local YWCA, to which we invited staff and membership of local women's groups such as Nine to Five, labor union women's committees, welfare-advocacy groups, and the National Organization of Women (NOW). The response to these early workshops was exciting, and in 1985 the project was in its sixth year of serving as an educational resource for women's organizations committed to social change. Today it consists of a collective of nine women economists. What we have learned about the role of radical education in popular movements for change serves as the basis for this essay. We begin by describing an example of critical education for welfare recipients and advocates and move to a discussion of its lessons.

A Session at Blue Mountain Lake

Twenty women gather on the shore of a lake in the Adirondacks on a beautiful weekend in June. We have been invited to use a conference center at Blue Mountain Lake as the setting for a three-day economic-literacy workshop, enabling us to fulfill a commitment to greater outreach to low-income women who might not otherwise be able to provide a site and materials for a workshop. The women gathered on the shore come from the project and from four welfare-rights organizations: Worker's Association for Guaranteed Employment (based in Rhode Island), Cape Alliance (Cape Cod), Downtown Welfare Advocacy Center (New York), and the Coalition for Basic Human Needs (Boston).

We are black, Latina, and white, with widely varying levels of education and literacy. Most of us are single mothers, and Women for Economic Justice raised additional funds from foundations to pay child-care and transportation expenses for those attending.

We are free to spend three days learning about and thinking about economics—from our perspective, based on our experience and our understanding of economic problems. The economists have come equipped with tables, charts, fact sheets, and films covering aspects of the domestic and international economy such as capital flight, women's poverty, the welfare state, and Reaganomics. The advocates have come with abounding testimony that the U.S. economy is their biggest problem and with experience in developing strategies to cope with the economic system. Our goal is to develop an understanding of the economy that is rooted in that experience and that builds the participants' confidence in their ability to analyze and change the economic system.

The setting is idyllic—a rural lodge on a placid lake, a recreation spot donated by a wealthy family for use by groups engaged in organizing for social change. Tennis courts and private planes on the lake are tangible evidence that poor people are at the bottom of a pyramid that has a lofty peak.

On a pier in midafternoon six women in bathing suits, diverse in age, race, and education, look at charts comparing benefit levels of Aid to Families with Dependent Children (AFDC) in several different states. We talk about the inadequacy of those benefits and share ways in which women on welfare scrape by from month to month. The discussion is heated; we are all angry at an economic system that is so punitive. Why are benefit levels so low, we ask?

"Because rich people don't give a damn about us. They're too caught up with their private boats and planes to want to give us more than the crumbs," says one young welfare recipient, newly active in the welfare-rights movement.

"This is all abstract. My problem is that I can't find day care for my two babies. How am I going to go back to school and get a decent education when I've got babies running around the house?" asks a teenage mother.

"Day care won't do me any good," answers a black woman. "All the day care in the world isn't going to get me a job. You know, all the high tech companies in my town hire only white people."

"Rich people run the system, and they hate us," says another. "The state legislature is in their pockets, and the only thing that will change them is if we organize and make their lives miserable," continues another women with several years of community organizing experience.

"It's capitalism. That's the problem," concludes one of the participants.

"Why are we letting men off the hook?" one of the women asks.

"If they shared the responsibility the way they share the fun, we wouldn't have to go begging to those guys in the state house."

The participants are interpreting their experiences differently, but each woman has an insight that will be part of the analysis we begin to build with this conversation. One of the economists asks the group what kind of welfare system they would design if they had the power, and a veteran organizer replies. "We need a guaranteed annual income. Give us enough money to live decently, and then we can do whatever we want to: go back to school, find day care, be independent, maybe get a part-time job."

"How high would you set the income grant?" asks another economist.

"Oh, about a hundred thousand," one of the organizers retorts quickly. After much discussion and laughter, we settle on a figure about twice the federal poverty level: our figure is roughly $20,000 for a family of three.

"Where would the money come from?" an economist probes.

"Rich people. You know, they don't pay any taxes," reminds one of the organizers.

"But if you raise their taxes, won't they fight back?"

"We'll pass a law that they have to pay taxes, and put the money they use now to catch welfare fraud into catching tax cheaters."

"But rich people get their money from owning or managing corporations. If corporations have to pay higher taxes, they might leave this country and set up shop overseas," contributes another economist who will later show slides of women working in Mexican border factories.

"Well, we'll pass another law that makes them stay here," volunteers one of the veteran organizers.

The discussion is like a quilting bee in which women bring to the group bits and pieces of the fabric of their lives and stitch, according to a pattern, a distinctive work of art. They begin with explanations of poverty and inadequate benefits rooted in terms of skills deficiencies, day-care scarcity, and discrimination—implying that if they'd gone to school more, had older children, and had benevolent employers, they might have made it to the bottom of the working-class system. Men and rich people seen as individuals are the villains in this scenario, but we gradually move toward a deeper, more structural analysis, piecing together the quilt. As the conversation continues, there is reference to capitalists' need for cheap labor and the process by which jobs are designed to depress wages and skill levels.

"If we had a guaranteed annual income, nobody would take the crummy jobs. That's why AFDC has to be so low, to force us to do all the work nobody else wants to do."

"Yeah, like raising babies!"

We began with disparate understandings rooted in different experiences, but as we share experiences, we move toward an explanation that incorporates all of our understandings. The awareness sinks deeper that skills do not assure jobs and that race, age, and gender largely determine one's position in the economy. As we work together and learn, our understandings converge.

The Role of Critical Education

This method of education is rooted in the lessons of feminism, of liberation theology, and of educators such as Paolo Freire. Central to the method is the conviction that we are all experts on our own experience and that learning comes out of that experience. Women without formal education often believe that they are personally inadequate and blame themselves for their poverty. When placed in a group with other women who have education but are poor, they begin to question this understanding. The presence of the economists who do have formal education raises another question: Why is it that some acquire education and others do not? Again, the experiences of those in the group lead us to a deeper understanding of the role of education.

We believe that critical economics education inevitably raises fundamental questions about the U.S. economic system and overturns the myths of individual solutions to poverty. Once embarked on a critical path, the women in our workshop at Blue Mountain started to build an agenda for economic change that began with distributional issues: who should receive how much from the workings of the system? But the agenda expanded to include questions about the system by which we produce the goods and services to be distributed: Who really controls the size of the economic pie? How can the poor begin to take control of that system?

By building on the issues most central to people's experiences, economics education can be introduced in a mode that is immediately applicable instead of in the traditional mode of principles and theories first, issues last (if ever). But this is not the kind of economics education that will immediately translate into job skills. The project is rooted in the belief that poor people's education must be two-pronged: one side stressing survival skills, which may include skills on the job and skills in dealing with the state bureaucracy, and another side stressing the need for collective action for social change. Our vision of social change is one in which collective, popular movements apply pressure to power structures. If these movements are to be effective, they need to challenge the popular understanding of the U.S. economy as a just and efficient system.

When carried to its fullest expression, critical economics education gives participants the ammunition with which to argue against the prevailing wisdom that rationalizes inequity and prevents collective action.

Participants in these workshops learn that the U.S. economy does not produce an adequate number of jobs, that government intervention to guarantee economic rights does not necessarily impinge on political rights, and that scarcity is not a natural fact but a social arrangement. Because we work with women, we also stress mathematical literacy, the ability to work with charts, graphs, and numbers in order to argue one's position. Most of the economists have had to confront their own anxiety about math, and recognize the way in which this anxiety can cripple women's efforts at advocacy. Later in the weekend, participants worked with charts showing the risk of poverty for women of different racial and ethnic groups:

"I don't understand this. This chart makes it look like most poor women are white. But I know that Latinas are very poor. Are the government numbers lying?" asks one Latina participant.

"Can anyone explain this?" an economist prompts.

One of the participants answers: "It's because there are more white people than people of color. See, the poverty rate is like a share of the pie, but the white pie is bigger." An economist asks if anyone could draw a diagram illustrating this point, and another participant walks over to an easel holding big sheets of newsprint, draws a series of large circles, and explains the disproportionate burden of poverty for women of color to the whole group. This kind of teaching breaks down the distinction between teacher and student and give participants the opportunity to demonstrate their new learning.

A related feature of critical education is a demystification of the idea of "expert." We often use role plays in which we take on the role of conservative, liberal, and radical economist. A team of economists will argue the differences of points of view, use conflicting statistics, bring out the differences in assumptions and values that undergird disagreements, and then ask the participants to choose the point of view that enables social change. This device has several positive effects. The debate gives life to all the points of view, not just those of one's preferences. People begin to identify with a point of view and feel less alone in their understanding. Finally, people see that they can use "experts" on their side and need not accept analyses that blame them for their poverty or that argue that poverty is a necessary incentive for participants in a market economy.

Building a Movement Against Women's Poverty

The Blue Mountain workshop formed the foundation for a working alliance between these welfare activists and the women economists in the project, which continues to this day. We participants believe that this alliance persists because it began in an atmosphere of nonhierarchical learning. The participants found their experiences confirmed in the economists' analysis, and the economists refined, and sometimes changed, their analysis on the basis of the participants' experience.

For the participating economists, the opportunity to work with poor women has produced a better analysis of the causes of women's poverty and a better strategic sense of how best to struggle against it. For instance, many of the economists came to the analysis with a "jobs first" strategy, which emphasized the role of full employment and adequate child care in eliminating women's poverty. We economists have been changed through our contact with welfare recipients and their strong affirmation of the unpaid work that they already do. We have come to realize that welfare recipients already have jobs but that these jobs are not remunerated. Some of us have shifted the focus of our analysis to the mechanisms by which the unpaid status of women's labor is reproduced over time and across societies. Strategically, this has meant that many of the economists now support strengthening the welfare state as a necessary condition for changes in jobs and production and have turned to building coalitions in defense of the welfare state.

Women everywhere, without benefit of sophisticated economic analyses, have recognized the value of their labor and applied it to the transformation of oppressive economic structures. As the project's economists more and more become participants in these struggles, we have seen our academic work develop in concreteness and commitment, and all of us now use our academic writings as a forum in which to make visible women's poverty and their organized collective and individual struggles against it.

Critical education demands a different kind of educator, one who is critical not only of the existing social order but also of the role of the educator in society. Radical educators, like radical social workers or health workers, often must struggle against the institutional constraints of their work places. Professional recognition, funding, and promotion are threatened by attempts to transform the educational process. Isolated within the university, radical educators turn to their students for support, but class differences and unequal power relationships can undermine student-teacher alliances. A similar problem occurs in the field of social work and is described in an earlier essay by Ann Withorn in this collection.

The Economic Literacy Project is an attempt to deal with these problems. Since we are not located within a university and are sponsored by a community-based group, we are not constrained by hierarchical mechanisms of promotion and professionalization. Most important, we have tried to develop teaching styles that revolve around the experience and expertise of all workshop participants.

The long-range vision implied in this kind of community education runs directly counter to current educational policy directed at poor women. Today's public and private educational resources are increasingly concentrated on short-term training programs for the poor. The single most important objective of these programs is to find employment—and end welfare recipiency—for the participants as quickly as possible. Professional evaluators receive contracts to compare the rate of "placement" (an appropriately objectifying term) against the rate of state expenditure without regard for the quality of employment or its long-term prospects. Programs are considered successful if they save the state money. Constrained by the fiscal realities of the contemporary welfare state, training and educational programs of this nature can only alleviate the income needs of individual women; they can never eliminate the structural mechanisms that generate poverty for women and their children.

TOWARD THE FEMINIZATION OF POLICY

Exit From an Ancient Trap by the Redefinition of Work

Deanne Bonnar

Throughout history, women have done most of the world's care-giving work, but this work has rarely entitled them to control over resources in their own right. While production and maintenance of the material basis of life have generally been the work of both males and females, the equally necessary reproduction and the physical care of people has remained almost exclusively a female activity. The Western definition of work, especially in the Judeo-Christian tradition, has focused on the system of the production and maintenance of goods; care of humans has been looked at as an aspect of love, duty, or biological destiny but rarely as work. The failure to

This essay builds on the author's Ph.D. dissertation, "When the Bough Breaks: A Feminist Critique of Income Support Policies for Female-Based Families" (Brandeis University, 1984).

regard care of humans as work has created the ancient trap of poverty for the female householder. Unless informed by a reconceptualization of women's work, future attempts to extricate women from that particular problem may simply create new traps with major consequences for human life.

Before I continue with a discussion of old and current problems with the definition of work, I would like to suggest why a redefinition of work is fundamental to an ability to move forward. Although the reconceptualization of a word may strike many as an academic exercise, it can actually be a powerful, revolutionary tool. Redefinition can produce the collective shift in perception necessary to break the dominant pattern of thinking and acting that reinforces the current system. Work in all contemporary industrial societies is the system through which rights, status, and entitlements are distributed. When women seek to redefine work, therefore, we seek to establish a new basis for people's relations to one another.

Old Traps

In 1980, the International Labor Organization, a United Nations agency, published findings that concluded: "Women do two-thirds of the world's work and get five percent of the wealth."[1] That same year, another United Nations Commission on the Status of Women arrived at slightly different figures, but with the same impact: "Women are one-third of the world's formal labor force and do four-fifths of all informal work, but receive only ten percent of the world's income and own less than one percent of the world's property."[2] International studies have also found that between one quarter and one third of all families worldwide are supported by women. Not surprisingly, these families are among the very poorest and suffer the greatest hardships. Universally, women and children, in spite of their work, remain the poorest of the earth's poor.[3]

Popular images to the contrary, the poverty of women unattached to male households is at least as old as Judeo-Christian tradition. In the Old Testament, Ruth gleaned the fields of Boaz to secure grain for herself and Naomi. In the New Testament, in the parable of the widow's mite, the widow serves clearly as a symbol of a person in poverty. In 1790, the city of Hamburg, Germany, declared, "Six sevenths of our poor being women and children, they shall be set to spinning flax in their houses."[4] And in 1939, the *Social Security Yearbook* stated:

> Economic insecurity is concentrated further in certain types of families. Since the husband is usually the principal wage earner, the problem of economic insecurity is particularly acute in broken families headed by a woman—that is families headed by a widow, a divorcee, or a wife whose husband was living elsewhere than in the household. . . . Per capita income is invariably the lowest of all in broken families.[5]

The yearbook went on to say that among those who were poor, women and children comprised the bulk of those living in absolute poverty, a state of having no money income at all.

The poverty of women is not new, but it has received remarkably little attention even in socialist and feminist traditions, in which one might expect to find it. Both traditions have generally concluded that, as women enter the labor market, housework will be collectivized and individual households will wither away—thereby ensuring equality of women.[6] But in this century, women have increased their work in the market sector the world over without the predicted disappearance of individual households. Every international study of women's labor, without exception, has found that women who work for wages necessarily have a dual work life in which wage work is added to their domestic labor. Responsibility for domestic labor is theirs regardless of what other type of work they do. In Sweden, China, and Cuba, it is official policy that males must share the housework, but that policy has been extremely hard to enforce. While the percentage of women working for wages has jumped, women remain overwhelmingly compressed into the lowest-paid positions in society.

The restriction of women to a narrow range of lowest-paid jobs is as true in self-designated socialist countries as it is in market economies. It is also true in countries with much older and stronger social-policy commitments to women's equality. For example, Sweden has long had an official policy that

> equality implies that both men and women shall have the same right and opportunity for a fully realized life. A job and financial independence are the basis for creating this equality.

And that

> the goal of our long-range program of womens' rights must be that every individual, regardless of sex, shall have the same opportunities and fundamentally the same responsibility for child upbringing and housework.[7]

Nonetheless, "sixty-seven percent of the extremely low paid workers in Sweden are women and one in every four women belongs to the low income bracket, while only one in every twelve men can be assigned to this category."[8] Published figures of wage rates for women in Sweden vary, but all observers agree that there is substantial discrepancy in incomes between men and women. Women are concentrated in a narrow range of occupations while men are found in more than three hundred. And in Hungary, one of most advanced socialist societies, everyone is guaranteed a job, but wages for men are about 30 percent higher than those for women. There too, women remain in a much narrower range of occupations, which generally pay lower wages.[9]

Further, nurturing jobs in all countries are held mainly by women and pay substantially less than jobs held by men even though such jobs may require even less skill or training. George Stocking, for example, comments on the ranking of jobs by the U.S. government:

> Foster Mothers, Child Care Attendants, and Nursery School and Kindergarten teachers supposedly required no more training or responsibility than Restroom or Parking Lot Attendants. What is even more appalling is that every one of these parenting jobs ranks well below Dog Trainer. The job of a Nurse who works in every major department of her hospital and assists with surgery and birth is ranked as slightly less demanding than that of a Hotel Clerk.[10]

The closer one comes to an activity requiring direct care, the less one earns. In the United States, high school teachers' salaries are twice that of preschool teachers, and doctors command more than five times the income of nurses, who are better paid than patient aides.

The Interaction of Domestic and Market Work

One major explanation for the low wages paid for nurturing jobs is that care-giving work and its attendant services in the home have traditionally been *unpaid* labor. In the early stages of the current feminist movement, feminists often uncritically adopted the view that housework was boring, trivial, and not real work. Most feminists shunned it in favor of market work, which was seen as more important, more challenging, and more rewarding. Yet the existence of paid employment for women did not make trivial homemaking labor disappear but instead compressed it into the hours counted as leisure, as poor women had known for a long time. Most women who took on market work, far from feeling liberated, felt that they held two jobs.

Investigators into women's work hours find that for employed married women in 1980, the work day is longer than it was for their grandmothers. Indeed, Joanne Vanek reports that nonemployed married women work fifty-six hours a week, employed wives seventy-one hours, and employed mothers of young children eighty hours (their husbands average sixty-five).[11] While there is a reduction in the amount of housework done by employed women, for those with young children the reduction does not compress domestic labor below forty hours a week, and for other women it is not compressed much below thirty hours. The assumption that the work in the home is trivial led many to believe that it would wither away in the face of "real" market work. That is has failed to fade is what now makes it worthy of attention.[12]

Both sociologists and insurance companies have begun to look at the realities of housework and its economic value.[13] But in spite of the increased attention, many recent studies of homemakers as workers continue to trivialize domestic work, defining it as a collection of rationalized tasks, as a series of physical jobs such as cooking, doing laundry, and cleaning. They ignore the intellectual, managerial, and emotional components that are among the most demanding aspects of the work. Cooking, for example, involves not only the actual purchase and preparation of food but decisions as to what to eat, and when, which are built on stores of information about food prices, nutrition, tastes, safety, schedules of household members, medical requirements, cooking techniques, and ethnic traditions. In addition, food preparation and serving carry messages of power and status, and food is expected to provide social and psychological nourishment as well as satisfying hunger.

The theoretical problems associated with any discussion of domestic-sector labor stem from the assumption that housework is the primary work that takes place in the home. I argue, instead, that the primary work of the household is care giving, of which housework is a part—not the other way around. Care giving is work that involves the supervision and care of another person who needs daily or frequent personal assistance in order to sustain life. Housework refers to the care given to things. Housework done in the process of care giving can be complex, time-consuming, and arduous, but it is the care of humans that is truly absorptive work and is most likely to impinge on the selection of market work. Housework is a vital and demanding part of care giving, but it is the care of humans that sets the basis and organizes the demands. Care giving is not a part of housework; housework is a part of the process of giving care to humans. It is care giving, not housework, that should be the focus. Care giving, whether raising children or enabling a disabled or frail adult to maintain himself or herself, is not a trivial pursuit, and it is more gratifying to some people and makes a greater social contribution than many types of work in the market sector.

Furthermore, nurture is work that the market sector has a very hard time organizing on a rationalized basis. Economies of scale, seemingly central to industrialized enterprises, prove to be antithetical to the nurturance that is fundamental to the care-giving process. Production-line systems may provide meals, but they cannot provide emotional sustenance. There is no reason that teams of people cannot come through residences and clean them, but there are reasons that teams of people should not take over the care of dependent humans. It matters little if tables are dusted by different people every week, but it matters a lot if children's care givers are repeatedly changed. It matters little if laundry is washed by one or a dozen people, but it matters a lot if an ailing or confused person is cared for by twenty different people in a week, as happens frequently in nursing homes. Caring for people and caring for things are not comparable activities. Because they go on in the household together, we must not be confused about their separate requirements and their different value.

Households in which there are people who need care—whether

they be children, the chronically ill, disabled adults, or the frail and elderly—require management. For many care givers, this unacknowledged management work uses a great deal of energy. Innumerable women who have taken on market work and have succeeded in sharing household tasks with their mates still feel oppressed by the work at home and have a difficult time articulating the problem. It is common to hear, "He does a lot more than he used to, but I'm still the responsible person." Thus, even if the spouse takes the child to buy shoes, it is generally the primary care giver who watches the state of the shoes, the growth of the child's feet, and the family budget; assesses the community resources for footwear; and makes the timing decisions. In addition, she is likely to maintain responsibility for the purchase if the spouse is somehow unable to take the child at the necessary point.

We need to recognize the amount of thought that goes into common care giving for three reasons. First, because the activities are so common, their very familiarity makes it easy to think we understand what is involved without, in fact, having conceptual clarity about the nature of work.

Second, the lack of clarity perpetuates a belief that the tasks can be transferred to the market, thereby eliminating the inequities between men and women in care-giving work and freeing women to compete equally in the market sector. While it is conceivable that much can occur through the purchase of services, the management issue is still not accounted for in such a scheme, and it represents a significant proportion of the work. The simple purchase of shoes for one child, for example, has all the elements of the managerial process: the gathering of information (on the child's feet, the shoes, the community resources, the family budget), the assessment of the information, the decision, and the evaluation of the decision made.

Third, I am increasingly convinced that unaddressed demands of care giving are a major factor in the type of work that many women seek outside the home. Recently, a well-educated, experienced professional woman with adolescent children told me she had turned down an offer of a challenging position in favor of a more routine job. She stated, "I can't afford a job that requires a lot of mental energy after hours because I then don't have the energy the family takes." While some might assess the decision as a "fear of success" or a "lack of achievement drive," neither seems to be operating. She added, "When the children are grown, I'll have the energy for that level of work."

This example suggests a deeper rationale for the decisions many women must weigh in seeking paid employment. Women are overwhelmingly concentrated in a narrow range of jobs. The reasons for this are complex, including the demands of capitalism, the universality of division of labor by gender, and discrimination. However, it may also reflect occupational choices women make. I am not arguing that women choose to be in poorly paid positions but that choices about market work are constrained not by housework but by the always demanding, sometimes satisfying, highly energy-absorbing care-giving work at home. As long as domestic care giving is primarily a female responsibility, many women, unless they have exceptional talents or interests, may continue to choose a market work life that complements the work they already do.

The critical dual home and market roles of women have not been significantly helped by any of the policies yet developed. Theoreticians treat this problem in a variety of ways from explanations about patriarchy to psychological and biological explanations, but few point out that when equality of the sexes has been promoted by policy, it has been directed only toward enabling women to assume traditional male work roles, with no concommitant effort toward enabling men to become care givers. It has been assumed that the activities of production were more valuable and complex than the activities of reproduction and care of humans.

By this time it should be clear that I consider it to be a grave mistake to consider the social product solely the result of those who work in market production. To do so ignores and devalues the work of reproduction and care giving without which no society can continue. The devalued laborer is then encouraged, pushed, or coerced into the valued labor and unwittingly becomes the bearer of two work loads rather than one. This burden has extensive negative consequences for care giving and social relations.

The dual work load for women is but one of the new traps society is setting up in an attempt to escape the ancient traps of female inequality and the poverty of female householders. By defining work as those activities that people call employment, many economists in industrial nations are in the bizarre position of suggesting that work is becoming scarce. Thus there are vast numbers of people who are unemployed while corresponding numbers of other people are overworked.

Perhaps an even more serious trap, however, is that both market economies and planned industrial economies have emphasized increasing material wealth, often at the expense of the nurture of human life. But one may well doubt the benefit of expanding material wealth if the capacity of people to care for one another is reduced. One of the tangible problems that has arisen from the split of market labor from domestic labor is the separation of men from the nurturant activities that sustain life. Because such activities have been increasingly removed from public view, many now regard them as nonexistent or unnecessary. But I maintain that *personal* nurturant work is both necessary and absolutely fundamental to lives that people value. Many women carry double work loads not because they have been overly socialized to concerns about "ring around the collar" but because they resist living in a world where personal care giving does not exist.

Alternatives

What alternatives do industrial wage economies have? I suggest two. Economists suggest that work decisions are influenced by trade-offs between time and money. I contend that industrial economies must consider *both* if real change is to occur in the definition and evaluation of women's work.

The first requirement is to manipulate the time side of the equation by reducing the length of the work day considered full-time employment from eight to perhaps six hours a day, assuming a five-day week. This change would make full-time employment available to the many care givers now employed "part-time." And by reducing the demands on male workers it holds the promise of allowing men to become more active care givers. In addition, it opens full-time employment to many people with infirmities for whom an eight-hour work day is too long. By redefining work to include the activities of care giving as well as those of material production, one can quickly see that I am not talking about trading work for leisure but about rearranging the overall conditions of work. Understanding care giving as part of human work makes more clear the direction that social policy should take.

The second requirement is to pay for domestic care giving directly. Building upon work by David Gil and the Wages for Housework campaign of Mariarosa Dalla Costa and Selma James, I propose instituting a system of wages for care givers.[14] What follows is a brief sketch of how such a policy would work.

Wages for Care Givers

Minimally, a policy recognizing the value of domestic labor would provide a basic wage, set at the level of the minimum wage for a full work week. Increments would be added to the basic wage based on the amount of time, the complexity of work, and the number of people cared for. The intensity of care and the amount of time required by an individual would be a factor in setting increments to the wage so that those caring for infants, very young children, and severely impaired people would also be eligible for more income. Calculating from a standard full-time work week, people might be considered to need care in units of one tenth time up to units of time-and-a-half, perhaps even double time. Thus care givers of school-age children and certain partially impaired adults might earn wages for half-time care, while someone who cared for a person with third-stage Alzheimer's disease might earn time-and-a-half wages.

Care-giver wages would also be increased by providing an increment to the wage in any situation in which the care giver is the household's only earner. The model might look as follows: A single woman with an infant would receive $3.35 an hour minimum wage, $1.00 an hour more for the care of an infant, and another $1.00 an hour as a single earner. Thus, a single mother's total wage would be $5.35 an hour, or a little over $11,000 a year (assuming the current forty-hour week). If she were to marry, her total wage would decrease by $1.00 an hour, but she would still earn $9,000 a year, which would be a significant contribution to her family income and a recognition of her own labor.

The specific amounts of money involved in the wage are used for illustrative purposes only. It is the principle of establishing the basic wage and adding increments for the complexity and intensity of the task that I am interested in demonstrating. Market wage discrimination is fundamentally flawed, but as long as it is the dominant way of recognizing work, treating care giving differently will keep it in the category of "not real work." A basic wage, with increments for circumstances in which the work is harder and the care giver less able to do other forms of work, permits flexibility in income and reflects the actual conditions of work for the care giver. Varying the amount of wage is important, for it acknowledges that work in the home is not an undifferentiated mass, and it directs money to those most likely to have the greatest need for it. At this point, there are at least four work factors that deserve increments. One is the intensity of the care; the second, the number of people cared for; the third, the lack of other supports in the care giver's household; and fourth, the amount of time spent in care giving.

A flexible wage system could enable an employed person to receive a half-time wage for looking after her mother half-time and to receive a full-time wage if her mother's condition deteriorated and she decided to quit her job to look after her. The woman's wage would be increased if the mother became bedridden and needed intense personal care. The increased income would permit the daughter to buy some services so that she has more choice about when and how she provides care.

Eligibility

A care giver would be considered to be any person who has the responsibility for the physical care and supervision of another person whose ability to look after himself or herself is limited by age; physical, emotional, or mental restrictions; or combinations of such factors. There would be no restrictions on eligibility by marital status, age, sex, or relationship to the cared-for person. Kin, friends, and strangers would be equally eligible to receive the wage on the condition they provide the actual care.

Certification for eligibility could be handled through the Social Security system. Parents and expectant parents would simply register as parents. People caring for the disabled would be expected to submit certifications for the level of care needed by the recipient. Medical eligibility criteria are already in place for levels of nursing home, and these might be adapted for home care. Changes in physical status requiring more or less care would also require certification or a system of declaration and random audits.

It might also be useful to consider instances in which wages are paid to individuals such as the mentally or physically disabled for providing self-care when the amount of time and energy involved in meeting the basic requirements for daily life precludes that person's participation in market work. There are many issues to be worked out with such a concept that there is not the space to follow here, but the idea is raised for further consideration if a system of wages for care giving is developed.

Financing and Administration

I suggest using the Social Security system, already in place, and building upon its procedures for payments, appeal hearings, random audits, and research. Care-giver wages would be subject to the same benefit and tax systems as other wages but would require some revision of the tax system, such as exemption of all income up to a moderate budget level with progressively steeper taxes after that. Without such revamping of the tax system, the proposal for care-giver wages would simply add income to higher-income families.

Integration with the tax system is a major issue in the development of an adequate care-giver wage and may well be the source of funding for such a wage. *Newsweek* (April 16, 1984) reported that more than $330 billion could be recouped if the tax system were restructured to eliminate the plethora of exemptions currently in place. Some 90 million people in the United States are receiving or are in need of some level of noninstitutional care. These people include children, adults with chronic limitations resulting from disease or disability, and frail elders. If a bill for proposed care-giver wages were enacted, at the levels I have suggested, the total price of the program presently would be $260 billion, including administrative costs. More than $120 billion of this would be recovered through the federal tax structure and from the phasing out of a variety of programs such as Social Security Survivor's Benefits for young beneficiaries, Aid to Families with Dependent Children, and Supplemental Social Security.

The size of the expenditures needed for paying wages to care givers highlights the potential for fundamental change. It has the capacity to effect genuine vertical transfer to the lowest-income groups in the population. The total proportion of national wealth enjoyed by the lowest groups in the population has been remarkably resistant to change over the last fifty years, in spite of Social Security and other antipoverty programs. It should be noted that bankers, economists, and insurance companies have already estimated that household work is worth between $500 and $650 billion a year to the economy. These figures represent the unpaid labor that is directly related to the poverty of most women and children in this country. The proposed national defense budget in 1985 is more than $300 billion, representing the national collective surplus. Much of the surplus is built on the unpaid labor of women. These connections should be kept in mind when those who profit from the maldistribution of resources (and the policy makers who represent them) argue that such a program proposal is unaffordable. Women cannot "afford" the current system.

Concerns

It is not surprising that proposals for waging domestic-sector work should raise intense opposition. They are, after all, radical proposals that involve shifts in views about work, the separation of market and domestic spheres, and the traditional relation of dependency between the sexes, and they would require major transfers of wealth. One would expect opposition from those who profit from the current social arrangements. Some of the strongest opposition, however, has come from quarters traditionally supportive of radical change. For example, the Communist party, Socialists, and feminists actively worked together against a proposal for wages for homemakers in Sweden in 1978. If discussion of wage policy for domestic labor is to advance, it must be able to deal with the objections raised by those who also are honestly concerned with changing women's situation.

Socialists and feminists are concerned about the social and psychological isolation of women in the home, as well as about the reinforcing of women's traditional roles. They point out that the need for contact with adults is one impetus for many women seeking outside employment. Leaving domestic work unpaid does not reduce the isolation. Rather, it is reasonable to believe that as workers in the domestic sector receive wages, their mobility, their identification as a class of workers, their possible unionization, and their political strength would be *increased.*[15] One way to address the isolation problem is to make the wage part of a larger package that envisions a new Social Security for women, much as the current Social Security was developed for men. Included in such a package should be increased funds for day-care centers, a network of community resource centers, something like the centers for older people now available, and training programs on care giving.

Paradoxically, paying women for housework may decrease traditional role rigidity, as the Wages for Housework campaign argues. Paying for care giving allows it to be seen as work, rather than as a moral imperative or biological destiny. As people come to understand that care giving is one form of work among others, they may be more free to choose between it and other labor, rather than feeling obliged to do it and market labor as well.

Others object to paid care because it would be "buying love." On the one hand, it is quite true that money cannot buy love. Money can buy food and fuel, but it cannot produce emotional caring. On the other hand, the lack of money cannot produce love either, but the lack of resources can substantially rob people of their ability to care. Paying for care giving is not "buying love" but buying the circumstances of life that make love possible. Society cannot continue a system where half the world works for love and the other half works for money, as long as money is the currency that buys food.

I have raised these concerns here not to dismiss them but to point out there are valid counter-arguments. There are serious problems, but keeping care unpaid does not solve them, and the concerns about pay for care giving should not foreclose further discussion.

The Future

The proposal to pay for care giving is not only a provocative policy alternative for the future, but it has also immediate use in that it brings attention to the basic societal work of care giving and acknowledges the massive amount of unpaid labor undergirding industrial economies. It clarifies important next steps, such as enacting Social Security credits for homemakers and the U.N. Decade for Women's proposal that unpaid labor be included in gross national products. The model also draws attention to the entire life cycle of care-giving responsibilities that have traditionally fallen to women and exposes the falsehood of referring to women in the domestic sector as "not working."

Interestingly, wages to care givers are already being paid to some degree. In the United States more than a dozen states have pilot projects for paying wages to family members who look after a disabled elderly person in their own home. In Britain, an Invalid Care Allowance was introduced in 1975. While it is available to married men and all other unpaid care givers except married women, the concept has much in common with the care-giver wage proposed. In China, in each commune the Brigade pays a member to care for an individual with chronic or disabling conditions. In a similar fashion in Hungary and Sweden problems and dissatisfactions with developing nurseries and day-care centers have led to paying parents for home care.[16] While each of these models addresses only one area of care giving, it is useful at this point to recognize that both market economies and planned economies have adopted systems for paying for home care. Rather than declining, these systems seem to be expanding.

Wages for care givers will not solve all circumstances of poverty, but they could make giant inroads into the unequal poverty burden borne by women, especially female heads of household. It should be kept clear that in the long run, the issue for women is not misfortune but injustice. At issue is the injustice of mothers having their needs for income defined as "dependency," while the unemployed, the veterans, or the retirees do not. At issue is the injustice of a work place that pays women fifty-nine cents for every dollar a man earns. At issue is the injustice of a dual antipoverty system in which people who tend machines are more protected than people who tend other people.

Finding an exit from the trap of female poverty entails more than patching the holes in the present "safety nets." It means, fundamentally, honoring the work that women contribute to the world. That will force all people to reconsider the grounds on which we build a collective life.

WHAT IF WE ALL WENT TO THE POLLS?

Politics and Poverty

Rochelle Lefkowitz

The young state rep looked down on the hundreds of women who filled the marble rotunda. He pursed his lips and nodded to the reporter. "Impressive," he conceded, "if it were any other group, that is."

The welfare mothers had come to the capital from cities and towns across the state. The cavernous entrance hall was full, but still more women streamed up the state house steps through the massive double doors. Each woman had come personally to tell her legislators how a vote to cut the state's Emergency Assistance program (EA) would affect her life.

"Unfortunately," the lawmaker shook his head, "in the end, when we vote on EA, it won't do them any good." He confided, "In my district, if you vote for welfare bills too often, you can kiss your seat goodby." He shrugged, "Besides, everybody knows, poor people don't vote."

Is he right? Is it true that poor Americans—two out of three of whom are women—really don't vote? And if so, will the massive voter-registration drive of the early 1980s change things and make elected officials like this state rep more responsive to poor women's needs?

Like the state legislator quoted above, many public officials dismiss poor women's concerns by citing their nonvoting record. Most poor women in the United States today, however, are citizens with the constitutional right to help hire and fire these same public officials. Would current and would-be officeholders act any differently if they saw poor women as likely voters, likely to replace officials who were deaf to their concerns with others who would listen?

So long as elected officials perceive poor people as nonvoters, that remains a pretty empty threat. But how accurate is that perception?

Unlike many myths about poor people, their reputation as nonvoters is a fairly accurate one. As of 1980, 163 million Americans were eligible to vote.[1] By 1984, poor people represented 15 percent of the national voting-age population.[2] Yet although many barriers to universal suffrage in this country, like poll taxes and literacy tests, have been lifted, just one in four of the 34 million American adults who live in households with annual incomes of under $10,000 a year actually votes.[3] Meanwhile, 70 to 75 percent of Americans who earn more than $25,000 a year cast their ballots[4]—a level of voter participation three times that of poor Americans.

Like many other problems that disproportionately affect poor people, and especially poor women, low voter turnout finally attracted national attention when it began to spread. For the past twenty years, Americans' overall voter participation has been declining. By the 1980 presidential elections, it had reached a new low. That year, 76.5 million, or 47 percent of all eligible voters, stayed home on Election Day.

Gender Gap

That same year, two other trends captured media attention in a way that promised to turn the political behavior of a forgotten minority, poor women, into a key ingredient for a new electoral majority.

First, there was the women's vote. Altogether, as of 1980, American women made up 53 percent of the electorate. Yet, for most of the time since women won the right to vote in 1920, they hadn't voted all that differently from their male counterparts. But in 1980, women equaled men in the percentage of voter turnout for the first time in peacetime.[5] That year, 6 million more women than men went to the polls.[6] And, for the first time, their votes reflected the distinctive views that they had begun to express in opinion polls. Among these was women's significantly greater support for elected officials who supported social programs.

While this so-called gender gap was grabbing headlines, so was the feminization of poverty. By 1980, according to those tracking income trends, two out of three American adults living in poverty were women. As postcards and posters from the Women's Economic Agenda Project, a California group, which, among its activities, registers low-income women to vote, asked: "What if we were all to go to the polls?"[7]

What, indeed? After the New Right's sweep of the 1980 elections, many political analysts, including some long-time supporters of poor people's struggles, began taking a closer look at election returns. What they found made some insist that the voting booth could become a key battleground for poor women—if only they'd go there.

The numbers they uncovered are compelling. Ronald Reagan claimed a landslide in 1980 and a mandate to dismantle social programs, especially those for poor women and their children. But the actual figures tell a different story. For one thing, just over one in four Americans who were eligible to vote in 1980 (27 percent) elected Ronald Reagan. Indeed, if one in every twenty Americans who voted for him had stayed home, he would have lost. What's more, his margin of victory in the ten most populous states was less than the number of all nonvoting white women in each of those states; less than the number of nonvoting black men and women in Michigan, New York, and California; less than the number of nonvoting Latino women and men in California, New York, and Texas.[8]

And it doesn't end there. In many races after the 1980 presidential elections, nonvoters remained the United States' largest political party, and they played a key role in many close contests. In 1982, thirteen congressional races were decided by margins of fewer than 7,000 votes. A shift of 44,000 ballots that year would have changed the results in five Senate races and twenty House races won by Republicans.

At the same time, in cities from Denver to Philadelphia, organized efforts to sign up new voters led to upsets in mayoral elections. In Chicago, for example, more than 100,000 new black and Latino voters were added to the rolls, and in 1983, Harold Washington, Chicago's first black mayor, was elected with a 40,000-vote margin.[9]

These results, and others like them, seemed to make the case for voter registration among poor women. By early 1983, many longtime supporters of poor people's struggles had joined groups such as the Southwest Voter Registration and Education Project, the National Association for the Advancement of Colored People (NAACP) voter registration project, and other longstanding voter-registration efforts and people from public and private human service organizations, women's groups, unions, and a wide array of activists from the peace, civil-rights, and environmental movements to launch a massive voter-registration drive. Their campaign attracted considerable time, resources, and energy. In its infancy, it added more voters to the rolls that any such effort since the Great Depression.[10] Much of the effort seemed aimed at poor women. According to Hulbert James, once a chief welfare-rights organizer in New York,[11] who became executive director of Human SERVE (Human Service Employees Registration, Voting and Education Campaign), a key group in the campaign: "The bulk of people we are registering are low income and minority—and more than 80 percent are women."[12]

Mobilizing Poor Women

How did poor women become the prime candidates of this new wave of voter-registration activity? In 1983, Frances Piven and Richard Cloward, leading theorists of the 1960s welfare-rights movement, joined the growing chorus of feminists, environmentalists, and civil-rights and peace activists, who were urging their under-registered consitutencies to sign up to vote.[13] While feminists stressed the potential impact of the gender gap and others emphasized the effect of sheer numbers of new voters on single issues or certain races, Piven and Cloward were saying, "We think this strategy could generate the political force to defend the popular victories of the past, such as the income maintenance programs that are now being cut."[14]

Their proposal generated much excitement. This new push to sign up voters promised to be more efficient than earlier door-to-door campaigns. The plan was to reach large groups of nonvoters at once: on cheese lines, at day-care centers, in clinic waiting rooms, and in the lobbies of welfare and unemployment offices. Among its early supporters were social workers; large, national nonprofit organizations from the NAACP to Planned Parenthood; unions; college students; and progressive elected officials—as well as some poor women and their advocates.

Why the sudden appeal of voter registration in these circles? Since the late 1970s, the right wing assault that began with Proposition 13 tax cut fever in California had dismantled services for poor people and countless other Americans—affecting voters and nonvoters profoundly. The subsequent election taught poor people and their supporters that elections mattered; Reagan's had changed their lives materially.

The New Right tidal wave that swept away large chunks of government programs painstakingly assembled over decades left many of the groups listed above depressed, even angry—and, for the most part, on the defensive. Voter registration was the first thing to come down the pike in a long time that seemed positive and energizing.

In fact, as Cloward and Piven proposed it, a voter-registration drive among poor people seemed to pack a triple punch: (1) it awakened a beaten-down sense of pride in human services and their providers; (2) it offered a specific set of actions to take, based on compassion for the clients of those services, which was intended to empower them to act on their own behalf; (3) it held out the promise of a new, broader coalition among those whom Reaganomics had attacked that would embrace poor people, their advocates, and other progressives to form a new majority.

As a strategy, it seemed as if voter registration could short-circuit the mighty New Right direct-mail machine, enabling progressives to forge a majority that could win city halls, state houses, Congress, even the White House in 1984 and end the reign of Reaganomics. As a tactic, it appeared unassailable: who, after all, could attack an approach as all-American as a voter-registration drive?

There seemed to be something particularly inspiring about mobilizing poor women to register and vote. Entitlement programs thrust millions of poor women into intimate relationships with government. These were hardly partnerships of equals. According to advocates of voter registration, though, poor women held one trump card: by voting in large numbers, they could conceivably replace some elected officials who had short-shrifted them with others more inclined to respond to their needs.

Elections, then, were cast as a kind of civic Sadie Hawkins Day for poor women, when all of a sudden the tables would be turned and the very people that poor women usually depend on would seek their help for once. What's more, the request would be in the form of an appeal to flex some muscle, to make poor women's voices heard for a change. Indeed, efforts to recruit new voters among poor women featured such slogans as: "Votes Mean Power" and "Register: Your Vote Is Your Voice."[15]

A voter-registration card, like a driver's license, is proof of having been pledged by a respected sorority. It publicly identifies its bearer as a solid citizen, a member of the respectable majority, in contrast to the stigma that a Medicaid card or food stamps confer. What's more, once you've actually pulled the curtain of the voting booth, it's a secret ballot. There's usually little reason to fear reprisals for expressing your views.

For all these reasons, many activists committed to social change began to view voting as a wedge for poor women, as a way for powerless individuals to act together on their own behalf. Some still questioned how many new voters would actually reach the polls; although some barriers such as property ownership or fluency in English were illegal, others, including the availability of transportation and child care and restricted hours of polling places, remained. But even these skeptics—and still others previously cynical about the social-change potential of electoral politics—found it hard to resist the argument made by a youth worker in East Harlem: "At least if they're registered," she said, "they'll have the choice."[16]

What's Behind the Curtain?

But will they? Poor women's choices tend to be limited. Medicaid, for instance, often won't pay to fix a broken pair of eyeglasses, but it will only cover the purchase of a new pair in a limited number of styles and only from places that accept Medicaid as payment. What will make voting any different? After all, if the prefix "welfare" is powerful enough to tarnish the otherwise sacred status "mother," then perhaps "poor" is strong enough to downgrade the all-American title "voter."

It's unfair, of course, to preach a double standard about voting, to insist that poor women, unlike the rest of the electorate, should abstain from voting until offered ideal candidates and a guarantee that their interests will be represented. Such demands would sentence poor women to the sidelines, uncorrupted by the tradeoffs of electoral politics but without any chance to act on their own behalf.

Still, some poor women and their advocates raise important questions about what was really behind the voting booth curtain for poor women. Their questions probe the proposal on all levels, from the practical to the philosophical, from the strategy's roots to its promised results. Some were answered, in part, by the 1984 elections. Others remain. Still others apply to any broad, developing strategy for social change through coalitions that put forward incremental demands. In all, they point to ways to strengthen voter registration as a strategy for social change.

Some early questions about voter registration were of the nuts-and-bolts variety. Could poor women who were homeless or in battered-women's shelters register to vote without conventional addresses? Would registrars be kicked out of welfare waiting rooms for loitering? Once registered, would poor women turn out at the polls, especially if they had no way to get there or no one to watch the children or might have to lose a day's pay?

While would-be registrars pondered how to reach poor women and how to get them to turn out on Election Day, some suggested that the difficulties really weren't technical at all. Instead, they wondered, were issues around outreach and turnout really symptoms of the fact that voter registration was yet another well-meaning effort on behalf of poor women—but not at their request? If poor women themselves had the urge to register and vote, these skeptics asked, would registrars be looking for new voters or running out of forms?

Some likened voter-registration drives aimed at poor women to previous efforts to protect Medicaid-funded abortions. In the late 1970s some feminist groups fought hard to save abortion funding for poor women—only to be told if they really wanted to show their support for poor women, they should also have been supporting efforts by welfare-rights groups to get welfare-grant increases. In the case of abortion rights, these poor women argued, it was a question of others choosing poor women's priorities. As Janet Diamond, former publicity director for the Coalition for Basic Human Needs, a Massachusetts welfare-rights group, put it, "It's the difference between saying we'll do it for you—or with you."[17] That, said some poor women, might also describe voter registration.

A *second question* grew out of this one: Would all the attention to a "respectable" voter-registration drive drain other efforts led by poor women of their cohorts' energy and other resources? Eventually, in fact, many foundations that traditionally funded poor women's services and organizing projects funded voter-registration drives in the early 1980s. The closest available barometer may be the fiscal health over the next several years of poor women's organizations and campaigns.

A *third question* involved voter registration's coercive potential. If women in clinic waiting rooms, for instance, were asked to register to vote, would voter registration simply become another condition of care? Would this vehicle for empowerment, once in the hands of human service workers, become another tool to harass clients? What's more, would administrators move to penalize workers who tried to register their clients?

While arrests of would-be registrars on cheese lines made headlines, as did stories of election officials "running out" of or "losing" ballots, or demanding that wheelchair-bound, would-be voters get up several flights of stairs, little emerged during pre-1984-election voter-registration drives to confirm suspicions that voter registration would be used against poor women by human service workers. However, a *fourth question,* even more difficult to document, remained harder to dismiss: By the time the electoral process embraced poor women, how meaningful were their choices?

Many elections in the 1980s were between Tweedledee conservatives and Tweedledum neoconservatives, putting new voters in the position of being all dressed up with nowhere to go. As activist Gary Delgado, of the Center for Third World Organizing, put it: "First there is the question of options—for whom or what will people be able to vote?"[18] In most elections, the real choices are made long before voters cast their ballots. Often, primaries, not general elections, are the true contests. Before that, nominating conventions and party platform meetings are the forums where the significant trade-offs are made. By Election Day, often all that remain are symbolic choices.

Beyond Election Day

A whole other set of questions about how much power poor women would gain by voting looked beyond Election Day. They revolved around whether voting could be translated for poor women into a group expression of new clout, with other voters and elected officials.

A *fifth question* that arose about voter registration, then, was this: If many poor women registered to vote, would this create a new voting bloc to be reckoned with, like the senior citizens' bloc, or would voting, like most other poor women's experiences, simply be downgraded to some new second-class act?

This question is complex. The act of voting itself, of course, is an individual one. No one is actually with a voter when he or she pulls the levers. Politicians, though, in campaigns and in office, act as if voters and nonvoters are part of groups. Yet the act of registering and voting does not make a group or voting bloc out of individual poor women.

Poverty, like age, gender, or other conditions, in and of itself is a status. Being poor does not automatically make a woman a member of a group. It simply puts her in the pool of women with low incomes. To forge a politically conscious group that can flex some muscle from an aggregate of individuals takes several steps. Critics questioned whether the drive to register poor women to vote could be set up for the task.

According to Ethel Klein, a professor of political science at Columbia University who has taken a close look at the gender gap, the rise of political group consciousness is a three-stage process.[19] The first stage, she says, is affiliation. Here, the individual needs to recognize that she's part of a group—not just an exception who happens to share certain characteristics with group members—and has common interests. Given the stigma attached to poverty in U.S.

society, this step is a giant one for a poor woman, compared, for instance, with the traumatic but less degrading acknowledgment of senior citizenship.

While one's status as a poor woman is objective, that is, it can be measured by income, assets, and other sources of support, membership in the group of poor women is subjective; it depends on an individual identifying with this group and making a commitment to others in it. Besides the self-hatred and prejudice against the poor that divide poor women from one another, poor women, like the rest of U.S. society, are kept apart by powerful strains of racism and homophobia, among other prejudices. Many poor women often feel responsible for their fate. The way services are structured—with rigid income cutoffs instead of sliding fee scales—also pits poor women who are employed at low wages against poor women who depend on state programs for sustenance.

Klein says that the second step toward political consciousness is rejecting the traditional definition of the group's status in society, in order to make way for a new definition. She describes this process of building a new group identity as one in which negative images are replaced by positive ones, such as "Gay is proud" or "Black is beautiful." At a time when even mainstream groups like labor unions are successfully attacked as "special interests," such a change in self-image and public identity isn't easy. For poor women, often portrayed as lazy welfare cheats who don't deserve to have their basic needs and their children's met, this might take the form of a new, more accurate image: that of hard-working mothers who are thrifty enough to make food stamps last the month and heroically sacrifice to be both mother and father to their children, whom they deeply love.

Although poor women are certainly forced to look to government for solutions, it is possible to be poor and hold the same rugged-individualist, blame-the-victim attitudes as most Americans. In other words, a poor woman can get food stamps without feeling entitled to them or without feeling she has the right to pressure elected officials to raise her monthly allotment.

Klein identifies the third stage of political consciousness as more than the belief that personal survival is more than simply a question of individual effort but the belief that you deserve equal treatment, which has been denied you because of discrimination. For poor women, this translates to the notion that the most reliable route out of poverty is not a man, a diploma, or a job—it's group action to improve women's economic status through societywide solutions such as equal pay for work of comparable worth.

While registering voters at government offices is less isolating than a door-to-door campaign, it does not necessarily forge such group consciousness. Perhaps if entire chapters of poor women's organizations signed up together, as neighbors who would have an impact on particular elections, politicians would be forced to recognize poor women as voting blocs.

Even then, a *sixth question,* which speaks to the very nature of winning elections, remains: How can elections, which are won by a small or large majority, protect the rights of minorities? According to political scientist Klein, "Minority groups rarely have enough initial resources to influence political decisions directly. They need to expand the scope of the conflict to include sympathetic members of the general public in hope that they, too, will exert pressure on politicians to address the concerns of the group."[20] This suggests the need for coalition politics. It also suggests that even after poor women become voters, their relative position of power doesn't change much. How can poor women enter coalitions around elections with enough clout from the start to ensure that their issues will be a firm part of the agenda, not to be compromised away?

A *seventh question* also plagues all electoral advocates: How can you turn votes into political leverage and prove it's your group that provided the winning margin for a candidate or referendum? Every group claims to represent the votes that made the difference in a close race. So far, there is no technology or exit poll that can definitively resolve the dispute. It falls to political pundits in the media and academia, as well as officeholders themselves, to decide who is owed what, decisions that occur in a society whose pecking order puts poor women far down on most lists. Even when it's clear that poor people must have elected some public officials (who else but poor people live in places like East New York or the South Bronx?) elected officials have other constituents to please, groups that can point to the funds, as well as the troops, that contribute to campaigns.

Thus, even candidates like Chicago Mayor Harold Washington, who acknowledge the role of newly registered poor voters in their victory, must answer to other interests and take actions like cutting General Relief budgets. For the most part, the effect of poor women's vote both in elections and on elected officials remains to be seen, since massive registration is so recent. It will be difficult to track, since most campaigns haven't the funds to keep detailed records that would show which issues moved voters to support a candidate. Even places like the Center for American Women in Government did not keep statistics as of the mid-1980s on voters' income or how women or the men they help elect act once in office.

Trade-Offs

This brings up yet an *eighth question* about voter registration. Because no elections concern a single issue or single constituency, after Election Day, officeholders must answer to a cacaphony of louder, usually wealthier voices than those of poor women. Since politics involves so many trade-offs at so many points, elected officials are often playing one set of constituents against another—oil companies against consumers, landlords against tenants. Even members of coalitions are pitted against one another, as seniors are told that their Social Security cost-of-living increases depend on higher taxes from their children. Voters are even caught in internal conflicts—the same person can be the teacher seeking higher pay from the board of education and the taxpayer seeking lower property taxes.

Such a divide-and-conquer mentality among public officials with budgets and interests to balance can lead to coalitions being torn apart by so many conflicting claims on members' loyalties at many stages, from the weaving together of party platforms, to candidate selection and lobbying on public budgets. As Gary Delgado, of the Center for Third World Organizing, asked: "If there are any concessions, who'll cut the deal for low income people of color?"[21]

While there is no shortage, then, of proposals that could benefit poor women, from rent control and national health insurance, to sliding-scale social services, welfare-grant increases, and care givers' wages, just to name a few, how can a coalition—which reflects these self-interests and the broad sense of a decent society—be held together long enough to elect officials and hold them accountable?

Clearly elections are just one key but early battle for poor women to gain a voice in public policy. A *ninth question* about the impact poor women would have as voters is, Just how much of the process of public policy making can voters affect? Many laws affecting poor women are actually regulations, make in an executive bureaucracy of appointed officials well insulated from the winds of elections. Even if poor women can convince enough other voters and legislators to pass certain laws, there's also the matter of enforcement and adjudication, now more difficult for poor women since the recent sweeping cutbacks in legal services.

A *tenth question* that skeptics raise about voter registration is not about the power of poor voters but about the power of their elected advocates. Particularly in a conservative era, where public attitudes about the role of government are so narrow, even if poor women help elect officials who are responsive, can these officeholders and poor women's "lobbyists" and advocates deliver?

Perhaps they could more often if there were more of them. From New York City Council member Ruth Messinger, to California State Assembly member Maxine Waters, state and local legislatures contain some stalwarts who support poor women. And there is certainly no shortage of proposals put forward by poor women through these advocates and others—creative plans for funding social services and benefits by closing real estate tax loopholes, reinstating stock-transfer taxes, and transferring military appropriations. But because these public officials are a minority, they are often unable to command the necessary support among their colleagues to deliver. As times become more conservative, and it becomes more radical to support welfare rights, some of these lawmakers' closest legislative allies claim to be supporting poor women by calling for new computer systems designed to uncover welfare fraud among recipients, instead of pushing delinquent corporations to pay their taxes, which could add far larger sums to the public coffers. And some of the lobbyists who began as welfare advocates become changed by the system in their definition of what it is feasible to fight for.

These concerns, and others along these lines, led many long-time welfare-rights activists such as Theresa Funiciello to question just how much poor women could expect to gain by voting—unless some of the changes suggested above come about.

For years, Funiciello had been active in the Downtown Welfare Advocacy Center (DWAC), a New York City welfare-rights organization. A former Aid to Families with Dependent Children recipient, she had become a special assistant to the New York State commissioner of social services under Governor Mario Cuomo. "Few academicians have so consistently lent their skills to oppressed people as have Frances Piven and Richard Cloward," notes Funiciello,[22] "[yet] even if the strategy succeeds, the conditions of the poor will not change; registering people to vote will not bring about social change."

Necessary but Not Sufficient

Certainly not by itself. As Gary Delgado notes, "While voter registration does have a tactical importance, it is clear the current campaign may not reach the strategic level of projected political significance unless political education, direct action and policy development become an integral part of the organizing."[23]

While all the foot soldiers in recent voter-registration drives might not have shared this view, it is perhaps where the architects and critics of the strategy would agree. Cloward and Piven themselves characterized voter registration from the start as "a strategy that is simultaneously a movement strategy and an electoral strategy. It is intended both to increase the electoral participation of people at the bottom and to politicize the terms of their participation."[24]

Yet if voter registration is to avoid being a top-down effort that raises expectations, sets up its intended beneficiaries to feel betrayed, then cynical if it fails to bring quick, extensive, definitive change, it must be clear about its promises. As Funiciello puts it, "The electoral mobilization against Reagan is not de facto a political mobilization to benefit the poor. . . . at best there will be some restoration of cuts and she will only be as poor as she was before. The poor," she observes, "having only been manipulated to vote, will be in no organized position to articulate or apply pressure for their own demands."[25]

The act of voting has a better chance, however, to contribute to changing poor women's lives if they themselves make voter registration part of a larger strategy that includes education, organizing, and other concerted activity. For poor women, electoral politics is only a subset of political activity, to bring about equity, not as an end, but as a step toward a changed role—just as for some feminists, reforms to secure women's rights are only a part of a strategy for women's liberation. Poor women's organizations, from the welfare-rights groups in the 1960s to their heirs in the 1980s, have developed a variety of political activities. In the 1960s they ranged from urging women to sign up for the benefits they were entitled to to sit-ins in welfare offices, storefront welfare-rights counseling centers, and support groups. In the 1980s, they included organizing guests and audience for a "Donahue" television show about welfare in the summer of 1985 and playing a key role in a coalition to organize "Up to Poverty," a Massachusetts campaign to raise welfare benefits to the poverty line and call public attention to the fact that no state in the union offers welfare benefits high enough to bring welfare recipients up to poverty level.

Since public officials are merely the gatekeepers for the powerful, to gain the necessary clout for social change, all these activities and others, too, must be part of poor women's strategy to mobilize public opinion—and power—to see that politicians cannot get away with simply paying lip service to poor women's aspirations while avoiding any commitment to specific policies for achieving those goals.

Short of complete change, there are two dimensions of power along which to evaluate political clout: access and influence. Access, having your phone calls answered, means that political decision makers recognize certain organizations as representatives of legitimate interests. Influence means you have some successes to show, such as relevant bills introduced and passed and progams saved from budget cuts.

To reach that point, coalitions with other women's groups hold promise, that is, if poor women are equal partners from the start and leaders when it comes to their concerns. Other women may need some education about poor women's lives and priorities, but the tendency to support public solutions to private problems is already strong among women in general and feminists in particular. Public opinion polls since 1976 show that women are less inclined to think people ought to get ahead on their own (notes Klein, 49 percent of men felt this compared to 38 percent of women).[26] In 1977, the year before the feminization of poverty was coined as a term, the National Women's Conference in Houston incorporated planks about poor women's issues in its agenda. And by 1980, only 28 percent of women were inclined to reduce government services compared with 38 percent of men.[27]

At best, voter registration, then, is a necessary but not sufficient part of a strategy for ameliorating women's poverty, in which poor women educate and organize themselves and others and maintain constant vigilence in coalitions and public policy arenas to win and preserve significant gains. It is patronizing to think that poor women would think otherwise. But it is only responsible for the proponents of voter registration to make sure not to promise more than they can deliver or raise expectations that would invite anger and apathy if they fail to materialize.

But if the issues touched on above are addressed, then poor women have a shot at having some clout in the next set of elections. As equal partners from the start in coalitions in a changing electorate, poor women might have a fighting chance to achieve some gains. Anything less means that poor women simply pay more than their share of the fare to stand in the back of a bus that will likely run out of gas before it reaches their stop.

Years from now, back at the state house, this might mean poor women would wear badges that said "Save EA for me—I'm poor and I vote." If the now-older state rep took a closer look at the crowd, he might see poor women in the lead, followed by waves of social workers, teachers, seniors, firefighters, even some utility company lobbyists. All these constituencies would have been educated and mobilized to fight for Emergency Assistance as part of a broad progressive agenda, which would include day care for state workers, reduced classroom size, and cost-of-living increases for Social Security—all of which would have poor women's support and none of which would be traded for the other. Instead of looking down, that state rep and his colleagues might have to look twice.

COMPARABLE WORTH, INCOMPARABLE PAY

Teresa Amott and Julie Matthaei

In 1983, 41 percent of the poor women who supported their children alone also worked in the labor force, averaging thirty weeks of work during the year. Looked at from another perspective, nearly 30 percent of employed women maintaining families alone are unable to raise their families above the poverty level.

Why isn't employment the way out of poverty for women? One answer can be found in the occupational distribution of women. Women cannot lift themselves out of poverty by working because most women work in underpaid women's jobs.

Under the banner of "pay equity," also known as "comparable worth," feminist activists have been struggling to raise the pay in women's jobs. In the early 1980s, pay equity was a central issue in a strike at Yale University, where women workers argued that their clerical and technical work received lower pay than other jobs that required comparable skill, training, and responsibility. At the conclusion of the strike, women workers did receive pay increases, which narrowed the gap between their salaries and those of men employed by the university.

Pay equity can contribute to ending poverty for women by rais-

---

This essay appeared in *Radical America* 18, no. 5. Used by permission.

ing the income of many of the working poor and by raising fundamental questions about the worth of work. Nonetheless, it suffers from the limitations of any piecemeal reform and needs to be pursued as part of a broader program of demands, which includes a stronger and less punitive welfare state. This chapter introduces the concept of pay equity and describes how it might be used as an element in a strategy to end poverty.

The Emergence of the Comparable-Worth Strategy

When the Equal Pay Act of 1963 prohibited unequal pay for equal work and the broader Civil Rights Act of 1964 set affirmative action into motion, many people assumed that the gap between men's and women's wages would close. Instead, the average salary for a woman working full-time year-round remained roughly 60 percent of the salary earned by a man. The constancy of the wage gap in the face of antidiscrimination legislation drew attention to the fact that women and men rarely hold the same jobs. Traditional sex roles and outright sex discrimination by employers and workers had the result of excluding women from most occupations other than homemaking and its extension in the labor market. Those paid occupations open to women shared low pay and few opportunities for advancement and often centered around nurturing and serving others. Throughout the decade of the 1970s, more than 40 percent of all women workers were concentrated in ten occupations, most of which were more than 70 percent female—for example, nursing, secretarial and clerical work, teaching, and food services. In contrast, men, especially white men, had more job options and more opportunity for high pay and promotion. For instance, stock clerks, predominantly male, earn more than bank tellers, who are predominantly female; and mail carriers earn more than registered nurses. As a result of this occupational segregation, legislation prohibiting unequal pay for equal jobs failed to address the heart of pay inequity between the sexes: men and women earning unequal pay for different jobs.

The idea of comparable worth was devised to raise women's wages in female-dominated occupations up to the level paid in male occupations of "comparable worth." Also known as pay equity, comparable worth means that jobs deemed to be of "equal value to the employer" should pay the same, regardless of their sex or race typing. The first wage comparability case before the courts was based on race.[1] However, subsequent attempts to apply the Civil Rights Act to nonidentical jobs have focused on wage differences based on job segregation according to gender.

Some of the first attempts to broaden the concept of equal pay emerged during World War II, when unions such as the United Auto Workers (UAW) and the International Union of Electronic, Electrical, Technical, Salaried and Machine Workers (IUE) fought differential pay for men and women workers in order to prevent an overall reduction in pay scales and to generate greater unity between men and women workers.[2] Since then, the ranks of advocates for pay equity have grown and a more feminist construction has been placed on the concept. Women's-rights groups, working-women's organizations, and unions representing women workers are currently pursuing three comparable-worth strategies for correcting pay inequities based on sex or race: litigation, collective bargaining, and legislation. Often a combination of these strategies is used.

Litigation

Prior to a 1981 Supreme Court decision, the courts were uniformly unfriendly to charges of sex discrimination. In Denver, where nurses charged discrimination because the city paid them less than tree trimmers and sign painters, the judge ruled against the nurses, arguing that the doctrine of comparable worth was "pregnant with the possibility of disrupting the entire economic system."[3] In 1981, however, the Supreme Court ruled that Title VII of the 1964 Civil Rights Act could be applied to prohibit wage differences in similar, but not identical, jobs.[4] Since then, there have been lower court decisions, such as the one in the state of Washington, which have awarded back pay to women whose jobs have been systematically undervalued. Although higher court decisions (such as one that challenged the Washington decision) have created a complex legal picture here, the point is that there *has* been some reason to hope for resolution through the courts.

Collective Bargaining

A variety of unions, including the UAW, IUE, AFSCME, CWA, SEIU, UE, and others, have adopted pay equity as a goal in bargaining, as well as in membership education and lobbying. Most efforts have focused on public employees, largely because information on pay scales for them is more accessible, and state agencies may be more vulnerable to public pressure brought through alliances of the community with labor. Local 101 of AFSCME in San José, California, is one of the public-sector success stories. These city employees struck to win a substantial pay increase and "special adjustments" to upgrade jobs held predominantly by women.[5] Unions often combine litigation with bargaining, as in the case of an IUE local that won pay-equity raises for women workers employed at a Massachusetts General Electric Plant.

Legislation

Many states have adopted legislation calling for a pay-equity study of state employment; others, including California, Minnesota, and Washington, have passed statutes that require public-sector wages to be set on the basis of comparable worth.[6] In Idaho, a law that assigns pay in state positions on the basis of skill and responsibility has produced a 16 percent increase in pay for female clerical workers. Other states have begun to raise wages in predominantly women's jobs without explicit recourse to the principle of comparable worth. In New Mexico, for instance, more than $3 million was appropriated in 1983 to raise the wages of the lowest-paid state employees, more than 80 percent of them women, even though a job evaluation study has not yet been completed.

Implementing Comparable Worth

The primary mechanism for implementing the principle of comparable worth in wage structures is the job analysis or job evaluation study. Efforts for pay equity usually involve ridding an existing study of inherent sex bias and/or demanding a formal job evaluation study where one does not exist.

Job evaluation studies were in use long before pay-equity advocates recognized their potential in comparable-worth struggles. Generally speaking, most large, bureaucratic firms and state agencies do not negotiate a wage directly with each employee but rather assign an employee to a particular rung of a job ladder. The worker's position on the job ladder determines his or her wages. Workers in the same job would thus receive the same salary, while workers in different jobs would be paid differently. To determine pay scales, large firms use fairly systematic job analysis or evaluation schemes, often prepared by outside consultants. The first step of the study analyzes jobs through examination of job descriptions and, sometimes, discussions with workers. In the most common type of evaluation, known as a point-factor system, points are assigned to each job on the basis of criteria (factors) such as skills, effort, responsibility, and working conditions. In the final stage of the process, dollar values are assigned to the points in each category of criteria. The same procedures, and often the same consultants, are used for job evaluations in pay-equity cases. In smaller firms, the process is much more informal, but rankings of jobs are still undertaken.

Despite the aura of objectivity surrounding these studies, there is no objective way to determine the relative productivity of jobs. Owing to the division of labor, a myriad of different workers contribute to the output of any product, and it is impossible to distinguish their different contributions. How can one technically measure the relative importance to a hospital of dietitians, nurses, or the pharmacological staff? Normally, hospital administrators pay market wages, the amount needed to attract workers, and infer the relative worth of these different workers from their wage rates. Job evaluation studies, however, attempt to determine the relative productivity of jobs apart from the market. To do this, they must subjectively choose a set of factors and weigh them. There are many ways in which sex, race, and class bias can enter into the calculations.

One critical area is the selection and definition of factors to be evaluated. For example, it is common to define responsibility as supervisory responsibility over other workers, machines, or money. In this instance, child-care workers would receive low points for responsibility, even though their jobs entail enormous responsibility for children under their care. Similarly, skilled activities such as nurturing and guiding are rarely counted, causing traditional women's jobs to receive lower points than men's jobs. Boredom from routinized work is not commonly considered worthy of points as an adverse working condition, although outdoor work and heavy lifting are.

Another critical area is the weighting of different factors, accomplished either through the number of points allocated to each factor or by the method that assigns dollars to points. Weighting has the effect of determining the relative worth of different factors and generally involves sophisticated statistical techniques such as multiple-regression analysis. In effect, consulting firms specializing in job evaluations rely on previous correlations between existing pay scales and measured factor points to predict for new clients what a job's salary should be. From the perspective of the employer, the best point rankings are those that duplicate the existing pay hierarchy as closely as possible, since this seemingly "objective" technique can then be used to legitimize pay differentials. Consequently, job evaluation schemes usually embody existing pay practices, complete with sex, race, or gender bias. For example, the maximum number of points assigned for responsibility may be two thousand, while adverse working conditions are awarded a maximum of only two hundred points; this weighting would ensure that managerial jobs pay more than service or operative jobs.

Despite these biased methods, current methods of evaluating jobs can still be used to win pay raises for those in "undervalued" work. For example, most studies have found that male and female jobs with equal point evaluations are paid differently because of the weighting of different factors mentioned above or because firms use different ranking schemes for different types of jobs. In these instances, legislation or bargaining agreements mandating equal pay for jobs of equal point value (under the same ranking scheme) can achieve somewhere between 5 and 25 percent pay increases.[7]

Much more can be won by eliminating bias from the weighting technique. To do so requires wide access to information about existing or contemplated job evaluation studies. Women need to disseminate information on how consulting firms such as Hay Associates, which serves approximately 40 percent of the Fortune 500 companies, conduct their studies, and we need to bargain for input at all stages of the evaluation process. The more we involve ourselves in the technique, taking power from the technocrats, the more success we will have. Progress has already been achieved in this area. Most unions that have staff members who are experts on the technique of feminist proponents of comparable worth are currently at work expanding the definitions of compensable factors so as to recognize the value of women's traditional work skills. (One of the most important redefinitions has been the inclusion of responsibility for children as a compensable factor.) More work needs to be done to rid the method of race and class bias.

How Radical Is Comparable Worth?

Not only does the comparable-worth principle directly challenge sexual inequality in the labor market, it may also have the potential for bringing about other radical change. Comparable worth promises to undermine male supremacy outside the labor market as well.

Feminists have long noted the way in which the lower wages of women have reinforced the traditional nuclear family and women's responsibility for unpaid work in the home. So long as women are denied access to men's jobs and few women's jobs pay a living wage, women are under strong economic pressure to marry. Married women's financial dependence upon their husbands contributes to sexual inequality within marriage. The economic costs of leaving or being left by one's husband are illustrated by the high percentage of women heading families on their own who live in poverty. The risk of poverty is highest for women of color; in 1982, 56.2 percent of black and 55.4 percent of Latino families headed by women were poor.

In addition, the principle of comparable worth subjects the pay structure to scrutiny it rarely receives. Conventional economic wisdom argues that in the "perfectly competitive market economy," workers are paid according to their "marginal product," that is, according to their contributions to the production process. (In graduate school, one of the authors' teachers built models that assumed that women were 60 percent as productive as men, justifying this assumption with the fact that full-time women workers earned on average, 60 percent as much as men!) Comparable worth debunks such convenient rationalizations of the pay structure, and the sexist assumptions they both reflect and create, by showing that the force behind pay differences has not been productivity differences but rather power and discrimination. Thus, the principle presents a radical critique of the U.S. system of income distribution through the "free market" and presents an alternative way of achieving what the market had promised: the distribution of income to workers according to their contributions in a manner that is fair and that provides incentives at the same time.

Finally, although the comparable-worth principle does not directly attack occupational segregation by sex, it may do so indirectly. On the one hand, by making traditionally feminine jobs palatable to women, comparable worth may reduce the incentives for women to seek entrance into male-dominated, more privileged jobs. On the other hand, as traditionally feminine jobs begin to offer wages comparable to those of masculine jobs, more men will find them attractive. Also, as women begin to fight for and expect working conditions comparable to those of men, they may find men's jobs more desirable and be more willing to fight to get them.

Broadening the Comparable-Worth Agenda

The principle of comparable worth gains effectiveness and constituency when combined with other progressive demands. Conservative economists have warned that raising wages for women's work would create uncontrollable inflation. The authors argue that although firms will try to increase their prices (and state agencies, their tax revenues), the inflationary impact would depend upon the magnitude and speed of the pay-equity adjustment, as well as on the ability of firms and governments to pass on the costs. (This ability, in turn, depends on the degree of monopoly power the firms have and on citizen resistance to tax increases.) Finally, inflation is not the worst of all evils, and it can be limited by using wage-price controls, long a demand of progressives.

What is more worrisome are the other possible reactions of firms and state agencies to an increase in the price of women's labor: automation, elimination of state programs, and the departure of factories to countries where women still provide a superexploitable labor force. Already, computerization is threatening clerical workers, and job flight has created massive structural unemployment in the United States. In order for comparable-worth struggles not to exacerbate these problems, they must be pursued in conjunction with demands for job security, retraining, and legislation forbidding arbitrary plant closings.

In order to aid all undervalued workers, pay equity must also be extended to include comparisons between comparable but racially segregated jobs. Even this extension will not solve all workers' problems. Workers without jobs will not benefit, nor will workers in those jobs calculated to have the least worth. Since these are the main job problems faced by men of color, comparable worth offers little to them. Raising pay for women in certain jobs reduces inequality between women and men on the same level of the job hierarchy, but it increases the relative poverty of those at the bottom of the hierarchy. Their problems can only be solved by a more comprehensive restructuring of work and by a deeper and more radical discussion of the worth of work.

As currently practiced, the doctrine of comparable worth accepts the idea of a hierarchy of workers, more or less "worthy" on the basis of some objective criteria. However, as radicals become involved in decisions about what factors should merit higher pay, one may well begin to question the rationale for the hierarchy itself. If the discussion of what makes work worthy is extended to the grass roots, it may well be determined that all jobs are equally worthy. It may be decided that workers in unskilled, routinized jobs may be doing the hardest work of all, for such work saps and denies their very humanity. Why should those whose jobs give them the most opportunity to develop and use their abilities also be paid the most? The traditional argument—that higher pay must be offered as an incentive for workers to gain skills and training—is contradicted by the fact that the present highly paid jobs attract many more workers than employers demand. And given the unequal access to education and training that exists in U.S. society, a hierarchial pay scheme becomes a mechanism for the intergenerational transmission of wealth and privilege historically linked with racism, sexism, and classism.

We see the doctrine of comparable worth as one of the most innovative and promising approaches to redressing sexual inequality in the work place and the home. In fact, given the present reactionary climate, it is one of the few struggles in which tangible progress against injustice is being achieved. Furthermore, it raises larger questions about the fairness of the free-market system, questions that may even undermine the rationale for inequality of income. For those many poor women who participate in the paid labor force, pay equity could ease poverty; for others, unable to participate because women's work does not pay enough to cover child-care and other work-related expenses, pay equity could open the door to participation in the labor force.

If poverty is to be eliminated, however, pay equity must be joined by other strategies described in this collection of essays. A movement to eliminate poverty must encompass demands for a radically different system of income maintenance, health care, education, and child care along with mechanisms promoting unionization in low-wage women's jobs.

WOMEN AND THE STATE
Ideology, Power, and Welfare

Frances Fox Piven

Much of the feminist literature of the last few years evinces an almost categorical antipathy to the state. Among socialist feminists, the antipathy is signaled by the use of such terms as "social patriarchy" or "public patriarchy" to describe state policies that bear on the lives of women.[1] And among cultural feminists, it takes form in the nostalgic evocation of the private world of women in an era before state programs intruded on the family.[2]

There is some irony in this situation. While women intellectuals characterize relationships with the state as "dependence," women activists turn increasingly to the state as the arena for political organization and influence. At least as important, the intellectual animus toward the state flies in the face of the attitudes of the mass

An earlier version of this essay was prepared for the Research Planning Group on Women and the Welfare State, sponsored by the Council for European Studies. Other versions of it have appeared in *Socialist Review* and in *Gender and the Life Course*, ed. Alice Rossi (Hawthorne, N.Y.: Aldine Publishing Co., 1948). Used by permission of the author. The author would like to thank members of that group as well as Richard A. Cloward, Barbara Ehrenreich, Temma Kaplan, Evelyn Fox Keller, Joel Rogers, and Alice Rossi for their comments. (See Notes.)

of American women evident in survey data. Although the data show that most women are opposed to a defense buildup and presumably, therefore, are hostile to the military aspects of state power, in areas of domestic policy they evidently believe in a large measure of state responsibility for economic and social well-being, suggesting a belief in the strong and interventionist state that some feminist intellectuals abjure.[3]

Of course, activist women may be erring "liberals," and popular attitudes, including the attitudes of women, can be wrong. But in this instance. I think it is an undiscriminating antipathy to the state that is wrong, for it is based on a series of misleading and simplistic alternatives. On the one hand, there is somehow the possibility of women's power and autonomy; on the other, dependence on a controlling state. But these polarities are unreal: all social relationships involve elements of social control, and yet there is no possibility for power except in social relationships. In fact, I think the main opportunities for women to exercise power today inhere precisely in their "dependent" relationships with the state, and in this essay I explain why.

Before I turn directly to this issue, I want to consider the shift in the political beliefs signaled by the gender gap, for I think it important as well as evidence of my main contentions about power. Of course, everyone agrees the gender gap is important as well as being evidence of something. The media have bombarded us with information on the gap and also have given us the main explanation for it, attributing the new cleavage of opinion and voting behavior between men and women to the policies of the Reagan administration.[4] This explanation is not wrong, for the Reagan administration policies may well have had a catalytic effect on the expression of women's political attitudes. The organized women's movement has also been given credit for generating the gap; despite the poor match between the largely middle-class constituency of the movement and the cross-class constituency of the gap, and between the issues emphasized by the movement and the issues that highlight the gap, this explanation is probably not entirely wrong either.[5] Nevertheless, I think a development of this magnitude is likely to have deeper roots than have heretofore been proposed. I will conclude that those roots are in the expanding relationships women have developed with the state and in the new possibilities for power yielded by those relationships. But because the connection between beliefs and this new institutional relationship is not simple and direct, I want first to evaluate and give due weight to other influences on the shift in political opinion that has occurred among women.

Rather than showing the imprint of the women's movement, with its clearly modernizing tendencies, the emphasis on peace, economic equality, and social needs associated with the women's side of the gender gap suggests the imprint of what are usually taken as traditional female values. This oft-made observation suggests that the gender gap is not a fleeting response to particular current events but has deep and authentic roots. At the same time, traditional values of themselves cannot account for this development. The care-giving values held by women are old, but the sharp divergence between women and men is entirely new. Much tradition, however, may color the politics of women. The fact that traditional values associated with the family are now being asserted as public values is a large transformation. Or, as Kathy Wilson told a reporter on the occasion of the convening of the National Women's Political Caucus in 1983, "Women are recognizing that their private values are good enough to be their public values." More than that, the beliefs associated with the gender gap are specifically about the obligations of government to protect these values. Women are asserting that the state should represent women, on their terms.

All of this suggests the possibility that a major transformation of consciousness is occurring on a scale that suggests powerful historical forces at work, whatever the precipitating role of Reagan administration policies. Although the comparisons may seem at first glance too grand, I think the public articulation and politicization of formerly insular female values may even be comparable to such historic developments as the emergence of the idea of personal freedom among a bonded European peasantry or the spread of the idea of democratic rights among the small farmers of the American colonies and the preindustrial workers of England and France or the emergence of the conviction among industrial workers at different times and places of their right to organize and strike. Each of these ideological developments reflected the interplay of traditional and transforming influences. And each brought enormous political consequences in its wake.

Change in the Objective Circumstances of Women

The gender gap simultaneously reflects the influence of women's traditional beliefs and the transformation of those beliefs in response to radical changes in the objective circumstances of American women. I want now to consider those objective circumstances—the way changes in the family, the labor market, and the state have altered the opportunities and constraints that confront women as political actors. If ideologies are, as I contend, forged in the crucible of memory and experience, then the scale of these institutional shifts lends weight to my opening contention that a major ideological transformation is at work.

One large change is in the family. Rising rates of divorce and separation, combined with growing numbers of women who bear children but do not marry, mean that fewer and fewer women are in situations that even outwardly resemble the traditional family. Moreover, even those women who remain within traditional families now confront the possibility, if not the probability, of desertion or divorce and the near-certainty of a long widowhood. Even within those shrinking numbers of apparently traditional families, relations have been altered by the face that many women no longer rely exclusively on the wages earned by men.

Even taken by itself, one should expect this large change in circumstance to have consequences for the politics of women. The firm contours of the insular and patriarchal family narrowly limited the options for action available to women, but they also created options for action, for exercising power in family relations, no matter how convoluted the ways. Now these options are contracting. They do not exist in families in which men are not present. And even when men are, the old forms of female power have almost surely been weakened if, as Barbara Ehrenreich argues, men in general are increasingly "liberated" from their obligations under the moral economy of domesticity and, thus, wield the threat of desertion or divorce.[6]

But if relations in the traditional family gave women some limited options for action, in the larger sense these relations made women dependent on men and, therefore, subject to them, even for access to the public world. It should not be surprising, therefore, that in the past the political opinions of women followed those of men so closely. The family was indeed an institution of social control, as of course all institutions are.

The shredding of marital bonds, together with the inability of families to maintain themselves on the wages earned by men, meant that more and more women were forced to enter the labor market. Women became wage workers on a mass scale. Whatever this change actually meant in the lives of women, it clearly meant that they had entered the mainstream of ideas about power simply because most of those ideas are about power in the marketplace. There are few analysts indeed who do not think that the economic resources and opportunities for organization generated by market relations are critical resources for power. In this very broad sense, the tradition of the political left is not different. For nearly a century, leftist intellectuals have looked almost exclusively to production relations as the arena in which popular power could be organized and exercised. Production, by bringing people together as workers in mass-production industries, generated the solidarities that made collective action possible. And, once organized, workers in the mass-production industries also gained leverage over capital.

But the prospects for women generated by their mass entry into the labor market are neither so simple nor so happy. The situation is, of course, different for different women. For those who are better educated and perhaps younger, liberation from the constraints of the family has meant an opportunity to move into and upward in the realms of the labor market and politics. These women, among whom I count myself, have tried to shake themselves free of the old moral economy of domesticity and in its place have developed new ideas to name their new opportunities and aspirations. These ideas include the women's movement, liberation, modernization, and market success. The women's movement not only took advantage of burgeoning opportunities for women in government, business, law, and medicine,[7] it helped create those opportunities. In this sense, changes in objective circumstances and ideology were interactive, as I think they always are. If new ideas reflect new conditions, new ideas in turn may well lead people to act in ways that help shape those conditions.

But most women did not become lawyers, nor will they. Most

women, forced to sell their labor, sold it in the expanding low-wage service sector as fast-food workers, hospital workers, or office-cleaning women. In these jobs, perhaps as a result of the influx of vulnerable women workers, wages and working conditions have actually deteriorated over the last decade.[8] The relative stability of the ratio of female earnings to male earnings, despite the large gains made by some women, is striking evidence of the weak position of these workers.[9] They are located in industries in which unionization has always been difficult; those unions that did form realized few gains because widely scattered work sites made organization difficult and a ready supply of unemployed workers weakened the power to strike. The prospect of long-term, high levels of unemployment in the U.S. economy makes it less likely than ever that these structural barriers, which prevented unionization and the use of the strike power in the past, can now be overcome.

Nor is it likely that women will gradually enter the manufacturing industries in which workers did succeed in unionizing, if only because these industries are shrinking. New jobs are being created not in steel, autos, or rubber, but in fast foods, data processing, and health care. Of course, even if this were not so, even if women were likely to enter the smokestack industries in large numbers, it would be too late, for international competition and robotization have combined to crush the historic power of mass-production workers. In fact, the broad shifts in the U.S. economy from manufacturing to services and from skilled work to unskilled work, combined with the likelihood of continuing high levels of unemployment, mean that the possibilities for the exercise of popular power in the work place are eroding for both men and women.

Women are thus losing their old rights and their limited forms of power within the family. In the marketplace, their position is weak, and prospects for improvement through individual mobility or the development of collective power are grim. These circumstances have combined to lead women to turn to the state, especially to the expanding programs of the welfare state. Income supports, social services, and government employment partly offset the deteriorating position of women in the family and the economy and have even given women a measure of protection and therefore power in these areas. In these ways, the state is turning out to be the main recourse for women.

Frances Fox Piven

Women in Relation to the Welfare State

The relationship of women to the welfare state hardly needs documenting. Women with children are the overwhelming majority among the beneficiaries of the main "means-tested" income-maintenance programs, such as Aid to Families with Dependent Children (AFDC), food stamps, and Medicaid.[10] Moreover, the numbers of women affected by these programs are far greater than the numbers of beneficiaries at any one time, for women in the low-wage service and clerical sectors of the labor force turn to welfare-state programs to tide them over during family emergencies or their frequent bouts of unemployment. Older women, for their part, depend on Social Security and Medicare benefits, without which most would be very poor. However inadequately, all of these programs moderate the extremes of poverty and insecurity among women.

More than that, the programs that make women a little less insecure also make them a little less powerless. The availability of benefits and services reduces the dependence of younger women with children on male breadwinners, as it reduces the dependence of older women on adult children. The same holds in the relations of working women with employers. Most women work in situations without unions or effective work rules to shield them from the raw power of their bosses. Social welfare programs provide some shield, for the availability of benefits reduces the fear that they and their children will go hungry and homeless if they are fired.

Women have also developed a large and important relationship to the welfare state as the employees of these programs. The proportion of such jobs held by women has actually increased, even as the total number of social welfare jobs has greatly expanded. By 1980, fully 70 percent of the 17.3 million social service jobs on all levels of government, including education, were held by women, accounting for about one third of all female non-agricultural employment and the larger part of all female job gain since 1960.[11] In these several ways, the welfare state has become critical in determining the lives and livelihood of women. Women's belief in the desirability of a responsible state, more widespread than men's belief, is partly a reflection of this institutional reality.

But will this new institutional context yield women the resources to participate in the creation of their own lives as historical actors? Can it, in a word, yield them power?

Women and Political Power

Very little that has been written about the relationship of women to the state suggests looking there for sources of power. On the contrary, the state is chiefly characterized as exercising social control over women, supplanting the eroding patriarchal relations of the family with a patriarchal relationship with the state. In my opinion, the determination to affirm this conclusion is generally much stronger than the evidence for it. Even in the nineteenth century, state policies had a more complicated bearing on the situation of women. Thus, although it is clearly true that changes in family law that granted women some rights as individuals, including the right to own property, did not alter their subordination to men, that is hardly evidence that the state by these actions was somehow moving "toward a new construction of male domination."[12]

This kind of argument is even more strongly made with regard to welfare-state programs. From widows' pensions and laws regulating female labor in the nineteenth century to AFDC today, state programs that provide income to women and children, or that regulate their treatment in the marketplace, are condemned as new forms of patriarchal social control. True, there is surely reason for not celebrating widows' pensions, or AFDC either, as emancipation. These programs never reached all of the women who needed suppport (widows' pensions reached hardly any), the benefits they provided were meager, and those who received them were made to pay a heavy price in loss of pride. Similarly, government regulation of family and market relations never overcame economic and social discrimination and in some instances reinforced it. But perhaps because some income would seem to be better than none, and even weak regulations can be a beginning, the definitive argument of the social-control perspective is not that the welfare state is weak and insufficient but that involvement with government exacts the price of dependence, somehow robbing women of their capacities for political action. It seems to follow that the massive expansion of these government programs in the past two decades and the massive involvement of women and their children in them are cause for great pessimism about the prospects for women exerting power and surely for pessimism about the prospects for women exerting power over the state.

In general, I think this mode of argument is a reflection of the eagerness with which U.S. society has embraced a simplistic social-control perspective on institutional life, straining to discover how every institutional change helps maintain a system of hierarchical relations and, therefore, is evidence of the power of ruling groups. Of course, ruling groups have power, they do try to exercise social control, and they usually succeed, at least for a time. But they are not all-powerful. They do not rule entirely on their terms, and they do not exercise social control without some accommodation to other forces. Even then, the institutional arrangements that achieve social control are never entirely secure, for people discover new resources and evolve new ideas, and sometimes these resources and ideas are generated by the very arrangements that, for a time, seemed to ensure their acquiescence.

The critique of the welfare state developed by radical feminists was surely strongly influenced by the major leftist analyses of these programs. Overall, and despite the complexities in some of their arguments, the Left disparaged social welfare programs not for maintaining patriarchy but for maintaining capitalism. Where in other arenas leftists were sometimes ready to see that institutional arrangements had been shaped by class conflict, and even to see a continuing capacity for class struggle, in the arena of social welfare they saw chiefly arrangements for social control. In part, this outlook reflected the view, almost axiomatic among many on the Left, that the only authentic popular power is working-class power arising out of relations to the means of production. It was at least consistent with this view to conclude that welfare-state programs weakened popular political capacities and weakened them in several ways. The complicated array of programs and categories of beneficiaries, combined with regressive taxation, fragmented working-class solidarity. The programs provided puny benefits but considerable opportunities for coopting popular leaders and absorbing popular energies; and the very existence of social welfare programs distracted working people from the main political issue, which, of course, was the control of capital. In this view, the welfare state was mainly understood as an imposition of power from above.

The Role of the State

But I do not think the evolution of the U.S. welfare state can be understood as the result only, or mainly, of a politics of domination. Rather it was the result of complex institutional and ideological changes that occurred in U.S. society and of the complex and conflictual politics associated with these changes. Over the course of the last century, the role of government (particularly the federal government) in U.S. economic life progressively increased. This development was largely a reflection of the demands of businessmen in an increasingly complex economy. But it had other consequences beyond creating the framework for industrial growth. As government penetration of the economy became more pervasive and more obvious, laissez-faire doctrine lost much of its vigor, although it still echoed strongly in the rhetoric of politicians. Few analysts dispute the significance of the doctrine in U.S. history. It was not that the actual role of government in the economy was so restricted, for the record in that respect is complicated. Rather, the doctrine of limited government was important because it restricted the spheres in which democratic political rights had bearing. Eventually, however, the doctrine became untenable. The political ideas of Americans, like the ideas of European peasants, gradually changed as they reflected changing reality. An economy increasingly penetrated by government gave rise to the wide recognition of the active role of the state in the economy and gradually to the idea of the fusion of economic rights and political rights.[13]

This shift in belief is evident in a wealth of survey data that show that Americans think government is responsible for reducing economic inequality, for coping with unemployment, for supporting the needy, for, in short, the economic well-being of its citizens. It is also evident in electoral politics, as E.R. Tufte's 1978 analyses of the efforts of political leaders to coordinate the business cycle with the election cycle make evident, as do exit poll data on the popular concerns that generated electoral shifts in the 1980 election.[14]

Ideas undergird political action. The emerging recognition that government played a major role in the economy, and that the democratic right to participate in government extended to economic demands, increasingly shaped the character of political movements. Beginning with the protests of the unemployed, the aged, and industrial workers in the Great Depression and continuing in the movements of blacks, women, and environmentalists in the 1960s and 1970s, government became the target of protest, and government action to redress grievances arising in economic spheres became the program. The gradually expanding U.S. welfare state was mainly a response to these movements. It is not by any means that the movements were the only force in shaping the welfare state. On the one hand, the success of the protestors was owed to the growing legitimacy of their demands in the eyes of a broader public and the threat they therefore wielded of precipitating electoral defections if government failed to respond. On the other hand, the programs that responded to protest demands were limited and modified by other powerful interests, mainly by business groups who resisted the programs or worked to shape them to their own ends. Nevertheless, popular movements were a critical force in creating and expanding the welfare state.[15]

If the welfare state was not an imposition from the top of society, if it was forged at least in part by politics from below, what then will be its consequences in the longer run for the continued exercise of political force from below? This, of course, is the main question raised by the social-control thesis, and it is of enormous significance for women, given their extensive involvement with the welfare state. Thus far, that involvement is not generating acquiescence. On the contrary, the differing male and female expectations of government revealed by the gender gap, as well as the indignation and activism of women's organizations in reaction to the policies of the Reagan administration, are not the attitudes of people who feel themselves helpless. Rather, they suggest that women think they have rights vis-à-vis the state and some power to realize those rights. If, however, the wide involvement of women in the welfare state as beneficiaries and workers erodes their capacities for political action, then what society is witnessing is a deluded flurry of activity that will soon pass.

Women and the Welfare State

But perhaps not. Perhaps this is the beginning of women's politics that draws both ideological strength and political resources from the existence of the welfare state. One sense in which this may be so is that the welfare state provides some objective institutional affirmation of women's political convictions. I said earlier that the welfare state was in large part a response to the demands of popular political movements of both men and women. These movements, in turn, had been made possible by changes in the relationship of government to the economy that had encouraged the idea that democratic rights included at least some economic rights. Once in existence, the social programs strengthen the conviction that economic issues belong in political spheres and that democratic rights include economic rights. In particular, the existence of the social programs are, for all their flaws, an objective and public affirmation of the values of economic security and nurturance that connect the moral economy of domesticity to the gender gap in political values and behavior.

This kind of affirmation may well strengthen women for political action. To use a phrase suggested by Jane Jensen in connection with the rise of the French women's movement, the "universe of political discourse" helps determine the likelihood and success of political mobilizations.[16] One can see the critical importance of the universe of political discourse or ideological context in determining not only the success but the scale of past expressions of oppositional politics among women. The participation of women in the food riots of the eighteenth and nineteenth centuries reflected the centrality of nurturance for women (as well as their access to the markets where collective action could take place). But perhaps women were able to act as they did on so large a scale because their distinctive values as women were reinforced by the traditional belief, held by men and women alike, that the local poor had a prior claim on the local food supply. By contrast, when middle-class women reformers in the nineteenth-century United States tried to "bring homelike nurturing into public life" they were pitted against the still very vigorous doctrines of American laissez-faire economics.[17] Not only were their causes largely lost, but their movement remained small, failing to secure much popular support even from women. The situation is vastly different today. The women reformers who are mobilizing now in defense of social welfare programs are not isolated voices challenging a dominant doctrine. The existence of the welfare state has contributed to the creation of an ideological context that has given them substantial influence in Congress as well as mass support from women.

Women have also gained political resources from their relationship with the state. One critical resource appears to be of very long standing. It is, quite simply, the vote and the potential electoral influence of women, given their large numbers. Of course, that resource is not new, and it is not owed to the welfare state. Women have been enfranchised for more than sixty years, but the promise of the franchise was never realized for the reason that women followed men in the voting booth as in much of their public life. Only today, with the emergence of the gender gap in politics, does the promise of women's electoral power seem real.

Part of the reason for the new significance of women's electoral power is in the institutional changes I have described. The "breakdown" of the family, although it stripped women of old resources for the exercise of power within the family, nevertheless freed them to use other resources. In fact, I think the breakdown of any institutional pattern of social control can generate resources for power. The disintegration of particular social relationships may well mean that people are released from subjugation to others and thus are freed to use resources that were previously effectively suppressed. The breakdown of the plantation system in the United States, for example, meant that rural blacks were removed from the virtually total power of the planter class, and only then was it possible for them to begin to use the infrastructure of the black Southern church as a focus for mobilization.

Similarly, only as women were at least partly liberated from the overweaning power of men by the breakdown of the family has the possibility of their electoral power become real. The size of the gender gap and the fact that it has persisted and widened in the face of the Reagan administration's ideological campaign suggest the enormous electoral potential of women. This, of course, is the media's preoccupation and was the preoccupation of contenders in the 1984 election as well. But its importance extends beyond 1984. Women have moved into the forefront of electoral calculations because they are an enormous constituency that is showing an unprecedented coherence and conviction about the key issues of the time, a coherence and conviction that, I have argued, is intertwined with the development of the welfare state. This electorate could change U.S. politics. In particular, it could change the politics of the welfare state, although not by itself.

The welfare state has generated other political resources that, it seems fair to say, are mainly women's resources. The expansion of social welfare programs has created a far-flung and complex infrastructure of agencies and organizations that are so far proving to be a resource in the defense of the welfare state and may have even larger potential. The historic involvement of women in social welfare and their concentration in social-welfare employment have combined to make women preponderant in this infrastructure and to give them a large share of leadership positions as well.[18] The political potential of these organizations cannot be dismissed because they are part of the state apparatus. Such organizations, whether public or private, are part of the state, in the elementary sense that they owe their funding to government. Nevertheless, the byzantine complexity of welfare-state organization, reflecting the fragmented and decentralized character of U.S. government generally, as well as the historic bias in favor of private implementation of public programs, may afford the organizations a considerable degree of autonomy from the state. That so many of these organizations have lobbied as hard as they have against the several rounds of Reagan budget cuts is testimony to this measure of autonomy. They did not win, of course. But mounting federal deficits are evidence they did not lose either, and that is something to wonder about.

There is another aspect of the politics generated by this organizational infrastructure that deserves note. The welfare state brings together millions of poor women who depend on its programs. These constituencies are not, as is often thought, simply atomized and, therefore, helpless people. Rather, the structure of the welfare state itself has helped to create new solidarities and has also generated the political issues that cement and galvanize these solidarities. One can see evidence of this in the welfare-rights movements of the 1960s, where people were brought together in welfare waiting rooms, and where they acted together in terms of common grievances generated by welfare practices. One can see it again today, most dramatically in the mobilization of the aged to defend Social Security. The solidarities and issues generated by the welfare state are, of course, different from the solidarities and issues generated in the work place. But that difference does not argue their insignificance as sources of power, as the Left often argues, and especially for women who have small hope of following the path of industrial workers.

The infrastructure of the welfare state also creates the basis for cross-class alliances among women. The infrastructure is dominated, of course, by better-educated and middle-class women. But these women are firmly linked by organizational self-interest to the poor women who depend on welfare-state programs. It is poor women who give the welfare state its raison d'être and who are ultimately its most reliable source of political support. Of course, the alliance between the organizational infrastructure and the beneficiaries of the welfare state is uneasy and difficult and sometimes overshadowed by antagonisms that are also natural. Nevertheless, the welfare state has generated powerful cross-class ties between the different groups of women who have stakes in protecting it.

The erosion of the traditional family and its deteriorating position on the labor market has concentrated women in the programs of the welfare state. The future of these women, workers and beneficiaries alike, hangs on the future of these programs. They need to defend the programs, expand them, and reform them. They need, in short, to exert political power. The determined and concerted opposition to welfare programs that has emerged among corporate leaders and their Republican allies and the weak defense offered by the Democratic Party suggest that the situation will require a formidable political mobilization by women. The programs of the welfare state were won when movements of mass protest, by raising issues that galvanized an electoral following, forced the hand of political leaders. The defense and reform of the welfare state is not likely to be accomplished by less. There is this difference, however. The electoral and organizational support needed to nourish and sustain the movements through which women can become a major force in American political life is potentially enormous.

TALKING ACROSS THE TABLE

Possibilities for Dialogue and Action Between Poor Women and Feminists

Ann Withorn and Rochelle Lefkowitz

We need the space and the time to develop definitions that are about us, not defined by white terms. We women of color have had to shape ourselves to their definition of womanhood, motherhood, and feminism. Perhaps it's time we came into our own.

———Black community activist

It's condescending to poor women to pick an issue (like Medicaid abortions) and decide to work on it. You don't choose my issues. I can do that myself. It's the difference between saying we'll do it for you—or with you.

———Welfare organizer

The media present feminism as something for women who are slender, white, educated, and upwardly mobile. But if you are over forty, perhaps overweight, and locked into a dead-end job or marriage, you may be more likely to see feminism as a put-down than a sisterly call to arms.

———Feminist

Maybe the first feminist consciousness-raising group didn't end with someone asking, "Why aren't we reaching more poor women?" But, almost from the start of the current women's movement, feminists in shelters, clinics, commissions, and support groups have been asking themselves why more poor women, especially women of color, aren't among them. At the same time, many poor women start sentences with the phrase, "I'm not for women's lib, but . . . ," embracing feminist ideas while rejecting the label.

There are, of course, no numbers to prove who is or isn't a card-carrying feminist. But anyone who has worked in coalitions including poor women and nonpoor feminists has felt the tension between them. Sometimes it erupts into accusations, walkouts, and angry manifestos. More often, there are silences, long looks, and dwindling numbers of poor women, so that finally the feminist advocates find themselves meeting alone, wondering once again why poor women aren't attracted to feminism.

Why aren't they? In many ways the women's movement has tried to be less exclusive than most political or ethnic groups. Many working-class women are feminists, across the spectrum of feminist perspectives. Many feminist issues would seem to speak to poor women. Violence against women—rape, battering, sexual harassment—doesn't discriminate on the basis of income, and it has been at the heart of the feminist agenda for the past decade, along with better health care, birth control, and job opportunities.

Yet other feminist concerns may have made poor women feel as if they lived on another planet. The early demand to escape from housewifery into a meaningful job can seem absurd to women stuck in low-paying, dead-end jobs to help support—or fully maintain—their families. And to women on welfare, and others whose care giving is an all-consuming task, it can seem like an argument for forcing them to take a second job. After the media are through with feminists (by tagging them as concerned either with burning bras or dressing for success), it seems as if no ground for dialogue exists.

Feminists have responded differently to this tension, depending on which wing of the movement they occupy. Some have simply accepted it as an unfortunate fact of life and gone on to seek power in the name of women. More have tried to research relevant issues themselves and devise positions or issues that would both explain and bridge the gap, issues such as Medicaid funding for abortions. Still others have become involved in providing various direct services for women, with a special emphasis on the needs of poor women—battered-women's shelters, for example. And, recently, a few theorists have tried to think through the meaning of poor women's increasing dependence on the capitalist state.

As white feminists from middle-class backgrounds, we have taken part in most of these strategies. We have also worked with many poor women and antipoverty activists over the years. Through it all we have seen the continuing differences in consciousness, trust, and operating assumptions between many poor women and most women who call themselves feminists. Over and over, we have heard women seeking welfare rights express their fear of being misunderstood, disregarded, or even betrayed by well-meaning feminists, their would-be allies. Among poor women of color, the distance has seemed even greater, sometimes even resulting in tensions among poor women because, among other reasons, white women on welfare are viewed as closer to feminism than black, Latina, Native American, or Asian women. And black feminists have found themselves placed at arm's length from everyone: "community" people distrust their feminism as identified with white interests, while white feminists tokenize or patronize them.

How did feminists, who have, above all, supported women's choice and autonomy, come to make other women feel so discounted? Perhaps some of the answer may come from the process of becoming a "feminist." For many middle-class white women, at least, feminism has meant dramatically stopping their constant service to men and children, while also attempting to identify with other women, as women. Both processes have been healthy—up to a point.

By insisting on an end to coffee service and the car pools, women asserted their right to make their own demands. If anything, feminism meant that women didn't always have to consider other people first, that they didn't need to wait until everyone else had spoken or achieved his or her personal and political demands. "Personal is political" meant seeing routes to power through changing old relationships and behaviors. But when poor women, especially women of color, heard such new-found assertiveness from women who appeared, in their lights, to be privileged, the stage was set for trouble. A black woman explains:

> They horn into affirmative action. After we struggle, they get themselves labeled a minority so they can get jobs before a black person,

> because we all know white men would rather hire a white woman over any person of color. And then they expect me to join them because we are both women? No way.

Perhaps the second process, whereby feminists seek to identify with other women, is especially infuriating. Poor women can identify with anyone's need to "get hers." But when feminists "get theirs" and then claim a victory for all women, it is grating, as is the "feminist empathy" that glosses over the racial and class *differences* that poor women never forget: "It really makes me mad when they keep saying they 'understand' and I know that they just can't," was a common complaint when welfare mothers discussed their feminist social workers.

For poor women, an equivalent barrier has sometimes been their vocal homophobia, perhaps fueled by the fear of losing any slight connection to respectability, to men and to men's money. Sometimes it has been easier for poor women to attack feminists as lesbians than to identify and acknowledge the depth of their class-based anger.

We have listened hard to the accusations and more often to the silences that reflect distrustful estrangement. We have come to see that it is not the place of middle-class feminists, once again, to hear all the evidence and then judge the extent of the damage. Neither is it the place of feminists to assume some kind of "sisterhood as social work" stance, whereby "difficulty with accepting feminism" becomes poor women's "presenting problem." All the big words and "rational" analysis learned from class privilege and/or educational advantages will not resolve the tension.

But it won't do either simply to generalize that "all women are one man away from welfare," or are likely candidates for rape and battering, and to sweep the evidence of diversity under the rug. To do so still asserts feminists' power to define the terms for discussion and denies legitimacy to the differences. And finally, feminists cannot hide behind a veil of "theory," which they acknowledge to be removed from the "experiences" of poor women. Poor women have theories to explain their situations too, and feminist theorists must admit to the influence of their own experiences on the theories they create.

This concluding chapter, then, attempts to summarize and explore the differing, but related, concerns that poor women and feminists bring to the table in any discussion about women's poverty. The goal is to suggest ways in which ground rules for collaboration can be developed and to identify common issues that may be approached from different directions. Out of this will come a laundry list of mutual demands that feminists and poor women, out of shared insights, could make together. Finally, we end by mentioning possible strategies for working together—or for supporting each other's work—which may lead to a more healthy interaction.

A Laundry List for Change

By talking and listening to one another, poor women and feminists will find quite a list of mutual concerns, an accounting that will, in turn, reveal underlying differences in perspective. Here we list five areas that seem especially crucial to achieving understanding and change.

The Family

The first area to discuss, as it is so often when women sit around a table, is the family. A simple phrase, "There is no place like home," has radically different meanings for different women. For some, home means warmth, a shelter from the heartless world, a place to give and receive love, even if the cupboard is bare. For others, home is a terrifying place of mixed messages, rejection, abuse, and intimate injustice that can crush the spirit.

In order to understand and end women's poverty, a recognition of both the family's positive and negative functions is central. "Family" has become a code word of the Right, often used to suggest that the beleaguered family would be fine if only "mommy would come back" and take care of the children, the elderly, and the infirm.

The conservative critique of the present-day family involves assumptions about motherhood, patriarchy, and the socialization of children that feminists have roughly and rightly condemned. Many feminists have tried to defend the family by examining and redefining it, but others have been impatient with such discussions. As feminists we have had the welcome mat pulled out from under us by conservative families because of our ideological and/or sexual preferences. We have been forced to escape from abusive families. So sometimes we dismissed, as culturally conservative, any attempts to defend the family.

But what does this hard line say to poor women? As many women of color assert most effectively, the family can also be a link to bedrock community and personal support, even as it may admittedly reproduce patriarchal relations. Many poor women will accept a feminist critique of the family only if it acknowledges the deep reasons why family "privacy" is often preferable to the more public welfare state, and if it recognizes how, for many people, the deepest emotional and social involvements are centered around family life.

We are certainly not suggesting that all poor women yearn for the privacy of traditional families. Nor are we arguing that all women need is a simple recognition of the "legitimacy" of female-headed households and extended families. Neither are we saying that all feminists want to "abolish the family," whatever that means. But we are suggesting that by exposing what has been the core experience of family life for so many women—the incest; the physical and emotional abuse; the stunting of political, economic, creative, and intellectual capacities and sexual identity—feminists may have given short shrift to the wide differences in women's experiences within families. To do so ultimately alienates especially those women of color and working-class women for whom the family has been, literally, a lifeline, as well as those lesbian mothers struggling valiantly to create healthy families in the midst of a homophobic society.

In many ways, poor women themselves may offer the corrective. Often, as Roberta Praeger points out forcefully elsewhere in this volume, an individual woman's poverty can be traced to a web of broad structural constraints woven together by the personal results of her private oppression within a family. Yet by continuing to try to create better worlds for their own children, poor women show a continuing hope for families. Perhaps their acceptance of contradictions can allow those who romanticize the family to give up illusions about its "natural" strength and also show to the toughest critics the family's continuing uses.

The Welfare State

Another arena for debate, again one that has come under the Right's harsh glare, is the welfare state. Here too, both feminists and poor women can bring together their differing experiences and ideas. No one can make more devastating mincemeat of welfare than poor women. Any welfare-rights group meeting will serve up enough hair-raising stories to supply a conservative speech writer for a month. Recently, feminist theorists have joined the critics' chorus with arguments about the dangerous role of the "public patriarchy" and the enforced dependence on a state that keeps women under its thumb.

But there are crucial distinctions to be made within the seeming convergence of criticisms. The Right attacks the welfare state because of its "costs" and "failures"—at least on the surface. Underlying its knee-jerk attack on big government are more powerful fears about the dangers of increasing claims on the right of business to make and increase profit—and about the worrisome freedom women gain if they live apart from men. Feminist theorists focus on the ways in which patriarchal relations are reproduced, rigidified, and strengthened when the welfare state takes on the duties of husband and father. And women on welfare focus their criticisms on how badly they are treated, even as they usually acknowledge their desire for more, not fewer, services and income supports. As one woman explains,

> It's too bad they make it so hard to get what you need. By the time I get my welfare check, or replace my lost Medicaid card, I am so mad I almost forget that I do really need them, and much more.

The task before feminists, then, is to develop a complex critique of the welfare state that does not deny the need for public services and income but clarifies, even expands, and certainly legitimizes it. Poor women—working women, together with welfare recipients, the elderly, and the physically disabled—need to overcome the social conditioning that makes them so afraid to be labeled "dependent" that they are too embarrassed to demand what they are entitled to. Here black women can often take the lead, since they are used to the tricks involved when whites try to make people ashamed of a condition that has been imposed upon them.

Such a dialogue could provide the backbone of an analysis for all progressive groups and help them better to expose and resist the Right's attempts to stifle social responsibility.

Race and Class Differences

The meaning of race and class differences among women is another painful area of discussion for feminists and poor women. In their own work the authors have been impressed by the deep well of class and racial distrust. This is a racist, class-bound society, and feminists will not make allies by trying to write off that reality under the concept of an all-embracing sisterhood.

Just as feminists must understand and resist being victimized, so they must also understand how they can themselves be victimizers. There are small ways—holding late night meetings far away from poor neighborhoods, leaving poor women stranded among strangers, or not thinking about the price of carfare or child care. Rules and structures that force white middle-class women to listen and self-consciously to admit to their areas of ignorance, may be necessary for real dialogue to take place, not because black and poor women will be intimidated without such rules but because they will simply refuse to participate in discussions with feminists who are insensitive. Many battered-women's shelters have been forced to engage in such self-conscious efforts for years, and there is much to learn from their efforts.

Obviously, everyone in U.S. society needs to confront racial and class differences. But they are the immediate barriers to developing either an analysis of or a movement for changing the world that poor women face. On the one hand, basic agreement on goals and tactics, for example, often cannot be reached because women on welfare assume that the feminist advocates in coalitions with them are "less committed," since some come to meetings as part of their paid work. On the other hand, it has been poor women whose demands for higher pay and benefits have been sometimes viewed as leading to "weakened politics" within feminist services.

Perhaps the key starting place is for feminists to accept that most black and poor women never forget their blackness or their class in discussions about their gender. If feminists seem to force women to "choose" their most critical form of oppression, by that very act of insensitivity, they will, almost certainly, force most women of color and poor women to reject them, or at least to avoid them except in the most formal encounters. When that happens, we have all lost, because it will only be out of informal, mutual experiences of working and honestly struggling together that real communication can occur.

Attitudes Toward Nurturance and Dependence

Another critical area for discussion is attitudes toward nurturance and dependence. Everyone hates "dependence," it seems. The Right wants to save women from depending on the state (the "womb of welfare," George Gilder calls it) and its cycle of poverty, in exchange for relying happily ever after on husbands or male employers, no doubt. Feminists, too, often view psychological and social dependence as holdovers from women's history as the supplicants of men. The only goal for personal fulfillment seems to be autonomy from men and the state, along with a withdrawal from an over-identification with traditional nurturing duties. And, certainly, poor women too don't want dependence if it means groveling before insensitive bureaucrats for inadequate resources for themselves and their families.

But maybe we women are all missing something. What if we redefine dependence as a natural state of obtaining some of the things you need from some other people some of the time? Then everyone is justifiably dependent, as human beings, and we can shift the stigma onto those who fail to meet their obligations to help—from the men who fail to live up to agreements regarding emotional or material support for children to the society that misallocates its collective resources. Until feminists and poor women consider whether the problem is really dependence itself—instead of the ways in which U.S. society regards and responds to natural human need—both groups may find themselves making the wrong basic demands.

Likewise, discussion needs to continue about the value of nurturance and the need for society to support it. Otherwise, the option of caring for others, at home or at certain work places, will continue to be devalued. Those feminists who see success only in terms of women's shedding their aprons for briefcases need to consider what their argument means for women and for society as a whole. At the same time poor women may need to consider the implications of being seen as nurturers only—one is a welfare *mother,* a displaced *homemaker*—for their own sense of personal balance, as well as for society's evaluation of their worth.

The Centrality of the Work Place

A final arena where feminists and poor women may already be finding important common ground is the work place. Both traditional Marxism and capitalism have placed the ultimate value in one's "productive labor." Conservative capitalists think women today should not seek serious, steady employment but should see the family as their primary—unpaid—work, participating in the market to supplement husbands' income or to meet employers' emergencies. Liberal capitalists want to help women find jobs but want them to be "realistic" abut their employment options within a class society. Even Marxists often see full employment outside the home as the main means by which women will gain economic legitimacy.

Some feminists are now questioning the idea that full employment is the only way to end women's poverty, at least under capitalism. As Deanne Bonnar argued powerfully earlier in this volume, care givers need supports outside the marketplace, and most care givers are women.

Poor women may rightfully get nervous if feminists go too far and seem to undervalue work-place changes that will allow them to have reasonably well-paid work when they choose it. But talking about what women need in addition to paid work, as well as ways to increase wages and benefits, should be a discussion in which poor women have a lot to say. One woman who is now a full-time student after years of raising five children on welfare put it thus:

> I raised my children well, but they were a handful. They were all less than two years apart, and one was disabled. There was no way I would have wanted *any* full-time job during most of those years—I had a job. But I wish I had had enough money to get what I needed for my family without always having a hassle. And now I need to go to school, for me, not just to get a job. I deserve it. Why is that so hard to understand?

Mutual Demands

Is it possible that if poor women and feminists listen to each other they may hear new ways to speak? And new things to say? And better ways to say them? A continuing dialogue that hears each position and responds to it respectfully may create a set of demands we can all fight for. They may not seem realistic at first, but together they may form a base for organizing and change. Here the authors can only outline the basic needs that can be articulated at this stage of the discussion.

Improvement in Benefits

Substantial improvement in basic benefits to poor women must be reaffirmed as a right. This is an immediate and primary demand. Poor women need more money now and can hardly trust anyone who fails to understand this. There is not a state in the union where welfare benefits enable a family to live at the poverty level. A campaign to bring welfare benefits "up to poverty," such as the one in Massachusetts, gives voice to this need by its very title. Constant efforts must be made to fight the punitive, degrading aspects of welfare. Otherwise women may not even apply for the inadequate "benefits" to which they are entitled. Obviously, poor women's organizations should take the lead, not feminist "experts," who may think they know best. At the same time, any and all feminists should make the demand for more benefits a "constant" in their discussions about any issue. Care givers' wages may be one way to talk about the need for general supports for women and their families. It is impossible to overestimate the importance of improved benefits as a starting place for convergence of feminist and poor women's concerns.

Higher Wages

Efforts to improve women's wages must be continued by all women's groups. Current campaigns to raise the minimum wage (minimum wage has been $3.35 an hour since 1981) are critical. Unionization, application of the comparable-worth principle, and media attention are essential here also if women are ever to earn breadwinners' wages. A word of caution, following on concerns raised by Amott and Matthaei regarding comparable worth: feminists need to avoid a class-based elitism in their evaluation of work. All too often, for example, advocates of comparable worth can induce snickers in their audiences by exposing the different rates of pay for secretaries and asphalt layers, as if it is a joke that an "uneducated," dirty asphalt layer should receive decent pay. The point is not that some male laborers are overpaid (they are not) but that women's work is undervalued, relative to men's work. Everyone's wages cannot be adequate until the pay gulfs resulting from the sexual division of labor are bridged.

What's more, demands for comparable worth must go along with demands for more union organizing. Women in unionized work places earn far better pay than nonunionized workers and have better benefits. Similarly, much as most demands for full employment may still leave out women's currently unpaid work in the home, they are still crucial as ways to create possibilities for women to work outside the home and to reduce the competition for jobs between white women and people of color.

Full Medical Coverage

Support for full and expanded medical coverage cannot be forgotten. In 1982, one in six Americans had no health insurance. In the 1960s many liberals had hoped for national health insurance, a demand that seems to have been erased from collective political memory in the face of "rising medical costs." The Right seems to have cowed the liberals on this point so that everyone "accepts" the need for cutback in care for the sake of "cost containment." Yet poor women are always clear that medical coverage is a major stumbling block to their employment, because even when they can live on "women's wages," they cannot obtain decent medical coverage. The legacy of poor health care—and inadequate coverage for the near poor—will cripple the next generation. It is time to rejuvenate old demands for some form of national medical supports, especially so that poor women will not be forced into charity wards as "cost effectiveness" measures progressively limit their options.

Public Day Care

Publicly funded day care for all children needs to be provided through local school systems. There is little "economic" argument against this demand, given decreasing numbers of school-age children; the physical plants and the teachers are there. For it to occur, though, society has to admit that most children can benefit from day care and that most mothers work. Instead, U.S. society now denies both these facts of life with another form of the "good woman-bad woman" split. Good, middle-class women discretely select from a wide variety of child-care options, while poor women can send their children only to a limited number of subsidized institutions. The current panic about child abuse in day-care centers must be challenged for what it is, a way to discredit day care and make women feel guilty about using it, instead of demanding more and better child care.

Better Housing

The crisis in urban housing for poor families needs to be acknowledged as a women's issue. Public housing projects are the new "poor houses." They have been increasingly allowed to run down, so that, later, private developers can make money "returning them to the market" through rehabilitation and a drastic decrease, if not elimination, in the number of poor residents. An increasing number of homeless people are women on welfare who simply cannot afford housing on their welfare budgets. It is time that housing issues, long separated from "social welfare" concerns, are linked together with other expectations of an expanded, more responsive, welfare state.

Consolidation of Social Services

The variety of social services that have been separated into specialized categories need to be relinked and made available to all women, perhaps on a sliding-scale fee basis. Now eligibility criteria for the few inadequate public services are so narrowly tied to income and status—as a senior citizen or as the parent of a "child at risk"—that social services seem less like a right to be fought for by all women and more like another scarce resource that divides women who must fight for it. Deanne Bonnar refers to such an approach as a new "social security for women," and it is critical if the women's care-giving activities—for children or for elderly or disabled relatives—are to be supplemented and supported.

Reduction of Domestic Violence

Domestic violence must be consistently addressed as a poor women's issue. Any woman can be battered in her home. A poor woman, however, has fewer resources to help her leave her home, and the fear of how poor women are treated may keep a middle-income woman in a violent home. So keeping and expanding services to battered women is another basic part of the "benefit package" poor women need.

Redefinition of Full-time Work

A changing definition of the full-time work day and work week is needed. One hundred years ago workers fought for and won what was originally thought to be a utopian demand, the eight-hour day and the forty-hour week. Today women need to insist that *all* workers be considered full-time and paid accordingly, for a six-hour day and a thirty-hour week. This calculation would allow for care giving *and* for work outside the home. It does not stigmatize women as "less serious workers" because they integrate work in the home and work outside. Finally, men might even have the time to become better nurturers if they could earn a decent living in thirty hours. The changing U.S. economy, with its constant unemployment should make the benefits of such a demand obvious.

Working Together

Most feminists and most poor women could quickly agree about the general value of each of the eight demands outlined above. Even the particulars of what should be demanded could be worked out, in theory, because of the harmony of goals. Yet unless an ninth, internal demand is added, the ability to fight for such far-reaching goals is in jeopardy.

Feminists and poor women, especially feminists, need to invent processes that are more sensitive to the great differences in class and race and culture that separate them. White women, middle- and upper-class women, need to stop talking and listen to women of color, and to poor and working-class women, if they wish to be real allies. Attention must be paid not only to the words about goals but also to the unspoken signs that show that women feel ignored, discounted, or overridden by the facts and analyses of feminist experts who speak "for them."

The final demand, the thread that must run through all the rest, can be best expressed in the words of one almost, but not quite, burned out Boston woman:

> Let us lead our own fight. Sure, we may want their help with information and ideas about strategy. But we can't accept help if at every moment we are afraid they will take over our struggle. If we win [the effort to raise benefits], then *our* everyday lives change—theirs don't. If we lose, then we are still stuck with less than we need to live. Why can't they see that we can't trust anyone to wage such an important war *for* us? We're fighting for our lives and for our children's lives; they have to respect us enough to let us make our own mistakes and learn our own lessons from them.
>
> Poor women are not afraid to ask for help; they have to help each other to survive. But when we help each other it's equal, not this "we've studied the issue and see the best way to go is . . ." If they can't learn this, then we will have to go our own way, without them, but we really don't want that. Just tell feminists to listen to us. If they do that long enough, and with the right attitude, then we can feel secure enough to listen to them.

Notes

What Makes Women Poor?

BARBARA EHRENREICH

1. See U.S., Department of Commerce, Bureau of the Census, "A Statistical Portrait of Women in the U.S.," *Current Population Reports,* Special Study, Series P-23, no. 56, 1976 and "Characteristics of the Population Below the Poverty Level," *Current Population Reports,* 1978, cited by Harriette McAdoo and Diana Pearce in "Women and Children: Alone and in Poverty," in National Advisory Council on Economic Opportunity, *Final Report* (National Advisory Council on Economic Opportunity, 1981); and *Current Population Survey* cited by the Children's Defense Fund, *A Children's Defense Budget: An Analysis of the President's Budget and Children* (Washington, D.C.: Children's Defense Fund, 1982).

2. *New York Times,* 19 December 1982; Alexander Cockburn and James Ridgeway, *Village Voice,* 1 March 1983, pp. 10–11.

3. Diana Pearce, "The Feminization of Poverty: Women, Work and Welfare," *Urban and Social Change Review,* February 1978; Statistics from an interview with Pearce, March 1982.

4. See Bureau of the Census, "Profile of the United States: 1981, *Current Population Reports,* Series P-20, no. 374 and "Families Maintained by Female Headed Householders 1970–79," *Current Population Reports,* Series P-23, no. 107 (Washington, D.C.: Government Printing Office, 1980).

5. Patricia C. Sexton, *Women and Work,* Research and Development Monograph no. 46 (Washington, D.C.: U.S. Department of Labor, Employment and Training Administration, 1977), cited in the National Advisory Council on Economic Opportunity, *Final Report* (Washington, D.C.: National Advisory Council on Economic Opportunity, 1981).

6. Barbara Ehrenreich, "The Male Revolt: After the Breadwinner Vanishes," *The Nation,* 26 February 1983, pp. 225, 240–42.

The Feminization of Poverty: Women, Work and Welfare

DIANA PEARCE

1. U.S., Department of Commerce, Bureau of the Census, "A Statistical Portrait of Women in the U.S.," *Current Population Reports,* Special Study, Series, P-23, no. 58 (Washington, D.C.: Government Printing Office, 1976).

2. Women's Bureau, 1977.

3. Bureau of the Census; Women's Bureau.

4. Ibid. This is probably an underestimate, for the poverty levels established by the Census Bureau assume that a male-headed family needs more money than a female-headed family of the same size; thus in 1972 the poverty threshold for a family of four (with three dependent children) was $3902 if the family was headed by a male but only $3715 if it was headed by a female. See U.S. Commission on Civil Rights, *Women and Poverty* (Washington, D.C.; Government Printing Office, 1974).

5. Women's Bureau.

6. Bureau of the Census.

7. R.L. Coser and G. Rokoff, "Women in the Occupational World: Social Disruption and Conflict," *Social Problems* 18 (1970); J.C. Darlan, "Factors Influencing the Rising Labor Force Participation Rates of Married Women With Pre-school Children," *Social Science Quarterly* 56 (1976); L.J. Waite, "Working Wives: 1940–1960," *American Sociological Review* (1976); D. Treiman and K. Terrell, "Sex and the Process of Status Attainment: A Comparison of Working Men and Women," *American Sociological Review* 40 (1970); L. Suter and H.P. Miller, "Income Differences Between Men and Career Women," *American Journal of Sociology* 78 (1973); A.S. Blinder, "Wage

Discrimination: Reduced Form and Structural Estimates," *Journal of Human Resources* 8 (1973); A.S. Sorkin, "On the Occupational Status of Women, 1870–1970," *American Journal of Economics and Sociology* 32 (1973).

8. V. Oppenheimer, *The Female Labor Force in the United States: Demographic and Economic Factors Governing Its Growth and Changing Composition* (Berkeley, Calif.: University of California, Institute of International Studies, 1970).

9. E. Gross, "Plus ça change . . .? The Sexual Structure of Occupations Over Time," *Social Problems* 16 (1969).

10. L.K. Howe, *Pink Collar Workers: Inside the World of Women's Work* (New York: Putnam, 1977).

11. D.S. Knudsen, "The Declining Status of Women: Popular Myths and the Failure of Functionalist Thought," *Social Forces* (1969).

12. V. Fuchs, "Differences in Hourly Earnings Between Men and Women," *Monthly Labor Review* (1971).

13. K. Shortridge, "Working Poor Women," in *Women: A Feminist Perspective,* ed. J. Freeman (Palo Alto, Calif.: Mayfield Publishing Co., 1976).

14. I. Sawhill, "Women With Low Incomes," in *Women and the Workplace: The Implications of Occupational Segregation,* ed. M. Blaxall and B. Reagan (Chicago: University of Chicago Press, 1976).

15. Ibid.

16. The ratio of female to male changes in an uneven pattern over time, as well as across industries.

17. H. Wilensky, "Orderly Careers and Social Participation: The Impact of Work History on Social Integration in the Middle Mass," *American Sociological Review* 26 (1961).

18. Women's Bureau.

19. R. Farley, "Trends in Racial Inequalities: Have the Gains of the 1960s Disappeared in the 1970s?" *American Sociological Review* 43 (1977).

20. U.S., Department of Health, Education, and Welfare, National Center for Social Statistics (NCSS) Social Rehabilitation Service, *Public As-*

sistance Statistics, December 1977 (Washington, D.C.: Government Printing Office, 1977).

21. Ibid.

22. H. Nicol, "Preliminary Findings of Child Support Enforcement Research" (Paper presented at the Fifteenth Annual Conference on Welfare Research Statistics, San Francisco, 1975).

23. Ibid.

24. Why is it that in a society that constantly investigates welfare recipients for fraud, no one enforces child support? It may be that this reveals something about the way in which marriage is still an economic institution. It is as if the husband's economic support before divorce was in "payment" for the wife's housekeeping, emotional support, and sexual access, but not for her child-rearing activities, for it is only child-rearing activity that is continued after divorce, typically by the wife—93 percent of mothers receive custody of the children. See Urban Institute, *Child Support Payments in the United States* (Washington, D.C.: Urban Institute, 1976).

25. C. Bell, "Women and Social Security: Contributions and Benefits," in U.S., Congress, Joint Economic Committee, Hearings, *Economic Problems of Women*, 93rd Congress, 1st sess., July 24–26, 30, 1973.

26. M.H. Dahm, "Unemployment Insurance and Women," in U.S., Congress, Joint Economic Committee, Hearings, *Economic Problems of Women*, 93rd Congress, 1st sess., July 24–26, 30, 1973.

27. M.D. Ornstein, *Entry Into the American Labor Force* (New York: Academic Press, 1976).

28. NCCS, 1977.

29. Joint Economic Committee, Hearings, *Economic Problems of Women*, 1976. Figures refer to 1974.

30. Ibid.

31. W. Bell and D.M. Bushe, "The Economic Efficiency of AFDC," *Social Science Review* 49 (1975).

32. Women's Bureau.

33. See Williams. This does not include those who are in training, awaiting training, awaiting placement, or looking for work. Thus the employment of a broader definition of "in the labor force" not limited to those currently and officially working would result in a much larger percentage of welfare mothers in the work force (however marginally).

34. Ibid.

35. Ibid.

36. S. Levitan, M. Rein, and D. Marwich, *Work and Welfare Go Together* (Baltimore: John Hopkins University Press, 1972).

37. G. Appel, "The AFDC Work Incentives in Michigan," in "Research and Statistics as a Management Tool" (Proceedings of the Eleventh Workshop on Public Welfare Research and Statistics, Las Vegas, Nev., August 8–11, 1971).

38. I. Garfinkel, "Welfare, What's Right and Wrong With It" (Paper presented at the Center for the Study of Democratic Institutions, Chicago, November 22, 1877). Two caveats about this anomally should be noted, however. First, there is little evidence that people consciously act in this way; rather it is probably an unconscious move that is difficult to reverse. Second, and perhaps more important, it only applies to women workers; men have an hours limitation (one hundred per month) on the amount that they can work and stay on welfare, whereas for women the only limitation is total earnings.

39. NCSS, *Findings of the 1973 AFDC Study, pt. 2-A, Financial Circumstances* (1974).

40. K. Polanyi, *The Great Transformation* (Boston: Beacon Press, 1957).

41. NCSS (1976); and Levitan, Rein, and Marwich, *Work and Welfare*.

42. Of course, this table is only a gross indicator; it is expected that a more detailed breakdown on both occupational distribution of AFDC mothers and WIN training positions would reveal even more reinforcement of occupational segregation. In addition, this limitation is carried through at the individual level.

43. A.D. Smith, A.E. Fortune, and W.J. Reig, "Notes on Policy and Practice: WIN, Work, and Welfare," *Social Service Review* 49 (1975); U.S.

Commission on Civil Rights, *Women and Poverty* (Washington, D.C.: Government Printing Office, 1974).

44. By law, WIN participants may be placed in jobs that pay as little as 75 percent of the minimum wage. U.S. Commission on Civil Rights, *Women and Poverty.*

45. Smith, Fortune, and Reid, "Notes on Policy and Practice." Figures are from the Department of Labor, 1976, cited in N. Gordon, "Women's Roles and Welfare Reform," *Challenge* 20 (1978). Figures are similar for men.

46. Ibid.

47. D. Street, "Bureaucratization, Professionalization, and the Poor," in *Poverty and Social Change,* ed. K.A. Gronbjerg, D. Street, and G.A. Suttles (Englewood Cliffs, N.J.: Prentice-Hall).

48. M.R. Holimer, "Excerpts from HEW, 'Synopsis of Selected Findings to Date from the Income Maintenance Experiments' " (in "Research and Statistics to Meet Today's Needs and Tomorrow's Challenges: Papers from the Sixteenth Annual Conference on Welfare Research and Statistics, New Orleans, August 15–18, 1976").

49. NCSS, 1976; see also L.A. Ferman, "Welfare Careers, Low Wage Workers, and Sexism," in *New Research on Women* (Ann Arbor, Mich.: University of Michigan Press, n.d.).

50. On the basis of a number of studies that the work ethic is alive and well among the poor, it is assumed that they want to work, so that what is taken as problematic is not whether the poor (or welfare mothers) are willing to work, but whether they can find jobs by which they can support themselves. See especially L. Goodwin, *Do the Poor Want to Work: A Social-Psychological Study of Work Orientations* (Washington, D.C.: Brookings Institution, 1972); and Holimer, "Excerpts from HEW."

Shortchanged: The Political Economy of Women's Poverty

ELAINE DONOVAN AND MARY HUFF STEVENSON

1. The statistics reported in this essay are from the 1980 census figures unless otherwise noted.

2. For a more detailed discussion of the shortcomings of the official definition of the poverty line, as well as an alternative definition of poverty, see D. Light, "Income Distribution: The First Stage in the Consideration of Poverty," *Occasional Papers of the Union for Radical Political Economics*, December 1969.

3. For an excellent and far more detailed discussion and critique of "the new home economics" see Isabelle Sawhill, "Economic Perspectives on the Family," *Daedalus* 106, no. 2 (Spring 1977).

4. M. Feber and B. Birnbaum, "The New Home Economics: Retrospects and Prospects," *Journal of Consumer Research* 4 (June 1977).

5. See, for example, R. Mancke, "Lower Pay for Women: A Case of Economic Discrimination?" *Industrial Relations*, October 1971.

6. "Courts Stay Benefits for Welfare Mothers," *Boston Globe*, 9 January 1979.

7. Isabelle Sawhill, "Discrimination and Poverty Among Women Who Head Families," in *Women and the Workplace: The Implications of Occupational Segregation*, ed. M. Blaxall and B. Regan (Chicago: University of Chicago Press, 1976).

8. Ibid., p. 211.

9. Two excellent sources on this topic are Joanne Vanek, "Housewives as Workers," in *Women Working*, ed. A. Stromberg and S. Harkness (Palo Alto, Calif.: Mayfield, 1978); and Heidi Hartmann, "The Family as the Locus of Gender, Class, and Political Struggle: The Example of Housework," *Signs: Journal of Women in Culture and Society* 6, no. 31 (1981).

10. See, for example, Jean Gardiner, "Women's Domestic Labor," *New Left Review*, no. 89 (January–February 1973).

11. Jane Humphries, "Class Struggle and the Persistence of the Working Class Family," *Cambridge Journal of Economics* 1 (September 1977).

Has Poverty Been Feminized in Black America?
LINDA BURNHAM

1. Democratic Socialists of America (DSA), *Bay Area Newsletter*, May 1983.

2. National Advisory Council on Economic Opportunity, quoted in Barbara Ehrenreich and Karin Stallard, "The Nouveau Poor," *Ms.*, July-August 1982, p. 20.

3. Barbara Ehrenreich and Karin Stallard, *Poverty in the American Dream* (Boston: South End Press, 1983), p. 9.

4. Census Bureau report, cited in *San Francisco Chronicle*, 11 April 1984; *Los Angeles Times*, 13 September 1984.

5. Ehrenreich and Stallard, *Poverty in the American Dream*, p. 9.

6. Center for the Study of Social Policy, *The "Flip-Side" of Black Families Headed by Women: The Economic Status of Black Men* (Washington, D.C.: Center for the Study of Social Policy, 1984), pp. 3–10.

7. U.S., Department of Labor, Women's Bureau, *Equal Employment Opportunity for Women: U.S. Policies* (Washington, D.C.: Government Printing Office, 1982), pp. 16–36.

8. Ibid., pp. 10–11.

9. Center for the Study of Social Policy, *A Dream Deferred: The Economic Status of Black Americans* (Washington, D.C.: Center for the Study of Social Policy, 1983), p. 9.

10. U.S. Commission on Civil Rights, *Disadvantaged Women and Their Children* (Washington, D.C.: U.S. Commission on Civil Rights, 1983), p. 11.

11. Center for the Study of Social Policy, *Working Female-Headed Families in Poverty* (Washington, D.C.: Center for the Study of Social Policy, 1982), p. 8. Female-headed households constitute an even higher proportion, 18.8 percent, of families with children below the age of eighteen. See U.S. Commission on Civil Rights, *Disadvantaged Women*, p. 5.

13. See, for example, Ehrenreich and Stallard, "The Nouveau Poor." The social democrats have been fairly frank, on this and other issues, about appealing to the "majoritarian" middle class. They do so on the grounds that the traditionally poor and the racial and national minorities are too few in number and too politically powerless to serve as the base for a broad social movement. Our problem is not with the breadth of the movement the social democrats envision but with the fact that, in attempting to organize the (white) middle class they opportunistically drop out the

question of racism, national chauvinism, and privilege, and the material privilege of the labor aristocracy within the working class.

14. Center for the Study of Social Policy, *A Dream Deferred*, p. 4. (This figure includes all forms of the family.)

15. Ibid., p. 5.

16. Ibid., p. 25.

17. Ibid., p. 18.

18. *New York Times*, 9 October 1984, p. 21. This trend has been exacerbated under Reagan's presidency. In general, the poor have grown poorer over the past few years. But the Reagan administration has made a careful political calculation—counting on the racism endemic among white Americans—and imposed cuts in social welfare in such a way as to ensure that the further decline in the condition of the poor is most concentrated in the more rapid deterioration in the standard of living of black Americans. Recently accumulated data indicate that blacks lost more ground under Reagan than any other group. According to the *New York Times* of 9 October 1984, the poverty rate for blacks rose from 32.5 percent at the beginning of his administration to 35.7 percent—an increase of 1.3 million people—and the median family income of blacks fell by 5 percent.

19. Center for the Study of Social Policy, *A Dream Deferred*, p. 25.

20. Center for the Study of Social Policy, *Working Female-Headed Families in Poverty*, pp. 7–13.

21. Center for the Study of Social Policy, *A Dream Deferred*, p. 26.

22. Ibid., p. 25.

We Were Never on a Pedestal: Women of Color Continue to Struggle With Poverty, Racism, and Sexism

ELIZABETH HIGGINBOTHAM

1. Few people are familiar with the histories of people of color. Yet, an appreciation of their experiences in this nation is critical for grasping the complications and multiple roles of women of color.

2. Elizabeth Higginbotham, "Laid Bare by the System: Work and Survival for Black and Hispanic Women," in *Class, Race, and Sex: The Dynamics of Control,* ed. Amy Swerdlow and Hanna Lessinger (Boston: G.K. Hall, 1983), pp. 200–15.

3. Angela Davis, *Women, Race, and Class* (New York: Random House, 1981), p. 5.

4. Bonnie Dill Thornton, "Our Mothers' Grief: Racial-Ethnic Women and the Maintenance of Families" (Research paper no. 4, Memphis State University, Center for Research on Women, 1986).

5. Maxine Hong Kingston, *Chinamen* (New York: Knopf, 1980); and Victor G. Nee and Brett De Bary Nee, *Longtime Californ': A Documentary Study of an American Chinatown* (New York: Pantheon, 1972).

6. Mario Barrera, *Race and Class in the Southwest* (South Bend, Ind.: University of Notre Dame Press, 1979).

7. Jacqueline Jones, *Labor of Love, Labor of Sorrow* (New York: Basic Books, 1985).

8. For more about this, see Elizabeth Clark-Lewis, "This Work Had A' End: The Transition from Live-in to Day Work" (Working paper no. 2: Southern Women: The Intersection of Race, Class, and Gender, Memphis State University, Center for Research on Women, 1985); David Katzman, *Seven Days a Week: Women and Domestic Service in Industrial America* (New York: Oxford University Press, 1978); Julia Kirk Blackwelder, "Women in the Work Force: Atlanta, New Orleans, and San Antonio, 1930–1940," *Journal of Urban History* 4, no. 3 (May 1978): 331–58; Alice Kessler-Harris, *Out to Work* (New York: Oxford University Press, 1982).

9. Barrera, *Race and Class in the Southwest;* and Albert Camarillo, *Chicanos in a Changing Society* (Cambridge, Mass.: Harvard University Press, 1979).

10. Evelyn Nakano Glenn, "The Dialectics of Wage Work: Japanese American Women and Domestic Service, 1905–1940," *Feminist Studies* 6 (Fall 1983): 432–71.

11. Elizabeth Higginbotham, "Employment for Professional Black Women in the Twentieth Century" (Research paper no. 3, Memphis State University, Center for Research on Women, 1985).

12. Barrera, *Race and Class in the Southwest;* and William J. Wilson, *The Declining Significance of Race* (Chicago: University of Chicago Press, 1978).

13. Dorothy Newman et al., *Protest, Politics, and Prosperity* (New York: Pantheon, 1978).

14. Karin Stallard, Barbara Ehrenreich, and Holly Sklar, *Poverty in the American Dream* (Boston: South End Press, 1983).

15. This table does not even begin to present a full appreciation of the extent of poverty, since these figures are for those people who have secured full-time employment. It is well known that there are high percentages of unemployment in racial-ethnic communities. Existence is often more precarious for those who experience short- and long-term unemployment. See Bettylou Valentine, *Hustling and Other Hard Work* (New York: Free Press, 1978).

16. Higginbotham, "Employment for Professional Black Women."

17. Julianne Malveaux, "The Status of Women of Color in the Economy: The Legacy of Being Other" (Paper presented at the National Conference on Women: "The Economy and Public Policy," Washington, D.C. June 19–20, 1984.

En La Lucha: Economic and Socioemotional Struggles of Puerto Rican Women

IRIS ZAVALA MARTINEZ

1. See Manuel Maldonado-Denis, *Puerto Rico y Estados Unidos: Emigracion y Colonialismo* (Mexico City: Siglo Veintiuno, 1976); Center for Puerto Rican Studies, *Labor Migration Under Capitalism: The Puerto Rican Experience* (New York: Monthly Review Press, 1979); and Centro de Estudios Puertorriquenos, *Los Puertorriquenos y la Cultura: Critica y Debate Conferencia de Historiografia, 1974* (New York: City University of New York, Research Foundation, 1976).

2. Some very good sources are Manuel Maldonado-Denis, *Puerto Rico: Una Interpretacion Historico-Social* (Mexico City: Siglo Veintiuno, 1969); Center for Puerto Rican Studies, *Labor Migration;* and J. Inclan, "Socioeconomic Changes in Puerto Rico: The Development of the Modern Proletarian Family" (Paper circulated by the Center for Puerto Rican Studies. 1978).

3. See Center for Puerto Rican Studies, *Labor Migration;* and Marcia Rivera Quintero, "The Development of Capitalism in Puerto Rico and the Incorporation of Women into the Labor Force," in *The Puerto Rican Woman,* ed. E. Acosta-Belen (New York: Praeger, 1979).

4. Yamila Azize, *Luchas de la Mujer en Puerto Rico, 1898–1919* (San Juan: Litografia Metropolitana, 1979); and Virginia Sanchez Korrol, "Survival of Puerto Rican Women in New York Before World War II," in *The Puerto Rican Struggle: Essays on Survival in the United States,* ed. C. Rodriguez, V. Sanchez Korrol, and J.O. Alers (New York: Puerto Rican Migration Research Consortium, 1980).

5. See R. Santana Cooney and A. Colon, "Work and Family: The Recent Struggles of Puerto Rican Females," in *The Puerto Rican Struggle,* ed. Rodgriguez, Sanchez Korrol, and Alers.

6. See E. Christensen, "The Puerto Rican Woman: A Profile," L. Miranda King, "Puertorriquenas in the United States: The Impact of Double Discrimination," and M. Vazquez, "The Effects of Role Expectations on the Marital Status of Urban Puerto Rican Women," all in *The Puerto Rican Woman,* ed. E. Acosta-Belen. See also E. Mizio, "Impact of External Systems on the Puerto Rican Family," *Social Casework* 55, no. 2 (1974): 76–89.

7. See R. Zambrana's introduction and S. Andrade's article "Family Roles of Hispanic Women: Stereotypes, Empirical Findings, and Implications for Research," in *Work, Family, and Health: Latina Women in Transition,* ed. R. Zambrana (New York: Hispanic Research Center, 1982).

8. A few women's names are mentioned in G. Baralt, *Esclavos Rebeldes: Conspiraciones y Sublevaciones de Esclavos in Puerto Rico (1795–1873)* (Rio Piedras: Ediciones Huracan, 1982).

9. For further descriptions of the Puerto Rican women's involvement in political and social movements see Azize, *Luchas de la Mujer en Puerto Rico;* N. Zayas and J. Silen, eds., *La Mujer en la Lucha Hoy* (Rio Piedras: Zayas and Silen, 1973); Isabel Pico, "The History of Women's Struggle for Equality in Puerto Rico," in *The Puerto Rican Woman,* ed. Acosta-Belen; and "Puerto Rico: Women, Culture, and Colonialism in Latin America" in *Slaves of Slaves: The Challenge of Latin American Women,* ed. Caribbean Women's Collective (London: ZED Press, 1980), pp. 132–46.

10. See U.S., Department of Commerce, Bureau of the Census, "A Statistical Portrait of Women in the United States," *Current Population*

Reports, Special Study, Series P-23, no. 100 (Washington, D.C.: Government Printing Office, 1980); and "A Description of Latinos in the United States: Demographic and Sociocultural Factors of the Past and the Future" in *Latino Families in the United States,* ed. S. Andrade (New York: Planned Parenthood Federation of America, 1983), p. 17.

11. See Santana Cooney and Colon, "Work and Family," pp. 65–66 for 1960 and 1970 data. See Council on Interracial Books for Children, *Fact Sheets on Institutional Racism,* November 1984, p. 7.

12. See W.R. Gove and J.F. Tudor, "Adult Sex Roles and Mental Illness," *American Journal of Sociology* 78 (1973): 812–35; and M. Weissman and L. Klerman, "Sex Differences and the Epidemiology of Depression," *Archives of General Psychiatry* 34 (1977): 98–111. See also G.W. Brown and T. Harris, *Social Origins of Depression: A Study of Psychiatric Disorder in Women* (New York; Free Press, 1978); B. Dohrenwend, "Social Status and Stressful Life Events," *Journal of Personality and Social Psychology* 28 (1973): 225–35; and I. Al-Issa, *The Psychopathology of Women* (Englewood Cliffs, N.J.: Prentice Hall, 1980).

13. See an excellent review by E. Carmen, N.F. Russo, and J.B. Miller, "Inequality and Women's Mental Health: An Overview," *American Journal of Psychiatry* 138, no. 10 (1981): 1319–30.

14. These case examples come from my clinical work with the Puerto Rican community in Massachusetts. The names and defining characteristics have been changed.

15. See I. Zavala-Martinez, ch. 2, "Puerto Ricans and Mental Health: An Overview of Research and Clinical Data," in "Mental Health and the Puerto Ricans in the United States: A Critical Literature," Manuscript available from the author or Hunter College, Library of Center for Puerto Rican Studies, New York; and L. Comas-Diaz, "Mental Health Needs of Puerto Rican Women in the United States," in *Work, Family, and Health,* ed. Zambrana.

16. See S. Urdang, *Fighting Two Colonialisms: Women in Guinea-Bissau* (New York: Monthly Review Press, 1979), pp. 12–17.

17. L. Miranda, "Puertorriquenas in the United States: The Impact of Double Discrimination," in *The Puerto Rican Woman,* ed. Acosta-Belen, pp. 124–33.

18. Refer to E. Soto and P. Shaver, "Sex-Role Traditionalism, Asser-

tiveness, and Symptoms of Puerto Rican Women Living in the United States," *Hispanic Journal of Behavioral Sciences* 4, no. 1 (1982): 1–20; C. Torres-Matrullo, "Acculturation and Psychopathology Among Puerto Rican Women in Mainland United States," *American Journal of Orthopsychiatry* 46, no. 4 (1976): 710–19; and J. Inclan, "Psychological Symptomatology in Second Generation Puerto Rican Women of Three Socioeconomic Groups," *Journal of Community Psychology* 11 (1983): 334–45. See also V. Abad and E. Boyce, "Issues in Psychiatric Evaluations of Puerto Ricans: A Sociocultural Perspective," *Journal of Operational Psychiatry* 10, no. 1 (1979): 28–39; and Comas-Diaz, "Mental Health Needs of Puerto Rican Women."

19. E. Chaney, *Supermadre: Women in Politics in Latin America* (Austin: University of Texas Press, 1979).

20. M. Lopez-Garriga, "Estrategias de Autoafirmacion en Mujeres Puertorriquenas," *Revista de Ciencias Sociales* 20, nos. 3, 4 (1978): 257–85.

21. V. Garrison, "Support Systems of Schizophrenic and Non-schizophrenic Puerto Rican Migrant Women in New York City," *Schizophrenia Bulletin* 4, no. 4 (1978): 561–95; and E. Vazquez NuHall, "The Support System and Coping Patterns of the Female Puerto Rican Single Parent," *Journal of Non-White Concerns* 7, no. 3 (1979): 128–37.

22. L. Morris, "Women Without Men: Domestic Organizations and the Welfare State as seen in a Coastal Community of Puerto Rico," *British Journal of Sociology* 30, no. 3 (1979): 322–40.

23. Personal communication with other colleagues, community workers, and individual women, 1985.

Teenage Mothers: Seduced and Abandoned

NANCY ARIES

1. *The Data Book: Summary* (Washington, D.C.: Children's Defense Fund, 1985), p. 2.

2. Susan Fischman and Howard Palley, "Preventing Adolescent Unwed Motherhood: Is a National Health Policy Sufficient?" *Health and Social Work* 3, no. 1 (February 1978):30–46.

3. *Preventing Children Having Children: A Special Conference Report*, Clearinghouse Paper no. 1 (Washington, D.C.: Children's Defense Fund, 1985), pp. 10–13.

4. Kristin Moore and Martha Burt, *Private Crisis, Public Cost: Policy Perspectives on Teenage Childbearing* (Washington, D.C.: Urban Institute Press, 1982), p. 109.

5. Sandra Hofferth and Kristin Moore, "Early Childbearing and Later Economic Well-Being," *American Sociologic Review* 44 (October 1979): 784–815.

6. Frank Furstenburg, "Social Consequences of Teenage Parenthood," *Family Planning Perspectives* 8, no. 4 (July 1976): 148–64.

7. James McCarthy and Ellen Radish, "Education and Childbearing Among Teenagers," *Family Planning Perspectives* 14, no. 3 (May/June 1982): 154–55.

8. Josefina Card and Laurell Wise, "Teenage Mothers and Teenage Fathers: The Impact of Early Childbearing on the Parents' Personal and Professional Lives," *Family Planning Perspectives* 10, no. 4 (July–August 1978): 200–01.

9. J.J. Conger and A.C. Peterson, *Adolescence and Youth: Psychological Development in a Changing World*, 3rd ed. (New York: Harper & Row, 1984), pp. 184–85.

10. Muriel Hammer, Linda Cutwirth, and Susan Philips, "Parenthood and Social Networks: A Preliminary View," *Social Science and Medicine* 16 (1982): 2091–2100.

11. Frank Furstenberg and Albert Crawford, "Family Support: Helping Teenage Mothers Cope," *Family Planning Perspectives* 10, no. 6 (November–December 1978): 322–333.

12. Carol Stack, *All Our Kin: Strategies for Survival in a Black Community* (New York: Harper & Row, 1974).

13. *Preventing Children Having Children*, p. 3.

14. Glick and Norton, cited in Moore and Burt, *Private Crisis, Public Cost*, pp. 82, 120.

15. *Preventing Children Having Children*, p. 5.

16. Elizabeth McGee, *Too Little, Too Late: Services for Teenage Parents* (New York: Ford Foundation, October 1981); Sylvia Perlman, "Nobody's Baby:

The Politics of Adolescent Pregnancy" (Ph.D. dissertation, Brandeis University, 1984).

17. Melvin Zelnik, John Kanter, and Kathleen Ford, *Sex and Pregnancy in Adolescence* (Beverly Hills, Calif.: Sage Publications, 1981).

18. *Preventing Children Having Children*, p. 5.

19. Virginia Cartoof, "The Challenge of Serving Teenage Mothers," (Paper presented at the National Florence Crittenton Association Conference, Colorado Springs, October, 1980).

20. Shelby Miller, *Children as Parents: Final Report on a Study of Childbearing and Childrearing Among 12 to 15-Year-Olds* (New York: Child Welfare League of America, 1983).

Growing Numbers, Growing Force: Older Women Organize

KATHLEEN KAUTZER

1. Tish Sommers, "Epilogue" in *Displaced Homemakers: Organizing for a New Life*, Laurie Shields (New York: McGraw Hill, 1981). This book is a firsthand account of the genesis and evolution of the displaced-homemakers' movement.

2. Arthur H. Miller, Patricia Gurin, and Gerald Gurin, "Age Consciousness and Political Mobilization of Older Americans" *The Gerontologist* 20 (September 1980): 691–700. It is interesting to note that the term "older women" evokes such negative reaction from many women that they resist joining an organization titled "The Older Women's League." Although OWL leaders are repeatedly advised to select a more "positive appealing" name, they insist on retaining their original name because they consider positive identification as older women to be an essential component of consciousness raising among their constituency.

3. U.S., Department of Commerce, Bureau of the Census, *Current Population Reports*, Series P-25, no. 927, table 33 (Washington, D.C.: Government Printing Office, 1983).

4. Bureau of the Census, *Current Population Reports*, Series P-60 no. 145, table 60 (1983).

5. Ibid.

6. Ibid., table 17.

7. Bureau of the Census, *Current Population Reports,* Series P-60, no. 147, table 15 (1983).

8. Bureau of the Census, *Current Population Reports,* Series P-20, no. 389, table 1 (1983).

9. These studies are summarized in Deanne Bonnar, "When the Bough Breaks: A Feminist Analysis of Income Maintenance Strategies for Female Based Households" (Ph.D. dissertation, Brandeis University, 1984).

10. The problems of older women care givers are detailed in "Till Death Do Us Part: Caregivers of Severely Disabled Husbands" (OWL Gray Paper no. 7, available from OWL, 1325 G. Street, N.W. Washington, DC 20005).

11. Bruce Bladeck, *Unloving Care* (New York: Basic Books, 1980).

12. "Older Women and Health Care" (OWL Gray Paper no. 3, available from OWL, 1325 G. Street, N.W. Washington, DC 20005).

13. Statistics on earning patterns and labor-force participation of older women are cited in "Not even for Dogcatcher: Employment Discrimination and Older Women" (OWL Gray Paper no. 8, available from OWL, 1325 G Street, N.W. Washington, DC 20005). This paper points out that unemployment statistics underestimate the employment problems faced by older women since they fail to include discouraged workers (who have ceased looking for work in the belief that they are not qualified for available jobs). The Department of Labor estimates that older women constitute 60 percent of all discouraged workers.

14. Valerie Kincade Oppenheimer, *The Female Labor Force in the U.S.,* Population Monograph Series No. 5 (Berkeley: University of California Press, 1970).

15. Myrna I. Lewis and Robert N. Butler, "Why Is Women's Lib Ignoring Older Women?" in *The Older Woman: Lavender Rose or Gray Panther,* ed. Marie Marschall Fuller and Cor Ann Martin (Springfield, Ill.: Charles C. Thomas, 1982), pp. 211–23.

16. These studies include Sara A. Matthews, *Social World of Older Women: Management of Self-Identity* (Beverley Hills, Calif.: Sage Publications, 1979); Lillian Rubin, *Women of a Certain Age* (New York: Basic Books, 1976); and Ruth Jacobs, *Life After Youth: Female, Forty—What Next?* (Boston: Beacon Press, 1979).

17. The Older Women's League has prepared a pamphlet entitled "Older Women and Job Discrimination—A Primer" to advise older women about their rights and the appropriate procedures for filing discrimination complaints. The pamphlet is available from OWL, 1325 G. Street, N.W., Washington, D.C. 20005.

18. Shields, *Displaced Homemakers*, p. 20.

19. James H. Schulz, *The Economics of Aging* (Belmont, Calif.: Wadsworth Publishing Co., 1980); and "Social Security: Adequacy and Equity for Older Women" (OWL Gray Paper no. 2, available from OWL, 1325 G. Street, N.W. Washington, DC 20005).

20. Unpublished data from Bureau of the Census, *Current Population Reports* (1983).

21. Ibid.

22. Maximilian Szinovacz, ed., *Women's Retirement* (Beverley Hills, Calif.; Sage Publications, 1982). This anthology documents and criticizes the sexist biases of many gerontologists and presents summaries of a variety of recent research studies focused exclusively on female retirees. Another excellent feminist critique of gerontological research is Diane Beeson, "Women in Studies of Aging: A Critique and Suggestion," *Social Problems* 23 (1975): 52–59. Since the Older Women's League Education Fund (OWLEF) was founded in 1978, gerontologists have expressed an increasing interest and concern with older women's issues. Owing to a recent influx of female scholars in the field, there has also been a dramatic expansion of research focused exclusively on older women. This research is summarized in *The Mature Women in America, A Selected Annotated Bibliography 1979–1982* (available from the National Council on the Aging, Inc., Washington, DC 20004).

23. Letter to Older Women's League membership "On Death and Dying" by Tish Sommers, May 1985. (Copies may be obtained from OWL, 1325 G. Street, N.W., Washington, DC 20005.)

And Sunday Lasts Too Long: Rural Women and Poverty

B. ELEANOR ANSTEY AND JANET PAIGE KULLER

1. A composite picture of America's angry farmers was written by journalists in the spring of 1985: "Bitter Harvest," *Newsweek*, 18 February 1985, p. 52.

2. See William Whitaker, "The Many Faces of Ephraim: In Search of a Functional Typology of Rural Areas," *Social Development Issues* 7, no. 1 (Spring 1983): 14; U.S., Department of Commerce, Bureau of the Census, "Social and Economic Characteristics of the Metropolitan and Nonmetropolitan Population," *Current Population Reports*, Special Studies, Series P-23, no. 55 (Washington, D.C.: Government Printing Office, 1975); Bureau of the Census, *Current Population Reports*, Series P-60, no. 138, "Appendix A: Characteristics of the Population Below the Poverty Level: 1981" (Washington, D.C.: Government Printing Office, 1983), p. 177; Richard Dewey, "The Rural-Urban Continuum: Real but Relatively Unimportant," *American Journal of Sociology* 66 (July 1960): 60–66.

Welfare: Death by Exhaustion

BETTY REID MANDELL

1. Winifred Bell, *Contemporary Social Welfare* (New York: Macmillan, 1983), pp. 127–28.

2. Coalition on Women and the Budget, *Inequality of Sacrifice: The Impact of the Reagan Budget on Women* (Washington, D.C.: National Women's Law Center, March 1984), p. 8.

3. Ibid., p. 61.

4. Deanne Bonnar, "The Genesis Paradigm: Income Transfers for Women" (Paper, Brandeis University).

5. Solidarity, a Socialist Feminist Network, *Socialist-Feminism* (Takoma Park, Md.: Solidarity, 1981), p. 64.

6. Grace Abbott, *The Child and the State*, vol. 1 (New York: Greenwood Press, [1938] 1968), pp. 7–8.

7. Deanne Bonnar, "The Genesis Paradigm," p. 31.

8. Ibid., pp. 30–31.

9. Ibid., p. 22.

10. Ibid., p. 10.

11. Ibid.

12. Winifred Bell, *Aid to Dependent Children* (New York: Columbia University Press, 1965), p. 16.

13. Massachusetts Advocacy Center, *For Want of a Nail: The Impact of Federal Budget Cuts on Children in Massachusetts* (Boston: Massachusetts Advocacy Center, 1982), pp. 3–4.

14. See, for example, Alfred Kadushin, *Child Welfare Services* (New York: Macmillan, 1967), p. 366.

15. Abbott, *The Child and the State*, p. 235.

16. Ibid., p. 233.

17. Ibid., p. 232.

18. Ibid., p. 238.

19. Ibid., pp. 237, 239.

20. Ibid., p. 234. Citing C.C. Carstens, secretary of the Massachusetts Society for the Prevention of Cruelty to Children in 1913.

21. Over the years this program has expanded to include more categories of need, so that now it covers dependents and survivors of workers and is called Retirement, Survivor, and Disability Insurance (RSDI). In 1965, it added Medicare, a program that provides limited health insurance for people sixty-five and over.

22. The Reagan administration attempted unsuccessfully to abolish this minimum. However, it did eliminate benefits for deceased workers' children who attend college.

23. Bell, *Aid to Dependent Children*, p. 130.

24. Abbott, *The Child and the State*, p. 271. Citing Annual Report of the Massachusetts Department of Public Welfare for the Year Ending November 30, 1933 (Public Document no. 17), *The Depression Years of 1933 and 1934 in Massachusetts*, p. 10.

25. Abbott, *The Child and the State*, pp. 248–249, 261.

26. Suitable-home laws were declared unconstitutional by the Supreme Court in the late 1960s.

27. Abbott, *The Child and the State*, p. 281.

28. For a full discussion of the welfare rights movement, see F.F. Piven and R.A. Cloward, *Regulating the Poor: The Functions of Public Welfare* (New York: Pantheon, 1971).

29. "The Equality Revolution," *New York Times Magazine*, 18 August 1968.

30. Abbott, *The Child and the State*, p. 240.

31. Coalition on Women and the Budget, *Inequality of Sacrifice: The Impact of the Reagan Budget on Women* (Washington, D.C.: National Women's Law Center, March 1984), pp. 9–10.

32. Massachusetts Advocacy Center, *For Want of a Nail*, p. 11.

33. See Piven and Cloward, *Regulating the Poor*, for a full discussion of this.

34. Abbott, *The Child and the State*, p. 238.

35. Coalition on Women and the Budget, *Inequality of Sacrifice*, p. 12.

36. The right of strikers to receive AFDC was also rescinded in 1981, as was the right of strikers to receive food stamps. This supports the contention of Frances Fox Piven and Richard Cloward *(The New Class War)* that the current administration wants to eliminate entitlements that provide a cushion for workers, thereby forcing workers to do any work at any price.

37. Coalition on Women and the Budget, *Inequality of Sacrifice*, p. 8, 9; and Henrietta J. Duvall, Laren W. Goudreau, and Robert E. Marsh, "Aid to Families With Dependent Children: Characteristics of Recipients in 1979," *Social Security Bulletin* 45, no. 4 (April 1982): 3–19.

38. Bell, *Aid to Dependent Children.*

39. For a full discussion of these practices, see Claudia Dreifus, "Sterilizing the Poor," in *Feminist Frameworks* ed by A.N. Jaggar and P.S. Rothenberg (New York: McGraw Hill, 1984), pp. 58–66.

40. Wilhelm Reich, *Function of the Orgasm*, T. Wolfe, trans., 2d ed. (New York: Orgone Institute Press, 1948), p. xxvi.

41. George Gilder, *Naked Nomads* (New York: Quadrangle, 1974).

42. My articles by this title were published in *Social Work*, Jan. 1971 and April 1971. The discussion that follows is taken from these articles. See *The Origins of Totalitarianism* (Cleveland: World Publishing, Meridian Books, 1958).

43. Ibid., p. 186.

44. Ibid., p. 474.

45. Ibid., p. 459.

For Better and for Worse: Women Against Women in the Welfare State

ANN WITHORN

1. See Michael Lipsky, *Street Level Bureaucracy* (New York: Basic Books, 1981).

2. For a summary of services offered by feminists see Naomi Gottlieb, ed., *Alternative Services for Women* (New York: Columbia University Press, 1980).

3. For a good summary of major works of this criticism see the notes to Frances Fox Piven's essay in this volume.

4. See Noel Timms, *The Client Speaks* (London: Routledge and Kegan Paul, 1974) for a good summary of worker-client attitudes, as well as my book *Serving the People.*

5. The source of this quote, and of many of the insights of this chapter, is Judy Gradford, who was a member of Advocacy for Resources for Modern Survival (ARMS) and now works in a feminist shelter for battered women in Cambridge.

6. See Elaine Norman and Arlene Mancuso, *Women's Issues and Social Work Practice* (Itasca, Ill.: F. E. Peacock, 1980); and Mimi Abramowitz, "Social Work and Women's Liberation: A mixed Response," *Catalyst* 1 (1978).

7. See Margalie S. Larson, *The Rise of Professionalism* (Berkeley, Calif.: University of California Press, 1977).

8. Jeffry Prottas' book *People Processing* (Lexington, Mass.: Lexington Books, 1979) is very useful in describing how one is forced to become a "client" in order to receive a needed service.

9. See the special issue of *Catalyst* on labor and human services, vol. 5, nos. 17, 18 (Summer 1985) mentioned above for more discussion of how progressives try to work in unions.

Daddy's Good Girls: Homeless Woman and "Mental Illness"

STEPHANIE GOLDEN

1. Testimony of Mary Ellen Hombs (U.S., Congress, House, Committee on Banking, Finance and Urban Affairs, Subcommittee on Housing and Community Development, *Homelessness in America,* Dec. 15, 1982, Hearing, p. 13. In my experience the number was closer to one half.

2. Inge K. Broverman et al., "Sex Role Stereotypes and Clinical Judgements of Mental Health," *Journal of Consulting and Clinical Psychology* 34 (1970): 3, 5, 6.

3. For a study that throws much light on how these norms operate see Shirley S. Angrist, Mark Lefton, Simon Dinitz, and Benjamin Pasamanick, *Women After Treatment: A Study of Former Mental Patients and Their Normal Neighbors* (New York: Appleton-Century-Crofts, 1968), pp. 10–11.

4. See Paul M. Roman and Harrison M. Trice, *Schizophrenia and the Poor* (Ithaca, N.Y.: New York State School of Industrial and Labor Relations, 1967), pp. 22, 43.

5. Theodore Lidz, *The Origin and Treatment of Schizophrenic Disorders* (New York: Basic Books, 1973), pp. 48, 68.

6. Ibid., p. 69.

7. See Thomas S. Szasz, *Schizophrenia: The Sacred Symbol of Psychiatry* (New York: Basic Books, 1976), pp. 148–49, 154–55.

8. *Butler's Lives of the Saints*, ed., revised, and supplemented by Herbert Thurston and Donald Attwater (New York: P.J. Kennedy, 1956), vol. 2, p. 321; see also R. Pierloot, "Belgium," in *World History of Psychiatry*, ed. John G. Howells (New York: Brunner/Mazel, 1975), pp. 1–38.

9. See George Ferguson, *Signs and Symbols in Christian Art* (New York: Oxford University Press, 1959), p. 64; also *Butler's Lives*, vol. 14.

Beyond the "Normal Family": A Cultural Critique of Women's Poverty

MARGARET CERULLO AND MARLA ERLIEN

1. Hans Mayer, *Outsiders: A Study in Life and Letters* (Cambridge, Mass.: M.I.T. Press, 1984).

2. We borrow this example from Judy Housman, "Mothering, the Unconscious, and Feminism," *Radical America* 16, no. 6 (November–December 1982).

3. See Angela Davis, *Women, Race, and Class* (New York: Random House, 1981); E. Frances White, "Listening to the Voices of Black Feminism," *Radical America* 18, nos. 2, 3 (1984); Hortense Spillers, "Interstices: A Small Drama of Words," in *Pleasure and Danger: Exploring Female Sexuality*, Carole S. Vance (Boston: Routledge and Kegan Paul, 1984).

4. We are drawing on some of the ideas of Michel Foucault, who has analyzed the significance of the historical shift of focus from crime to "the criminal" as a type of person, from madness to "the madman," and from sexual perversion to the "pervert." See *Discipline and Punish* (New York: Vintage, 1969); *Madness and Civilization* (New York: Vintage, 1972); *The History of Sexuality* (New York: Vintage, 1980).

5. See, for example, Carlyle C. Douglas, "Urban League to Debate U.S. Aid and Self-Help," *New York Times*, 21 July 1985.

6. Quoted in Salim Muakkill, "Black Family's Ills Provoke New Concern," *In These Times*, 12 June 1985, p. 5.

7. Salim Muakkill, "Civil Rights Leaders Shift Course Inward," *In These Times*, 7 August 1985, p. 5.

8. Daniel Patrick Moynihan, *The Negro Family: The Case for National Action*, prepared for the U.S. Department of Labor, Office of Policy Planning and Research (Washington D.C.: Government Printing Office, 1965).

9. See Robert Staples, *The Black Family, Essays and Studies*, rev. ed. (Belmont, Calif.: Wadsworth, 1978); Lee Rainwater and William Yancey, *The Moynihan Report and the Politics of Controversy*, (Cambridge, Mass.: M.I.T. Press, 1967); Charles Vert Willie, *A New Look at Black Families*, 2d ed. (Bayside, N.Y.: General Hall, 1981).

10. See, e.g., Herbert Gutman, *The Black Family in Slavery and in Freedom* (New York: Pantheon, 1976); Carol Stack, *All Our Kin: Strategies for Survival in a Black Community* (New York: Harper and Row, 1974).

11. Quoted in Louise Meriwether, "To Be Young, Black, and Pregnant," *Essence*, April, 1984, p. 68.

12. E.H. Norton, "An Open Letter From a Black Woman to a Black Man," Speech to the National Convention of the Urban League, July 1975, quoted in *The Underclass*, Ken Auletta (New York: Vintage Books, 1983), p. 263.

13. Dorothy Height, "What Must Be Done About Our Children Having Children?" *Ebony*, May 1985, p. 101.

14. See both Barbara Ehrenreich and Karin Stallard, "The Nouveau Poor," *Ms.*, July–August 1982, pp. 217–24; and Karin Stallard, Barbara Ehrenreich, and Holly Sklar, *Poverty in the American Dream: Women and Children First* (Boston: South End Press, 1983), as well as the excerpt in this volume. The quotations that follow are all from "The Nouveau Poor."

15. For an elaboration of this point, see E. Frances White, "Listening to the Voices"; and Jacqueline Dowd Hall, *Revolt Against Chivalry* (New York: Columbia University Press, 1983).

Toward the Feminization of Policy: Exit From an Ancient Trap by the Redefinition of Work

DEANNE BONNAR

1. International Labor Organization, *Women at Work* (New York: United Nations Publications, 1980).

2. Cited in Lisa Leghorn and Katherine Parker, *Woman's Worth: Sexual Economics and the World of Women* (Boston: Routledge and Kegan Paul, 1981).

3. See especially Kathleen Newland, *The Sisterhood of Man* (New York: W.W. Norton and Co., 1979).

4. Frances Fox Piven and Richard A. Cloward, *Regulating the Poor: The Functions of Public Welfare* (New York: Vintage Books, 1971), p. 25.

5. Social Security Board, *Social Security Yearbook: 1939* (Washington, D.C.: Social Security Board, 1940), p. 20.

6. For a discussion of these predictions and their inadequacy see Hilde Scott, *Does Socialism Liberate Women?* (Boston: Beacon Press, 1974).

7. The Swedish Institute, *Equality Between Men and Women in Sweden* (Stockholm: The Swedish Institute, 1982), p. 1; and a Swedish government report to the United Nations cited in Rita Liljestrom, "Sweden" in *Family Policy Government and Families in Fourteen Countries,* ed. Sheila Kamerman and Alfred Kahn (New York: Columbia University Press, 1978), 33.

8. Liljestrom, "Sweden," p. 37.

9. Zsuza Ferge, *A Society in the Making: Hungarian Social and Societal Polichy 1945–75* (White Plains, N.Y.: M.E. Sharpe, 1979), p. 184.

10. Quoted in Leghorn and Parker, *Woman's Worth,* p. 177.

11. Joanne Vanek, "The Time Spent in Housework," in *The Economics of Women and Work,* ed. Alice Amsden (New York: St. Martin's Press, 1980), p. 277.

12. See Alice Amsden, ed., *The Economics of Women and Work* (New York: St. Martin's Press, 1980); Rae Andre, *Homemakers: The Forgotten Workers,* (Chicago: University of Chicago Press, 1981); Wendy Edmond and Susie

Fleming, eds., *All Work and No Pay* (Bristol, England: Falling Wall Press, 1975); Ellen Malos, ed. *The Politics of Housework* (London: Allison and Busby, 1980); and Ann Oakley, *The Sociology of Housework,* (New York: Pantheon Books, 1974).

13. See Andre, *Homemakers;* Leghorn and Parker *Woman's Worth;* and Newland, *Sisterhood of Man* for further discussion.

14. See David G. Gil, "Mother's Wages: An Alternative Attack on Poverty," Reprint no. 45 from *Social Work Practice: 1969;* David G. Gil, *Unravelling Social Policy* (Cambridge, Mass., Schenkman Publishing Co., 1973); David G. Gil, *Beyond the Jungle* (Cambridge, Mass.: Schenkman, 1979); and Mariarosa Della Costa and Selma James, *The Power of Women and the Subversion of the Community,* 3d ed. (Bristol, England: Falling Wall Press, 1972).

15. See Della Costa and James, *The Power of Women.*

16. Bong-Ho Mok, "In the Service of Socialism: Social Welfare in China," *Social Work* 28, no. 4 (July–August 1983): 269–73; Ferge, *A Society in the Making;* and Liljestrom, "Sweden."

What if We All Went to the Polls? Politics and Poverty

ROCHELLE LEFKOWITZ

1. Richard Cloward and Frances Piven, "Realigning the Democrats," *The Organizer,* 9, no. 4 (Winter 1983):21.

2. Bella Abzug and Mim Kelber, *Gender Gap* (Boston: Houghton Mifflin, 1984), p. 204.

3. Ibid., p. 225.

4. Hulbert James, Maxine Phillips, and Don Hazen, "The New Voter Registration Strategy," in *Beyond Reagan: Alternatives for the 80s,* ed. Alan Gartner, Colin Greer, and Frank Reissman (New York: Harper & Row, 1984), p. 228.

5. Adam Clymer, "Women's Political Habits Show Sharp Change," *New York Times,* 30 June 1982, p. D21.

6. Abzug and Kelber, *Gender Gap,* p. 96.

7. Tee shirts, posters, and postcards with the message: "2 out of 3 adults in poverty are women. What if we all went to the polls," © 1983 Designed by Sandra Chelnov and Alice Denny for the East Bay Women's Coalition, a California group that organized the Women's Economic Agenda Project, an outgrowth of Women USA's 1982 voter-registration project in the East Bay.

8. "Three Scenarios for the '84 Election," Bella Abzug and Mim Kelber, *Ms.*, March 1984, p. 40.

9. James, Phillips, and Hazen, "The New Voter Registration Strategy," p. 227–28.

10. Don Hazen and Rochelle Lefkowitz, "Voter Registration: Including the Excluded," *The Organizer,* Spring 1984, p. 23.

11. Frances Fox Piven and Richard Cloward, *Poor People's Movements* (New York: Random House, 1977), p. 306.

12. Stefanie Weiss, "What If They Gave an Election and We All Came," *Ms.*, March 1984, p. 92.

13. Among the early groups involved in voter registration were Women USA, Freeze Voter '84, NAACP, Southwest Voter Registration and Education Project and scores of other civil-rights groups such as Project Big Vote, Project VOTE, and more than fifty women's groups under the umbrella of the Women's Vote Project.

14. Cloward and Piven, "Realigning the Democrats," p. 22.

15. Ruth B. Mandel, "How Women Vote: The New Gender Gap," *Working Woman,* September, 1982, p. 131. The author is director of the Center for the American Woman and Politics, Rutgers University.

16. Joanmarie Kalter, "Voter Registration," Pacific News Service, December 27, 1983, draft, p. 3.

17. Rochelle Lefkowitz, "Their Voices Will Grow Louder," *In These Times,* 27 April 1983, p. 8.

18. Gary Delgado, "Registration Won't Realign the Democrats," *The Organizer,* Spring 1984, p. 29.

19. Ethel Klein, *Gender Politics* (Cambridge, Mass.: Harvard University Press, 1984), p. 3.

20. Ibid., p. 123.

21. Delgado, "Registration Won't Realign the Democrats," p. 29.

22. Tom Sanzillo and Theresa Funiciello, "Critique of a Movement to Transform the Democratic Party," draft, p. 1.

23. Delgado, "Registration Won't Realign the Democrats," p. 30.

24. Cloward and Piven, "Realigning the Democrats," p. 22.

25. Sanzillo and Funicello, "Critique of a Movement," p. 17–18.

26. Klein, *Gender Politics*, p. 158.

27. Ibid.

Comparable Worth, Incomparable Pay
TERESA AMOTT AND JULIE MATTHAEI

1. The case was *Quarles* v. *Phillip Morris*. For more information, see Judy Scales-Trent, "Comparable Worth: Is This a Theory for Black Workers?" (Paper, State University of New York at Buffalo Law School, 1984).

2. Ruth Milkman, "The Reproduction of Job Segregation by Sex: A Study of the Sexual Division in the Auto and Electrical Manufacturing Industries in the 1960s" (Ph.D. dissertation, University of California at Berkeley, 1981).

3. League of Women Voters Education Fund, "Women and Work: Pay Equity," Publication no. 110, 1982.

4. Ibid. The decision was *County of Washington, Oregon* v. *Gunther.* It involved female jail matrons who were paid 70 per cent of the salary for male guards.

5. Ibid.

6. A good source of information on state and local government pay equity initiatives is *Who's Working for Working Women* (Comparable Worth

Project, National Committee on Pay Equity and the National Women's Political Caucus, Comparable Worth Project, in 1984). The pamphlet contains an excellent bibliography and a list of resource groups in each state. To order, write the National Committee on Pay Equity, 1201 165h Street, N.W., Suite 422, Washington, DC, 20036.

7. For more information on the uses and limitations of job evaluation schemes, see Helen Remick, ed., *Comparable Worth and Wage Discrimination, Technical Possibilities and Political Realities* (Philadelphia: Temple University Press, 1984); and Donald Treiman and Heidi Hartman, *Women, Work and Wages: Equal Pay for Jobs of Equal Value* (Washington, D.C.: National Academy of Sciences, 1981).

8. Ronnie Steinberg, "A Want of Harmony: Perspectives on Wage Discrimination," in Remick, *Comparable Worth.*

Women and the State: Ideology, Power, and Welfare

FRANCES FOX PIVEN

1. See, for example, N.B. Barrett, "The Welfare System as State Paternalism" (Paper presented to Conference on Women and Structural Transformation, Rutgers University, Institute for Research on Women, November 1983); E. Boris and P. Bardaglio, "The Transformation of Patriarchy: The Historic Role of the State, in *Families, Politics, and Public Policy,* ed. I. Diamond (New York: Longman, Green, 1983), pp. 70–93; C. Brown, "Mothers, Fathers and Children: From Private to Public Patriarchy," in *Women and Revolution,* ed. L. Sargent (Boston: South End Press, 1980), pp. 239–67.

See also Z. Eisenstein, *The Radical Future of Liberal Feminism* (New York: Longman, Green, 1981); Z. Eisenstein, "The State, the Patriarchal Family and Working Mothers," in *Families, Politics and Public Policy,* ed. I. Diamond (New York: Longman, Green, 1983), pp. 41–58; M. McIntosh, "The State and the Oppression of Women," in *Feminism and Materialism,* ed. A. Kuhn and A. Wolpe (London: Routledge and Kegan Paul, 1978), pp. 254–89; and J. G. Schirmer, *The Limits of Reform: Women, Capital and Welfare* (Cambridge, Mass.: Schenkman Publishing Co., 1982).

Happily, however, some of the most recent work has begun to explore the political and ideological resources yielded by women in and through the welfare state. See, for example, L. Balbo, "Crazy Guilts: Rethinking the Welfare State Debate from a Woman's Perspective" (Paper, 1981); and Balbo,Untitled (Paper presented at the conference "The Transformation of the Welfare State: Dangers and Potentialities for Women," Bellagio, Italy, August 1983). See also A. Borchorst and B. Siim, "The Danish Welfare State: A Case for a Strong Social Patriarchy; D. Dahlerup, "Feminism and the State: An Essay with a Scandinavian Perspective"; Y. Ergas, "The Disintegrative Revolution: Welfare Politics and Emergent Collective Identities"; H.M. Hernes, "Women and the Welfare State: The Transition from Private to Public Dependence"; and J.G. Schirmer, "Cut off at the Impasse: Women and the Welfare State in Denmark" (Papers presented at the conference "The Transformation of the Welfare State: Dangers and Potentialities for Women," Bellagio, Italy, August, 1983). See also A.S. Rossi, "Beyond the Gender Gap: Women's Bid for Political Power, *Social Science Quarterly* 64 (1983):718–33.

2. J.B. Elshtain, "Feminism, Family and Community," *Dissent*, Fall, 1982, pp. 442–50; and J.B. Elshtain, "Antigone's Daughters: Reflections on Female Identity and the State," in *Families, Politics, and Public Policy,* ed. I. Diamond (New York: Longman, Green, 1983), pp. 298–309.

3. Attitudes towards defense spending accounted for a good part of the difference between male and female preferences in the 1980 election. This pattern persisted into 1982, when 40 percent of men favored increased defense spending but only 25 percent of women did. However, by 1982 women had come to place concerns about defense second to their concerns about the economy. See A. H. Miller and O. Malanchuk, "The Gender Gap in the 1982 Elections" and M. Schlichting and P. Tuckel, "Beyond the Gender Gap: Working Women and the 1982 Election (Papers presented to the Thirty-eighth Annual Conference of the American Association for Public Opinion Research, Buck Hills Falls, Pa., May 19–22, 1983) for an examination of differences in the attitudes of married and unmarried and employed and unemployed women; they conclude that the gender gap holds regardless of marital or labor-force status.

4. Rossi in "Beyond the Gender Gap" reviews studies that show the beginning of a gender gap as early as the 1950s. However, exit poll data after the 1980 election revealed an unprecedented 9 percent spread in the voting choices of men and women. In subsequent polls, the spread substantially widened to a 15 percent difference between men and women in response to the question whether Ronald Reagan deserved reelection asked in a *New York Times* poll reported in December 1983. Moreover, while male ratings of the President rose with the upturn in economic indicators and the invasion of Grenada, the unfavorable ratings by women remained virtually unchanged.

5. Attitudes about the reproductive and legal rights of women, which have been the central issues of the movement, do not differentiate male

and female respondents in the surveys. Single women, however, are much more likely than men to support the women's-rights issues.

6. B. Ehrenreich, *The Hearts of Men* (New York, Anchor Books, 1983).

7. Where only 4 percent of the nation's lawyers and judges were women in 1971, women accounted for 14 percent in 1981. In the same period, the percentage of physicians who are women rose from 9 to 22, and the percentage of female engineers increased from 1 to 4.

8. L. Peattie and M. Rein, "Women's Claims: A study in political economy" (Paper, 1981); and E. Rothschild, "Reagan and the Real America," *New York Review of Books*, 5 February 1981, p. 28.

9. See Peattie and Rein, "Women's Claims" for a review of data on women's participation in the labor force that shows the persistence of part-time and irregular employment as well as the concentration of women in low-paid jobs.

10. More than one third of female-headed families, or 3.3 million, received Aid to Families with Dependent Children in 1979 (Census Bureau). An almost equal number received Medicaid, and 2.6 million were enrolled in the food stamp program. See S.P. Erie, M. Rein, M. and B. Wiget, "Women and the Reagan Revolution: Thermidor for the Social Welfare Economy," in *Families, Politics, and Public Policy,* ed. I. Diamond (New York, Longman, Green, 1983), pp. 94–123.

11. Ibid.

12. Boris and Bardaglio, "The Transformation of Patriarchy," p. 75.

13. F.F. Piven and R.A. Cloward, *The New Class War: Reagan's Attack on the Welfare State and Its Consequences* (New York: Pantheon, 1982).

14. E.R. Tufte, *Political Control of the Economy* (Princeton, N.J.: Princeton University Press, 1978). See W.D. Burnham, "The 1980 Earthquake: Realignment, Reaction, or What?" in *The Hidden Election: Politics and Economics in the 1980 Presidential Campaign,* ed. T. Ferguson and J. Rogers (New York: Pantheon, 1981), pp. 98–140 for an excellent discussion of the issues that determine the outcome of the 1980 election. He concludes that worry over unemployment was the critical issue leading voters who had supported Carter in 1978 to defect to Reagan in 1980.

15. F.F. Piven, and R.A. Cloward, *Regulating the Poor: The Functions of Public Welfare* (New York, Pantheon, 1971); and F.F. Piven and R.A.

Cloward, *Poor People's Movements: Why They Succeed, How They Fail* (New York: Pantheon, 1977).

16. J. Jenson, " 'Success' Without Struggle? The Modern Women's Movement in France" (Paper presented to a workshop at Cornell University, "The Women's Movement in Comparative Perspective: Resource Mobilization, Cycles of Protest, and Movement Success," May 6–8, 1983).

17. D. Hayden, *The Grand Domestic Revolution* (Cambridge, Mass.: The MIT Press, 1981), pp. 4–5.

18. Rossi in an 1982 analysis of the first National Women's Conference at Houston in 1977, reports that 72 percent of the delegates were employed either by government or by nonprofit social welfare organizations. See also Rossi, "Beyond the Gender Gap," for a discussion of "insider-outsider" coalitions made possible by government employment.

Contributors

Teresa Amott teaches economics at Wellesley College, works on the Economic Literacy Project of the Massachusetts organization Women for Economic Justice (WEJ), and provides technical assistance to women's and community groups around the country. She writes about women, poverty, and militarism in various national publications.

B. Eleanor Anstey teaches in the School of Social Work at the University of Iowa, where she is also active in women's issues. She grew up on a family farm in the Midwest and is currently doing work on international issues of development and their effect on women.

Nancy Aries teaches health policy at Baruch College at the City University of New York (CUNY) and writes about health and management issues.

Deanne Bonnar is Boston regional director of the Office for Children. She speaks and writes about "care givers' wages" for various audiences and publications.

Linda Burnham, a California-based writer and activist, is a member of the National Council of the San Francisco group Alliance Against Women's Oppression and is on the editorial board of the Marxist journal *Line of March.* She has written extensively about oppression of blacks, women's liberation, and socialist feminism in several periodicals.

Margaret Cerullo teaches sociology at Hampshire College in Amherst, Massachusetts. She is active in feminist and leftist politics in the Boston area and writes about her concerns for various publications.

Janet Diamond is assistant director of publications and outreach for the Massachusetts Department of Public Welfare. Before that she was a welfare-rights activist and co-founder and media coordinator for the Coalition for Basic Human Needs (CBHN), a Massachusetts welfare-advocacy group.

Elaine Donovan teaches economics at the University of Massachusetts/Boston and works with WEJ. She writes about economic problems facing employed and poor women.

Diane Dujon teaches about welfare organizing and is an administrator at the College of Public and Community Service of the University of Massachusetts/Boston. She is a co-founder of Advocacy for Resources for Modern Survival (ARMS), a Boston welfare-rights group.

Barbara Ehrenreich is a New York-based feminist and activist who has written extensively about women, men, and the welfare state for many national publications. She is co-chair of Democratic Socialists of America and the author of such books as *The Hearts of Men* and *Poverty and the American Dream.*

Marla Erlien is a Boston-area activist who has worked in many areas of feminist, socialist, and anti-imperialist politics. She currently works with the Jefferson Park Writing Project, which promotes writing and creative development among women in Cambridge, Massachusetts, public housing.

Stephanie Golden is a New York writer and editor who has worked at several New York shelters while writing a book on homeless women.

Judy Gradford works with Transition House, a Cambridge, Massachusetts, battered-women's shelter. She is a co-founder of ARMS and a board member of CBHN.

Marion Graham is a staff member and union steward at the University of Massachusetts/Boston. She was also a co-founder of ARMS.

Elizabeth Higginbotham is an assistant professor in the Department of Sociology and Social Work and a research associate at the Center for Research on Women at Memphis State University. She has published material on many aspects of the lives of women of color. She is currently completing a manuscript on class differences in black women's routes to college.

Pat Jerabek teaches at the College of Public and Community Service and works with the Economic Literacy Project of WEJ.

Kathleen Kautzer is currently writing a Ph.D dissertation for Brandeis University about the Older Women's League. She has been a union organizer of clerical workers and is the daughter of a displaced homemaker.

Janet Paige Kuller is a social worker who now lives in the state of Washington. She has done field work in rural communities and grew up on a farm in the Midwest.

Rochelle Lefkowitz is a New York journalist, editor, and publicist who has worked with community and women's groups. She has written articles in various publications as well as commentaries for Cable News Network.

Betty Reid Mandell teaches at Bridgewater State College and is a long-time welfare-rights advocate. She writes about a range of social-welfare issues in books such as *Welfare in America: Controlling the Dangerous Classes* and *Where Are the Children? A Class Analysis of Foster Care and Adoption.*

Julie Matthaei teaches economics at Wellesley College and writes extensively about women and economics. She is author of *An Economic History of Women in America.*

Diana Pearce is senior research analyst at Catholic University in Washington, D.C. She has spoken and written extensively about the "feminization of poverty" since she coined the term in 1978.

Frances Fox Piven teaches at City University of New York. She has been active in welfare advocacy since the early 1960s. She has written about the welfare state in books such as *The New Class War, Poor People's Movements,* and *Regulating the Poor.*

Roberta Praeger is a long-time Cambridge, Massachusetts, activist who has worked on housing, welfare, and women's issues.

Pamela Sparr is an economist and journalist who is co-founder of the New York Women's Economic Literacy Project.

Dottie Stevens is a Boston area welfare-rights and poor people's activist, a co-founder of ARMS, and a board member of CBHN.

Mary Huff Stevenson teaches economics at the University of Massachusetts/Boson and works with WEJ. She has written extensively about women and the economy for various publications.

Ann Withorn teaches at the College of Public and Community Service, University of Mass/Boston. She is an editor of *Radical America* as well as author of *Serving the People: Social Services and Social Change* and *The Circle Game: Services for the Poor in Massachusetts, 1966–1978.*

Iris Zavala Martinez is a Puerto Rican clinical psychologist and director of a strategic mental-health program for Latino children and families in Worcester, Massachussetts. She has much experience working in the Puerto Rican community and has spoken and written on issues relevant to it both from a mental-health and sociopolitical perspective.

Selected Sources

Part One—POVERTY'S PINK COLLAR

Center for the Study of Social Policy. *A Dream Deferred: The Economic Status of Black Americans*. Washington, D.C.: Center for the Study of Social Policy, 1983.

Coalition on Women and the Budget. *Inequality of Sacrifice: The Impact of the Reagan Budget on Women*. Washington, D.C.: National Women's Law Center, 1982, 1983, 1984.

Ehrenreich, Barbara, and Stallard, Karin. "The Nouveau Poor." *Ms.* August 1982, p. 20.

Howe, Louise, K. *Pink Collar Workers*. New York: Putnam, 1977.

Murray, Charles. *Losing Ground*. New York: Basic Books, 1984. New Right critique of the welfare system.

Pearce, Diana, and MacAdoo, Harriette. "Women and Children: Alone and in Poverty." In National Advisory Council on Economic Opportunity. *Final Report*. Washington, D.C.: National Advisory Council on Economic Opportunity, September 1981.

Sawhill, Isabelle. "Discrimination and Poverty Among Women Who Head Families." In *Women and the Workforce,* edited by M. Blaxall and B. Regan. Chicago: University of Chicago Press, 1976.

Scott, Hilda. *Working Your Way to the Bottom: The Feminization of Poverty.* Boston: Routledge and Kegan Paul, 1984.

Stallard, Karin; Ehrenreich, Barbara; and Sklar, Holly. *Poverty in the American Dream.* Boston: South End Press, 1983.

U.S., Department of Commerce, Bureau of the Census. "A Statistical Portrait of Women in the U.S." *Current Population Reports,* Series P-23, no. 58. Washington, D.C.: Government Printing Office, 1976.

Part Two—SISTER STRUGGLE

Acosta-Belen, E., ed. *The Puerto Rican Woman,* New York: Praeger, 1979.

Children's Defense Fund. *Preventing Children Having Children: A Special Conference Report, Clearinghouse Paper No. 1.* Washington D.C.: Children's Defense Fund, 1985.

Cloward, Raymond, and Smith, William Jr., eds. *The Family in Rural Society.* Colorado: Westview Press, 1981.

Coalition on Women and Employment. *First Friday Report—Joblessness Among Women: A Portrait of Female Unemployment.* Washington D.C.: Full Employment Action Council, 1985.

Jacobsen, Mike, ed. *Nourishing People and Communities Through the Lean Years.* Iowa City: University Printing Press, 1982.

Jones, Jacqueline. *Labor of Love, Labor of Sorrow.* New York: Basic Books, 1985.

Smith, Ralph E. *The Subtle Revolution: Women at Work.* Washington D.C.: The Urban Institute, 1979.

Swerdlow, Amy, and Lessinger, Hanna. *Class, Race and Sex: The Dynamics of Control.* Boston: G.K. Hall, 1983.

Wallace, Phyllis. *Black Women in the Labor Force.* Wellesley, Mass.: Wellesley College Center for Research on Women, 1981.

Zambrana, R., ed. *Work, Family and Health: Latina Women in Transition.* New York: Hispanic Research Center, 1982.

Part Three—THE TIES THAT BIND

Auletta, Ken. *The Underclass.* New York: Vintage, 1983. Neoliberal thesis of a permanent underclass.

Cloward, Richard, and Piven, Frances Fox. *Regulating the Poor: The Functions of Public Welfare.* New York: Pantheon, 1971.

Davis, Angela. *Women, Race, and Class.* New York: Random House, 1981.

Ehrenreich, Barbara. *The Hearts of Men.* Garden City, N.Y.: Anchor, 1983.

Gottlieb, Naomi. *Alternative Services for Women.* New York: Columbia University Press, 1981.

U.S., Department of Labor, Office of Policy Planning and Research. *The Negro Family: The Case for National Action* by Daniel Patrick Moynihan. Washington, D.C.: Government Printing Office, March, 1965.

Vance, Carol S. *Pleasure and Danger: Exploring Female Sexuality.* Boston: Routledge and Kegan Paul, 1984.

Willie, Charles Vert. *A New Look at Black Families,* 2d ed. Bayside, N.Y.: General Hall, 1981.

Withorn, Ann. *The Circle Game: Services for the Poor in Massachusetts 1966–1978.* Amherst, Mass.: University of Massachusetts Press, 1982.

Part Four—AND STILL I RISE

Abzug, Bella, and Kelber, Mim. *Gender Gap.* Boston: Houghton Mifflin, 1984.

Diamond, Irene, ed. *Families, Politics and Social Policy.* New York: Longman, 1983.

Eisenstein, Zillah. *The Radical Future of Liberal Feminism.* New York: Longman, Green, 1981.

Ford Foundation. *Women, Children, and Poverty in America,* New York: Ford Foundation, 1985.

Klein, Ethel. *Gender Politics.* Cambridge, Mass.: Harvard University Press, 1984.

Leghorn, Lisa, and Parker, Katherine. *Woman's Worth: Sexual Economics and the World of Women.* Boston: Routledge and Kegan Paul, 1981.

Piven, Frances Fox, and Cloward, Richard A. *The New Class War: Reagan's Attack on the Welfare State and Its Consequences.* New York: Pantheon, 1982.

Remick, Helen, ed. *Comparable Worth and Wage Discrimination: Technical Possibilities and Political Realities.* Philadelphia: Temple University Press, 1984.

Treiman, Donald, and Hartmann, Heidi. *Women, Work and Wages: Equal Pay for Jobs of Equal Value.* Washington, D.C.: National Academy of Sciences, 1981.

Withorn, Ann. *Serving the People: Social Services and Social Change.* New York: Columbia University Press, 1984.